Enhancing Capabilities through Labour Law

In 2002 the International Labour Organization issued a report entitled 'Decent work and the informal economy' in which it stressed the need to ensure appropriate employment and income, rights at work and effective social protection in informal economic activities. Such a call by the ILO is urgent in the context of countries such as India, where the majority of workers are engaged in informal economic activities, and where expansion of informal economic activities is coupled with deteriorating working conditions and living standards.

This book explores the informal economic activity of India as a case study to examine typical requirements in the work-lives of informal workers, and to develop a means to institutionalise the promotion of these requirements through labour law. Drawing upon Amartya Sen's theoretical outlook, the book considers whether a capability approach to human development may be able to promote recognition and work-life conditions of a specific category of informal workers in India by integrating specific informal workers within a social dialogue framework, along with a range of other social partners including state and non-state institutions. While examining the viability of a human development based labour law in an Indian context, the book also indicates how the proposals put forth in the book may be relevant for informal workers in other developing countries.

This research monograph will be of great interest to scholars of labour law, informal work and workers, law and development, social justice and labour studies.

Supriya Routh is a France-ILO Chair at the Nantes Institute for Advanced Study, Nantes, France. Formerly he was an Assistant Professor of Law at the West Bengal National University of Juridical Sciences, Kolkata, India. His research interests are labour law, informal economic activities, law and development, human rights, and the capability approach.

Enhancing Capabilities through Labour Law

Informal Workers in India

Supriya Routh

Routledge
Taylor & Francis Group

LONDON AND NEW YORK

First published 2014
by Routledge
2 Park Square, Milton Park, Abingdon, Oxon, OX14 4RN

and by Routledge
711 Third Avenue, New York, NY 10017

Routledge is an imprint of the Taylor & Francis Group, an informa business

© 2014 Supriya Routh

British Library Cataloguing in Publication Data
A catalogue record for this book is available from the British Library

Library of Congress Cataloging-in-Publication Data
1. Labor laws and legislation – India.   2. Social security – India.
3. Informal sector (Economics) – India.   4. Refuse and refuse disposal –
India.   I. Title.
    KNS1220.R68 2014
    344.5401 – dc23
    2013035987

ISBN: 978-0-415-72605-4 (hbk)
ISBN: 978-1-315-84970-6 (ebk)

Typeset in Baskerville
by Florence Production Ltd, Stoodleigh, Devon, UK

To
Sumangal, Sandhya
and Gangotri

Contents

Acknowledgements

Creation of knowledge is a collective endeavour. During the present study I acquired debts from many individuals, which I can never repay. I can only acknowledge the contributions that others have made to this book. I would like to put on record my appreciation for Professor Judy Fudge, who has been an enormous intellectual influence. Whenever I was content with my work, she challenged me to think further; whenever I was in doubt, she encouraged me to move ahead; whenever there was an obstacle, she helped me remove it. I thank Professor William Carroll for his guidance, support and friendship. He provided me with the fieldwork tools and helped me to successfully integrate my fieldwork into the book. I also learned from him that an academic's duty needs to extend beyond the four walls of the university. I am thankful to Professor Jeremy Webber for his unconditional support, advice and friendship. I also became very fond of the Webber family during my association with them. I thank Professor Andrew Harding for offering me the much-needed emotional support during my study. The discussions on the ups and downs of the Indian and the English cricket teams were stress relievers for me. Occasionally, we also discussed law and development, and labour migration issues.

My friends Mike and Kathy Large have been a constant source of support. I cherish our (sometimes heated) discussions on several issues. A special thank you to Mike for going through my draft chapters and giving his comments. I thank my friend Agnieszka Zajaczkowska for her help with the planning and execution of my fieldwork. I am grateful to my friends Anne-Marie Delagrave, Ania Zbyszewska, Areli Valencia, Jan Clerk, Carey Johannesson, Jing Qian, Kaitlyn Matulewickz and Heather Jensen for their critical comments on the various chapters. I thank Professor Gangotri Chakraborty for her comments on the draft manuscript. I also thank the three anonymous reviewers of this book for their helpful comments on the draft manuscript. I thank my friend Kerry Sloan for her help with the editorial improvements on my draft chapters. I also thank the editorial team at Routledge for their help during the editing process of the book.

I thankfully acknowledge the support and help offered by Uma Rani Amara, Coen Kompier, Dr Nandan Nawn, Rukmini Sen, Dr Surajit C. Mukhopadhyay, Professor Mahendra P. Singh, Professor Kamala Sankaran, Dr Kaveri Gill, Sabir Ahmed and Reshmi Ganguly during my fieldwork in India and Geneva. I am grateful to my research participants, especially the waste-picker participants who made this research possible. I tried to express their perspectives in this book.

I thank the University of Victoria, the Inter-University Centre on Work and Globalization (CRIMT), the International Development Research Centre (IDRC), the Hari Sharma Foundation, the Law Foundation of British Columbia and the Rechtskulturen for funding my research and keeping me free from financial concerns.

My partner Bidisa Chaki has been a constant source of support and constructive criticism. She never objected to the interference of my professional life in our personal one. I am indebted to her for the sacrifices she made so that I am free to do what I value doing. Finally, I thank my mother Sandhya Routh, my father Sumangal Routh and my *guru* Gangotri Chakraborty for shaping my life the way it is – I dedicate this book to them.

Abbreviations

AMM	*Annapurna Mahila Mandal*
ASI	Annual Survey of Industries
AWWRI	Association of Workers engaged in Waste Recycling Industry
BMS	*Bharatiya Mazdoor Sangh*
BPL	Below the Poverty Line
BPSSS	*Barjya Punarbyawaharikaran Shilpa Shramik Sangathan*
CITU	Centre of Indian Trade Unions
Congress-I	Indian National Congress Party
CPI	Communist Party of India
CPM	Communist Party of India (Marxist)
DGET	Directorate General of Employment and Training
DW	Decent Work
EMI	Employment Market Information
EU	European Union
FB	Forward Block
GDP	Gross Domestic Product
HMS	*Hind Mazdoor Sabha*
HUDCO	Housing and Urban Development Corporation
ICLS	International Conference of Labour Statisticians
ILC	International Labour Conference
ILO	International Labour Organization
IMF	International Monetary Fund
INTUC	Indian National Trade Union Congress
IRC	Interest Reconciliation Council
JSK	*Jan Sangati Kendra*
KKPKP	*Kagad Kach Patra Kashtakari Panchayat*
KMC	Kolkata Municipal Corporation
NAS	National Accounts Statistics
NCEUS	National Commission for Enterprises in the Unorganised Sector
NGO	non-governmental organisation
NSS	National Sample Surveys
NSSO	National Sample Survey Organisation

PBKMS	*Paschim Banga Khet Majdoor Samity*
RIHS	Revised Integrated Housing Scheme
RSBY	*Rashtriya Swastha Bima Yojana*
RSP	Revolutionary Socialist Party
SASPFUW	State Assisted Scheme of Provident Fund for Unorganised Workers in West Bengal
SEWA	Self Employed Women's Association
SEWA Bank	*Swashrayi Mahila Sewa Sahakari Bank*
SMS	*Sramajibee Mahila Samiti*
SMVSS	*Sakti Mahila Vikas Swavlambi Co-operative Society*
SMVSSS	*Sakti Mahila Vikas Swavlambi Sarkari Samiti*
SNA	System of National Accounts
UF	United Front
UN	United Nations
UNDP	United Nations Development Programme
USA	United States of America
WB	West Bengal
WBBWWS	West Bengal Beedi Workers' Welfare Scheme
WBNUJS	West Bengal National University of Juridical Sciences
WBUSWHS	West Bengal Unorganised Sector Workers' Health Security Scheme
WBUSWWB	West Bengal Unorganised Sector Workers' Welfare Board
WIEGO	Women in Informal Employment: Globalizing and Organizing
WTO	World Trade Organization

International conventions, recommendations and declarations

Charter of the United Nations 1945.
Constitution of the International Labour Organization 1919.
ILO, Unemployment Indemnity (Shipwreck) Convention 1920.
ILO, No 29, Forced Labour Convention 1930.
ILO, No 87, Freedom of Association and Protection of the Right to Organise Convention 1948.
ILO, No 98, Right to Organise and Collective Bargaining Convention 1949.
ILO, No 100, Equal Remuneration Convention 1951.
ILO, No 105, Abolition of Forced Labour Convention 1957.
ILO, No 111, Discrimination (Employment and Occupation) Convention 1958.
ILO, No 138, Minimum Age Convention 1973.
ILO, Labour Statistics Recommendation 1985.
ILO, Declaration on Fundamental Principles and Rights at Work 1998.
ILO, No 182, Worst Forms of Child Labour Convention 1999.
ILO, Declaration on Social Justice for a Fair Globalization 2008.
ILO, No 189, Domestic Workers Convention 2011.
ILO, No 201, Domestic Workers Recommendation 2011.
Treaty of Versailles 1919.
WTO, Singapore Ministerial Declaration 1996.

Legislation

The Indian Trusts Act 1882.
The Co-operative Societies Act 1912.
The Charitable and Religious Trusts Act 1920.
The Trade Unions Act 1926.
The Industrial Disputes Act 1947.
The Minimum Wages Act 1948.
The Factories Act 1948.
The Employees' State Insurance Act 1948.
The Constitution of India 1949.
The Companies Act 1956.
The Indian Penal Code 1860.
The Societies Registration Act 1860.
The Motor Vehicles Act 1939.
The Maternity Benefit Act 1961.
The Contract Labour (Regulation and Abolition) Act 1970.
The Code of Criminal Procedure 1973.
The Constitution (Forty-second Amendment) Act 1976.
The Constitution (Forty-fifth Amendment) Bill 1978.
The Kolkata Municipal Corporation Act 1980.
The Kerala Fishermen's Welfare Fund Act 1985.
The Environment (Protection) Act 1986.
The Employment of Manual Scavengers and Construction of Dry Latrines (Prohibition) Act 1993.
The Building and Other Construction Workers' (Regulation of Employment and Conditions of Service) Act 1996.
The Bio-medical Waste (Management and Handling) Rules 1998.
The Municipal Solid Wastes (Management and Handling) Rules 2000.
The National Rural Employment Guarantee Act 2005.
The Kerala Fishermen's and Allied Workers' Welfare Cess Act 2007.
The West Bengal Unorganised Sector Workers' Welfare Act 2007.
The Unorganised Sector Social Security Act 2008.

Cases

Akhil Bharatiya Soshit Karamchari Sangh (Railway) v Union of India [1980] MANU 0058 (SC)

Bandhua Mukti Morcha v Union of India [1983] MANU 0051 (SC)

Bangalore Water Supply & Sewerage Board v A. Rajappa and Others [1978] MANU 0257 (SC)

Consumer Education and Research Centre v Union of India [1995] MANU 0175 (SC)

Francis Coralie v Union Territory of Delhi [1981] MANU 0517 (SC)

His Holiness Kesavananda Bharati Sripadagalvaru v State of Kerala [1973] MANU 0445 (SC)

Indra Sawhney v Union of India [1992] MANU 0665 (SC)

K. Kunhikoman v State of Kerala [1961] MANU 0095 (SC)

Kharak Singh v State of Uttar Pradesh [1962] MANU 0085 (SC)

Kirloskar Brothers Ltd v Employees' State Insurance Corpn [1996] MANU 0873 (SC)

M. Chhaganlal v Greater Bombay Municipality [1974] MANU 0052 (SC)

Minerva Mills Ltd v Union of India [1980] MANU 0075 (SC)

Miss Mohini Jain v State of Karnataka [1992] MANU 0357 (SC)

Mrs Maneka Gandhi v Union of India [1978] MANU 0133 (SC)

Municipal Corporation of the City of Ahmedabad v Jan Mohammed Usmanbhai [1986] MANU 0099 (SC)

Munn v Illinois, 1876 WL 19615 (U.S.Ill.)

Olga Tellis v Bombay Municipal Corporation [1985] MANU 0039 (SC)

P. Rathinam v Union of India [1994] MANU 0433 (SC)

People's Union for Democratic Rights v Union of India [1982] MANU 0038 (SC)

Prem Shankar Shukla v Delhi Administration [1980] MANU 0084 (SC)

Regional Director, Employees State Insurance Corporation v Suvarna Saw Mills, 1979 Lab. I.C. 1335 (Karnataka)

Royal Talkies, Hyderabad v Employees State Insurance Corporation [1978] MANU 0282 (SC)

Sheela Barse v State of Maharashtra [1987] MANU 0139 (SC)

Shri Ram Krishna Dalmia v Justice S.R. Tendolkar [1958] MANU 0024 (SC)

Siddheswar, Hubli v ESI, 1998 Lab. I.C. 212 (Orissa)

Sodan Singh v New Delhi Municipal Committee [1989] MANU 0521 (SC); and its follow-up decision [1992] MANU 0489 (SC)

Introduction

When the term 'informal sector' was used by Keith Hart in the early 1970s,[1] it referred to the wide range of activities that were not regulated, documented, or required government permission and interference to operate.[2] The International Labour Organization (ILO) hoped that through informal self-employment and small-scale entrepreneurship workers would have more control over their working conditions and living standards.[3] Accordingly, the ILO's policy stand was to encourage and promote informal economic activities in developing countries.[4] At this time scholars predicted that informal economic activities were only a transient phase, and that, along with industrial and economic development, workers engaged in informal economic activities would eventually become part of the formal economy.[5]

However, this prediction of formal economy assimilating informal workers in the course of development did not materialise. Instead of withering away, informal economic activities have experienced enormous growth around the globe.[6] Developing countries experienced the majority of this expansion of informal

---

1 Keith Hart, 'Informal income opportunities and urban employment in Ghana' (1973) 11(1) *The Journal of Modern African Studies* 61.
2 ILO, 'Employment, incomes and equality: a strategy for increasing productive employment in Kenya', report of an inter-agency team financed by the United Nations Development Programme and organised by the International Labour Office (Geneva: ILO, 1972).
3 Ibid 6, 503–504; Hart, 'Ghana' (n 1) 68–70.
4 Keith Hart, 'Bureaucratic form and the informal economy' in Basudeb Guha-Khasnobis, Ravi Kanbur and Elinor Ostrom (eds), *Linking the Formal and Informal Economy Concepts and Policies* (New York: Oxford University Press, 2006) 23 at 25–26. Even though I will be questioning the predominant idea of development as *economic development*, I use the binary of developing and developed because these terms have attained specific meanings in the context of informality.
5 See Neema Kudva, Lourdes Beneria, 'Introduction' in Neema Kudva, Lourdes Beneria (eds), *Rethinking Informalization: Poverty, Precarious Jobs and Social Protection* (Cornell University Open Access Repository, 2005) 6 at 6–7; Judy Fudge, 'Blurring legal boundaries' in Judy Fudge, Shae McCrystal and Kamala Sankaran (eds), *Challenging the Legal Boundaries of Work Regulation* (Oxford & Portland, Oregon: Hart Publishing, 2012) 1 at 5–6; also see Martha Alter Chen, 'The informal economy: definitions, theories and policies' (2012) WIEGO Working Paper No 1, available at http://wiego.org/sites/wiego.org/files/publications/files/Chen_WIEGO_WP1.pdf (last visited 2 November 2012).
6 Kudva and Beneria, *Rethinking Informalization* (n 5) 6; also see James Heintz, Robert Pollin, 'Informalization, economic growth, and the challenge of creating viable labor standards in developing countries' in Kudva, Beneria, *Rethinking Informalization* (n 5) 44 at 52–57; see also Martha

economic activities,[7] which was coupled with deteriorating working conditions and living standards of informal workers.[8] In view of the deplorable working conditions and living standards of informal workers, the ILO's initial enthusiasm for the informal sector was short-lived.[9]

In 1991, the ILO noted that, although the informal sector is an easily available alternative to job creation in the formal economy, conditions of work in the informal sector are far from appropriate.[10] Accordingly, the ILO declared that easy informal job creation cannot help workers if such jobs do not provide decent work.[11] In 1999, the ILO developed the Decent Work (DW) agenda, which constitutes the ILO's '[m]ission and objectives', and comprises the pillars of decent employment and income, rights at work, effective social protection and social dialogue.[12] Noting that decent work deficiency is a problem for informal workers globally, in its 2002 Report entitled *Decent Work and the Informal Economy*, the ILO calls for the need to integrate the DW agenda in informal economic activities.[13]

Such a call by the ILO is urgent in the context of countries such as India, where approximately 92 per cent of the workers are engaged in informal economic activities.[14] Informal workers in India suffer from multiple deprivations such as insecurity, uncertainty, longer working hours, lower wages, poor living standards, poor health, illiteracy and lower life expectancy in connection with their work-lives.[15]

Alter Chen, Renana Jhabvala and Frances Lund, 'Supporting workers in the informal economy', Working Paper on the Informal Economy (Geneva: International Labour Office Employment Sector, 2002) 1–3.

7   See ILO, *Women and Men in the Informal Economy: a Statistical Picture* (Geneva: ILO, 2002) 17–25.

8   See generally ILO, 'The dilemma of the informal sector', report of the Director-General, International Labour Conference, 78th Session (Geneva: ILO, 1991).

9   ibid.

10   ibid.

11   See ILO, *Decent Work and the Informal Economy*, International Labour Conference, 90th Session, 2002 (Geneva: International Labour Office, 2002) 4–5, 29–32, available at http://www.ilo.org/ public/english/standards/relm/ilc/ilc90/pdf/rep-vi.pdf (last visited 20 July 2010). The Decent Work Agenda developed by the ILO envisages a strategy to improve the living and working conditions of workers globally, irrespective of their formal or informal status. See ILO, 'Decent work agenda: promoting decent work for all', available at http://www.ilo.org/global/about-the-ilo/decent-work-agenda/lang--en/index.htm (last visited 1 December 2010); see also Dharam Ghai (ed), *Decent Work: Objectives and Strategies* (Geneva: ILO, 2006).

12   ILO, 'Mission and objectives', available at http://www.ilo.org/global/about-the-ilo/mission-and-objectives/lang--en/index.htm (last visited 4 August 2012).

13   See ILO, *Informal Economy* (n 11).

14   National Commission for Enterprises in the Unorganised Sector (NCEUS), *Report on Definitional and Statistical Issues Relating to Informal Economy* (New Delhi: NCEUS, 2008) 44.

15   Jan Breman describes the precarious plight of informal workers in India. Based on his case study of workers in Ahmedabad, Gujarat, he describes how informality contributes to precariousness by tracing the shift of workers from formal textile industry to informal economic activities. He lays specific emphasis on deskilling of informal workers, increasing working hours, decreasing income and the absence of unionisation. See Jan Breman, *The Making and Unmaking of an Industrial Working Class: Sliding Down the Labour Hierarchy in Ahmedabad, India* (New Delhi: Oxford University Press, 2004) 174–89, 260–68, 279; see also Jeemol Unni, Uma Rani, *Insecurities of Informal Workers in Gujarat, India* (Geneva: ILO, 2002).

There is a definite link between informal economic activity and abject economic poverty in India.[16] Scholarly studies on India have mainly been concerned with the effects of the increasing economic-policy-induced informality on conditions of informal workers.[17] Although these studies focus on the working and living conditions of informal workers, they do not explore the possibility of, or mechanism for, introducing and institutionalising the DW agenda for informal workers in India. Some recent studies conclude that informal economic activities in India are far from being compliant with the DW agenda.[18] Some studies point out that there is desperate need of law to regulate the informal activities in India.[19] Others indicate that informal workers' organisations are strategically significant in improving conditions for the workers in India.[20]

The Government of India's response to the conditions of informal workers in the country has been a delayed one. While the First National Commission on

16 NCEUS, *Report on Conditions of Work and Promotion of Livelihoods in the Unorganised Sector* (New Delhi: NCEUS, 2007), available at http://nceus.gov.in/Condition_of_workers_sep_2007.pdf (last visited 21 June 2010) 1, 8–9, 24–25, 43, 114; see also Breman (n 15) 254–58; Barbara Harriss-White, 'Globalization, the financial crisis and petty production in India's socially regulated informal economy' (2010) 1(1) *Global Labour Journal* 152; R K A Subrahmanya, Renana Jhabvala, 'Meeting basic needs: the unorganised sector and social security' in Renana Jhabvala, R K A Subrahmanya (eds), *The Unorganised Sector: Work Security and Social Protection* (New Delhi: Sage Publications, 2001) 17 at 18; Kaveri Gill, *Of Poverty and Plastic: Scavenging and Scrap Trading Entrepreneurs in India's Urban Informal Economy* (New Delhi: Oxford University Press, 2010) 59, 70–72.

17 See Barbara Harriss-White, Anushree Sinha (eds), *Trade Liberalization and India's Informal Economy* (New Delhi: Oxford University Press, 2007); Jan Breman, *Footloose Labour: Working in India's Informal Economy* (Cambridge: Cambridge University Press, 1996); Uma Rani, Jeemol Unni, 'Do economic reforms influence home-based work? Evidence from India' (2009) 15(3) *Feminist Economics* 191; Jeemol Unni, Namrata Bali, 'Subcontracted women workers in the garment industry in India' in R. Balakrishnan (ed), *The Hidden Assembly Line: Gender Dynamics of Subcontracted Work in a Global Economy* (Bloomfield, Connecticut: Kumarian Press, 2002) 115; Sujata Gothoskar, *New Initiatives in Organizing Strategy in the Informal Economy: a Case Study of Domestic Workers Organizing in India* (Bangkok: Committee for Asian Women, 2005).

18 See Rina Agarwala, 'From work to welfare: informal worker's organizations and the state in India' (unpublished PhD Thesis, Faculty of Princeton University, 2006); Bharati Chaturvedi, 'Santraj Maurya and Lipi in India: tales of two waste pickers in Delhi, India' in Melanie Samson (ed), *Refusing to be Cast Aside: Waste Pickers Organising Around the World* (Cambridge, MA: WIEGO, 2009) 8.

19 See Kamala Sankaran, Shalini Sinha and Roopa Madhav, 'WIEGO law pilot project on the informal economy domestic workers: background document', available at http://www.wiego.org/informal_economy_law/india/content/dw_background_note.pdf (last visited 24 April 2010); Kamala Sankaran, Shalini Sinha and Roopa Madhav, 'WIEGO law pilot project on the informal economy waste pickers background note', available at http://www.wiego.org/informal_economy_law/india/content/wp_background_note.pdf (last visited 24 April 2010).

20 See Agarwala (n 18); Elizabeth Hill, *Worker Identity, Agency and Economic Development: Women's Empowerment in the Indian Informal Economy* (New York: Routledge, 2010); Poornima Chikarmane, Laxmi Narayan, 'Organising the unorganised: a case study of the Kagad Kach Patra Kashtakari Panchayat' (Trade Union of Waste Pickers), available at http://www.wiego.org/program_areas/org_rep/case-kkpkp.pdf (last visited 23 April 2010); Nalini Shekar, 'Suman More: KKPKP, Pune, India' in Samson (n 18) 11; Arbind Singh, Rakesh Saran, 'NIDAN Swachdhara Private Ltd: forming a company with waste pickers in India' in Samson (n 18) 17; Janhavi Dave, Manali Shah and Yamini Parikh, 'Through union and co-operative in India, SEWA' in Samson (n 18) 27.

Labour (1969) did not mention informal workers, the Second National Commission on Labour (2002) was constituted 'to suggest an Umbrella Legislation for ensuring a minimum level of protection to the workers in the unorganised [informal] sector'.[21] The enormity of the numbers of informal workers in India and their poor predicament, which is comprehensively charted by the recently constituted Government of India commission, the National Commission for Enterprises in the Unorganised Sector (NCEUS), demonstrates the need for legislative protection for informal workers.[22]

Although some groups of informal workers, such as *bidi*[23] workers, construction workers etc enjoy legislative protection, such protections are principally directed towards waged informal workers.[24] The majority of informal workers in India do not enjoy productive employment in any meaningful sense; they encounter extremely adverse conditions at work, they are excluded from social protection mechanisms of the state and do not have any voice to air their grievances.[25] Many of these conditions could be secured for informal workers with the help of protective legislation. However, as the NCEUS shows, precarious conditions of informal workers in India are a fallout of the workers' exclusion from legislative protection in the country.[26]

In view of the decent work deficiency, and deplorable working and living conditions of informal workers in India, this book is concerned with ameliorating conditions of informal workers in India. More specifically, the objective of this book is to see whether a human development-inspired legislative framework might be able to promote overall development of a specific category of informal workers in India. As I discuss later, informal economic activities manifest activity-specific and region-specific heterogeneity. Because of this heterogeneity it is difficult, if not impossible, to categorise all informal economic activities together for analytical purposes. Accordingly, I adopt the approach of selecting one specific informal economic activity – waste picking – as my informal activity frame of reference.

In this introductory chapter, I situate my study within the existing scholarly and policy debates, and identify the research questions guiding my study. I explain how my theoretical and conceptual approaches will help me answer my research questions, and contribute to the debates on informal economic activities, human development and DW, and law. In the following section (secton 1), I identify scholarly contributions to the debates I mentioned above. In section 2, I locate my study within the law and policy debates on informal economic activities in India. In section 3, I discuss my theoretical frame of reference, which is Amartya Sen's

---

21   National Commission on Labour, *The Terms of Reference* (New Delhi: Government of India, 2002) ch 1 at 6, available at http://labour.nic.in/lcomm2/2nlc-pdfs/Chap1-2.pdf (last visited 28 May 2012).
22   See NCEUS, Definitional and Statistical Issues (n 14); see also NCEUS, Conditions of Work (n 16).
23   *Bidi* means hand-rolled cigarette in many Indian languages.
24   See NCEUS, *Conditions of Work* (n 16).
25   ibid.
26   ibid.

capability approach. As I will explain, since the objective of my study is to promote overall development of informal workers in India, I adopt the capability approach, which is a non-paternalistic and multi-dimensional approach to human development. I also discuss the existing scholarship that employs the capability approach in reconceptualising labour law and I identify the gaps left unaddressed by such studies.

In section 4, I outline some of the literature on the ILO's DW agenda and, specifically, the social dialogue pillar of that agenda. As I argue in Chapters 4 and 5, the democratic underpinning of the capability approach as conceived by Sen is compatible with the social dialogue pillar of the DW agenda. In section 5, I identify the research questions guiding my study and discuss my methodology with reference to my fieldwork in India. I adopt an integrated methodology for my study, which employs both textual analysis and empirical fieldwork to answer the key questions of the study. Finally, in section 6, I provide an outline of the book.

I.1 Informal economic activities, human development and decent work, and law

My study relies on the contribution of other scholars engaged in the analysis of working conditions and living standards of informal workers, the ILO formulated DW agenda and the capability approach-based labour law reconceptualisation. Since the aim of my study is human development of informal workers through legislative means, I have primarily relied on legal and socio-legal studies on labour law and how such law can promote human development of informal workers. I have also drawn upon sociological studies looking at the conditions of informal workers in developing countries and specifically in India, and economic studies engaged in the analysis of the capability-based human development approach. Since I am also interested in analysing the role of the social dialogue pillar of the DW agenda in the overall development of informal workers, I draw on policy studies on the DW agenda.

Despite the prominence of informal economic activities and informal workers in scholarly and policy debates[27] there is a dearth of legal studies on the topic. Very few legal studies have attempted to look at the role of law on conditions of informal workers. Prominent exceptions are Hernando de Soto and Kamala Sankaran's work on the relationship between law and informal economic activities in Peru and in India respectively.[28] De Soto looks at how complicated, costly

27 See for example ILO, *Informal Economy* (n 11); Marc Bacchetta, Ekkehard Ernst and Juana P Bustamante, *Globalization and Informal Jobs in Developing Countries* (Geneva: WTO & ILO, 2009); Kudva and Beneria (n 5); and Women in Informal Employment: Globalizing & Organizing (WIEGO), available at http://wiego.org (last visited 20 October 2010), for research and advocacy on comprehensive issues related to informal workers.

28 See generally Hernando de Soto, *The Other Path: the Invisible Revolution in the Third World* (New York: Harper & Row, 1989); Kamala Sankaran, 'Informal employment and the challenges for labour

and time-consuming laws and legal frameworks force entrepreneurs to operate informally.[29] However, he is not concerned about ways in which law might be able to improve conditions of informal workers.[30]

On the other hand, although Sankaran analyses the exclusion of informal workers from the scope of labour law in India, she does not look at how an effective legislative framework could be developed in order to improve conditions of informal workers in India.[31] Legal scholar and former ILO official Anne Trebilcock indicates how different development approaches could become possible candidates for the development of labour law for informal economic activities.[32] However, her study remains inconclusive about the choice of the development approach and does not analyse how a human development-inspired labour law might work in the context of informal economic activities.[33]

Labour law scholars (and economists) Bob Hepple, Robert Salais, Simon Deakin, Frank Wilkinson, Jude Browne, Judy Fudge, Brian Langille and Kevin Kolben are interested in the reconceptualisation of labour law so that law could promote human development of workers.[34] These scholars invoke the capability approach to human development formulated by Sen in reconceptualising labour law.[35] However, with the exception of Hepple they are not concerned with informal economic activities

law' in Guy Davidov, Brian Langille (eds), *The Idea of Labour Law* (Oxford and New York: Oxford University Press, 2011) 223; Kamala Sankaran, *Labour Laws in South Asia: the Need for an Inclusive Approach* (Geneva: International Institute for Labour Studies, 2007); Kamala Sankaran, 'Protecting the worker in the informal economy: the role of labour law' in Guy Davidov, Brian Langille (eds), *Boundaries and Frontiers of Labour Law* (Portland, OR: Hart Publishing, 2006) 205; Kamala Sankaran, 'Labour laws in South Asia: the need for an inclusive approach' in Tzehainesh Tekle (ed), *Labour Law and Worker Protection in Developing Countries* (Oxford and Portland, OR: Hart, Geneva: ILO, 2010) 225.

29   de Soto, *The Other Path* (n 28).
30   ibid.
31   Sankaran, 'Informal employment' (n 28); Sankaran, 'Protecting the worker' (n 28); Sankaran, 'The need for an inclusive approach' (n 28).
32   See Anne Trebilcock, 'Using development approaches to address the challenge of the informal economy for labour law' in Davidov and Langille *Boundaries and Frontiers* (n 28) 63.
33   See generally ibid.
34   See Bob Hepple, *Labour Law, Inequality and Global Trade*, Sinzheimer Lecture 2002 (Amsterdam: Hugo Sinzheimer Instituut, 2002); Robert Salais, 'Incorporating the CA into social and employment policies' in Robert Salais, Robert Villeneuve (eds), *Europe and the Politics of Capabilities* (New York: Cambridge University Press, 2004) 287; Jude Browne, Simon Deakin and Frank Wilkinson, 'Capabilities, social rights and European market integration' in Salais and Villeneuve (ibid) 205; Simon Deakin, 'The contribution of labour law to economic and human development' in Davidov and Langille, *Idea of Labour Law* (n 28) 156; Brian A. Langille, 'Core labour rights: the true story (reply to Alston)' (2005) 16(3) *European Journal of International Law* 409; Judy Fudge, 'The new discourse of labor rights' (2007) 29 *Comparative Labor Law and Policy Journal* 29; Judy Fudge, 'Labour as a "fictive commodity": radically reconceptualizing labour law' in Davidov and Langille, *Idea of Labour Law* (n 28) 120; Brian Langille, 'Labour law's theory of justice' in Davidov and Langille, *Idea of Labour Law* (n 28) 101; Kevin Kolben, 'A development approach to trade and labor regimes' (2010) 45(2) *Wake Forest Law Review* 355.
35   ibid; see also Amartya Sen, *Development as Freedom* (New York: Alfred A. Knopf, 1999).

in developing countries, and accordingly, their reconceptualisation effort remains confined to issues involving workers in developed countries.

On the other hand, sociologists, economists and development scholars have shown interest in analysing working conditions and living standards of informal workers from a capability approach-based human development point of view,[36] but their approach remains non-legal. Few ILO reports note the urgency of promoting DW for informal workers,[37] but the organisation leaves it to the member states to develop their own mechanism for the same.[38]

As this brief overview of scholarly literature suggests, scholars from different disciplines have been interested in informal economic activities, a human development approach and labour law, but an analysis of informal economic activities with a view to promote the human development of informal workers through legislative means remains absent from scholarly debates. Such an analysis is important because informal workers remain excluded from legislative benefits in developing countries,[39] including India.[40]

Such an analysis can also indicate whether it is possible to institutionalise human development-enhancing factors through legislative means. Accordingly, in this book I analyse the informal activity of waste picking in India as an example of informal economic activity in order to see whether it is possible to promote human development of waste pickers through a human development-inspired labour law conceptualisation. In the following sub-sections I locate my study within the three categories of scholarly literatures that I engage with in my study, which are informal workers, law and policy in India; the capability approach; and the DW agenda and social dialogue.

I.1.1 Informal workers, law and policy in India

In India, scholarly studies undertaken mainly by economists focus principally on the contribution of the informal sector to the overall economy.[41] Economists are interested in ascertaining the share of informal economic activities on the gross domestic product (GDP) of the country.[42] They are concerned with the productivity

---

36   Hill, *Worker Identity* (n 20); see also Elizabeth Hill, 'Women in the Indian informal economy: collective strategies for work life improvement and development' (2001) 15(3) *Work, Employment & Society* 443; Sabina Alkire, *Valuing Freedoms: Sen's CA and Poverty Reduction* (New York: Oxford University Press, 2002); Agarwala *From Work to Welfare* (n 18).

37   ILO, *The Dilemma* (n 8); see also ILO, *Informal Economy* (n 11).

38   ILO, *Informal Economy* (n 11).

39   See Tekle, *Labour Law* (n 28); de Soto, *The Other Path* (n 28); Guillermo E Perry and others (eds), *Informality: Exit and Exclusion* (Washington DC: The World Bank, 2007).

40   See NCEUS, *Conditions of Work* (n 16); Tekle, *Labour Law* (n 28); also see note 31.

41   See Sugata Marjit, Saibal Kar, *The Outsiders: Economic Reforms and Informal Labour in a Developing Economy* (New Delhi: Oxford University Press, 2011); also see Renana Jhabvala, Ratna M Sudarshan and Jeemol Unni (eds), *Informal Economy Centrestage: New Structures of Employment* (New Delhi: Sage Publications, 2003).

42   See N Lalitha, 'Unorganised manufacturing and the gross domestic product' in Jhabvala, Sudarshan and Unni, *Informal Economy Centrestage* (n 41) 157.

and employment generation capacity of the informal sector.[43] Even the recently constituted high-powered government commission, the NCEUS, was constituted in order to determine how the informal sector in India can contribute to the growth, employment generation, exports promotion, productivity improvement and competitiveness of the country.[44]

Scholarly concern for conditions of informal workers has received scant attention in informality debates in India. Such lack of attention led one commentator to note that the 'ongoing debates' on informal economic activities 'are directed almost exclusively by the interests and concerns of the entrepreneurs, and are practically silent on the right of workers to safety and security'.[45]

However, scholars mainly outside India show that workers' rights, their safety, security, vulnerability, marginalisation and exclusion concerns are central problems in informality debates around the globe.[46] They note that in some countries the majority of informal activities are 'moderately or highly precarious' – devoid of stability and security.[47] Some studies document the vulnerability and struggle of specific categories of informal workers.[48] For certain categories of informal workers, such as homeworkers, there is a link between working in the informal activity and being poor.[49] Martha Alter Chen, Renana Jhabvala and Frances Lund note that informal economic activities are a manifestation of deteriorating bargaining power of workers worldwide.[50]

Through her sociological study in India, Rina Agarwala shows that, while some informal workers in India have successfully bargained with the state in order to

---

43   See generally Ratna M Sudarshan, Jeemol Unni, 'Measuring the informal economy' in Jhabvala, Sudarshan and Unni, *Informal Economy Centrestage* (n 41) 19; Jeemol Unni, Uma Rani, 'Employment and income in the informal economy: a micro-perspective' in Jhabvala, Sudarshan and Unni, *Informal Economy Centrestage* (n 41) 39; Keshab Das, 'Income and employment in informal manufacturing: a case study' in Jhabvala, Sudarshan and Unni, *Informal Economy Centrestage* (n 41) 62; see also generally Marjit and Kar *The Outsiders* (n 41). Such scholarly interest is part of a global trend of linking informal activities with growth and development issues. For example see Bacchetta, Ernst and Bustamante, *Globalization and Informal Jobs* (n 27).

44   'Terms of Reference of the Commission', Annexure 3 in NCEUS, *Conditions of Work* (n 16) 342. However, it is a relief that once constituted the commission did not strictly adhere to the terms of reference, as I will discuss presently.

45   Das, 'Income and employment' (n 43) 98.

46   Kudva and Beneria, *Rethinking Informalization* (n 5); also see Chen, Jhabvala and Lund, *Supporting Workers in the Informal Economy* (n 6) 13–14.

47   Lourdes Beneria, Maria Floro, 'Distribution, gender, and labor market informalization: a conceptual framework with a focus on homeworkers' in Kudva and Beneria, *Rethinking Informalization* (n 5) 9 at 19.

48   See Samson, *Refusing to be Cast Aside* (n 18); also see generally Martha Chen, Jennefer Sebstad and Lesley O'Connell, 'Counting the invisible workforce: the case of homebased workers' (1999) 27(3) *World Development* 603.

49   Marty Chen, 'Rethinking the informal economy: from enterprise characteristics to employment relations' in Kudva and Beneria, *Rethinking Informalization* (n 5) 28 at 40–42; see also Heintz and Pollin, 'Informalization' (n 6) 44; also see Chen, Jhabvala and Lund, *Supporting Workers in the Informal Economy* (n 6) 12.

50   Chen, Jhabvala and Lund, *Supporting Workers in the Informal Economy* (n 6) 29; see also Chen, 'Definitions, theories and policies' (n 5).

avail themselves of some legislative benefits, such benefits remain restricted to certain Indian states, and only to some specific categories of informal workers.[51] Sankaran shows that being based on the juridical notion of the employment relationship, Indian labour laws are not particularly suited to the needs of informal workers in the country.[52] However, Sankaran's work did not focus on the possibility of an informal activity-specific labour law model.[53] Like Sankaran, since I am also interested in ascertaining whether informal workers could avail themselves of appropriate legislative safeguards, in this book I examine the possibility of a labour law model suited to the conditions of a specific category of informal workers in India in order to fill the gap in the existing literature that looks at the possibility of improving informal workers' conditions through legislative means. Because I am interested in legislation-induced overall human development of informal workers, my theoretical framework is based on Sen's capability approach.

I.1.2 The capability approach

Sen offers an encompassing idea of human development that permeates working conditions and living standards of informal workers, making it possible to conceptualise overall development of such workers. Sen's capability approach emerged as a response to the mainstream human development approaches.[54] Different mainstream human development theories attribute development to the possession and enjoyment of goods, resources and wealth, and measure development in terms of happiness or utility.[55] Some theoretical approaches prioritise institutions, rights and liberties.[56] As an alternative to these approaches that concentrate on the availability of resources, Sen offers a multi-dimensional approach to human development known as the capability approach.

Instead of prioritising the role of resources, the capability approach looks at what different resources do for individuals, as I discuss in detail in Chapter 3. This approach evaluates development on the basis of multiple factors – resources, institutions, environment and physical features – that enhance an individual's opportunity. According to the capability approach, there need not be any predetermined set of resources or institutions which can guarantee human development, as Sen argues that necessary resources and institutions for the purpose of human development will depend on actual circumstances that surround specific individuals. Such a multi-dimensional non-paternalistic idea of human development

---

51 See generally Agarwala, *From Work to Welfare* (n 18).
52 See note 31.
53 Ibid.
54 David A Clark, 'The capability approach: its development, critiques and recent advances' GPRG-WPS-032 (November 2005) 1 at 2–3.
55 ibid. Also see generally Amartya Sen, 'Equality of what?' The Tanner Lecture on Human Values, delivered at Stanford University (22 May 1979) in *The Tanner Lectures On Human Values Vol I* (Salt Lake City: University of Utah Press/Cambridge, London, Melbourne and Sydney: Cambridge University Press, 1980).
56 Ibid. For example see John Rawls, *A Theory of Justice* (Cambridge, MA: Harvard University Press, 1971).

is especially useful for the purpose of analysing working conditions and living standards of specific categories of informal workers.

According to Sen, human development entails freedom to choose the life people have reasons to value.[57] The idea of democratic participation and dialogue is central to Sen's capability approach. He calls for active participation of people mediated by multiple institutions of a democratic society in order to decide conditions that a society should provide to facilitate individual capabilities.[58]

The capability approach offers multiple advantages as a theoretical basis for the analysis of informal economic activities. First, the reference point of the capability approach is the working and living conditions of workers – the approach is concerned with human development. This focus on human development of workers helps in thinking about informal workers as complete individual entities, not necessarily tied to an employment relationship on which the traditional idea of labour law is based. Secondly, the capability approach is non-paternalistic. Non-paternalism allows workers to decide for themselves what development means to them. Thirdly, according to Sen, policy decisions should be arrived at through a democratic deliberation process with wide participation of all stakeholders in a society.[59] Multiple institutions of the democratic society such as the government, opposition, political parties, legislature, media, civil society and judiciary should mediate such a democratic culture.[60]

These advantages have drawn scholars such as Hepple, Salais, Deakin, Wilkinson, Browne, Fudge and Langille to reconceptualise labour law on the basis of the capability approach. However, as Fudge notes, the efforts to reconceptualise labour law's normative foundations through the capability approach are focused on developed countries.[61] Although some studies employ the capability approach in the context of informal economic activities in the developing world, they do not undertake an analysis of the institution of law itself.[62] The few scholarly studies that are concerned with labour law in this particular context note that there is an urgent need to debate and analyse labour law specifically contextualised in developing country informality issues.[63]

Against this backdrop, I examine whether the capability approach can be invoked to develop a normative goal of labour law for a particular variety of informal economic activities in India. Since the capability approach as conceptualised by Sen has a strong democratic component I analyse how far the

---

57   Sen, *Development* (n 35) 18.
58   ibid 155–57; Amartya Sen, *The Idea of Justice* (Cambridge, MA: Harvard University Press, 2009) 388–415.
59   Sen, *Development* (n 35) 155–57; Sen, *Idea of Justice* (n 58) 388–415.
60   Sen, *Development* (n 35) xii–xiii; Jean Drèze, Amartya Sen, *India: Development and Participation* (New Delhi: Oxford University Press, 2002) 20.
61   Fudge, 'The new discourse' (n 34) 31.
62   See for example Hill, *Worker Identity* (n 20); see also Hill, 'Women' (n 36); Alkire, *Valuing Freedoms* (n 36); also see Trebilcock, 'Using development approaches' (n 32) 63.
63   See generally Tekle, *Labour Law* (n 28); Sankaran, Sinha and Madhav, 'Domestic workers' (n 19); Sankaran, Sinha and Madhav, 'Waste pickers' (n 19).

strategy of social dialogue, which is one of the pillars of the DW agenda promoted by the ILO,[64] could be successfully employed to integrate informal workers into the process of institutionalisation of capability-enhancing factors. My goal is to determine whether and, if so, how the process of social dialogue can promote a non-paternalistic idea of labour law for informal economic activities. For this reason I explore the literature that debates the role of the DW pillar of social dialogue in improving conditions of workers, including informal workers.

I.1.3 The decent work (DW) agenda and social dialogue

In 1999, the ILO devised the DW agenda as a global goal for workers around the world. The DW agenda was envisaged as a policy goal to improve conditions of workers irrespective of the nature of the work and status of the industry within which they work.[65] It comprises four basic pillars: productive employment, fundamental rights and principles at work, social protection and social dialogue.[66] Thus, decency of work is dependent on the productive and satisfactory nature of work (or employment), availability of labour rights at work, provision for social security and effectiveness of social dialogue.[67]

The objective of the DW agenda is to promote 'people's well-being'.[68] Decent work 'can pave the way for broader social and economic advancement, strengthening individuals, their families and communities'.[69] What the capability approach envisages in the larger political context, the DW agenda conceptualises in the narrower context of work and worker welfare. Sen's capability approach can be specified in policy terms with the help of the DW agenda developed by the ILO.

In Chapter 4, I focus on the social dialogue pillar of the DW agenda. The ILO asserts that giving voice to informal workers is one of the most important measures in making decent work available to informal workers.[70] Voice (democratic deliberation) and public participation are central to the idea of social dialogue. I analyse the pillar of social dialogue from a two-pronged perspective. First, I assess the conditions necessary to institutionalise social dialogue in informal economic activities. Secondly, I look at how the pillar of social dialogue might help promote conditions of a specific category of informal workers in India.

The principle of social dialogue is based on the understanding that workers can decide for themselves what constitutes a decent life for them, and can help

---

64   The ILO defines social dialogue as tripartite negotiation, consultation or exchange of information about social and economic policy between governments, employers and workers. See ILO, 'Social dialogue sector', available at http://www.ilo.org/public/english/dialogue/ (last visited 4 August 2012).
65   ILO, 'Promoting decent work for all' (n 11).
66   Ghai, *Decent Work* (n 11); ILO, *Informal Economy* (n 11).
67   Ghai, *Decent Work* (n 11).
68   ibid.
69   ibid.
70   ILO, *Informal Economy* (n 11).

determine the policies that promote their decent life by effective democratic participation. The pillar of social dialogue refers to a wide range of mechanisms of discussion, consultation, negotiation and information exchange in matters of common interest between the workers, employers and government.[71] The purpose of social dialogue is to promote democratic participation by principal stakeholders in the world of work.[72] Workers' perceptions of what constitutes a decent life for them, and their capacity to represent their view through the processes of democratic deliberation that are part of social dialogue fit within the capabilities approach developed by Sen.[73]

The principle of democratic deliberation and public participation is foundational in Sen's capability approach.[74] Sen envisages a continuous process of democratic deliberation in furtherance of social and economic policy measures that are instrumental in enhancing capabilities of individuals.[75] Thus, it is possible to conceptualise social dialogue as a component of democratic deliberation and public participation process that is central to Sen's capability approach and his idea of justice.[76] Social dialogue, which promotes the idea of effective exchange of information, opinions and participation in the democratic deliberation process amongst all the stakeholders related to work,[77] is a manifestation of workers' capabilities and, in turn, also promotes capabilities of the workers.

To date, the ILO has not been able to devise mechanisms to promote social dialogue in the informal economy.[78] According to Sarosh Kuruvilla, the ILO's focus on social dialogue is still rooted in the bipartite and tripartite institutional mechanism that has been the reference point of traditional labour law.[79] Although the ILO recognises that social dialogue need not be limited only to collective bargaining,[80] in conceptualising social dialogue the ILO emphasises the role of labour unions, employers and governments.[81] The problem with this bipartite or tripartite conceptualisation is that a large number of informal workers are left out because of the absence of labour unions or employers.[82]

---

71 ILO, Freedom of Association and Collective Bargaining (Geneva: ILO, 1994); ILO, Conclusions Concerning Tripartite Consultation at the National Level on Economic and Social Policy (Geneva: ILO, 1996); ILO, Decent Work: Report of the Director General (Geneva: ILO, 1999); A V Jose, The ILO Declaration on Fundamental Principles and Rights at Work: Role of Social Partners in South Asia (Geneva: ILO, IILS, 2002) 2.
72 ILO, 1994 (n 71); ILO, 1996 (n 71); ILO, 1999 (n 71).
73 Amartya Sen, *Inequality Re-examined* (New York: Russell Sage Foundation/Cambridge, MA: Harvard University Press, 1992); Sen, *Development* (n 35).
74 Sen, *Development* (n 35) 31–32, 36–40, 51–53, 123, 147–48, 152–55; Sen, *Idea of Justice* (n 58) 91, 324–27, 388–415.
75 Sen, *Development* (n 35); Sen, *Idea of Justice* (n 58).
76 Sen, *Idea of Justice* (n 58) 388–415.
77 Ghai, *Decent Work* (n 11); ILO, *Informal Economy* (n 11).
78 Sarosh Kuruvilla, 'Social dialogue for decent work' in Ghai, *Decent Work* (n 11) 179–80.
79 ibid.
80 ILO, *Informal Economy* (n 11).
81 Kuruvilla, 'Social dialogue' (n 78) 180–81.
82 ibid 181–83.

Therefore, it is imperative to move beyond the limited concepts of bipartite and tripartite dialogue process mediated by unions, to give voice and allow participation to informal workers. Therefore, in this book I explore the possibility of integrating a specific group of informal workers into the social dialogue process. Situated at the intersection of the scholarly literature noted above, the following are the aims and methods of my study.

I.2 Aims and methods

In this study I want to ascertain the extent to which the integrated framework of the capability approach and the social dialogue pillar of the DW agenda can effectively contribute to the design of a labour law model that is responsive to the problems of informal workers in India. What mechanism might be devised in the furtherance of legislative institutionalisation of factors that can enhance capabilities of the specific category of informal workers (waste pickers) in India? As a corollary to these issues I seek to ascertain the capability deficiencies of the waste pickers in India. Which desirable capabilities do the waste pickers identify as valuable to them? What role can unionisation/organisation of informal workers play during the legislative institutionalisation of capability-enhancing factors? What could be the role of multiple institutions of a democratic society in the process of institutionalisation of capability-enhancing factors for informal workers in India?

In order to address these issues, I adopt an interdisciplinary approach to my study. My study is situated at the intersection of the disciplines of law, sociology and political economy, with a case study of a specific informal economic activity in India. Although the central focus of the study is legal, it is not a legal study in the traditional sense of the term. My study is not concerned solely with the analysis and interpretation of legislative texts and judicial decisions, but rather conceptualises and contextualises law in social interactions. It understands law as one amongst many of the institutions of society that shape social interactions. My case study employs the methods of qualitative interviewing and participant observation.

I undertake a socio-legal approach[83] to my study, which analyses law in the larger context of the society.[84] Such an approach allows me to question the interrelationship between law and society; evolutionary influences of law and society on each other; assumptions underlying the relation between law and society.[85] The socio-legal approach is specifically important for these purposes because my

---

83 Scholars distinguish between socio-legal approach, an interdisciplinary research approach in the United Kingdom, from the law and society approach prevalent in the United States, and the legal sociology tradition of continental Western European countries. While these distinctions are based on very subtle premises, what is common in all these traditions is that all of them promote interdisciplinary research involving law – law is studied in the context of the society. See Reza Banakar, Max Travers, 'Introduction' in Reza Banakar and Max Travers (eds), *Theory and Method in Socio-Legal Research* (Oxford & Portland, OR: Hart, 2005) ix at xi–xiii.

84 ibid 1–2.

85 See Reza Banakar, Max Travers, 'Law, sociology and method' in Banakar and Travers, *Theory and Method* (n 83) 1 at 5.

study questions the fundamental basis of (labour) law – it questions the assumptions underlying labour law and its role in society – it discusses the inadequacies of labour law to address problems of informal economic activities – and it advocates the reconceptualisation of labour law so that it remains a relevant institution for the betterment of the society at large. In order to analyse law in the context of the society, my study undertakes a theoretical analysis, which is supplemented by empirical research.

I develop the theoretical underpinnings of my study in Chapters 3, 4 and 5. I employ my theoretical analysis in order to propose a new approach to labour law, which is more attuned to the necessities of informal workers. As I alluded to earlier, the theoretical approach that I propose in the interest of developing a labour law model for informal workers integrates the capability approach formulated by Sen with the strategic pillar of social dialogue developed by the ILO. I then test this theoretical proposal through my empirical study, which I discuss in Chapters 6 and 7. Specifically, I employ the analytical perspective of the capability approach in order to evaluate the nature and extent of deprivation of a specific category of informal workers in India. With the help of this empirical study I show how my theoretical approach might work in the specific context of the informal economic activity of waste collection in India.

I have selected waste picking as the subject of my case study for two different reasons: first, waste picking is an informal activity that is directly linked to the formal economy through the process of production;[86] and, secondly, waste picking is one of the most marginalised and volatile of all informal activities (waste pickers are primarily temporarily engaged in waste-picking activity in the absence of better work – it is hardly considered proper work even by waste pickers themselves). Although both of these characteristics might be true for some other informal activities, waste picking is the classic case of the lower rung of informal activity that is transient in nature, which posits a serious challenge to the institutionalisation of capability-enhancing factors and operationalisation of the social dialogue principle.

Moreover, women constitute the majority of the waste pickers in India.[87] Women waste pickers manifest the work-life challenges of informal economic activities where work and family responsibilities are interwoven into each other. Accordingly, in order to understand the complexities of my research participants' work-lives, during the case study, my interviewing focus was narrative and intended to elicit interpretative accounts of the experiences of the interviewee stakeholders. As a participant observer, although I participated during the unionisation effort

---

86   See generally Alejandro Portes, Lauren Benton, 'Industrial development and labor absorption: a reinterpretation' (1984) 10(4) *Population and Development Review* 589; also see generally Alejandro Portes, Manuel Castells and Lauren A Benton (eds), *The Informal Economy: Studies in Advanced and Less Developed Countries* (Baltimore & London: The Johns Hopkins University Press, 1989).

87   See generally Poornima Chikarmane, Lakshmi Narayanan, 'Transform or perish: changing conceptions of work in recycling' in Fudge, McCrystal and Sankaran, *Challenging the Legal Boundaries* (n 5) 49.

of the waste pickers (discussed in Chapter 7), I attempted to be non-interfering in the decision-making processes. The approach of the empirical study was to preserve the naturalness of the case studied in Kolkata, India.

Since the activity of waste picking is linked to the formal recycling production process, such linkage could indicate that informality might not necessarily be a strategic cost–benefit decision at all times as argued by some scholars and international organisations[88] and more of a survival need of informal workers. Such linkage will also help to illustrate the continuity between formal and informal activities, if any, and its effect on informal workers. Waste pickers are self-employed workers who do not have a fixed employer. Such a framework of operation of the activity adversely affects waste pickers' bargaining power.

However, workers engaged in the waste picking activity are beginning to organise for their rights. Such organisation initiative has helped me understand the role of informal workers' union in their capability development. I conducted my case study in Kolkata (state of West Bengal), India. During the course of my fieldwork in Kolkata, waste pickers in the city organised themselves into a trade union. The formation of the trade union in Kolkata has helped me probe the relation between unionisation of waste pickers and enhancement (or the possibility thereof) of their capabilities.

The state of West Bengal is a particularly interesting jurisdiction for a case study of informal waste pickers. Ruled by the Left Front government led by the Communist Party of India (Marxist) for a long time, the state provides some limited nature of support to informal workers.[89] Since 2001, the state has instituted a contributory provident fund scheme for informal workers.[90] In 2007 the state enacted the West Bengal Unorganised Sector Workers' Welfare Act, 2007. A Labour Welfare Board constituted under the statute would conceive and execute health insurance schemes, pension schemes, house building loans, educational assistance for workers' children, maternity benefit schemes and other welfare schemes for informal workers.[91] However, what is striking is that waste pickers as a category of informal workers are totally excluded from the purview of the scheme, as well as the statute. Accordingly, waste pickers in Kolkata do not receive any kind of government assistance or social protection. Against this backdrop I analyse deprivations of waste pickers in Kolkata, the capital of the state of West Bengal, through my case study. In the following section, I provide a chapter outline of my study.

88　See generally ILO, *Informal Economy* (n 11); Perry and others, *Informality* (n 39); de Soto, *The Other Path* (n 28).

89　Agarwala, *From Work to Welfare* (n 18) 120–121.

90　'State Assisted Scheme of Provident Fund for Unorganised Workers in West Bengal' (SASPFUW), Labour Department Resolution Nos 180-IR (24 January 2001) and 305-IR (19 February 2001) of the Government of West Bengal.

91　See Government of West Bengal, *Labour in West Bengal 2010: Annual Report* (Kolkata: Government of West Bengal) 74.

I.3 Chapter outline

Informal economic activities are defined in different ways,[92] depending on the nature and purpose of scholarly analyses. In Chapter 1, I engage with the debate on the different conceptual understandings related to informal economic activities, and analyse terminologies used in the context of informal activities.

In Chapter 2, I discuss the report of the high-level commission, the NCEUS, established by the Government of India,[93] which shows the scarcity and sometimes total lack of legislative protection for informal workers in India.[94] Although India's constitution provides for labour welfare guarantees,[95] such guarantees largely remain unrealised for informal workers. In the absence of legislative protection of informal workers in India, I document the efforts of informal workers' trade unions, and other NGOs in promoting informal workers' interests. I argue that through socio-economic provisioning and political action these organisations promote human development of informal workers, and ensure a dignified life for these workers, as envisaged by the Constitution of India. I link the Indian judiciary-developed idea of dignified life to the concept of human development envisaged by Amartya Sen.

In Chapter 3, I elaborate on the concept of human development envisaged by Sen. He adopts an *institutionally integrated approach*, wherein the different institutions of the democratic society would interact in order to ensure appropriate conditions for human development in terms of promotion of capabilities.[96] Sen envisages continuous public participation and democratic dialogue involving individuals and integrated institutions in furtherance of promotion of capabilities within a particular society.[97] Social dialogue and public participation play a constructive role in the promotion of capabilities within a particular society. I discuss the nuances of social dialogue and public participation in a democratic society as envisaged by Sen. I also indicate the link between the ILO's DW pillar of social dialogue and Sen's notion of democratic dialogue and public participation in this chapter.

In Chapter 4, I discuss the strategic agenda of DW envisaged by the ILO in order to ameliorate conditions for informal workers. I argue that the social dialogue pillar is the ILO's strategic equivalent of the democratic dialogue principle central to the capability approach. However, social dialogue promoted by the ILO remains faithful to the tripartite structure, integrating government, workers and employers into the dialogue process. In the absence of representative organisation of informal workers, a tripartite social dialogue framework cannot integrate informal workers into the policy-making process. Thus, I argue that the social

---

92   NCEUS, *Definitional and Statistical Issues* (n 14) 13–16.

93   See Government of India Resolution No 5(2)/2004-ICC (20 September 2004).

94   See generally NCEUS, *Conditions of Work* (n 16); NCEUS, *The Challenge of Employment in India: an Informal Economy Perspective*, vol 1 Main Report (New Delhi: NCEUS, 2009).

95   P B Gajendragadkar, *The Constitution of India: Its Philosophy and Basic Postulates*, Gandhi Memorial Lectures, University College, Nairobi, First Series (Nairobi: Oxford University Press, 1969) 51.

96   Sen, *Development* (n 35) xii–xiii; Drèze and Sen, *India: Development and Participation* (n 60) 20.

97   Sen, *Idea of Justice* (n 58) 345–46.

dialogue framework needs to integrate multiple institutions in order to allow informal workers to participate in the policy-making process involving them. I conclude the chapter with a comparison of the DW agenda and the capability approach as possible frameworks to analyse the case study of informal workers in Kolkata, India.

In Chapter 5, based on Sen's capability approach, I offer a theoretical framework to think about labour law for informal economic activities, which is not tied to the juridical concept of employment relationship. I use elements of Sen's theory discussed in Chapter 3 to conceptualise labour law for informal economic activities.

Chapter 6 is based on my case study of the informal waste pickers in Kolkata, India. In this chapter I analyse the capability deficiencies of a specific category of informal workers – waste pickers in Kolkata. I also ascertain what the waste pickers in Kolkata deem to be *desirable capabilities* for their work-lives. In Chapter 7, I propose a framework through which labour law for specific categories of informal workers could be developed. This chapter is aimed at putting the theory into work with a specific example. The book ends with a concluding chapter, where I briefly review my main arguments and research findings.

1 Informality in India

A workers' perspective

1.1 Introduction

In the Introduction to this book, I charted the context and delineated the aim of my book. In this chapter, I discuss the concepts that I engage with in my book. I discuss the different terminologies and the underlying theoretical justifications, which are used in the context of the generic concept of *informality*. I identify the terminology that is most appropriate for the purpose of my study, which, as I pointed out in the introductory chapter, is amelioration of conditions of informal workers in India. Accordingly, while identifying the appropriate terminology for policy-making purposes, I focus on its appropriateness in the Indian context.

The majority of workers globally work under extremely precarious conditions.[1] Insecurity looms large over every aspect of their work. These workers lack guaranteed regular work, they can barely secure minimum wages, they do not have any social protection and the conditions at work defy the notion of dignity for workers.[2] Despite their precarious condition, informal workers have largely remained outside government policy initiatives.

Policy-making in the informal economy is marred by the way informal economic activities are variously defined with differing perspectives in view. Economists and statisticians are interested in measuring the contribution of the informal economic activities in the overall economy. Labour activists are concerned with the improvement of the living standards and working conditions of workers engaged in informal activities. Amongst these differing perspectives each of the constituents

---

1 See ILO, *Decent Work and the Informal Economy*, International Labour Conference, 90th Session (Geneva: International Labour Office, 2002) 1–4, 31–33, available at http://www.ilo.org/public/english/standards/relm/ilc/ilc90/pdf/rep-vi.pdf (last visited 20 July 2010); Kristina Flodman Becker, 'The informal economy' Sida fact finding study (March 2004) 21, available at http://rru.worldbank.org/Documents/PapersLinks/Sida.pdf (last visited 20 July 2010); *National Commission for Enterprises in the Unorganised Sector* (NCEUS), 'Report on conditions of work and promotion of livelihoods in the unorganised sector' (New Delhi: NCEUS, 2007), available at http://nceus.gov.in/Condition_of_workers_sep_2007.pdf (last visited 21 June 2010); Jeemol Unni, 'Gender and informality in labour market in South Asia' (2001) 36(26) *Economic and Political Weekly* 2360.

2 ILO, *Informal Economy* (n 1) at 2–4, 16–27; Becker (n 1) at 8–10; NCEUS, 'Conditions of work' (n 1).

chooses their own definition and terminology to work their way in furthering their objectives. Accordingly, I engage with the different concepts and propose the use of a terminology for a worker-centric informality conceptualisation.

Before discussing the conceptual nuances of informality in the Indian context, it is useful to clarify the terms that I shall be using in this book. I will be using the term 'informal employment' to suggest informal economic activities, irrespective of whether workers engaged in such activities are waged-workers or self-employed workers. I will use the terms 'informal employment' and 'informal economic activities' interchangeably. I will use the term *work* to suggest all kinds of paid and unpaid labour – such as self-employment, wage-employment, disguised employment, unpaid family work. To denote workers in an employment relationship, I will use the terms 'waged-workers' or 'workers in employment-relationship'. To denote workers who are not employed by an employer, I will use the terms 'self-employed workers', 'own account workers', and 'unwaged workers'.

I begin my task by analysing the formal/informal divide on the basis of the dominant theories offered to explain it. There are two major theoretical conceptualisations that explain the formal/informal dichotomy – *dualism* and *structuralism*. The dualist theory is based on the rural/urban, agriculture/industry, and non-capitalist/capitalist dichotomy, and delineates the simultaneous but unrelated existence of the formal and the informal sectors. On the contrary, structuralists argue that the formal and the informal economies are inherently related to each other. According to the structuralist viewpoint the informal economy is part of the process of production that the formal economy employs in the modern world. I argue that both of these theories exclude a number of informal workers from the scope of their analysis. I contend that a better theoretical basis of the informal economy could be achieved by merging the insights from both of these theoretical points of view. Since my purpose is to address the predicament of informal workers engaged in wide-ranging heterogeneous informal economic activities, I argue for the merger of insights of these theoretical conceptualisations. Such merger can help build an inclusive characterisation of informal workers.

I argue that a worker-centric approach (rather than an economy-centric approach) to informal economic activities is essential to improve the conditions of informal workers. The concept of informal employment provides the conceptual basis for such worker-centric policy. The advantage of the concept of informal employment is that it relates the worker to their *work*, which does away with the necessity of finding a definite workplace or an employer–employee relation to ameliorate the conditions of informal workers.

My analysis throughout the chapter has a definite country focus – I focus on the Indian informal economy in building my argument with respect to the terminology and concepts of the informal economy. More than 90 per cent of the working population in India is engaged in informal economic activities, making India a central concern in the policy-making debates with respect to the informal economy. It is within this background that I analyse the definitions and concepts related to informal economic activities in India.

The chapter is divided in two principal parts. In the first part of the chapter,[3] which is divided into five sections, I discuss the theories offered to explain the formal/informal dichotomy. First, I look into the logic of the dualist model of the formal/informal divide. Secondly, I analyse the structuralist conceptualisation of the formal/informal linkage. Thirdly, I argue that both the theories leave a vital section of informal workers (and informal economic activities) outside their analytical purview. I argue that for an inclusive coverage of informal workers (for policy purposes) it is important to draw insights from both of the theoretical premises that help explain the complexities of the modern informal economic activities. Such an exercise would entail surpassing the boundaries of any one of the leading theories and visualising the theories as interrelated concepts which, taken together, are capable of explaining the informality problematic. Fourthly, I discuss how the ILO has been instrumental in developing terminologies related to informal economic activities. Finally, this part of the chapter concludes with the contention that the conceptualisation of informal employment is the most efficacious concept (among the competing concepts of informal sector and informal economy) so far as informal workers are concerned.

The second part of the chapter is India-specific. This part consists of three sections. After briefly pointing out the typical conditions of the country in which informal economic activities engage the majority of the workers in the country, I then discuss the definitions used in the informal economy domain in India. Informality is defined and conceptualised in terms of informal sector, informal employment, and informal economy.

I particularly look into the definitions proposed by the National Commission for Enterprises in the Unorganised Sector (NCEUS), which was established by the Government of India in 2004 for the purpose of ascertaining the spread of the informal sector and assessing the informal employment scenario in the country. The Commission (NCEUS) notes the different conceptualisation of the informal economy and related concepts in the country, and offers a wider conceptualisation of the terminologies used in the informal economy context. Finally, I focus on the concept of informal employment defined by the Commission (NCEUS), and I argue that the policy-makers should focus on the concept of informal employment in order to improve the conditions of informal workers in India. I argue that to improve the living standards and working conditions of informal workers a labour-centric approach to informality should be preferred to an economy-centric approach.

I.1.2 Conceptualising informality

Conceptual clarity is a precondition for any efficient and successful policy intervention. The concept of informality largely lacks such clarity. The term

---

3   The first part of the chapter has appeared as an article: Supriya Routh, 'Building informal workers agenda: imagining "Informal employment" in conceptual resolution of "Informality" ' (2011) 2(3) *Global Labour Journal* 208–27.

'informal' is used in different contexts that do not necessarily resemble each other. It is used to signify the nature of entrepreneurship (sector), type of job (employment), or a section of the economy. Scholars have sought to define informality from diverse perspectives, and it is often difficult to ascertain a converging point in all these conceptual ideas.[4] Sometimes the theoretical concepts appear to be in conflict with each other.[5] Thus, some commentators have quite aptly pointed out that the expression 'informality' seems to signify a very subjective opinion based on a scholar's understanding of the issue at a definite point of time.[6]

At a very general level informal economic activities can be defined as activities that are not regulated, monitored or controlled directly or indirectly by the state. The idea of informality has come to be associated with adversity – characterised by less productivity, precarious conditions of work, regulatory avoidance, and stealthy ways of operation.[7] When the term 'informal sector' first emerged from an anthropological study in Ghana, it did not necessarily have a negative connotation.[8] It was rather a picture of self-sufficient economic transactions not dependent on organised capital.[9] Over the course of time informality came to be identified with undesirable economic transactions and exploitative employment conditions.

Economic activity outside the (regulated and monitored) formal mode of organised production was not identified as productive. Workers who were not part of the formal economy were categorised as unemployed.[10] When British anthropologist Keith Hart identified economic activities that were outside bureaucratic control and state regulation scholars no longer assumed that the workers not employed in formal undertakings were unemployed and instead recharacterised the economy as dual.[11] The dual-economy thesis propounded that informal unregulated economic activities exist alongside the formal organised

4   Alice Sindzingre, 'The relevance of the concepts of formality and informality: a theoretical appraisal' in Basudeb Guha-Khasnobis, Ravi Kanbur and Elinor Ostrom (eds), *Linking the Formal and Informal Economy Concepts and Policies* (New York: Oxford University Press, 2006) 59.

5   Basudeb Guha-Khasnobis, Ravi Kanbur and Elinor Ostrom, 'Beyond formality and informality' in Guha-Khasnobis, Kanbur and Ostrom (n 4) 3–4; also Sindzingre (n 4) 58–59, 62–63, 71; also M R Narayana, 'Formal and informal enterprises: concept, definition, and measurement issues in India' in Guha-Khasnobis, Kanbur and Ostrom (n 4) 93–94.

6   Guha-Khasnobis, Kanbur and Ostrom (n 4) 3.

7   Note 1.

8   Keith Hart, 'Informal income opportunities and urban employment in Ghana' (1973) 11(1) *The Journal of Modern African Studies* 61–89; ILO, *Employment, incomes and equality: a strategy for increasing productive employment in Kenya*, report of an inter-agency team financed by the United Nations Development Programme and organised by the International Labour Office (Geneva: ILO, 1972) 5, 224–25, 505.

9   Hart (n 8); ILO, 'Employment' (n 8).

10 Hart (n 8); Guha-Khasnobis, Kanbur and Ostrom (n 5) 1; Keith Hart, 'Bureaucratic form and the informal economy' in Guha-Khasnobis, Kanbur and Ostrom (n 4) 23–28; ILO, 'Employment' (n 8) at 3–8.

11 See Hart, 'Ghana' (n 8); Guha-Khasnobis, Kanbur and Ostrom (n 5) 1; Hart, 'Bureaucratic form' (n 10) 24–26; ILO, 'Employment' (n 8) 3–8.

and regulated economic activities.[12] These two categories of activity were seen in isolation and perceived not to be related to each other.[13]

Hart named the non-regulated economic activities outside the formal economy collectively as the informal sector in his study in Ghana.[14] He made no effort to ascertain any link or interaction between the informal sector and the formal economy.[15] The dualist thesis of simultaneous but unrelated existence of the formal economy and the informal sector was simply accepted.

The dualist assumption came to be challenged during late 1980s. In what came to be known as the structuralist theory, Alejandro Portes, Manuel Castells, and Lauren A. Benton identified the linkage between the formal and the informal economy.[16] They argued that under the competitive pressure of the global market formal firms engage in informal practices to reduce their cost of production.[17] In the next two sections, I elaborate these concepts. I begin with the dualist concept.

1.2.1 Dualism and the formal/informal divide

With the spread of capitalism across the non-European world the existing modes of pre-capitalist and feudal production came under increasing pressure. Workers were forced to shift to industrial wage-work, leaving their respective agricultural and artisanal activities. Independent farmers were increasingly marginalised.[18] Because of uneven competition from the capitalist mode of production, the traditional modes of production disintegrated.[19] The independent traditional societies gave way to the newer mode of production and social relation.[20] Even if the traditional modes of production were not completely supplanted they suffered tremendous setback that resulted in large-scale unemployment from the traditional industries.[21] Nonetheless, the pre-capitalist traditional modes of production (howsoever fragile and disintegrated) persisted alongside the imported capitalist

---

12   Sindzingre (n 4) 60.

13   Guha-Khasnobis, Kanbur and Ostrom (n 5) 1–2.

14   Hart, 'Ghana' (n 8).

15   Hart, 'Bureaucratic form' (n 10) 23–26.

16   Manuel Castells, Alejandro Portes, 'World underneath: the origins, dynamics, and effects of the informal economy' in Alejandro Portes, Manuel Castells and Lauren A Benton (eds), *The Informal Economy: Studies in Advanced and Less Developed Countries* (Baltimore & London: Johns Hopkins University Press, 1989); also Alejandro Portes, Lauren Benton, 'Industrial development and labor absorption: a reinterpretation' (1984) 10(4) *Population and Development Review* 589.

17   Castells and Portes (n 16) 12–15, 26–31; also Lauren A Benton, 'Industrial subcontracting and the informal sector: the politics of restructuring in the Madrid electronics industry' in Portes, Castells and Benton (n 16) 228 at 228–30.

18   Michael Perelman, 'The history of capitalism' in Alfredo Saad-Filho (ed), *Anti-Capitalism* (London: Pluto Press, 2003) 119 at 120.

19   Tamás Szentes, *The Transformation of the World Economy: New Directions and New Interests* (London & New Jersey: Zed Books, 1988) 36, 50, 72.

20   ibid 36.

21   ibid 72.

mode of production, which had a destabilising effect on the socio-economic conditions in the periphery.[22]

It is within the context of the relationship between the capitalist mode of production and traditional economic activities in developing countries that W A Lewis propounded his two-sector development model. He described the source of surplus labour (because labour is unlimited) in 'agricultural activities', 'petty retail trading', 'domestic servants', 'the workers on the docks', 'the young men who rush forward asking to carry your bag as you appear', 'the jobbing gardener', 'and the like'[23] in the developing countries. He argued that the output in these temporary and occasional activities can remain constant even if the number of workers involved is halved.[24]

He then invoked the concepts of capitalist sector and subsistence sector to suggest the simultaneous existence of capitalist and non-capitalist modes of production.[25] He argued that the capitalist sector will keep on absorbing surplus labour from the subsistence sector until there is no surplus labour to absorb, thereby ensuring the development of the capitalist sector and the (national) economy as a whole.[26] He envisaged that the two sectors (subsistence and capitalist) run parallel to each other and are only connected to each other on the basis of flow of surplus labour or final product.[27] The Lewis model did not assert any inherent links between the subsistence and capitalist sectors in the production process.[28]

John R Harris and Michael P Todaro developed the two-sector model further. Unlike the Lewis model, their model explains rural to urban (agriculture to industry) migration, even in the absence of labour surplus.[29] They applied the two-sector concept in explaining urban migration and resultant unemployment.[30] Their basic thesis is that the rural to urban migration happens because of the rural urban difference in expected earnings, which is higher in urban areas and is

22 Karl Marx, 'Chapter 20: Historical facts about merchant's capital', Part IV: conversion of commodity-capital and money-capital into commercial capital and money-dealing capital (Merchant's capital) in *Capital Vol. III: The Process of Capitalist Production as a Whole*, available at http://www.marxists.org/archive/marx/works/1894-c3/ch20.htm (last visited 13 August 2010); Tom Kemp, *Historical Patterns of Industrialization* (London & New York: Longman, 1993) 40–41.

23 W A Lewis, 'Economic development with unlimited supplies of labour' (1954) 22(2) *The Manchester School* 139 at 141–42.

24 ibid 141.

25 ibid 146–47.

26 ibid 151–52.

27 ibid 139.

28 ibid. This is something that has been asserted by later theorists. See Castells and Portes (n 16) 27–32.

29 John R Harris, Michael P Todaro, 'Migration, unemployment and development: a two-sector analysis' (1970) 60(1) *The American Economic Review* 126.

30 ibid. The urban unemployment that the Harris and Todaro model propounds actually results in the creation of the urban informal employment outside the organised capitalist mode of production. They themselves, however, did not provide any account of the urban unemployment scenario per se. Their model did not touch upon the question of what these migrant unemployed people did to survive.

politically determined.[31] Although the expected earnings induce rural to urban migration, such migration results in urban unemployment because migration exceeds available jobs in urban industries.[32]

What follows from these two models is that the economy has two sectors – the formal capitalist sector (urban in nature) and the informal non-capitalist (subsistence) sector (mostly rural in nature).[33] There is a flow of workforce from the rural informal (non-capitalist) sector to the urban formal (capitalist) sector. When the urban formal sector is saturated and cannot absorb workers any more, urban unemployment is created because of migration from the rural informal sector.[34]

The unemployed workforce was seen as the residual workforce that did not participate in the industrial production process.[35] It was assumed that large pools of working-age people are unemployed because they do not participate in the factory-based production process. However, such an understanding was challenged by the empirical phenomenon in large parts of the Third World where the working-age population (who were excluded from the organised economic process) were engaged in some or other economic activity for their subsistence.[36] The myriad of activities people were engaged in were described as informal economic activities.[37] These informal activities existed alongside the organised formal capitalist market, thereby giving an impression of a dual economy.[38]

It was, however, not until 1971 that Hart coined the term 'informal sector'.[39] The idea of the informal sector instantly became so popular that the ILO employed the concept in its study of the Kenyan economy.[40] The informal sector was described as self-employment activities and small-scale entrepreneurship outside the organised capitalist market and free from government interference or support.[41] In 1993 the International Conference of Labour Statisticians (ICLS) adopted the definition of informal sector.[42]

The analytical categorisation of the informal sector (developed by the ILO) sought to identify the informal self-employment, own-account activities and

---

31   ibid.
32   ibid.
33   See Lewis (n 23) 139; Sindzingre (n 4) 60; Harris and Todaro (n 29) 126–42.
34   Harris and Todaro (n 29).
35   Hart, 'Bureaucratic form' (n 10) 23–28.
36   ibid 23–28; Hart, 'Ghana' (n 8).
37   See ILO, 'Employment' (n 8) 1–8, 223–32, 503–508; Saugata Mukherji, 'Evolution of the non-agrarian formal sector of the Indian economy through the nineteenth and twentieth century' in Binay Bhushan Chaudhuri (ed), *Economic History of India from Eighteenth to Twentieth Century* (New Delhi: Centre for Studies in Civilizations, 2005) 356.
38   See ILO, 'Employment' (n 8) 503–506; Mukherji (n 37).
39   Hart, 'Ghana' (n 8).
40   See ILO, 'Employment' (n 8).
41   See Hart, 'Ghana' (n 8) 68–70; ILO, 'Employment' (n 8) 6, 503–504.
42   See 'About the informal economy: definitions and theories', Women in Informal Employment: Globalizing and Organizing, available at http://www.wiego.org/about_ie/definitionsAnd Theories.php (last visited 22 June 2010).

entrepreneurship, and promote these activities in order to reduce the unequal income distribution[43] that might result from non-participation in the formal sector because of which informal sector workers are deprived of market returns and social protection. However, the emphasis of sector-specific analysis (of informality) is on informal entrepreneurship. Such an understanding failed to capture the heterogeneity of the informal economic activities. With the growing understanding of the informal economic activities, it was increasingly perceived that the sector-specific definition was inadequate.[44] Thus, the sector-specific understanding of informality was rejected in favour of informal economy,[45] which incorporates all activities (informal employment) and entrepreneurships (informal sector) that are not part of the formal economy.

The ILO's conception of informality during this period was based on the dual-economy model that was developed by Lewis. The dual-economy model had come under sharp criticism from Immanuel Wallerstein, who argued that dualism is only a falsity in a capitalist world.[46] Instead, he proposed the concept of a world system that is wholly capitalist in nature.[47] However, he did admit that there may be mini-systems of non-capitalist modes of production within the capitalist economy.[48] It is these mini-systems that are the precursors of the informal economy. With further evolution of the political economy, the dual system theory of unlinked coexistence of informal non-capitalist and formal capitalist modes of production came to be refined by structuralist arguments. Structuralist theory was envisaged within the context of increasing globalisation of capitalism and *laissez-faire* policy.

1.2.2 Structuralism and the formal/informal linkages

Neo-liberal policies recommend privatisation, free movement of capital and goods, reregulation in favour of capital, and restructuring of the state to facilitate these policies.[49] In the 1980s neo-liberalism became the official doctrine of the

43   Hart, 'Bureaucratic form' (n 10) 25–26.
44   Martha Alter Chen, 'Rethinking the informal economy: linkages with the formal economy and the formal regulatory environment' in Guha-Khasnobis, Kanbur and Ostrom (n 4) 75 at 76–80; Hart, 'Bureau form' (n 10) 22.
45   Chen (n 44) 76–80.
46   See Immanuel Wallerstein, 'The rise and future demise of the world capitalist system: concepts for comparative analysis' (1974) 16(4) *Comparative Studies in Society and History* 387 at 389–90; Immanuel Wallerstein, *The Modern World-System Capitalist Agriculture and the Origins of the European World-Economy in the Sixteenth Century* (New York and London: Academic Press, 1974) at 17–18.
47   Wallerstein, 'The rise' (n 46) 390–91, 398, 403–404; also Wallerstein, *The Modern World-System* (n 46) 2–11, 347–57.
48   Wallerstein, 'The rise' (n 46) 390, 398; also Wallerstein, *The Modern World-System* (n 46) 58, 87–129, 351.
49   See David Harvey, 'Neo-liberalism and the restoration of class power' in David Harvey, *Spaces of Global Capitalism: towards a Theory of Uneven Geographical Development* (London: Verso, 2006) 9 at 11–25; David Harvey, 'From globalization to the new imperialism' in R Appelbaum and W I Robinson (eds), *Critical Globalization Studies* (New York: Routledge, 2005) 91 at 98.

international (financial) agencies.[50] The World Bank and the International Monetary Fund (IMF) became instrumental in promoting neo-liberalism generally, and in developing countries in particular.[51] Social democratic states were made to withdraw from capitalist market operations.[52]

Neo-liberalism facilitated unrestricted export of (accumulated) national surplus capital throughout the globe.[53] Capitalists could export capital to profitable locations characterised by low-wage labour or low-cost raw materials.[54] The United States and the United Kingdom pioneered (with the help of the international financial institutions) the opening up of markets throughout the world by introducing policies with respect to the removal of quantitative restrictions, simplification or removal of tariffs etc. These policies were pursued through the World Bank, the IMF and the World Trade Organization (WTO).[55] Such policies at the global level resulted in industrial restructuring of the capitalist mode of production.[56] This industrial restructuring promoted intense competition amongst the capitalists globally in exploiting the most efficacious production process.

State withdrawal from the market fundamentally changed the power equilibrium in the market. Enterprises now have virtually unrestricted freedom to determine their policies that would keep them competitive in a free market. In this context, Portes and Benton argued that it was more expensive for the modern industrial sector to generate regular formal jobs within the industry than to generate informal jobs (by shifting such jobs) outside the industrial infrastructure where abundant numbers of low-wage workers were available.[57] They argued that in order to reduce the cost of generating regular employment industries began employing temporary and contractual workers.[58] Some of these new hirings were monitored by the state bureaucracy, while others were not.[59]

This new mechanism of industrial employment introduced informality into the formal organised industrial production process. The neo-liberal policy of global trade ensured that this new form of employment (temporary and contractual) could be generated anywhere in the world that provides the best conditions for the economies of scale by an industry situated anywhere in the world in the form of sweatshops, subcontracting etc.[60]

---

50 A Payne, *The Global Politics of Unequal Development* (New York: Palgrave Macmillan, 2005) 76–79; Harvey, 'Neo-liberalism' (n 49) 23–24.
51 Payne (n 50); Kemp (n 22) 90–91; Harvey (n 49).
52 Harvey (n 49) 23–29.
53 Harvey, 'From globalization' (n 49) 94.
54 ibid.
55 Harvey, 'Neo-liberalism' (n 49) 26–29.
56 Castells and Portes (n 16) 27–30; Lourdes Beneria, 'Subcontracting and employment dynamics in Mexico City' in Portes, Castells and Benton (n 16) 173.
57 Portes and Benton (n 16) 595–98.
58 ibid 596.
59 ibid.
60 David McNally, 'The colour of money: race, gender, and the many oppressions of global capital' in David McNally (ed), *Another World is Possible: Globalization and Anti-Capitalism* (revised edn Winnipeg: Arbeiter Ring Publishing, 2006) 137 at 178–90.

The Portes and Benton argument has been developed further by Castells and Portes.[61] They noted that informality is part of a production process that is linked to the formal capitalist mode of production,[62] and this link is an outcome of the neo-liberal globalisation process.

Dualists were content to study the individual informal transactions without bothering to explain the expansion of informality. By contrast, the structuralists took upon themselves the task of explaining the reason for gradual expansion of the informal sector. In order to explain the expansion of the informal sector they contextualised the formal/informal distinction against the backdrop of the changes in the formal production process.[63] Their analysis of the evolution of production processes is premised on the ascertainment of the shifting role of the state in mediating the relationship between capital and labour.[64] Thus, it was analytically necessary for them to employ the terminology of the informal economy as an overarching expression to denote the heterogeneous informal sectors that are linked to the formal economy.

Although Castells and Portes acknowledge that the informal economy is heterogeneous in nature, they identify three principal characteristics of informal economy: 'the systemic connection with the formal economy'; 'the special characteristics of labour employed in informal activities'; and the 'government's tolerant attitude toward the non-regulated sector'.[65] The analytical novelty of the structuralist understanding of the informal economy is its ability to explain the growing informality phenomenon in urban areas.[66] Subcontracted work and sweatshops are increasingly found in cities such as New York,[67] Miami,[68] Mexico City[69] and Madrid.[70] Thus, while the dualist economic model underlies the rural/urban division of informality and formality, the structuralist thesis accounts for the urban informality/formality divide on a national and international scale. Castells and Portes observed that, although the expression 'informal economy' falls short in explaining the heterogeneity of informal activities around the globe, each of which has historical, social and political origins, the concept is nonetheless analytically useful in the absence of a better expression that encompasses the informal activities as a whole.[71]

61 Castells and Portes (n 16) 11–33.
62 ibid.
63 ibid.
64 ibid 12–15.
65 ibid 25–27.
66 See Portes, Castells and Benton (n 16).
67 Saskia Sassen-Koob, 'New York City's informal economy' in Portes, Castells and Benton (n 16) 60.
68 Alex Stepick, 'Miami's two informal sectors' in Portes, Castells and Benton (n 16) 111.
69 Beneria (n 56) 173.
70 Benton (n 17) 228.
71 See Castells and Portes (n 16) 11–33.

Dualists failed to note the inherent links between formality and informality.[72] For dualists the informal sector needed to be seen as an exclusive characteristic of the rural economy. They are unable to account for the links between the sectors and the consistent growth of the informal sector. By contrast, the structuralist argument ignores subsistence and own-account activities from the analytical purview of the informal economy.[73] For structuralists, subsistence activities are analytically relevant for poverty studies, and are essentially a problem of distribution.[74] The informal economy, on the other hand, is a problem of production rather than distribution.[75] Therefore, even if studies of poverty and subsistence are important, they are not relevant for an analysis of the informal economy.[76]

Thus, structuralists leave out a significant section of informal activity from their analytical purview. Significant numbers of subsistence activities, especially in the Third World, such as subsistence agriculture, domestic work, street vending etc are not linked to the formal economy in their production process and, thus, would not be captured in the structuralist account. In an attempt to address this gap, some scholars[77] argue that formality and informality should be seen as a continuum, rather than disjunctive economic activities. However, even those scholars proposing the continuum idea do not elaborate on how the subsistence activities could be accounted for.

Any study of informality has to account for both subsistence activities unconnected to the formal economy (or sector) and subcontracted entrepreneurships linked to the formal economy. If either subsistence or subcontract employment is not accounted for in informality analysis, a large section of the workers would perpetually remain outside any analytical category – formal or informal – and be devoid of workers' rights. Even if some of these workers (especially subsistence workers) might be able to receive social protection from the state, they will be devoid of labour rights that arise from their relationship to their work. It is clear from the above account that the theories on the nature of informality are located in definite time and social spaces; since informality is varied across the globe and differs from country to country, it is difficult to explain such informality exclusively by reference to one theory or the other. To lay down a generalised characterisation of informality it would be necessary to invoke both the theories offered to explain the nature of informality.

Either of the theories by itself only partially explains the informality phenomenon. An overall conceptualisation of the formal/informal divide needs to have

---

72 However, an indirect cursory reference to outsourcing mechanisms could be traced in Lewis's arguments when he discusses movement of capital to labour-abundant countries. Lewis was not very inclined to develop this issue in terms of a link between the formal and informal 'sectors'. He maintained the dualism of the sectors. See Lewis (n 23) 176–86.

73 Castells and Portes (n 16) 12.

74 ibid 11–15.

75 ibid.

76 ibid.

77 Guha-Khasnobis, Kanbur and Ostrom (n 5) 2–3, 7, 16; also Sindzingre (n 4) 58, 64–65; Chen (n 44) 77, 84–87.

insights from both the theoretical premises. The following section draws from empirical observations of the formal and informal economic activities in the modern world and argues for the convergence of the dualist theory with the structuralist theory.

1.2.3 Informal economic activities and the convergence of the theoretical premises

Philip Harding and Richard Jenkins bridge the gap between the dualist and structuralist conceptualisations of formal/informal divide.[78] The analytical framework offered by Harding and Jenkins situates informality in a continuum of what they term as *real life* situations.[79] They argue that the straightforward dichotomy of formality/informality is a myth, not reality.[80] They describe the real life situations of informality, acknowledging that it is analytically difficult to draw clear boundaries between formal and informal activity.[81] They describe the varieties of informal and formal activities under the categories of: self-employment, household work, homework and outwork, work and employment, on-job informality, formal wage employment, corruption and crime.[82] While some of these activities are linked to the informal as well as the formal economy, many others are stand-alone informal or formal activity.[83] Thus, in the actual political economy space stand-alone informal activities (eg subsistence agriculture) coexist with exclusive formal economic activities (eg public companies) and formal activities linked to informal activities (eg outsourcing).[84]

In the same vein, J K Gibson-Graham argues that the non-capitalist modes of production exist side by side with the capitalist mode of production,[85] especially in the so-called Third World.[86] Although Gibson-Graham's theoretical framework is not consistent with the Wallersteinian unitary world capitalist system or the

---

78 Philip Harding, Richard Jenkins, *The Myth of the Hidden Economy: Towards a New Understanding of Informal Economic Activity* (Philadelphia: Open University Press, 1989) at 51.

79 ibid.

80 ibid. Referring to a study of the Detroit informal economy (conducted by Ferman and Berndt in 1981, in which they term 'informal economy' as 'irregular economy') Harding and Jenkins charted four functions that the informal economy has for the formal economy. They observe that the informal economy is a consumer of the goods produced in the formal economy – the formal economy is also the source of raw materials for the informal economy; the informal economy acts as a mechanism to distribute goods produced by the formal economy; the informal economy provides for the economic maintenance services for the formal economy; and the informal economy produces goods and services that are distributed through the formal economy. See ibid at 38–40.

81 ibid 103–49.

82 ibid 103.

83 ibid 103–49.

84 ibid.

85 See J K Gibson-Graham, *Postcapitalist Politics* (Minneapolis & London: University of Minnesota Press, 2006); J K Gibson-Graham, *The End of Capitalism (As We Knew It) – A Feminist Critique of Political Economy* (Oxford: Blackwell, 1996) 241–44, 259–65.

86 Gibson-Graham, *The End of Capitalism* (n 85) 257; Merilee S Grindle, 'Agrarian class structures and state policies: past, present and future' (1993) 28(1) *Latin American Research Review* 174–87.

Marxian idea of capitalist evolution, it is descriptively useful in identifying the non-capitalist modes of production that coexist with the capitalist system. It is also comparable with the Wallersteinian description of mini-systems. Gibson-Graham suggests that the contemporary economy is in reality a mixed system of coexistence of pre-capitalist and capitalist modes of production:

> What haunts the capitalist commodity is not only non-commodity production (those home-cooked meals and made beds, those inputs produced internally within enterprises and transacted there) but non-capitalist commodity production – independent commodity production by the self-employed, slave commodities (what pure and strange moment is this, that slavery is only infrequently imagined to exist?), family-based relations of commodity production and exploitation, commodity production in collective and communal enterprises, to name just a few of the non-capitalist forms for which there are names and therefore histories. How is it that these are often confidently banished from the present – which is thereby rendered purely capitalist – or depicted as relatively marginal and inconsequential? (On this point the right and the left seem to be in some kind of imperfect but widespread agreement.)[87]

Harding and Jenkins, and Gibson-Graham chart the reality of the complex modern economy. Their analysis is based on the empirical reality of multifarious economic activities that defy a straightforward formal/informal division. It is in this context of empirical reality that we need to juxtapose real life (a phrase used by Harding and Jenkins to describe modern economic activities) economic experience in the background of the theories offered to explain informality empirically to verify the theories. While dualism explains the pre-capitalist and non-capitalist stand-alone subsistence activities outside the bureaucratic monitoring of the state, it fails to address those activities that are related to the formal economy but outside the purview of the bureaucratic control or monitoring.

Structuralism, on the other hand, analytically explains activities that are linked to the formal economy but are not monitored by the state bureaucracy, but it does not explain the subsistence and own-account activities. It is therefore necessary to look beyond the confines of each of the theories and seek insights from both the theoretical premises so far as they are attuned to the complexities of the varieties of economic activities – formal and informal. The ILO-initiated concept of informal employment offers a more complete picture of the formal/informal conundrum that conforms to the real life political economy as charted by Harding and Jenkins, and Gibson-Graham.

1.2.4 Informal employment and the ILO

The analytical inadequacy of the previous conceptions of informal economic activities in promoting a worker-centric conceptualisation of informality designed to protect workers' rights propelled the development of the employment-

---

87   Gibson-Graham, *The End of Capitalism* (n 85) 245–46.

specific definition of informality by the International Labour Conference (ILC) in 2002.[88] The ILO has been working with the concept of the informal sector ever since it employed the concept to study economic activities in Africa in 1972.[89] An international statistical definition of the informal sector was adopted by the ICLS at its 15th Conference in 1993 to enable countries to measure economic activity generated in the informal sector in their national accounts.[90] The 1993 resolution defined the informal sector as household or unincorporated enterprises that may be own-account enterprises, or enterprises of informal employers, irrespective of the nature of the workplace, the extent of capital invested or the duration of the operation.[91] The definition was accepted by the international System of National Accounts (SNA),[92] thereby generating the possibility of maintaining separate informal-sector statistics in national accounts of individual countries. The informal sector was identified in national accounts based on the characteristics of the enterprise, rather than the work performed by the workers.[93]

The sector-based understanding of informality, however, fell short in explaining the heterogeneity of informal activities. The sector-based concept did not account for some informal activities. It became difficult, therefore, to measure the contribution of all informal activities in the overall economy. Moreover, workers employed in very small undertakings, or self-employed workers were excluded from the informal sector.[94] A sector-based definition did not distinguish between the various categories of informal employments, eg outsourcing, casual jobs, irregular work or precarious subsistence employment.[95] Such categorisation also did not serve well the borderline cases of informal employments, such as freelancers, subcontractors etc.[96] Hence, from the perspective of the ILO, this definition failed to capture the universe of informal workers.

In view of these criticisms against the analytical concept of the informal sector the Expert Group on Informal Sector Statistics (the Delhi Group, 2001)[97] proposed

---

88 See 'Matrix and glossary of terms', in ILO, *Informal Economy* (n 1) 121–27; see also Arturo Bronstein, 'Labour law and the informal sector' (1999) Workshop on Regulatory Frameworks and their Economic and Social Impact (unpublished paper), Geneva (4–5 February); Ralf Hussmanns, 'Measuring the informal economy: from employment in the informal sector to informal employment' Working Paper No 53, Policy Integration Department, Bureau of Statistics (Geneva: ILO, 2004) 1; 'About the informal economy' (n 42).

89 See ILO, 'Employment' (n 8).

90 See Hussmanns, 'Measuring' (n 88) 1–2.

91 See Fifteenth International Conference of Labour Statisticians Geneva (19–28 January 1993) (ICLS/15/D.6 (Rev.1)), Resolution II: Resolution concerning statistics of employment in the informal sector (Geneva: ILO, 1993) 53.

92 See Ralf Hussmanns, *Statistical Definition of Informal Employment: Guidelines Endorsed by the Seventeenth International Conference of Labour Statisticians 2003* (Geneva: ILO, 2004) 1.

93 Ibid 1–2; Hussmanns, 'Measuring' (n 88) 3–4.

94 Hussmanns, 'Measuring' (n 88) 1–3.

95 ibid.

96 ibid.

97 The Delhi Group on Informal Sector Statistics was established by the United Nations Statistical Commission in 1997 as an international forum to assess the definitions and measurements used in the informal sector, and to suggest improved sophisticated definitions and measurement in the informal sector.

the measurement of informal employment to complement measurement of the informal sector in national accounts.[98] Accordingly, for the purpose of collecting informal economy statistics the ILC (2002) defined informal economy as 'all economic activities by workers [informal employment] and economic units [informal sector] that are not covered or insufficiently covered by formal arrangements'.[99] The ILC definition was based on the ILO Report on Decent Work and the Informal Economy (2002).[100] The ILO report defined *employment in the informal economy* as employment in the informal sector, and informal employment outside the informal sector.[101] Thus, the concept of employment in the informal economy was much wider than the scope of the informal sector – it covers employment in the informal sector, as well as informal employment outside the informal sector.

This conceptual framework for the measurement of informal employment developed by the ILO report[102] was submitted to the 17th ICLS for its adoption. The 17th ICLS adopted the definition and statistical methodology (albeit with some modifications) as proposed by the ILO report.[103] The 17th ICLS did not endorse the phrase 'employment in the informal economy' as proposed by the ILO report.[104] Instead, it endorsed the term 'informal employment' to signify employment in the informal sector and informal employment outside the informal sector.[105] In this conceptualisation:

[e]mployment includes paid employment as well as self-employment, including unpaid work in an enterprise owned and operated by another member of the household or family, and the production of goods for own final use by households. The production of services (e.g. housework, caring for family members) for own final consumption by households is excluded.[106]

The 15th ICLS had adopted an enterprise approach to statistical definition; the 17th ICLS added a labour approach to the existing enterprise approach.[107]

98   Hussmanns, *Statistical* (n 92) 1.
99   ibid 2.
100 ILO, *Informal Economy* (n 1) 121–27.
101 ibid; Hussmanns, *Statistical* (n 92) 2.
102 ILO, *Informal Economy* (n 1); Anne Trebilcock, 'Decent work and the informal economy', Discussion Paper No 2005/04 (January 2005), available at http://62.237.131.23/publications/dps/dps2005/dp2005%2004%20Trebilcock.pdf (last visited 20 July 2010) 15.
103 Trebilcock (n 102) 15; ILO, 'Working out of poverty', Report of the Director General, International Labour Conference, 91st Session (Geneva: ILO, 2003), available at http://www.ilo.org/wcmsp5/groups/public/---dgreports/---dcomm/documents/publication/kd00116.pdf (last visited 20 July 2010).
104 Ralf Hussmanns, 'ILO guidelines on the measurement of employment in the informal sector and of the informal economy', presentation to the Goskomstat of Russia/GUS seminar on the non-observed economy: issues of measurement, St Petersburg (23–25 June 2004) as cited in Trebilcock (n 102) 14–15.
105 See Trebilcock (n 102) 15, 31–33.
106 ILO, *Informal Economy* (n 1) 126.
107 ibid 121.

The labour approach-based concept of informal employment is not only necessary in analytical terms so far as the measurement of the informal economy is concerned, but it is also apt for policy formulation purposes that are concerned with the social protection of workers, as I argue in the following sub-section.

1.2.5 A conceptual resolution

The sector-based definition of informality is essentially targeted at measuring the informal entrepreneurship in the economy and ascertaining its contribution in the overall economy. The concerns that surround the conceptualisation of the informal sector are: what is the contribution of the informal sector to the overall gross domestic product (GDP)? How productive is the informal sector in comparison with the formal sector? How to enhance the productivity of the informal sector? How technologically efficient is the informal sector? How much revenue generation is forgone because of the informal sector? Thus, the purpose of the sector-based definition is locating informality within the overall economy.

The concept of informal employment is devised primarily from the necessity of measuring informal activities in the informal sector as well as informal activities outside the informal sector (as discussed earlier). Although the principal purpose of the concept of informal employment is measurement, the concept connects informal workers with the *work* they perform, irrespective of whether or not they have a definite workplace or an employer. Informal employment or work can be performed in an informal entrepreneurship or in a formal enterprise or outside either of these enterprises. It is, therefore, the site for the ascertainment of working conditions and living standards of informal workers. Thus, for a study concerning the conditions of informal workers it is the concept of informal employment that is analytically the most useful one. It is because of such usefulness that the ILO has opted to use the concept of informal employment for policy-making purposes concerning the amelioration of the conditions of workers involved in informal employment. Women in Informal Employment: Globalizing and Organizing (WIEGO), the global research-policy network, also heavily relies on the concept of informal employment in its research documents and policy guidelines.[108] Thus the concept of informal employment holds analytical edge over other concepts so far as workers are the focus of policy concerns.

The ILO's policy focus is the worker rather than the economy per se. The improvement of living standards of workers globally is the principal concern of the ILO. It promotes adherence to labour standards to improve the conditions of workers.[109] The concept of informal employment helps the ILO to concentrate on the workers, rather than on the enterprise. Therefore, the concept of informal employment, which is a variation of the concept of work, is the most suitable

---

108 See Women in Informal Employment: Globalizing and Organizing (WIEGO), available at http://wiego.org/wiego/about-wiego (last visited 26 May 2012).
109 David Kucera, Leanne Roncolato, 'Informal employment: two contested policy issues' (2008) 147(4) *International Labour Review* 321 at 322.

concept of informality for ILO purposes. The concept of informal employment fills in the gap left by the structuralist analysis of the informal economy. Structuralists left subsistence and own-account activities outside their analytical scope of the informal economy. The concept of informal employment brings the subsistence activities within the central debate surrounding the informal economy, along with the informal enterprises linked to the formal economy.

Informal employment has country-specific characteristics.[110] Therefore, attempts to link the concept of informal employment to the overall economy have to be premised in a country-specific context so as to arrive at a policy agenda that is analytically appropriate in that specific country context. Thus, I examine the concept of informality in the Indian context in the next part of the chapter to attain an in-depth understanding of the nature and extent of informality in India.

1.3 India and informal work

In this part, I examine the definitions and concepts associated with informality in India. I analyse the concepts of informal economy, informal sector and informal employment in the country's context to ascertain the conceptual background upon which policy decisions could be taken. I conclude this part by scrutinising the terminology that could be successfully used to analyse and address the conditions of the informal workers in India.

1.3.1 Background of informal economic activities in India

India manifests characteristics of both the dualist and the structuralist model. Non-capitalist modes of production coexist with capitalist mode of production.[111] It was the British who brought in the concept of formality in India through bureaucratic regulation of economic activities.[112] Before the British Raj government bureaucracy through civil servants was unknown in India. However, informal modes of pre-capitalist production did not become obsolete at the introduction

---

110 ibid 325–28, where the authors point out (just as with informal enterprise) that 'voluntary informal employment' is also a country-specific phenomenon and is a characteristic of more developed countries amongst the developing countries – such employment might be a reality in Mexico, but the same cannot be said of India; World Bank Report by Guillermo E Perry and others (eds), *Informality: Exit and Exclusion* (Washington DC: The World Bank, 2007), wherein the bank studies the Latin American informality and reports the voluntary nature of informal activities in some Latin American countries. However, the report acknowledges that such finding might not be true for most countries where informality is a problem. See Klarita Gerxhani, 'The informal sector in developed and less developed countries: a literature survey' (2004) 120(3/4) *Public Choice* 267.

111 See Anupam Sen, *The State, Industrialization and Class Formations in India – a Neo-Marxist Perspective on Colonialism, Underdevelopment and Development* (London: Routledge & Kegan Paul, 1982) 64–66, 70, 85–86, 88, 102–103, 194–208; Kemp (n 22) 40–41, 139; Gibson-Graham, *The End of Capitalism* (n 85) 245–46, 257–65.

112 Jan Breman, *Footloose Labour – Working in India's Informal Economy* (Cambridge: Cambridge University Press, 1996) 5.

of the formal mode of production; those coexisted with the formal mode of production.[113]

After independence the country resorted to a Soviet-style planned economy.[114] State regulation and monitoring was the benchmark of this stage of industrial evolution.[115] The state took primary responsibility for industrialisation.[116] The formal economy was characterised by the nationalised industries and the private entrepreneurships heavily regulated by the state.[117] State regulation diminished when India became part of the free market trading system from the early 1990s.[118] In the meantime, however, agriculture remained the backbone of the Indian economy: 65 per cent of the population continues to be engaged in agricultural activities.[119] Because of rural to urban migration (and the absence of urban jobs for all) a portion of the workforce is perpetually under-employed and informally employed.[120]

This under-employed and informally employed pool of workers became the country's asset in the global free trade regime. After 1991, when India became part of the world free trade regime, this huge pool of cheap labour constituted a comparative advantage for the country in global trade.[121] India increasingly became one of the most popular destinations of global outsourcing and sub-contracting business along with China.[122] Outsourcing and subcontracting activities juxtapose formal employment with informality.[123] Formal or informal firms could

---

113 See Sen (n 111) 64–66, 70, 85–86, 194–208; Kemp (n 22) 12–13, 40–41, 128–39; Sindzingre (n 4) 60.

114 Tom Kemp, *Industrialization in the non-Western World* (New York: Longman, 1983) 85–94.

115 See Sen (n 111) 87–105.

116 ibid 91–99.

117 ibid.

118 See Barbara Harriss-White, Anushree Sinha, 'Introduction' in Barbara Harriss-White, Anushree Sinha (eds), *Trade Liberalization and India's Informal Economy* (New Delhi: Oxford University Press, 2007) 5–11; Montek Singh Ahluwalia, 'Economic reforms in India since 1991: has gradualism worked?' (2002) 16(3) *The Journal of Economic Perspectives* 67 at 71–73.

119 Ahluwalia (n 118) 76–77; Raghbendra Jha, 'The Indian economy: current performance and short-term prospects' in Raghbendra Jha (ed), *The Indian Economy Sixty Years after Independence* (London: Palgrave Macmillan, 2008) 20. A portion of this agriculture is unregulated subsistence and exchange activities performed at a family or community level. See David Ludden, 'The formation of modern agrarian economies in South India' in Chaudhuri (n 37) 1–7; S C Srivastava, 'Development and disparity: agriculture in north east India' (1998) 79(313) *Indian Journal of Economics* 195; J S Kanwar, S M Virmani and S K Das, 'Farming systems research in India: a historical perspective' (1992) 28(1) *Experimental Agriculture* 1–17.

120 Hart, 'Bureaucratic form' (n 10) 26–27; Mukherji (n 37) 418.

121 See Andrew D Foster, Mark R Rosenzweig, 'Comparative advantage, information and the allocation of workers to tasks: evidence from an agricultural labour market' (1996) 63(3) *The Review of Economic Studies* 347; Mohd Afaq Khan, 'India's comparative advantage in business process outsourcing' (2004) 1(2) *Aim Explore* 33; S Dash, 'Human capital as a basis of comparative advantage equations in services outsourcing: a cross country comparative study' (2006) *International Conference on Information and Communication Technologies and Development* 165.

122 See Khan (n 121) 33–39.

123 See Castells and Portes (n 16); Portes and Benton (n 16); Eckhard Siggel, 'The Indian informal sector: the impact of globalization and reform' (2010) 149(1) *International Labour Review* 93.

outsource and subcontract to either formal or informal entrepreneurships. Some scholars also argue that apart from outsourcing and subcontracting activities the economic reforms of 1991 gave rise to the informal sector because of relocation of capital from the formal sector to the informal sector and the relocation of downsized formal sector labour to the informal sector.[124]

Thus, the contemporary Indian economy is characterised by formal industries, informal entrepreneurships, and informal subsistence activities.[125] It is against this backdrop that the terminology and concepts related to informality in the country need to be examined. In the following section, I examine the concepts and terminologies with respect to informality in the country and analyse their usefulness for the purpose of policy-making so far as the improvement of the conditions of workers is concerned.

1.3.2 Definition and concepts relating to informality

India is an oft-cited example of an enormous and ever-growing informal economy. The extent and enormity of informality in the country is in part determined by the way informality is defined and measured in the country. Scholars have pointed out that the definition and measurement of the informal economy and informal employment in the country inflate the concept.[126] Both agricultural and non-agricultural activities are measured as part of the informal economy in the country. Since agricultural activities constitute the majority of economic activities in India their inclusion in the definition means that India has a very large informal economy and informal employment.[127]

The informal economy in India is also referred to as the unorganised economy.[128] The Annual Labour Report of the Ministry of Labour 2008–2009 defines unorganised labour as: 'workers who have not been able to organize themselves in pursuit of their common interests due to certain constraints, like, casual nature of employment, ignorance and illiteracy, small and scattered size of establishments, etc'.[129]

According to the National Sample Survey Organisation (NSSO) data (2004–2005) only 7.6 per cent of the total workers in the country are formal workers. The rest of the 92.4 per cent of workers are unorganised (informal) workers and 99.2 per cent of all agricultural employment, 75 per cent of all manufacturing

---

124 Siggel (n 123) 94–97.
125 Harriss-White and Sinha (n 118) 1–5; Sheila Bhalla, 'Definitional and statistical issues relating to workers in informal employment' Working Paper No 3, National Commission for Enterprises in the Unorganised Sector (New Delhi: NCEUS, 2008) 3; Siggel (n 123).
126 Keith Hart argues that the formal/informal dichotomy would be overstretched if the peasant economy is brought within the rubric of informality. See Hart, 'Bureaucratic form' (n 10) 31; see also Chen (n 44) 82–83.
127 ILO, *Women and Men in the Informal Economy: a Statistical Picture* (Geneva: ILO, 2002).
128 See NCEUS, 'Conditions of work' (n 1).
129 Ministry of Labour Annual Report 2008–2009 (Chapter 8: Unorganised labour para 8.1), available at http://labour.nic.in/annrep/annrep0809/Chapter-8.pdf (last visited 17 December 2009).

employment, 78 per cent of all building and construction employment and 98 per cent of all employment in trade and commerce are in the informal economy.[130]

The Government of India established the NCEUS in 2004 for the purposes *inter alia* of ascertaining the spread, size and scope of the informal sector, and estimating the employment and unemployment scenario in the sector.[131] While setting the terms of reference to the Commission, the Government of India was only concerned with the informal sector, not with informal employment. However, it is to the credit of the Commission that, instead of being restricted by the sector-based conception of informality, it defined and conceptualised the informal sector as well as informal employment in the country.[132]

The Commission noted that in India the term 'informal sector' had lacked any uniform identifying factor or definition; the term is used differently by different organisations to determine and measure informality according to the organisation's requirements.[133] The Directorate of National Sample Surveys (NSS) surveyed household enterprises under terminologies including *small scale manufacture and handicrafts*, and *non-registered small scale manufacture and handicrafts* until the mid-1970s.[134] The survey was revised thenceforth under the overarching theme of economic census to include data on unorganised manufacturing, service, trade, transport etc.[135] These surveys essentially included undertakings that were not covered by the Annual Survey of Industries (ASI).[136]

---

130 ibid; 'Legal empowerment and the informal economy – SEWA experience' Paper presented at the Regional Dialogue on Legal Empowerment for the Poor, Bangkok, Thailand (3–5 March 2009), available at http://www.snap-undp.org/lepknowledgebank/Public%20Document%20 Library/SEWA%20-%20Legal%20Empowerment%20and%20the%20informal%20economy. pdf (last visited 18 December 2009).

131 NCEUS, 'Report on definitional and statistical issues relating to informal economy' (New Delhi: NCEUS, 2008) 9. The terms of reference for the Commission were: '(i) Review of the status of unorganized/informal sector in India including the nature of enterprises, their size, spread and scope, and magnitude of employment; (ii) Identify constraints faced by small enterprises with regard to freedom of carrying out the enterprise, access to raw materials, finance, skills, entrepreneurship development, infrastructure, technology and markets and suggest measures to provide institutional support and linkages to facilitate easy access to them; (iii) Suggest the legal and policy environment that should govern the informal/unorganized sector for growth, employment, exports and promotion; (iv) Examine the range of existing programmes that relate to employment generation in the informal/unorganized sector and suggest improvement for their redesign; (v) Identify innovative legal and financial instruments to promote the growth of the informal sector; (vi) Review the existing arrangements for estimating employment and unemployment in the informal sector, and examine why the rate of growth in employment has stagnated in the 1990s; (vii) Suggest elements of an employment strategy focusing on the informal sector.' See Appendix – I of the report at 144.

132 ibid 9.

133 ibid 13–16.

134 ibid.

135 ibid. These surveys were guided by the Central Statistical Organisation (CSO), and fieldwork was conducted by the National Sample Survey Organisation (NSSO).

136 ibid.

A shift in the survey index was made in 1999 when informal sector enterprises in the non-agricultural sector were surveyed instead of the previously used concept of unorganised sectors.[137] The new conceptualisation of informal sector enterprises in the country was in keeping with the international definition of the informal sector, except for the fact that the concept in India was also based on the maximum number of workers employed in an enterprise.[138] The latest NSS survey (61st Round Survey on Employment and Unemployment) refined the concept of informality by introducing additional characteristics to identify informal employment.[139] Thus, the informal sector meant manufacturing establishments not included in the ASI and services not incorporated in the public sector.[140]

The National Accounts Statistics (NAS) categorised the unorganised sector as enterprises that are not part of the organised sector.[141] Thus, the identification of the unorganised sector was indirect and was based on the measurement of the organised sector. NAS identifies the organised sector from available official documents. According to the NAS criterion, any enterprise that is required to be registered or report its constitution and activities under law, regulation, notification, ordinance etc and has so reported is in the organised sector.[142] Thus, the entirety of the NAS visualisation of organised sector statistics is based on the available administrative documents, and not on first-hand verifiable empirical phenomena. The NCEUS report criticises such categorisation by the NAS:

[t]he application of such varying criteria, make it impossible to have comparable statistics across the sectors either for the organized or for the unorganized sector. The division is also artificial in nature and cannot be linked to any physical characteristics.[143]

Further, the Directorate General of Employment and Training (DGET) of the Ministry of Labour and Employment, Government of India collects employment

---

137   ibid.
138   ibid. However, since the NSS survey excluded manufacturing enterprises covered by the ASI, the effect was the exclusion of enterprises that employed at least 10 workers (if electricity was not used in the particular enterprise employing these workers) or 20 workers (if electricity was used in the enterprise employing these workers). These numerical maximums (10 or 20 workers depending on whether an establishment is using power or not) are fixed in the country by legislation. The Factories Act 1948, Employees' Provident Fund and Miscellaneous Provisions Act 1952, Contract Labour (Regulation and Abolition) Act 1970, Payment of Gratuity Act 1972 restrict the size of the entrepreneurship for the application of its provisions. These laws, therefore, create the formal/informal divide so far as legislative protections are concerned. There are, however, some laws, namely the Minimum Wages Act 1948, the Equal Remuneration Act 1976 etc that are applicable without any restriction with respect to size of the establishments. Therefore, these laws are applicable to both formal as well as informal establishments in the country.
139   ibid.
140   ibid.
141   ibid.
142   ibid 15.
143   ibid.

statistics under its Employment Market Information (EMI) programme.[144] The EMI programme is comprehensively designed to estimate the nature, scope and extent of employment and unemployment in the organised sector in the country with a view to formulating policy to address unemployment.[145] Although the programme seeks to provide comprehensive coverage of employment in the organised sector, it excludes a significant portion of organised sector employment from its scope, either due to its voluntary reporting mechanism or to its relatively limited territorial or subject-matter coverage.[146] Most significantly, the EMI programme does not cover a major portion of organised agricultural employment.[147] However, in spite of these limitations EMI data is used to compile national accounts for organised employment.[148]

In this maze of different conceptualisation of the formal and informal (organised and unorganised in India) sector, and formal and informal employment, the Commission decided that it was necessary to streamline the definition of the terms 'informal sector' and 'informal employment'. To address the confusion resulting from the multiplicity of conceptualisations of the phrases 'informal sector' and 'informal employment' the Commission proposed definitions of key terms.

The NCEUS recommended a very broad definition of the informal sector and informal employment. According to the Commission:

> [t]he informal sector consists of all unincorporated private enterprises owned by individuals or households engaged in the sale and production of goods and services operated on a proprietary or partnership basis and with less than ten total workers.[149]

Since the concept of enterprise is understood in India as excluding agricultural and related enterprises, the Commission's definition expressly includes agricultural and plantation activities within the scope of enterprise and, hence, as part of the informal sector definition.[150]

Thus, the informal sector in India consists of all unincorporated enterprises (agricultural or non-agricultural) where fewer than a total of 10 workers are employed. The definition is dependent on the legal status and size of the undertaking.[151] K P Kannan and T S Papola observe that the definition is generic and is the broadest one ever adopted.[152] The definition does away with the concept of

---

144 ibid 15–16.
145 ibid.
146 ibid.
147 ibid.
148 ibid 16.
149 ibid 61.
150 ibid.
151 ibid.
152 K P Kannan, T S Papola, 'Workers in the informal sector: initiatives by India's National Commission for Enterprises in the Unorganized Sector (NCEUS)' (2007) 146(3–4) *International Labour Review* 321 at 323.

separate legal personality of informal undertakings as distinguished from its owners.[153] Because of the enormous agricultural sector in India the overall informal sector is very large compared with the formal sector.[154]

The Commission defines informal workers as follows:

> informal workers consist of those working in the informal sector or households, excluding regular workers with social security benefits provided by the employers and the workers in the formal sector without any employment and social security benefits provided by the employers.[155]

Kannan and Papola further observe that the definition of informal worker is also a generic one that is characterised by the absence of job security and social protection, irrespective of the employment being in the formal or the informal sector.[156] This definition of informal workers (and thereby informal employment) corresponds to the conceptual framework delineated by the 17th ICLS.[157] The definition of informal worker depends upon the definition of worker in formal waged employment; workers who are not part of the formal sector or protected by employment benefits are informal workers engaged in informal employment. The definition is, therefore, largely dependent on the legal status of formal employment.

According to the definitions proposed by the Commission, the informal sector in India accounts for 86 per cent of total employment and contributes 50 per cent of total GDP.[158] It is on the basis of the Commission's definition that 92 per cent of total employment is informal employment.[159]

1.3.3 Informality in India

The Commission suggests the principal reasons why the definition and measurement of the informal sector was necessary was to ascertain the sector's contribution to the overall economy of the country, to enhance the competitiveness of the sector in the global market and to generate employment opportunities in the sector.[160] Thus, the focus of the exercise was to devise macroeconomic policy in order to

---

153 ibid.
154 ILO, *Women and Men* (n 127).
155 NCEUS, 'Definitional and statistical issues' (n 131) 61.
156 Kannan and Papola (n 152) 323.
157 NCEUS, 'Definitional and statistical issues' (n 131) 61.
158 ibid 62. However, some other accounts estimate the contribution of the informal economy ('informal sector' and 'informal employment') as more than 60%; see Harriss-White and Sinha (n 118) 2.
159 NCEUS, 'Definitional and statistical issues' (n 131) 62.
160 ibid 9; 'Contribution of the unorganised sector to GDP Report of the sub-committee of a NCEUS task force', Working Paper No 2 (June 2008) National Commission for Enterprises in the Unorganised Sector (New Delhi: NCEUS, 2008), available at http://nceus.gov.in/Final_Booklet_Working_Paper_2.pdf (last visited 22 June 2010).

improve the productivity and competitiveness of the informal sector. Although generation of employment in the sector was one of the concerns of the Commission, it recognised that mere generation of employment would not serve any fruitful purpose in improving the livelihoods of the informal workers.

The Commission noted that the real challenge of informal employment is to improve the overall conditions of employment and livelihood of the workers in the informal economy.[161] It recognised that the problem with employment in the informal sector is essentially a problem of quality of employment.[162] The Commission argued that employment means *job security, income security, social security* and *decent conditions of work*.[163] The Commission[164] moves away from the assumption that growth of the economy and competitiveness of informal activities will have a trickledown effect and by itself is capable of improving the conditions of the workers working informally.

The Commission Report entitled 'The Challenge of Employment in India: An Informal Economy Perspective'[165] notes that the growth in the economy and improving living standards for the working population may not be conjoined, and, therefore, solvable with identical policies. Economic growth need not necessarily improve the conditions of the population, especially the most impoverished and marginalised ones. The Indian economy has seen consistent growth in the last 25 years.[166] However, the growth of the economy did not result in the improvement, growth or development of the population of the country.[167]

The actual situation in the country corroborates the Commission's position that for overall development of the population focused attention needs to be given to specific groups in addition to macroeconomic policies directed at economic development. Recently, the Planning Commission of the Government of India accepted a new definition of (and methodology to estimate) poverty.[168] According to the new definition, 37 per cent of the population lives below the poverty line.[169] In spite of a growing middle class[170] India is still crippled with a significantly

161 NCEUS, 'The challenge of employment in India: an informal economy perspective', vol 1 main report (New Delhi: NCEUS, 2009).
162 ibid v.
163 ibid 7.
164 ibid.
165 ibid i–iv, 1.
166 Jha (n 119) 19–21.
167 ibid 17–37; NCEUS, 'Challenge of employment' (n 161). The report observes that the growth of the economy has benefited only the first 23% of middle class and higher income groups in the country. ibid iii.
168 See 'Planning Commission accepts 37% live below poverty line' (19 April 2010) OneWorld South Asia, available at http://southasia.oneworld.net/todaysheadlines/planning-commission-accepts-37-pc-live-below-poverty-line (last visited 21 June 2010).
169 See 'Report of the expert group to review the methodology for estimation of poverty', Government of India, Planning Commission (2009), available at http://www.planningcommission.nic.in/reports/genrep/rep_pov.pdf (last visited 21 June 2010); Himanshu, 'Poverty's definitional woes' (27 May 2010) Livemint.com and *The Wall Street Journal*, available at http://www.livemint.com/2010/05/27001014/Poverty8217s-definitional-w.html (last visited 21 June 2010).
170 Jha (n 119) 21.

large impoverished population and ranks very low on the human development index.[171]

The Human Development Report 2009 ranks India at a dismally low 134th position among 182 countries.[172] The country's rank has deteriorated from 127 in 2005[173] to 134 in 2009. The determinants of the index are life expectancy, literacy rate, survival until 40 years of age, usage of improved water resources, malnutrition etc.[174] At the macroeconomic level some of the biggest problems crippling the country's development are regional inequality, unemployment and underemployment, fiscal deficit, and lack of infrastructure.[175] Indicators such as infant mortality, child malnutrition, nutrient intakes, educational attainment and sex ratio suggest that economic development has failed to address these ground-level problems of the impoverished and marginalised population.[176] Economic development did not percolate down to the lower strata of society. Therefore, analytically the informal sector as a contributor to the economy needs to be viewed differently from that of the conditions of workers working in informal activities.

What is required in the context of informality is not generation of employment; rather, improvement of conditions at work and betterment of standards of living of the working population. That is what the NCEUS meant when it conceptualised employment generation in the informal sector.[177] To improve the conditions of workers employed in informal activities the NCEUS looked beyond mere employment generation in the informal sector and invoked the concept of Decent Work (DW) in informal employment. Thus, conceptualisation of informal employment helps in analytically framing the problem of informal employment in terms of the DW Agenda developed by the ILO.

The concept of informal employment is further analytically useful so far as the conceptualisation distinguishes work from employment under an employment relationship. Traditionally labour policy has been centred on the employer–employee relationship so far as conditions of service and provision for welfare benefits were concerned. However, the nature of informal activities falls outside of the employer–employee relationship to a great extent, thereby making it difficult for policy-makers to depend on the employer–employee relationship to

---

171 See Human Development Report 2009, 'India – the human development index: going beyond income', available at http://hdrstats.undp.org/en/countries/country_fact_sheets/cty_fs_IND. html (last visited 21 June 2010).

172 See Human Development Report 2009, 'Overcoming barriers: human mobility and development' (New York: UNDP, 2009) 145, available at http://hdr.undp.org/en/media/HDR_2009_ EN_Complete.pdf (last visited 21 June 2010).

173 See Human Development Report 2005, 'International cooperation at a crossroads: aid, trade and security in an unequal world' 264, available at http://hdr.undp.org/en/media/HDR05_ complete.pdf (last visited 21 June 2010).

174 See Human Development Report 2009, 'India' (n 171).

175 Jha (n 119) 31–35.

176 See Anil B Deolalikar, 'Human development in India: past trends and future challenges' in Jha (n 119) 155.

177 See NCEUS, 'Challenge of employment' (n 161).

ameliorate the conditions of those workers working informally. Therefore, we need to concentrate not only on informal workers in an employer–employee relation, but also on the informal workers who are not in such a relationship. We need to concentrate on the lives of the workers and their work, rather than employment in entrepreneurships if what we are concerned with is improving all informal workers' conditions (and not only workers who are employed in informal or formal enterprises). To shift focus from the traditional basis of the employer–employee relationship and social security guarantees to the life and work of the workers the concept of informal employment is analytically helpful.

A broad concept of informal employment encompasses employment in the informal sector, informal employment in the formal sector, employment of unpaid family labour,[178] beneficial self-employment and self-employment for subsistence purposes. The notion of informal employment places *work* (irrespective of any employer–employee relationship) at the centre of the informal employment debate. A significant portion of informal employment consists of activities that are performed by the workers from their homes, street corners and other diverse places. A workplace is absent for a large number of informal workers. The concept of informal employment offers a conceptual framework to relate workers with their work also in the absence of a workplace.

If the purpose of such analytical categorisation is the amelioration of the conditions of the workers engaged in informal employment it is useful to incorporate as many workers engaged in informal economic activities as possible within the purview of the concept. For example, although agriculture contributes only 25 per cent of India's GDP, it employs 65 per cent of the working population of the country.[179] If the purpose of informality analysis is the improvement of the conditions of the workers there is no reason why a proportion of these 65 per cent of working population should be excluded from such analysis.

However, a clarificatory note needs to be added here: although I propose the incorporation of all informal workers (including agricultural workers) within the analytical concept of informal employment, I am far from arguing that a single policy framework could be effective for all these diverse types of workers (and their work) categorised together. Even if all workers working informally are categorised together under the concept of informal employment, for policy-making purposes each category of work needs to be analysed separately. For example, it is impossible that waste picking, which is self-employed survival work without a definite workplace, could be equated with construction work, which is waged employment performed in a definite workplace, for policy-making purposes for the workers. Thus, while the concept of informal employment could be general and broadly defined (to give some generality to the concept), a worker-oriented

---

178 Unpaid family labour providing service (eg care work) is excluded from the definition of 'informal employment', but unpaid family labour producing goods is included within the concept of 'informal employment'. See ILO, *Informal Economy* (n 1) 121–27.

179 Jha (n 119) 20.

policy needs to analyse each category of informal work separately to devise appropriate means to improve the conditions of the workers engaged in different informal employments.

1.4 Conclusion

This chapter has two objectives. The first is to show that neither of the two leading theories explaining the formal/informal divide offers a complete picture of the varieties of informal economic activities. The second is to analyse the efficacy of the terminology and definitions related to informality for policy-making purposes from the point of view of improving the lives of the workers. I argue that the concept of informal employment is an appropriate one if the purpose is to ameliorate the conditions of informal workers. The concept of informal employment is not only useful for policy-making purposes for the workers but it also bridges the gap between the dualist and the structuralist theories in analytically providing a much wider coverage to workers working informally.

I also examine the usefulness of the concept of informal employment from an Indian informal economy perspective. The focus of the Indian approach has traditionally been on the concept of the informal sector, wherein the concept of informal employment is only a subsidiary and supplementary one. However, if the situation of informal workers is to be analysed and their conditions are to be improved, the concept of informal employment needs to form the core of the informality analysis.

The concept of informal employment embraces informal workers working in the informal sector, the formal sector or subsistence activities. Although formal sector workers enjoy legislative and executive benefits, informal workers engaged in the formal sector are generally excluded from such benefits, and so are informal workers engaged in the informal sector or subsistence activities. The NCEUS notes that irrespective of the sector where informal workers are engaged, the real challenges for informal workers in India are job security, income security and decent working conditions.

The constitution of India directs the governments (union and state governments) to provide job security, income security and decent working conditions to workers. For formal workers, these constitutional guarantees are at least theoretically ensured to some extent through legislative means. However such legislative benefit is absent in the case of informal workers. The NCEUS documents the absence of legislative benefits for informal workers in India. So far as legislative or executive benefits are concerned, informal workers are unequally treated from formal workers in the country. Such inequality not only undermines the socialist guarantees of the constitution of India, but it is in conflict with the express constitutional right to equality.

As I discuss in the next chapter, in India labour rights such as the rights to association and collective bargaining, freedom of expression, right against forced and child labour, right to work, appropriate conditions at work, equality of wage and maternity benefits are constitutionally guaranteed. However, the state has failed to realise these constitutional guarantees for informal workers in the country. In the next chapter, I consider the predicament of informal workers in India. Although labour rights are constitutionally protected, it is only formal workers employed in industrial establishments who receive legislative and executive protection in furtherance of their overall development. In the next chapter, I show how organisations of informal workers are promoting overall development of informal workers in the absence of any state action in that respect.

2 Constitutional rights and informal workers' struggle

2.1 Introduction

In Chapter 1, I discuss different theoretical concepts and terminologies relating to informal economic activities in general and with specific reference to India. In this chapter I discuss how (mainly self-employed) informal workers' collective initiative promotes their human development. I contrast the role performed by informal workers' organisations with the implementation of constitutional labour rights in India, because the constitution too envisages promotion of human development through the juridical concept of dignified wholesome work-lives. However, as I argue in this chapter, the constitutional guarantees remain unrealised for informal workers in India. It is the organisations of informal workers rather than the state that are promoting workers' interests.

My discussion of informal workers' organisations in this chapter will set the stage for the discussion of the trade union initiative of waste pickers in Kolkata that I describe in Chapter 7. In this chapter the discussion of the constitutional goal of dignified life and the absence of such dignity in the lives of informal workers will help me link the constitutional objective to an approach to human development that I discuss in Chapter 3. Moreover, the discussion in this chapter is also relevant for the purpose of analysing factors necessary for the human development of informal waste pickers, which I discuss in Chapters 6 and 7.

The National Commission for Enterprises in the Unorganised Sector (NCEUS) tries to capture workers who are excluded from protective labour and social security legislation, which are enacted largely to promote the interests of formal workers in an employment relationship. Since the point of departure for analysing informality in the Indian context is the availability and applicability of law, in this chapter I discuss the exclusion of informal workers from legislative protection. Labour legislation is unevenly applied to workers in India. While formal workers in an employment relationship receive comprehensive benefits under protective legislation, informal workers remain excluded from legislative protection. Despite a constitutional guarantee of a positive right to equality, informal workers do not receive treatment that is equal to that of formal workers. The Constitution of India is the source of labour jurisprudence in the country.

Labour welfare guarantees are categorised as civil-political and socio-economic rights under the constitution. Civil-political rights such as the right to equality, the right to speech and expression, the right to assembly and the right to form associations and unions are categorised under the Fundamental Rights chapter.[1] Socio-economic rights such as the right to work, the right to unemployment assistance, the right to livelihood, equal pay for equal work, the right to appropriate conditions of work and maternity relief are listed under the category of Directive Principles of State Policy.[2] While fundamental rights are enforceable by the judiciary, directive principles of state policy are goals set for the government(s) and are not enforceable by the judiciary.

The enforceable fundamental rights and the unenforceable directive principles together seek to promote dignified lives for workers. I point out that a dignified life for informal workers means an overall human development of such workers. I use my discussion in this chapter as a launching pad for my discussion of a theoretical approach to human development, which I argue that organisations of informal workers are promoting. In the next chapter, I move on to the discussion of human development, which I envisage as a normative goal of labour law.

The rest of this chapter is divided into four sections and a conclusion. In section 2.2, I look into the judicially mediated evolution of the relationship between the civil-political rights (fundamental rights) and social-economic rights (directive principles). This discussion is relevant because it is useful to ascertain what the directive principles, which contain most of the labour welfare guarantees, entail for informal workers in reality. In this section, I also discuss how the positive right to equality (a fundamental right) has remained unrealised for informal workers in India. Informal workers are unequally treated from formal workers so far as legislative provisioning is concerned. Using such unequal treatment as a starting point, in section 2.3 I describe the extent to which informal workers are protected under different labour legislation in India.

In section 2.4, through a description of labour unions and non-governmental organisation (NGO) activities, I show that the existing legislative vacuum is being filled by these private unions and NGO initiatives in order to improve the condition of informal workers in India. While discussing organisation initiatives of informal workers, I have chosen organisations that vary in their legal status – trade unions, companies, cooperatives, registered societies, and charitable trusts – in representing informal workers. I have also chosen organisations that are representative of self-employed informal workers. I do so for two reasons: first, because self-employed informal workers receive less protection under existing legislation; and, secondly, because I undertake a case study of self-employed informal waste pickers in Kolkata, India, which I report in Chapter 6. In this section, I also look into how organisations of waste pickers are seeking to promote a dignified life for waste pickers in India.

In section 2.5, I link the concept of *dignified life* envisaged in the Constitution of India to a concept of *human development* in order to examine the role of resources

---

1   Constitution of India pt III.
2   ibid pt IV.

provided by unions and NGOs to improve the lives of informal workers. I conclude this chapter with a roadmap leading to the next chapter.

2.2 Constitutional protection for labour

The constitutional protection afforded to labour is the basis of labour jurisprudence in India. In this section, I analyse how far constitutional guarantees for labour have been able to promote informal workers' interests in the country. Labour rights are categorised under two different parts of the Constitution of India. One of these parts of the constitution enlists civil and political rights; the other part enumerates social and economic rights.

While civil and political rights could be enforced through the judiciary, there is no provision for judicial enforcement of social and economic rights. However, most of the constitutional guarantees for labour are made of social and economic rights. The Supreme Court of India, by innovatively reading socio-economic guarantees as part of the civil-political rights, has tried to promote the interests of the weaker sections of the society. In this section, I analyse whether the Supreme Court has been able to promote informal workers' constitutional rights in India. I also analyse whether the right to equality, which is a fundamental civil-political right that can be enforced by the judiciary, can be used by informal workers to compare themselves with formal workers so far as legislative and executive benefits are concerned.

In this section, I first introduce the socialist orientation of the Constitution of India and discuss how such orientation finds expression in Parts III and IV of the constitution. I then discuss the relationship between the civil-political and socio-economic rights in the constitution. The relationship between the civil-political and socio-economic rights has evolved since the adoption of the constitution. I chart this evolution in order to show that the Supreme Court has sought to protect weaker sections of the population, including informal workers, through an innovative interplay of civil-political and socio-economic rights. However, I argue that the Supreme Court has failed to realise equal treatment of informal workers *vis-à-vis* formal workers and, accordingly, judicial action falls short of ensuring a dignified life for informal workers. My discussion in this section leads to the discussion of the next section on the coverage of informal workers under labour laws in India.

Workers in India are protected under the *socialist* Constitution of India, one that envisages providing *social justice* for its citizens.[3] The term 'socialist' was introduced into the constitution through the Forty-second Amendment of the Constitution of India in 1976. The Constitution (Forty-fifth Amendments) Bill 1978 defined

---

3   Constitution of India preamble. Jawaharlal Nehru, India's first Prime Minister, addressing the Constituent Assembly members, noted that: 'The first task of this Assembly is to free India through a new constitution to feed the starving people and clothe the naked masses and to give every Indian fullest opportunity to develop himself according to his capacity'. See *Constituent Assembly of India Debates (Proceedings)* Vol II(3) (22 January 1947), available at http://164.100.47.132/lssnew/constituent/vol2p3.html (last visited 5 March 2012).

socialist as 'a republic in which there is freedom from all forms of exploitation, social, political and economic'. While this definition was not adopted, the Constitution of India declared its socialist philosophy in the governance of the country in its preamble.

The philosophy declared in the preamble has been elaborated throughout the rest of the document. The Constitution of India distinguishes between *rights* and *goals*.[4] The fundamental rights guaranteed in Part III of the constitution are enforceable rights, whereas the directive principles in Part IV are unenforceable goals or aspirations.[5] If a citizen of (or a person in) the country is deprived of her fundamental rights (which are mostly civil and political rights, for which the state does not need to undertake a positive act to avail the citizen/person of the right), the deprived person can ask the court to enforce her rights through the issuance of appropriate writs (such as habeas corpus, mandamus, quo warranto, prohibition, certiorari). However, on the other hand, the directives in Part IV (which are principally economic and social rights) need some proactive action and economic expenditure on the state's part. Therefore, these rights have been made conditional upon the availability of resources at the state's disposal. Accordingly, the courts cannot enforce goals declared under this part of the constitution.

The chapters on the fundamental rights and directive principles of state policy constitute the heart and soul of the preamble's philosophy. The enforceable fundamental rights chapter guarantees:

- principles of equality and non-discrimination[6]
- protection of life and liberty[7]
- freedom of expression, assembly, union formation, movement and vocation[8]
- the right to free education[9]
- protection from forced labour[10] and
- a prohibition on the employment of children.[11]

Directives, on the other hand, are fundamental in the governance of the country.[12] States are directed to ensure (to the extent reasonably possible within economic and other limitations) the following:

---

4 See Shylashri Shankar, *Scaling Justice: India's Supreme Court, Anti-Terror Laws, and Social Rights* (New Delhi: Oxford University Press, 2009) xiii.

5 Although the Constituent Assembly vigorously debated whether directive principles of state policy should be made enforceable or not, they finally settled on the unenforceability of directive principles. See Granville Austin, *The Indian Constitution: Cornerstone of a Nation* (Bombay: Oxford University Press, 1976) 75–83.

6 Constitution of India arts 14, 15, 16.

7 ibid art 21.

8 ibid art 19.

9 ibid art 21-A.

10 ibid art 23.

11 ibid art 24.

12 ibid art 37.

- the right to work[13]
- adequate means of livelihood[14]
- equality of wages[15]
- fair distribution of material resources[16]
- adequate protection of workers (especially children)[17]
- provision for living wage[18]
- decent standard of life[19]
- provision for education, leisure and social and cultural development[20]
- appropriate conditions of work[21]
- maternity relief[22]
- assistance during old age and unemployment[23]
- promotion of weaker sections of the population[24]
- appropriate nutrition and health provision[25]
- workers' participation in management[26] and
- equal justice and legal aid.[27]

By providing for constitutional rights to life, health, education, social protection etc, the Constitution of India seeks to provide enabling conditions for dignified human existence.[28] A careful perusal of the fundamental rights and the directive principles with respect to work and workers would clarify that most of the guarantees are aimed at promoting a well rounded dignified human life for workers. The directive principles are particularly important in promoting such a dignified life.

Upendra Baxi notes that despite the uncomfortable juxtaposition of unenforceable directive principles with enforceable fundamental rights, 'at least upon the

---

13 ibid art 41.
14 ibid art 39.
15 ibid arts 38, 39.
16 ibid art 39.
17 ibid art 39.
18 ibid art 42.
19 ibid art 43.
20 ibid art 41.
21 ibid art 42.
22 ibid art 42.
23 ibid art 41.
24 ibid art 46.
25 ibid art 47.
26 ibid art 43-A.
27 ibid arts 38, 39-A.
28 See Justice Bhagwati in *Francis Coralie v Union Territory of Delhi* [1981] MANU 0517 (SC) para 8. *Manupatra* is an online reporter of Indian court judgments, abbreviated as MANU. The database cites cases in the style: MANU/SC/0517/1981; however, I shall be citing the reported cases as [1981] MANU 0517 (SC). The concept of dignified human life was developed by the Supreme Court in *Francis Coralie* in order to determine the content of the right to life and liberty under art 21 of the Constitution of India.

fulfillment of some of the major directives now depends not merely the "success" of the Constitution but also the destiny of India'.[29] Granville Austin defines directive principles as 'statements of the social revolution', which aim to promote positive freedom of the masses.[30]

The constitutional distinction between rights and goals (or directives) is premised on certain theoretical underpinnings. Rights signify the absence of state interference in matters of 'autonomous and fully capable agent[s]'.[31] Goals, on the other hand, imply dependent agents requiring positive action initiated by the state for their assistance.[32] Accordingly, rights could be enforced by the courts in the sense that the state could be compelled to refrain from interfering in individual (and collective) fundamental rights. It would be difficult for the courts to enforce goals because goals would require the state to invest resources and undertake proactive initiatives. Therefore, judgment on goals is left to the electorate – the electorate can judge the performance of the governments on the basis of the directive principles.[33]

Directive principles have been variously termed as: *election manifestos, new year resolutions, pious superfluities* and *veritable dustbins of sentiment.*[34] Although fundamental rights directly or indirectly promote workers' interests under the Constitution of India, directive principles are principal repositories of labour welfare guarantees and constitute the source of industrial jurisprudence in India.[35] The unenforceability of directive principles posed a challenge to the judiciary in promoting labour welfare. From its early years, the Indian judiciary had to face the challenge of determining the relationship between directive principles and fundamental rights in order to facilitate labour welfare. If directive principles could be enforced in the same manner as fundamental rights, states could be compelled to ensure labour welfare; but if directive principles were only aspirational goals, workers would have no effective remedy for their (directive principles') violation.

---

29 Upendra Baxi, "'The little done, the vast undone": some reflections on reading Glanville Austin's *The Indian Constitution*' (1967) 9 *Journal of the Indian Law Institute* 323 at 344.

30 Austin, *Cornerstone of a Nation* (n 5) 51.

31 Shankar (n 4) 120.

32 ibid.

33 ibid 123. While a section of the Constituent Assembly proposed enforceability of goals enumerated in the directive principles, the majority of the Constituent Assembly members were not in favour of making directive principles enforceable. See ibid 121–23. Explaining the justification of directive principles, chairman of the Constituent Assembly B R Ambedkar observed: 'In my judgment, the directive principles have a great value, for they lay down that our ideal is economic democracy. . . . [O]ur object in framing this Constitution is really twofold: (i) to lay down the form of political democracy, and (ii) to lay down that our ideal is economic democracy and also to prescribe that every government whoever it is in power, shall strive to bring about economic democracy . . .' See *Constituent Assembly Debates* vol VII 494–95; O Chinnappa Reddy, *The Court and the Constitution of India: Summits and Shallows* (New Delhi: Oxford University Press, 2010) 76–77.

34 Reddy (n 33) 17.

35 P B Gajendragadkar, *The Constitution of India: Its Philosophy and Basic Postulates*, Gandhi Memorial Lectures, University College, Nairobi, First Series (Nairobi: Oxford University Press, 1969) 51.

The Indian Supreme Court's approach in establishing the relationship between fundamental rights and directive principles evolved over three phases.[36] During the first three decades after Indian independence, the Supreme Court held that directive principles were subservient to fundamental rights.[37] During the 1970s, the court proposed harmonious relationships between directive principles and fundamental rights.[38] During the 1980s and 1990s, the court interpreted several directive principles as part of the fundamental rights in order to make those directive principles enforceable.[39]

In a judgment delivered in 1951, *State of Madras v Champakam Dorairajan*,[40] the Supreme Court, established a hierarchy between the directive principles and fundamental rights, observing that:

> The directive principles of the State policy, which by article 37 are expressly made unenforceable by a Court, cannot override the provisions found in Part III [fundamental rights] . . . The directive principles of State policy have to conform to and run as subsidiary to the Chapter of Fundamental Rights.[41]

However, the early 1970s witnessed one of the most famous decisions of the Supreme Court, popularly known as the *Fundamental Rights* case, in which a 13-judge bench of the Supreme Court[42] rewrote the relation between fundamental rights and directive principles. The court noted that in order to achieve the dignity of people as enshrined in the Constitution of India, Part III (fundamental rights) and Part IV (directive principles) have to be balanced and harmoniously construed.[43]

Fundamental rights and directive principles supplement each other[44] – fundamental rights are not superior to directive principles.[45] Fundamental rights and directive principles are the conscience of the constitution, and are constitutive of the *basic structure* of the Constitution of India.[46] While directive principles lay down goals to be achieved, fundamental rights provide for the means of achieving such goals.[47] The court noted: 'Is it that the rights reflected in the provisions of

---

36   Shankar (n 4) 124.
37   ibid 124–28.
38   ibid.
39   ibid.
40   [1951] MANU 0007 (SC).
41   ibid para 10. This judgment of the court is contrary to what Jawaharlal Nehru had in mind. Nehru noted: 'It is up to this Parliament to remove the contradiction [between fundamental rights and directive principles] and make the Fundamental Rights subserve the Directive Principles of the State Policy'. As cited in Reddy (n 33) 19.
42   *His Holiness Kesavananda Bharati Sripadagalvaru v State of Kerala* [1973] MANU 0445 (SC).
43   ibid paras 564, 634.
44   ibid para 634.
45   ibid para 906.
46   ibid paras 634, 672, 1206.
47   ibid para 634.

Part III are somehow superior to the moral claims and aspirations reflected in the provisions of Part IV? I think not . . . Freedom from starvation is as important as right to life.'[48]

Thus, in the *Fundamental Rights* case, both fundamental rights and directive principles were held to be part of the basic structure of the constitution. Several years later, the court elaborated in the *Minerva Mills Ltd v Union of India* case[49] that: 'the "harmony and balance" between fundamental rights and directive principles were also parts of that basic structure'.[50] Justice Bhagwati asserted:

> The crucial test which has to be applied is whether the Directive Principles impose any obligations or duties on the State; if they do, the State would be bound by a constitutional mandate to carry out such obligations or duties, even though no corresponding right is created in any one which can be enforced in a court of law.[51]

Following the *Fundamental Rights* case and *Minerva Mills Ltd*, the Supreme Court held that courts should seek assistance from directive principles while interpreting fundamental rights and that directive principles should be read into fundamental rights whenever possible.[52] Accordingly, the court began to read directive principles as part of fundamental rights. The advantage of interpreting directive principles as part of fundamental rights is that directive principles would become enforceable as part of fundamental rights. The Supreme Court read directive principles as part of Article 21 of the constitution, protecting right to life and liberty. In a number of judgments,[53] the Supreme Court of India quoted the US Supreme Court in *Munn v Illinois*,[54] noting that the right to life (under Article 21) means more than mere animal existence. The Supreme Court of India elaborated:

> We think that the right to life includes the right to live with human dignity and all that goes along with it, namely, the bare necessaries of life such as

---

48 ibid para 1762.
49 [1980] MANU 0075 (SC).
50 ibid para 61.
51 ibid para 116.
52 *Akhil Bharatiya Soshit Karamchari Sangh (Railway) v Union of India* [1980] MANU 0058 (SC) para 122.
53 Such as *Kharak Singh v State of Uttar Pradesh* [1962] MANU 0085 (SC); *Sunil Batra v Delhi Administration* [1978] MANU 0184 (SC); *Olga Tellis v Bombay Municipal Corporation* [1985] MANU 0039 (SC).
54 1876 WL 19615 (US Ill). In his dissenting opinion Mr Justice Field observed: 'By the term "life", as here used, something more is meant than mere animal existence. The inhibition against its deprivation extends to all those limbs and faculties by which life is enjoyed. . . . The deprivation not only of life, but of whatever God has given to everyone with life, for its growth and enjoyment, is prohibited by the provision in question, if its efficacy be not frittered away by judicial decision. . . . [Liberty] means freedom to go where one may choose, and to act in such manner, not inconsistent with the equal rights of others, as his judgment may dictate for the promotion of his happiness; that is, to pursue such callings and avocations as may be most suitable to develop his capacities, and give to them their highest enjoyment.'

adequate nutrition, clothing and shelter and facilities for reading, writing and expressing one-self in diverse forms, freely moving about and mixing and commingling with fellow human beings. Of course, the magnitude and content of the components of this right would depend upon the extent of the economic development of the country, but it must, in any view of the matter, include the right to the basic necessities of life and also the right to carry on such functions and activities as constitute the bare minimum expression of the human-self.[55]

A dignified human existence requires adequate nutrition, clothing, shelter, education, socialisation, socio-political participation, freedom of movement and economic development.

Following the trend, the Supreme Court in *Bandhua Mukti Morcha v Union of India*[56] developed a direct relation between Article 21 and directive principles such as Articles 39, 41 and 42. This case specifically dealt with informal forced labour under a debt bond system.[57] The court noted that the right to live with human dignity derives its content from clauses (e) and (f) of Article 39, Article 41 and Article 42.[58] Therefore, the right to life (Article 21) includes *protection of the health and strength of workers, protection of children against abuse, all-round development of children, educational facilities, just and humane conditions of work*, and *maternity relief*.[59]

According to the court these directives are minimum necessities for a life with human dignity.[60] This interpretation shows an indirect way of enforcing directive principles with the help of the fundamental rights. Similarly, the Supreme Court has held that the right to health and medical assistance, which promotes dignified life to workers, is part of Article 21 (a fundamental right), and derives its content from Articles 39(e), 41, 43 and 48(a) (directive principles).[61] In *Olga Tellis v Bombay Municipal Corporation*,[62] dealing with the plight of pavement dwellers, the Supreme Court held that the right to life (under Article 21) includes the right to a livelihood (Article 39(a)), because 'no person can live without the means of living, that is, the means of livelihood'.[63] The court further noted that directive principles enshrined in Article 39(a) and Article 41 are fundamental in the understanding and interpretation of fundamental rights.[64]

---

55 Justice Bhagwati in *Francis Coralie* (n 28) para 8.
56 [1983] MANU 0051 (SC).
57 ibid para 6.
58 ibid para 14.
59 ibid para 14.
60 ibid para 14.
61 See *Consumer Education and Research Centre v Union of India* [1995] MANU 0175 (SC); *Kirloskar Brothers Ltd v Employees' State Insurance Corpn* [1996] MANU 0873 (SC).
62 [1985] MANU 0039 (SC).
63 ibid para 32.
64 ibid para 33. Upendra Baxi commends the judiciary for asserting directive principles through fundamental rights, and thereby upholding their (directive principles and fundamental rights) *basic unity*. See Baxi, '"The little done, the vast undone"' (n 29) 367, 409. However, M P Singh sounds a note of caution against the judicial strategy. He argues that by increasingly reading

In another decision protecting informal workers' right to work, *Sodan Singh v New Delhi Municipal Committee*,[65] the Supreme Court held that street vending constitutes a *profession, occupation, trade,* or *business* (Article 19(1)(g)), and therefore is a fundamental right protected under a citizen's right 'to practise any profession, or to carry on any occupation, trade or business'. The Supreme Court has delineated a comprehensive list of factors in order to formulate the idea of dignified life for workers. However, the problem with interpretation-based judicial innovation in promoting workers' interests is that it suffers from several limitations. A primary limitation is that courts can provide relief through judicial policy-making only when an aggrieved party moves the court. In this sense, the courts are ill-equipped to address systematic deprivations that cause informal workers to suffer.

There is, however, another more fundamental and structural limitation in any judicial (constitutional) enforcement-based model of worker welfare. This limitation of the judiciary-dependent promotion of workers' benefits has been partially described by the Supreme Court in the *Fundamental Rights* case: '[I]f a State voluntarily were to implement the Directive Principles, a Court would be failing in its duty, if it did not give effect to the provisions of the law at the instance of a person who has obtained a right under the legislation.'[66] In *Bandhua Mukti Morcha*, the court further noted: '[N]o State neither the Central Government nor any State Government has the right to take any action which will deprive a person of the enjoyment of these [workers' constitutional rights enshrined in directive principles] basic essentials.'[67]

The court in *Bandhua Mukti Morcha* noted that government(s) cannot interfere to deprive an individual of her constitutional rights enumerated as directives under the Constitution of India. This assertion is problematic at two levels. First, since directive principles are not enforceable by the judiciary, even if a government deprives an individual from the enjoyment of these rights (ie directives), courts are in no position to enforce these rights. Secondly, since these constitutional rights are directives, and are therefore not realisable as fundamental rights, in order to enjoy these constitutional rights (such as the right to work or maternity benefit) people need to possess legal rights emanating from a statute. It is only when directive principles are enumerated in law that courts can enforce such constitutional rights 'at the instance of a person who has obtained a right under the legislation', as noted by the Supreme Court in the *Fundamental Rights* case.[68]

When combined, these two observations of the Supreme Court reveal the fundamental limitation in enforcing constitutional labour welfare guarantees for

directive principles into fundamental rights, the judiciary is diluting the seriousness and effectiveness of directive principles. See M P Singh, 'The statics and the dynamics of the fundamental rights and the directive principles: a human rights perspective' (2003) 5 *Supreme Court Cases Journal* 1.

65   [1989] MANU 0521 (SC) and its follow-up decision [1992] MANU 0489 (SC).
66   [1973] MANU 0445 (SC) para 1764.
67   [1983] MANU 0051 (SC) para 14.
68   [1973] MANU 0445 (SC) para 1764.

workers (including informal workers). The court pointed out that the judiciary can only enforce directive principles *when such principles find expression in enacted legislation*. Thus, even when workers' benefits (provided as directive principles) are read into fundamental rights, and even when specific workers are willing and able to move the court, the judiciary can enforce workers' rights only when such rights are obtained under legislation.[69]

The court has also noted that the state's responsibility in promoting workers' constitutional rights is, at best, a negative responsibility of non-interference in the enjoyment of workers' rights. In the context of labour rights, which are mainly directive principles, however, such a question arises only when workers have a legal right arising from a statute that seeks to implement specific directive principles. It is only when the state undertakes any action depriving workers of their constitutional rights that finds expression in statute(s) that the courts can step in to protect such rights. Thus, in order to realise constitutional labour rights, such rights need to be enumerated in statute(s) and the judiciary can enforce them only at the instance of an individual who possesses a legal right and moves the court to realise her legal right.

Informal workers suffer from systematic deprivations in part because of the juridical nature of constitutional labour welfare guarantees. Although the Supreme Court has taken progressive steps, such as upholding informal street vendors' fundamental right to carry on their economic activity, judicial remedies remain far too inadequate in addressing the overall human-development concerns of informal workers in India. Apart from upholding informal workers' right to livelihood and freedom of trade in certain parts of the country, the judiciary has been unable to promote constitutional welfare guarantees for informal workers as a class.[70] The Supreme Court, therefore, lamented:

> 'Justice, social, economic and political' and 'citizens, men and women equally, have the right to an adequate means to livelihood' which the Constitution of India promises is still a distant dream. This Court, in various judgments, has reminded the Government of its constitutional obligations to ameliorate the lot of the poor in India. Nothing much has been achieved. An alarming percentage of population in India is still living below poverty-line. There are millions of registered unemployed. The Government, in spite of constitutional mandate is unable to provide them with employment.[71]

---

69   Madhav Khosla shows that in the absence of state-formulated policy implementing directive principles, the judiciary is unable to enforce such directives even when the judiciary agrees that such directives are part of fundamental rights. See Madhav Khosla, 'Making social rights conditional: lessons from India' (2010) 8(4) *I.CON* 739.

70   I use 'class' as synonymous with 'group', rather than to suggest a distinction from an employer class. My choice of the expression 'class' is based on the equality clause of the Constitution of India (art 14), which permits justifiable *classification* and *class legislation* (discussed below).

71   [1989] MANU 0521 (SC) para 4. In this context, see E M S Namboodiripad, *The Republican Constitution in the Struggle for Socialism*, R R Kale Memorial Lecture (1968) Gokhale Institute of Politics and Economics, Poona (Bombay: Asia Publishing House, 1968) 8–11, 13; Upendra Baxi, 'The

The court noted that equality in matters of an adequate means of livelihood is still a distant dream for an alarming percentage of the population in India, who live below the poverty line. It is mainly informal workers who live below the poverty line in India. Informal workers have failed to receive equal treatment to that of their formal counterparts from the government(s) in India so far as protection and promotion of their means of livelihood are concerned. As a class, informal workers suffer from multiple deprivations compared with formal workers in India. There are more than 100 pieces of (central, and state government) labour welfare legislation in force in the country, mostly targeted towards formal workers. Formal workers receive comprehensive benefits ranging from *employees' state insurance* to *maternity benefits* under a plethora of labour welfare statutes. Informal workers, on the other hand, mostly remain outside the scope of these laws.[72] Such inequality between informal and formal workers exists in spite of the fact that the right to equality is a fundamental right under Article 14 of the constitution.

Article 14 of the Constitution of India declares: 'The State shall not deny to any person equality before the law or the equal protection of the laws within the territory of India.' Thus, the fundamental right to equality, available to any person living in India, is expressed in two ways forming a corollary to each other.[73] The first part of the provision reads that 'the state shall not deny to any person equality before the law', suggesting a negative burden of non-interference, while the second part of the Article reads that 'the state shall not deny to any person equal protection of the laws', imposing a positive responsibility on the state to protect all persons equally.[74] The positive responsibility imposed on the state is reinforced by Articles 15 and 16, which call upon the state to make 'special provision for the advancement of any socially and educationally backward classes of citizens'.[75] Further, Article 14 envisages a 'classless egalitarian socio-economic order'.[76] For the promotion of the right to equality, the state may undertake reasonable classification systems distinguishing people similarly situated from people differently situated. Any such classification must have a nexus to the purpose sought to be achieved through legislation.[77]

The Supreme Court laid down conditions for reasonable classification in *State of West Bengal v Anwar Ali Sarkar*.[78]

(im)possibility of constitutional justice: seismographic notes on Indian constitutionalism' in Zoya Hasan, E Sridharan and R Sudarshan (eds), *India's Living Constitution: Ideas, Practices, Controversies* (London: Anthem Press, 2005) 31 at 43–46.

72 Praveen Jha, 'Globalization and labour in India: the emerging challenges', available at http://www.nottingham.ac.uk/shared/shared_scpolitics/documents/gwcprojectPapers/India.pdf (last visited 16 June 2012).

73 *State of West Bengal v Anwar Ali Sarkar* [1952] MANU 0033 (SC) para 8.

74 M P Singh, *V N Shukla's Constitution of India* (10th edn Lucknow: Eastern Book Company, 2001) 37; Reddy (n 33) 85–86.

75 Constitution of India art 15(4) Reddy (n 33).

76 *M Chhaganlal v Greater Bombay Municipality* [1974] MANU 0052 (SC) para 32.

77 *St Stephen's College v The University of Delhi* [1991] MANU 0319 (SC) para 103.

78 [1952] MANU 0033 (SC) para 58.

- such classification 'must be founded on an intelligible differentia which distinguishes' persons or things 'that are grouped together from others' left out of the group, and
- the 'differentia must have a rational relation to the object sought to be achieved' by the statute in question.[79]

What should ideally follow from these conditions is that all persons under similar circumstances should receive equal protection from laws.[80] However, courts in India determine reasonable classification within a very narrow range that is based on technical considerations relevant to an impugned piece of legislation.[81] The principle of reasonable classification is relevant *only* to judge the constitutionality of existing legislation.

Therefore, even if informal workers are unequally treated in comparison to formal workers as far as employment, working conditions and social protection are concerned, it would be very difficult to enforce their right to equality through the judiciary in the absence of (beneficial) legislation. The principle of reasonable classification would be of no help in dealing with such unequal treatment. The approach of the courts in India has shown that they might be able to judge inequality between one group of informal workers and another when they possess legal rights, but when they do not possess legal rights the judiciary is unwilling to promote constitutional labour guarantees for informal workers.[82]

In this context, Justice Chinnappa Reddy, a former judge of the Supreme Court, argues that the Indian Supreme Court wrongly perceived that by merely laying down the principle of reasonable classification the court is able to secure the fundamental right to equality of Indian masses.[83] Justice Reddy asserts that *real equality* 'requires and provides for the establishment of a just society in which no one is hungry or despised or deprived of the decencies and amenities of life, and all men are free from insecurity and oppression and are allowed to enjoy the plenitude of life'.[84] Such a broad understanding of equality is missing from the Indian judiciary's approach towards informal workers, although the judiciary has promoted equality amongst formal workers, albeit within the narrow juridical framework of reasonable classification.

---

79 *Shri Ram Krishna Dalmia v Justice S R Tendolkar* [1958] MANU 0024 (SC) paras 13, 16.
80 *State of West Bengal* [1952] MANU 0033 paras 25, 38, 45, 47, 58.
81 *K Kunhikoman v State of Kerala* [1961] MANU 0095 (SC), for a debate on classification between rubber, tea, and coffee plantation owners on one hand, and pepper and areca plantation owners on the other; see also (1959) SCR 629 for a classification between butchers who slaughter cattle, on one hand, and butchers who slaughter sheep or goats on the other (on usefulness of different animals to society).
82 It should be noted here that the judiciary may be unwilling but is not unable to develop beneficial guarantees for people/workers. The case of *Vishaka v State of Rajastan* [1997] MANU 0786 (SC) is a case in point (discussed below).
83 Reddy (n 33) 89–95.
84 ibid 90.

In striking down a law on unequal pay, the Supreme Court in *State of Madhya Pradesh v Pramod Bhartiya*[85] declared that equal pay for equal work, irrespective of the technical details or designation of employees, flows from Article 14. Further, in *State of Uttar Pradesh v J P Chaurasia*[86] the Supreme Court noted:

> In matters of employment the government of socialist State must protect the weaker sections. It must be ensured that there is no exploitation of poor and ignorant. It is the duty of the State to see that the underprivileged or weaker sections get their due. Even if they have voluntarily accepted the employment on unequal terms, the State should not deny their basic rights of equal treatment.

Thus, although the judiciary has been concerned with the exploitation of workers who are compelled to work on unequal terms, the judiciary can play only a very limited role in improving the lot of vulnerable workers. However, the real problem is that such judicial concern has not percolated through the government or to the legislature. The above-mentioned observation of the Supreme Court urges the government and the state to improve conditions of workers who are in a disadvantageous bargaining position. However, as I will show in the next section, the government and the legislature of the country have largely failed to promote the interests of informal workers in India.

In spite of the fact that informal workers suffer from vulnerability and marginalisation when their formal counterparts enjoy comprehensive labour welfare guarantees, informal workers who are in dire need of legislative protection have not received equal treatment with their formal counterparts in terms of legislative protection. I discuss the absence of legislative protection for informal workers in the next section. By analysing labour laws in India, I show that informal workers are mostly left out of the country's legislative framework. It is only very recently that the government and the legislature have become active in order to promote social protection for informal workers.

2.3 Coverage of informal economic activities (informal workers) under labour law in India

As a general rule, the Parliament of India makes laws for the entire territory of India, while the state legislatures make laws for the whole or part of the state.[87] Thus, there is an overlap of law-making powers with respect to a state where both the Parliament and the state legislature are entitled to make laws. This overlap is resolved by Article 246 of the constitution, which lists subject matters into three categories to divide law-making power between the Parliament and the states.[88]

---

85 [1993] MANU 0060 (SC).
86 [1988] MANU 0502 (SC) para 29.
87 Constitution of India art 245.
88 ibid art 246.

The Parliament has exclusive law-making power with respect to the *Union List* (List I), state legislatures have exclusive power to make laws on subject matters listed in the *State List* (List II), and both the Parliament and the state legislature(s) are entitled to make laws on subject matters specified in the *Concurrent List* (List III).[89] Labour welfare and industrial relations are part of the Concurrent List of Schedule VII, enabling both the Parliament and the state legislature(s) to enact laws for workers.[90] Accordingly, in addition to numerous pieces of state legislation regulating industrial relations and promoting workers' welfare, there are about 43 central statutes on labour and industrial relations.[91]

The NCEUS defined the informal sector on the basis of two criteria: an ownership criterion and a size criterion.[92] According to the ownership criterion, an enterprise must not be a separate legal entity, such as a company[93] or a registered society,[94] apart from its owner, to qualify as an informal sector enterprise. Additionally, such proprietary enterprise must have a total of a maximum of nine workers engaged in its activity. The NCEUS reached the ownership and size criteria on the basis of legislative coverage of establishments and protection of workers. While establishments such as a company or a registered society are to adhere to legislative requirements, establishments employing 10 or more workers are covered by labour and social security legislation. Similarly, the NCEUS defines informal workers as workers who are excluded from 'any employment and social security benefits'.[95]

In its different reports, the NCEUS has conducted comprehensive reviews of Indian labour welfare and social protection laws in order to ascertain the coverage of informal workers under those laws. In one of its reports,[96] the Commission

---

89   ibid Schedule 7.
90   Entry 22 of the Concurrent List enumerates: '[t]rade unions, industrial and labour disputes'; Entry 23 of the List enumerates: '[s]ocial security and social insurance; employment and unemployment'; and Entry 24 provides: '[w]elfare of labour including conditions of work, provident funds, employers' liability, workmen's compensation, invalidity and old age pensions and maternity benefits'.
91   NCEUS, *The challenge of employment in India: an informal economy perspective*, vol 1 Main Report (New Delhi: NCEUS, 2009) 169.
92   NCEUS, *Report on Definitional and Statistical Issues Relating to Informal Economy* (New Delhi: NCEUS, 2008) 23.
93   Registered under the Companies Act 1956.
94   Registered under the Societies Registration Act 1860. The Societies Registration Act is an 'Act for the Registration of Literary, Scientific and Charitable Societies'. See short title of the Act. Section 1 of the Act explains the legal status of a society: '[a]ny seven or more persons associated for any literary, scientific, or charitable purpose, or for any such purpose as is described in section 20 of this Act, may, by subscribing their names to a memorandum of association, and filing the same with Registrar of Joint-stock Companies form themselves into a society under this Act'. Section 20 delineates the different kinds of societies, which could be registered under the Act: '[c]haritable societies, the military orphan fund or societies established at the several presidencies of India, societies established for the promotion of science, literature, or the fine arts . . .'.
95   NCEUS, *Definitional and Statistical Issues* (n 92) 27.
96   NCEUS, *Report on conditions of work and promotion of livelihoods in the unorganised sector* (New Delhi: NCEUS, 2007).

divides central legislation into three groups, based on their applicability to informal economic activities. The first of these groups contains laws that 'apply to all sections of the unorganised sector labour', such as the Equal Remuneration Act 1976, and the Bonded Labour System (Abolition) Act 1976.[97]

The second of these groups consists of 'laws which apply to some sections of the unorganised sector labour' such as the Minimum Wages Act 1948, Child Labour (Prohibition and Regulation) Act 1986, Dangerous Machines (Regulation) Act 1983, the Employment of Manual Scavengers and Construction of Dry Latrines (Prohibition) Act 1993, Inter-State Migrant Workmen (Regulation of Employment and Conditions of Service) Act 1979, Motor Transport Workers Act 1961, Sales Promotion Employees (Conditions of Service) Act 1976, and the Trade Unions Act 1926.[98]

The third of these groups consists of legislation 'which can be extended to the unorganised sector', such as the Beedi and Cigar Workers (Conditions of Employment) Act 1966, Payment of Wages Act 1936, the Building and Other Construction Workers (Regulation of Employment and Conditions of Service) Act 1996, the Contract Labour (Regulation and Abolition) Act 1970, the Maternity Benefit Act 1961, Workmen's Compensation Act 1923 and the Weekly Holidays Act 1942.[99]

For example, with respect to the first of the three groups, the Commission notes that under the Equal Remuneration Act 1976, employers cannot discriminate between men and women workers in hiring or payment, irrespective of whether such workers are engaged formally or informally.[100] Similarly, the Commission notes that the bonded labour system, whether employed formally or informally, is abolished under the Bonded Labour System (Abolition) Act 1976.[101]

With respect to the second group of laws, the Commission observes that the Minimum Wages Act 1948 specifies the categories of employment in its schedule, and determines wages for workers engaged in specific activities.[102] The categories of employment listed in the Act's schedule could be modified at any time by the government.[103] The Act lists both agricultural and non-agricultural activities, where employers are mandated to pay specified wages to their employees.[104] Since the Act lists certain informal economic activities in its schedule, the Commission groups it under laws that are applicable to some sections of informal sector workers. Similarly, the Commission shows that other legislation grouped under the second category addresses some sections of informal workers.[105] However, it

---

97   ibid 155.
98   ibid.
99   ibid 155, 157.
100   ibid 158.
101   ibid.
102   ibid.
103   Minimum Wages Act 1948 s 27 (Power of State Government to Add to Schedule).
104   For example 'Employment in any rice mill, flour mill or dal mill' (pt I) or 'Employment in agriculture' (pt II) Minimum Wages Act 1948 Schedule ss 2(g), 27.
105   NCEUS, 'Conditions of work' (n 96) 158–60.

is surprising that the Commission places the Trade Unions Act 1926 in this second group of laws instead of the first group because the Trade Unions Act is one of the very few pieces of legislation that is applicable to all formal as well as informal workers. I will discuss the scope of the Trade Unions Act in a later part of this section.

Finally, the Commission lists legislation that could be *extended* to informal workers, even if the laws do not specifically address informal workers.[106] In this category, the Commission lists laws such as the Contract Labour (Regulation and Abolition) Act 1970, Maternity Benefit Act 1961 etc. Under the Contract Labour Act, both the principal employer and the contractor employing contract labour are responsible for ensuring appropriate conditions at work and payment of wages to workers they employ.[107] Such protection is available to all workers, formal or informal.[108] In similar vein, the Maternity Benefit Act mandates that employers ensure maternity benefits to women workers formally or informally employed.[109] Although these statutes are applicable to establishments employing a specified minimum number of workers (10 or 20), the government, by order, can extend these statutory requirements to any group of formal or informal workers.[110]

The Commission also surveys state legislation having a bearing on informal workers, and is quick to note that these laws afford protection to only a small section of informal workers in the country.[111] The NCEUS also documents the 'abysmally poor' implementation of labour laws in India.[112] The small size of labour administration personnel, the exclusive focus on the formal sector, the inadequacy of infrastructure and the lack of representative voices for informal workers are factors responsible for poor enforcement of labour law.[113] Thus, the exclusion of informal workers from legislative protection happens at two stages. First, informal workers are largely excluded from beneficial legislation and, secondly, even when they are allowed legislative protection, such protection does not materialise because of non-enforcement.[114]

---

106   ibid 161–63.
107   Contract Labour (Regulation and Abolition) Act 1970 s 20 mandates that in case of failure of a contractor to provide legally mandated benefits to contract workers it is the responsibility of the principal employer to provide those benefits to such workers.
108   According to section 1(4) of the Contract Labour (Regulation and Abolition) Act 1970, the statute is applicable to all establishments where 20 or more workers are employed and to all employers (contractors) who employ 20 or more workers.
109   According to section 2 of the Maternity Benefit Act 1961, the statute is applicable to every factory, mine or plantation and to any other establishment employing at least 10 workers.
110   See s 31 (Power to exempt in special cases) of the Contract Labour (Regulation and Abolition) Act 1970 and s 2(1) Proviso (Application of Act) of the Maternity Benefit Act 1961.
111   NCEUS, 'Conditions of work' (n 96) 163–64, 284–87; Rohini Hensman, 'Labour and globalization: union responses in India' in Paul Bowles, John Harriss (eds), *Globalization and Labour in China and India: Impacts and Responses* (New York: Palgrave Macmillan, 2010) 189 at 193–96.
112   NCEUS, 'Conditions of work' (n 96) 164–71; NCEUS, 'Challenge of employment' (n 91) 186–87.
113   NCEUS, 'Conditions of work' (n 96) 166–67.
114   NCEUS, 'Challenge of employment' (n 91) 180; Hensman (n 111) 193–96.

In the 2009 Report prepared by the NCEUS, named 'The challenge of employment in India: an informal economy perspective',[115] the Commission discusses three of the major labour laws that regulate industrial relations and labour welfare in India.[116] Those are the Industrial Disputes Act 1947, Industrial Employment (Standing Orders) Act 1946, and the Factories Act 1948. These statutes, however, are problematic so far as informal workers are concerned. These Acts are meant to protect conditions of service,[117] employment security for formal workers,[118] promote amicable industrial relations in the formal sector,[119] and they are concerned with factories or industries where employers are mandated to provide for workers' benefits.

These Acts are based on the juridical concept of an employment relationship between workers and the employer and, as such, self-employed own-account workers are excluded from the scope of these statutes. Similarly, statutes categorised by the NCEUS 'Report on conditions of work and promotion of livelihoods in the unorganised sector'[120] (such as the Equal Remuneration Act, Contract Labour Act etc) as applicable to informal workers are also based on an employment relationship between workers and employers. Most of the legislation surveyed in that NCEUS report excludes self-employed own-account informal workers. By contrast, laws such as the Trade Unions Act 1926 apply to both formal and informal workers (including self-employed informal workers), although there are indications that this legislation is also biased towards formal workers.[121]

What follows from the Commission's review of Indian labour laws is that labour laws in India are biased towards formal workers employed in an industry. Although it is possible to argue that some of these laws address some informal workers, the majority of the statutes are not designed for them. Many of the Acts mentioned earlier have a numerical threshold for their applicability; they apply to an industry where at least 20 workers are employed (10 workers if electricity is used, and five workers for the applicability of the Migrant Workmen Act and the Motor Transport Workers Act).[122] Therefore, although it is possible to argue that some of the labour laws are applicable to informal workers who are in an employment relationship

115 NCEUS, 'Challenge of employment' (n 91).
116 ibid 169–70.
117 Factories Act 1948; Industrial Disputes Act 1947.
118 Industrial Disputes Act 1947 ch VA (Lay-off and Retrenchment) and ch VB (Special provisions Relating to lay-off, Retrenchment and closure in certain establishments).
119 Industrial Disputes Act 1947 ch IIB (Grievance Redressal Machinery) and ch III (Reference of disputes to boards, courts or tribunals).
120 NCEUS, 'Conditions of work' (n 96).
121 See the Trade Unions Act 1926. It defines a trade union as 'any combination . . . formed . . . for the purpose of regulating the relations between workmen and employers or between workmen and workmen, or between employers and employers . . .' (s 2(h)). The Act defines a trade dispute as 'any dispute between employers and workmen or between workmen and workmen, or between employers and employers which is connected with the employment or non-employment, or the terms of employment or the conditions of labour, of any person . . .' (s 2(g)). Both of these definitions are centred on employment relationship and waged workers. However, there is scope to argue that the Act is applicable to self-employed informal workers as well.
122 NCEUS, 'Challenge of employment' (n 91) 178–80.

(or disguised employment relationship), once the legislative threshold is set for industries employing at least 10 or 20 workers, 92 per cent of the total workforce remains outside such legislative protection.[123]

In this context it is worthwhile to take note of how the judiciary has defined industry, which has reduced the strict numerical threshold for the applicability of the Industrial Disputes Act. In *Bangalore Water Supply & Sewerage Board v A Rajappa and Others*,[124] the Supreme Court was called upon to determine the true import of the term *industry* as used in the 1947 statute.[125] Working under a socialist constitution and a context in which a significant majority of the workers were (and still are) excluded from legislative protection, the court could have interpreted the term 'industry' in such a manner that the majority of the work-relations (and thereby, the majority of the workers) could be brought under its definition and, thereby, brought under the protective umbrella of the statute. The majority of the court, speaking through Justice Krishna Iyer, interpreted the definition provided in the statute in the following manner:

(i) systematic activity, (ii) organized by co-operation between employer and employee . . . (iii) for the production and/or distribution of goods and services . . . The true focus is functional and the decisive test is the nature of the activity with special emphasis on employer–employee relations.[126]

Although the definition would still go on to exclude self-employed informal workers because of its focus on the employment relationship, it broadens the coverage of the term 'industry'. The term 'industry' now embraces waged workers who were left outside the beneficial scope of statutes that have a numerical threshold for their applicability. This definition makes the Industrial Disputes Act applicable even to small establishments where employer–employee relations exist. Justice Iyer passionately asserted one of the foundational aspects of Indian labour jurisprudence:

[the statute's] goal is amelioration of the conditions of workers, not from a neutral position but from a concern for the welfare of the weaker lot.[127]

123   ibid 180.
124   [1978] MANU 0257 (SC).
125   Industrial Disputes Act 1947 s 2(j) defines: '"industry" means any business, trade, undertaking, manufacture or calling of employers and includes any calling service, employment, handicraft, or industrial occupation or avocation of workmen'.
126   [1978] MANU 0257 (SC) para 111.
127   *Bangalore* para 43. However, it must be noted that, although the Supreme Court has given an extremely liberal interpretation to the concept of 'industry' so that the term can cover even small establishments, the expression 'worker' under the Act still has limiting effect on workers' rights. The Supreme Court has repeatedly observed that everyone who is employed in an 'industry' need not be workers. ibid paras 117–25. However, without overruling the 1978 decision of the court, the Supreme Court in 2005 challenged the expansive interpretation given to the definition

Thus, in accordance with the 1978 decision of the Supreme Court, it could be argued that informal waged workers should receive protection under the Industrial Disputes Act. Likewise, the Supreme Court and some of the High Courts have held that the expression 'employees'[128] in the Employees' State Insurance Act 1948 is wide enough to include casual and temporary workers such as canteen workers or bicycle stand operators, even if such workers are employed for only a day.[129] However, the Employees' State Insurance Act is applicable to establishments employing at least 10 workers.[130]

Thus, although it is possible to argue that informal waged workers could be brought within the purview of some of the major labour welfare legislation in India, the NCEUS reports demonstrate that enforcement of these Acts effectively excludes the majority of informal workers. Moreover, these Acts ignore self-employed informal workers, who are significant in number.[131] In view of the widespread exclusion of informal workers from legislative protection, the NCEUS proposed two Bills to the Government of India: the Unorganised Sector Workers Social Security Bill 2005 and the Unorganised Sector Workers (Conditions of Work and Livelihood Promotion) Bill 2005.[132]

Based on the Commission's recommended Bill on social security, the Indian Parliament enacted the Unorganised Sector Social Security Act 2008. Now, although the Central Government and some of the state governments have executed social protection schemes for informal workers,[133] a large number of

of industry by the 1978 decision. See *State of Uttar Pradesh v Jai Bir Singh* [2005] MANU 0360 (SC) paras 35–42.

128 Employees' State Insurance Act 1948 s 2(9).

129 *Royal Talkies, Hyderabad v Employees State Insurance Corporation* [1978] MANU 0282 (SC); *Siddheswar, Hubli v ESI* (1998) Lab IC 212 (Orissa); *Regional Director, Employees State Insurance Corporation v Suvarna Saw Mills* (1979) Lab IC 1335 (Karnataka).

130 Employees' State Insurance Act 1948 s 1 (short title, extent, commencement and application) and s 2(12) (Definitions). Prior to the Employees' State Insurance (Amendment) Act 2010, the statute was applicable to establishments employing 10 or more workers if electricity was used, or 20 or more workers if electricity was not used (in the particular establishment).

131 Barbara Harriss-White, 'Globalization, the financial crisis and petty commodity production in India's socially regulated informal economy' in Bowles and Harris (n 111) 131 at 134; Kalyan Sanyal, Rajesh Bhattacharya, 'Beyond the factory: globalization, informalization of production and the changing locations of labour' in Bowles and Harriss (n 111) 151 at 152, 158, 160.

132 Reserve Bank of India, *Internal working group to review the recommendations of the NCEUS report on conditions of work and promotion of livelihoods in the unorganised sector* (Mumbai: Reserve Bank of India, 2008).

133 For a comprehensive list of the Central Government and state governments' social security schemes and their scope, see S Mahendra Dev, 'Social security in the unorganized sector in India' in Ramgopal Agarwala, Nagesh Kumar and Michelle Riboud (eds), *Reforms, Labour Markets, and Social Security in India* (New Delhi: Oxford University Press, 2004) 198 at 200–27, 231–35; R K A Subrahmanya, 'Strategies for protective social security' in Renana Jhabvala, R K A Subrahmanya (eds), *The Unorganised Sector: Work Security and Social Protection* (New Delhi: Sage Publications, 2001) 38 at 42–44; Mina Swaminathan, 'Worker, mother or both: maternity and child care services for women in the unorganised sector' in Jhabvala and Subrahmanya *The Unorganised Sector* (ibid) 122 at 123–35.

informal workers remain excluded from the purview of such schemes because of inappropriate and inefficient implementation of the schemes.[134] Social security schemes in India are mainly targeted towards the *poor* rather than *workers*.[135] Even when social protection schemes are targeted towards workers, they do not provide *any legal right* to social security for informal workers,[136] something that the Unorganised Sector Social Security Act 2008 purportedly seeks to guarantee.

The 2008 Act is applicable to both waged[137] and self-employed[138] informal workers[139] who work either in the informal sector[140] or the formal sector.[141] The Central Government is to formulate social protection schemes providing for 'life and disability cover', 'health and maternity benefits', 'old age protection' and 'any other benefit' under the law.[142] The state governments are mandated to provide for 'provident fund', 'employment injury benefit', 'housing', 'educational schemes for children', 'skill upgradation of workers', 'funeral assistance', and 'old age homes' under the law.[143] The law requires the composition of National and State Social Security Boards for Unorganised Workers (Chapters III, IV) in order to implement the legislative mandate.[144]

Upon a self-declaration, informal workers are registered under the law, and an identity card is issued against such registration.[145] However, the law excludes informal workers who are receiving benefits under the Workmen's Compensation

For a discussion on employment generation schemes, see Alakh N Sharma, 'Employment generation policy and social safety nets in India' in Agarwala, Kumar and Riboud (ibid) 236 at 261–70; R K A Subrahmanya, 'Support for the unorganised sector: existing social security measures' in Jhabvala and Subrahmanya, *The Unorganised Sector* (ibid) 45 at 53–58; R K A Subrahmanya, 'Welfare funds: an Indian model for workers in the unorganised sector' in Jhabvala and Subrahmanya, *The Unorganised Sector* (ibid) 65 at 66–69.

134   Harriss-White, 'Socially regulated informal economy' (n 131) 145; Ramgopal Agarwala, Nagesh Kumar and Michelle Riboud, 'Reforms, labour markets, and social security policy in India: an introduction' in Agarwala, Kumar and Riboud (n 133) 1 at 2–3, 5, 8; R K A Subrahmanya, Renana Jhabvala, 'Meeting basic needs: the unorganised sector and social security' in Jhabvala and Subrahmanya, *The Unorganised Sector* (n 133) 17 at 19; Swaminathan (n 133) 124. Many of the social protection schemes are rendered ineffective because of the rampant corruption during the implementation of the schemes; see Wouter van Ginnekenn, 'Social protection for the informal sector in India' in Agarwala, Kumar and Riboud (n 133) 186 at 194.

135   Renana Jhabvala, 'Participatory approaches: emerging trend in social security' in Jhabvala and Subrahmanya, *The Unorganised Sector* (n 133) 30 at 31–34; Subrahmanya, 'Support' (n 133) 52–58. One recent right-based employment guarantee scheme for poor rural households is the National Rural Employment Guarantee Act 2005.

136   This is because most of the existing social protection schemes do not emanate from legislative mandates.

137   Unorganised Sector Social Security Act 2008 ss 2(a) 2(n) 2(b).

138   ibid s 2(k).

139   ibid s 2(m).

140   ibid s 2(l).

141   ibid s 2(f).

142   ibid s 3(1).

143   ibid 3(4).

144   ibid chs III, IV. In particular, see ss 5(8) and 6(8).

145   ibid s 10.

Act, Industrial Disputes Act, Employees' State Insurance Act, Employees' Provident Fund and Miscellaneous Provisions Act, Maternity Benefit Act and Payment of Gratuity Act from its purview.[146] In July 2011 the Central Government approved Rupees 1000 *Crore* (10,000,000,000) as a national social security fund for the execution of the law.[147]

Apart from the exclusion of informal workers who are covered under other social protection statutes, Kamala Sankaran points out that the 2008 Act excludes 'unpaid family workers', a vital sub-group of informal workers, from its purview.[148] She is also sceptical as to whether the diverse range of self-employed informal workers (such as informal entrepreneurs and own-account workers) would be covered under the 2008 Act, although the law does not expressly exclude any category of self-employed informal workers from its purview.[149] Rohini Hensman argues that lumping informal employees and informal self-employed workers together in the same legislation is a recipe for failure because the needs of informal waged workers and informal self-employed workers are different.[150] She also points out that, in the absence of the more powerful formal sector unions' interest in the legislation, 'it has less chance of success'.[151] Even if successful, Hensman notes, the law will leave informal workers with much weaker rights than their formal counterparts.[152]

Sankaran points out that the labour law is inadequate for the promotion of workers' interests in the Indian context.[153] She observes that Indian labour laws exclude informal workers on the basis of numerical thresholds, functional criteria and wage ceiling criteria.[154] Poor enforcement of labour laws adds to the exclusion of informal workers in India.[155] According to Sankaran, a multiplicity of labour laws dealing with the same or similar concepts and terminologies differently[156] further complicates their application to informal workers.[157] This multiplicity of

146   ibid s 2(m), Schedule II.
147   See 'Cabinet okays fund for unorganized sector' *The Times of India* (29 July 2011) available at http://articles.timesofindia.indiatimes.com/2011-07-29/india/29828840_1_unorganized-sector-workers-national-social-security-fund (last visited 29 January 2012).
148   Kamala Sankaran, 'Informal employment and the challenges for labour law' in Guy Davidov, Brian Langille (eds), *The Idea of Labour Law* (Oxford & New York: Oxford University Press, 2011) 223 at 229.
149   ibid 232.
150   Hensman (n 111) 198.
151   ibid.
152   ibid.
153   Sankaran, 'Informal employment' (n 148) 224; also see Kamala Sankaran, *Labour Laws in South Asia: the Need for an Inclusive Approach* (Geneva: International Institute for Labour Studies, 2007) 3–6.
154   Kamala Sankaran, 'Protecting the worker in the informal economy: the role of labour law' in Guy Davidov and Brian Langille (eds), *Boundaries and Frontiers of Labour Law* (Portland: Hart Publishing, 2006) 205 at 206–207.
155   ibid; Sankaran, *The Need for an Inclusive Approach* (n 153) 7, 14–16.
156   Such as the concepts of worker, employee, employer, establishment, industry, are defined differently under different statutes. See Sankaran, *The Need for an Inclusive Approach*, ibid 6.
157   ibid.

competing concepts means that informal workers may receive coverage under one statute (such as the Trade Unions Act), while being excluded from the purview of other statutes (such as the Factories Act). The global research and advocacy network, Women in Informal Employment Globalizing and Organizing (WIEGO), has conducted law pilot projects on informal economic activities in India.[158] The law pilot project on waste pickers shows how, in the absence of labour laws and appropriate policy,[159] waste pickers' organisations have innovatively leveraged the existing waste management law and policy to their best advantage.[160] However, the law pilot project on domestic workers points towards the inadequacy of law and policy for the promotion of domestic workers' interests.[161] Although some states such as Kerala and Karnataka have minimum wage laws for domestic workers,[162] there are no central or state statutes regulating service conditions or social protection for domestic workers.[163]

Thus, existing labour and social protection laws in India have largely failed to protect informal workers' interests, and promote their dignified life, which is a constitutional goal.[164] Sankaran points out that, despite the inadequacy of labour laws in the informal work context in India, some existing labour laws could prove to be vital in promoting informal workers' interests. She notes that the Trade Unions Act 1926 is one such statute.[165] Citing the example of the Self Employed Women's Association, Sankaran argues that the Trade Unions Act has evolved to include self-employment within the scope of the expression 'worker' under the Act.[166]

158   India Pilot Project: 'Law and informality, women in informal employment: globalizing and organizing', available at http://wiego.org/informal_economy_law/india-pilot-project (last visited 16 June 2012).

159   Renana Jhabvala, 'Opening remarks', workshop to discuss policy on community-based and decentralised integrated sustainable solid waste management in the country (22–23 July 2008), available at http://wiego.org/sites/wiego.org/files/resources/files/wp_consultation_report.pdf (last visited 16 June 2012); Poornima Chikarmane, 'Policy outline', Workshop to discuss policy (ibid).

160   Kamala Sankaran, Shalini Sinha and Roopa Madhav, 'Waste pickers background note', WIEGO Law Pilot Project on the Informal Economy, available at http://wiego.org/sites/wiego.org/files/resources/files/wp_background_note.pdf (last visited 16 June 2012); Kamala Sankaran, Shalini Sinha and Roopa Madhav, 'Concept note: national consultation of waste pickers' (22–23 July 2008) KKPKP and WIEGO Pilot Project, available at http://wiego.org/sites/wiego.org/files/resources/files/wp_consultation_concept_note.pdf (last visited 16 June 2012); 'Integrated solid waste management' and 'Municipal and organizational arrangements' Thematic Session I, Session chaired by Dr Kamala Sankaran, workshop to discuss policy (n 159).

161   Kamala Sankaran, Shalini Sinha and Roopa Madhav, 'Domestic workers: background document', WIEGO Law Pilot Project on the Informal Economy, available at http://wiego.org/sites/wiego.org/files/resources/files/dw_background_note.pdf (last visited 16 June 2012).

162   ibid 3.

163   ibid 1–3, 9.

164   *Francis Coralie* (n 28).

165   Sankaran, 'Informal employment' (n 148) 227.

166   ibid 227; Sankaran, 'Protecting the worker' (n 154) 211.

In the absence of legal protection for informal workers' constitutional rights, workers have undertaken to promote their (well-rounded) dignified life by themselves, through organisational initiatives. In this respect, informal workers have used the Trade Unions Act to their advantage. Informal workers have not only organised themselves under the Trade Unions Act, they have also organised themselves as cooperatives (under the Cooperative Societies Act 1912), societies (under the Societies Registration Act 1860), and trusts (under the Charitable and Religious Trusts Act 1920), thereby innovatively using the existing legislative framework in the country.

These workers' organisations promote dignified life for workers by providing for comprehensive social, economic, political and cultural resources that are guaranteed to workers under the Constitution of India. In the absence of adequate state initiatives for the promotion of the constitutional rights of informal workers, the private membership-based and non-membership organisations seek to promote workers' constitutional rights. In the next section of the chapter I discuss private initiatives aimed at realising constitutional guarantees, which the workers derive through the formation of membership-based and non-membership organisations.

2.4 Unionisation/organisation as a strategy for the realisation of constitutional labour guarantees for informal workers

As I have shown in the previous sections, the Indian constitutional and legislative frameworks have failed to meet expectations of its large working population,[167] with the result that there is growing inequality between formal and informal workers.[168] In the absence of legislative protection for informal workers generally and self-employed workers in particular, informal workers have organised themselves into trade unions and cooperatives in order to attain a life of dignity.[169]

In this section I discuss the *modus operandi* of informal workers' organisations in India. Informal workers' organisations in India simultaneously perform multiple functions for the overall development of informal workers. On the one hand, these organisations make provision for socio-economic resources for informal workers and, on the other, they enable informal workers effectively to exercise their civil-political rights. Organisations of informal workers do not always take the legal form of trade unions – informal workers organise themselves as cooperatives, registered societies, charitable trusts and companies. In this section, I show that, despite having a different legal status, functionally informal workers' organisations in India are strikingly similar. I discuss the nature and functioning of five

167 A Vaidyanathan, 'The pursuit of social justice' in Hasan, Sridharan and Sudarshan (n 71) 284 at 288–89; Granville Austin, 'The expected and the unintended in working a democratic constitution' in Hasan, Sridharan, and Sudarshan (n 71) 319 at 334–39.

168 Vaidyanathan (n 167) 290; Kaveri Gill, *Of Poverty and Plastic: Scavenging and Scrap Trading Entrepreneurs in India's Urban Informal Economy* (New Delhi: Oxford University Press, 2010) 98–100, 107.

169 Austin, 'The expected and the unintended' (n 167) 337; Vaidyanathan (n 167) 300.

self-employed informal workers' organisations. These five organisations represent different varieties of legal status: two trade unions; one registered society; one charitable trust; and one cooperative, and are some of the biggest organisation initiatives of informal workers.

For reasons mentioned earlier, my focus is on self-employed informal workers' organisations. I conclude this section with a discussion of informal waste pickers' organisation initiatives in India. I hope to show that by organising themselves into trade-based associations waste pickers have been able to achieve conditions that are capable of promoting their dignified life. My discussion of waste pickers' organisation initiatives will set the stage for my analysis of work-lives of waste pickers in Kolkata, India, which I present in Chapter 6.

The Self Employed Women's Association (SEWA) is an internationally renowned organisation for women informal workers.[170] SEWA is a trade union registered under the Trade Unions Act 1926. Registered in 1972, SEWA is an organisation of self-employed poor women workers.[171] Based on the ideals of *satya* (truth), *ahimsa* (non-violence), *sarvadharma* (integration of all faiths) and *khadi* (self-reliance), SEWA aims to promote full employment for its members 'whereby workers obtain work security, income security, food security and social security (at least health care, child care and shelter)'.[172] In 2009, SEWA had 1,256,944 members across India, and 631,345 members in the state of Gujarat.

Despite its large membership SEWA's registration as a trade union was not smooth. According to the Trade Unions Act 1926: '[t]rade [u]nion means any combination, whether temporary or permanent, formed primarily for the purpose of regulating the relations between workmen and employers or between workmen and workmen, or between employers and employers'.[173] On the basis of this definition the Labour Department refused to register SEWA as a trade union, reasoning that, since there were no recognised employers, workers of the union would have no one to bargain with or struggle against.[174] SEWA argued that a trade union does not need to be opposed to employer(s) since the primary purpose of a trade union is the promotion of unity amongst workers.[175]

The SEWA is a trade union that organises self-employed women workers engaged in various economic activities.[176] SEWA members pay an annual

---

170   Self Employed Women's Association (SEWA) http://www.sewa.org/ (last visited 5 January 2012); Aditi Kapoor, 'The SEWA way: shaping another future for informal labour' (2007) 39 *Futures* 554 at 555.

171   Self Employed Women's Association (SEWA) (n 170); see Kapoor (n 170) 560, for the different kinds of informal economic activities that SEWA members are engaged in.

172   SEWA, 'About us' http://www.sewa.org/About_Us.asp (last visited 5 January 2012); Elizabeth Hill, *Worker Identity, Agency and Economic Development: Women's Empowerment in the Indian Informal Economy* (New York: Routledge, 2010) 46–47.

173   Trade Unions Act 1926 s 2(h).

174   SEWA, 'About us' (n 172).

175   Ela R Bhat, *We Are Poor But So Many: the Story of Self-Employed Women in India* (New York: Oxford University Press, 2006) 9–10, 17–18; SEWA, 'About us' (n 172); also see Kapoor (n 170) 561.

176   SEWA, 'SEWA's structure', available at http://www.sewa.org/About_Us_Structure.asp (last visited 7 June 2012); John Blaxall, 'India's Self Employed Women's Association (SEWA):

membership fee of 5 rupees.[177] SEWA also accepts donations from a range of government and private donors, both Indian and foreign.[178] The union is governed by a two-tier representation model.[179] SEWA members directly elect trade council representatives and members of the executive committee.[180] The union governance is carried on by a mix of professional cadres and informal worker-members.[181] However, SEWA is different from the traditional concept of a trade union.[182] SEWA's functional emphasis is on an internally constructive role, rather than an external adversarial agenda.[183] High levels of participation in all aspects of the union characterise SEWA membership; SEWA offers specialist skills such as legal advocacy, financial and vocational training, and organisation and policy orientation to its members.[184]

SEWA functions through the constitution of trade and service cooperatives[185] and it is composed of around 90 trade and service cooperatives in India.[186] The *Swashrayi Mahila Sewa Sahakari Bank* (SEWA Bank) is the largest cooperative of SEWA members with 93,000 savings accounts, and it is run by the members themselves.[187] SEWA's health care initiative is a combination of health education and curative care, which is also run by the members.[188] SEWA's child care initiatives are run by local cooperatives and organisations.[189] SEWA initiated its integrated insurance scheme in 1992 with the help of the national insurance companies.[190] SEWA also provides legal services including legal education and legal

empowerment through mobilization of poor women on a large scale' 1 at 7, available at http://info.worldbank.org/etools/docs/reducingpoverty/case/79/fullcase/India%20SEWA %20Full%20Case.pdf (last visited 6 June 2012).

177 SEWA, 'SEWA's structure' (n 176).
178 Blaxall (n 176) 16.
179 SEWA, 'SEWA's structure' (n 176).
180 ibid.
181 Blaxall (n 176) 6, 13–14, 16–18.
182 Hill, *Worker Identity* (n 172) 75.
183 Bhat (n 175) in particular at 70, 99–122; also see Jan Breman, *The Making and Unmaking of an Industrial Working Class: Sliding Down the Labour Hierarchy in Ahmedabad, India* (New Delhi: Oxford University Press, 2004) 282–86.
184 Bhat (n 175); SEWA, 'Sewa services', available at http://www.sewa.org/Sewa_Services.asp (last visited 5 January 2012); Hill, *Worker Identity* (n 172) 75–76.
185 Bhat (n 175) 16–17, 53–54, 99–122; Janhavi Dave, Manali Shah and Yamini Parikh, 'The Self-Employed Women's Association (SEWA) organising through union and co-operative in India' in Melanie Samson (ed), *Refusing to be Cast Aside: Waste Pickers Organising Around the World* (Cambridge, MA: WIEGO, 2009) 27.
186 Dave, Shah and Parikh (n 185).
187 Bhat (n 175) 99–122.
188 SEWA, 'Sewa services: health care', available at http://www.sewa.org/Services_Health_Care.asp (last visited 5 January 2012).
189 SEWA, 'Sewa services: child care', available at http://www.sewa.org/Services_Child_Care.asp (last visited 5 January 2012).
190 SEWA, 'Sewa services: VimoSEWA (SEWA insurance)' http://www.sewa.org/Services_Work_Security_Insurance.asp (last visited 5 January 2012); Ginnekenn, 'Social protection' (n 134) 192–93; Mirai Chatterjee, Jayshree Vyas, 'Organising insurance for women workers' in Jhabvala and Subrahmanya, *The Unorganised Sector* (n 133) 74.

assistance during litigation through its legal advisory centre.[191] The SEWA Academy promotes its members' education and capacity building.[192] SEWA established the *Mahila Housing SEWA Trust* in 1994 in order to improve 'housing and infrastructural conditions' of women engaged in informal economic activities.[193]

SEWA's role is not limited to the services it provides to its members. SEWA has a strong external presence (both national and international) in the policy-development sphere.[194] With the members' full participation, SEWA lobbies the government on several issues.[195] SEWA has lobbied the government on matters such as the inclusion of the informal economy in official government statistics and policy; ascertainment of the contribution that informal economic activities make to the economy; promotion of legislative protection of informal economic activities; and promotion of institutional platforms for women's participation in the public sphere.[196]

As a matter of strategy, SEWA also resorts to direct struggle and agitation against myriad forms of discrimination against women informal workers.[197] Moreover, at a fundamental level, SEWA unionisation provides for the much-needed legitimation and recognition of informal workers and their activities.[198] Based on her extensive study of SEWA unionisation, Elizabeth Hill demonstrates that SEWA intervenes at three levels in the work-lives of informal workers.[199] The three levels are the *macro* or societal level, the *meso* or industry (enterprise) level and the *micro* or individual worker (interpersonal) level.[200]

From this summary, it is clear that SEWA organises to provide a range of socio-economic services to its members.[201] SEWA banking, insurance, health care, child care and housing services are remarkable as social protection schemes. SEWA also promotes its members' education, financial and vocational training, capacity building and legal advocacy. Moreover, SEWA is active in direct action (such as street action and agitation) and lobbying nationally and internationally. In effect, SEWA aims at socio-economic-political justice for informal women workers,[202] consistent with the foundational principles of the Indian constitution.

---

191   SEWA, 'Sewa services: legal services' http://www.sewa.org/Services_Legal_Services.asp (last visited 5 January 2012).
192   SEWA, 'Sewa services: capacity building of SEWA members' http://www.sewa.org/Services_Capacity_Building.asp (last visited 5 January 2012).
193   SEWA, 'Sewa services: housing and infrastructure' http://www.sewahousing.org/ (last visited 5 January 2012).
194   See Bhat (n 175) 70, 213; also see Hill, *Worker Identity* (n 172) 139–42; also see Kapoor (n 170) 564–66.
195   See Bhat (n 175) 70; also see Hill (n 172) 76–77, 139–42; Dave, Shah and Parikh (n 185) 32.
196   Hill (n 172) 76–77; Bhat (n 175).
197   Bhat (n 175) 70; Hill (n 172) 76–77, 89–93.
198   Hill (n 172) 76–83.
199   ibid 58–72, 76–94.
200   ibid 59–72, 77.
201   Kapoor (n 170) 556–57, 559.
202   ibid 561; Dave, Shah and Parikh (n 185) 32.

Although SEWA's socio-economic programme initiatives are the most visible ones, Hill argues that SEWA performs a significantly more important function. By organising the most vulnerable, marginalised and impoverished women workers, SEWA addresses their inherent insecurity, hesitation, fear, exclusion, anxiety and oppression.[203] According to Hill, SEWA's collective action has a positive psychological impact on its members, which is central for multi-dimensional human development.[204] SEWA membership is a source of recognition and respect for women informal workers.[205] Hill shows how psychological wellbeing becomes a source of overall human development of women informal workers, thanks to their recognition as workers and respect emanating from economic independence.[206]

Hill documents the confidence, self-respect, poise, self-assurance, sense of public status, identity and esteem amongst members of SEWA.[207] She makes a connection between these positive psychological traits and SEWA members' *agency* or reflexive human action.[208] Agency, according to Hill, is important for informal workers because agency enables workers to formulate strategies effectively to bargain 'relations of production, social security and political participation' [footnote omitted].[209] Agency is, therefore, a primary factor in the socio-economic transformation of informal workers.[210] In this sense, SEWA is not only responsible for socio-economic provisioning for informal workers, but it also promotes the psychological wellbeing of workers and enables them to act as independent agents in improving their lives and livelihoods.

While SEWA is a trade union of self-employed informal women workers engaged in a diverse range of activities, the Kagad Kach Patra Kashtakari Panchayat (KKPKP) is a trade union of waste pickers in Pune, Maharashtra.[211] KKPKP registered itself as a trade union in 1993.[212] Unlike SEWA, KKPKP admits both men and women members.[213] A membership-based organisation, annual fee-paying KKPKP members elect their representative council for the governance of the union.[214] While the council membership is mainly drawn from waste picker members, there are a few members who do not share the socio-economic

---

203   Hill, *Worker Identity* (n 172) 98.
204   ibid 95.
205   ibid 96.
206   ibid 95–99, 104–13.
207   ibid 104–12.
208   ibid 107–12, 115–17.
209   ibid 117.
210   ibid 119–25.
211   Kagad Kach Patra Kashtakari Panchayat (KKPKP), available at http://www.wastepickers collective.org/ (last visited 7 June 2012).
212   Piush Antony, *Towards Empowerment: Experiences of Organizing Women Workers* (New Delhi: ILO, 2001) 17.
213   Poornima Chikarmane, Laxmi Narayan, 'Organising the unorganised: a case study of the Kagad Kach Patra Kashtakari Panchayat (Trade Union of Waste Pickers)' 1 at 4, available at http://wiego.org/sites/wiego.org/files/resources/files/Chikarmane_Narayan_case-kkpkp.pdf (last visited 7 June 2012).
214   ibid 5, 7–8.

background of waste pickers, but are involved in the governance of the union.[215] One of the principal purposes of the union is to promote waste picking as productive, valuable and meaningful work in order to ensure that waste pickers are recognised and respected as workers.[216]

The KKPKP works on the same principles as SEWA. While on the one hand the KKPKP provides socio-economic benefits to its members, on the other hand it mobilises its members for direct political action and lobbying. In order to promote recognition of waste pickers, KKPKP persuaded the municipalities of Pune and Pimpri Chinchwad to endorse identity cards for its members.[217] Identity cards are not only important for the recognition of workers; the cards also secure access to waste and public services (including medical services) for waste pickers.[218]

The KKPKP has institutionalised socio-economic promotion programmes for its members. The union has instituted credit cooperatives, group insurance and a cooperative store for its members.[219] The KKPKP has also promoted self-help groups for its members. Members receive loans under reasonable interest rates from the credit cooperative registered by the KKPKP.[220] In 1995, the KKPKP established a cooperative shop for waste trade run by its members.[221] Between 20 and 30 members are engaged in the shop that sells waste for recycling.[222] This cooperative enterprise (ie the 'waste shop') arranges for provision of paid leave, provident funds, bonuses and other social security benefits to the workers engaged in the shop.[223] Additionally, in collaboration with the Life Insurance Corporation in India the KKPKP has arranged for a contributory group insurance programme, whereby its members are insured against disability, accidental death and natural death.[224] All credit takers are automatically insured under the insurance scheme.

The KKPKP undertakes educational and literacy programmes. Whilst adult members of the union pursue functional literacy (so that they can sign and maintain their accounts) and vocational training, non-formal educational initiatives are also undertaken for the children of the waste pickers.[225] The union undertakes awareness initiatives on issues such as child labour, discrimination of female children, domestic violence, child marriage etc; the union also pressures its members to refrain from child marriage.[226] The KKPKP also organises direct action and protest marches against the government. Since 1999, the KKPKP has

---

215 ibid 7–8.
216 Antony (n 212) 17–18; Nalini Shekar, 'Suman more: KKPKP, Pune, India' in Samson (n 185) 11.
217 Antony (n 212) 63.
218 ibid 63, 66.
219 Chikarmane and Narayan, 'Organising' (n 213) 37–40, 63.
220 Antony (n 212) 63.
221 ibid.
222 ibid.
223 ibid 63–64.
224 ibid 64.
225 ibid 63–64, 66.
226 ibid 62–63.

been organising annual protest rallies with its members.[227] The KKPKP has been lobbying the government for the incorporation of waste pickers under the scope of the Maharashtra Hamal Mathadi and Unprotected Manual Workers (Regulation of Employment and Welfare) Act.[228]

Although the union has so far been unsuccessful in its attempt to include waste pickers under the purview of that law, the union has kept up pressure on the government by organising annual rallies, networking with other organisations and publishing a newspaper.[229] As a testimony to the KKPKP's growing influence, the union is represented in a number of decision-making bodies such as the Collector's Child Labour Committee, Apex Committee on Sanitation (Pune Municipal Corporation), Advisory Committee on Domestic Workers Act and others.[230]

The Sramajibee Mahila Samiti (SMS) is a registered society[231] of women agricultural workers in West Bengal.[232] According to 2004–2005 data, 98.9 per cent of workers in the agricultural sector in India are informal workers.[233] A leftist ideology underlies the SMS's functioning; class- and gender-based political action is more important than socio-economic provisioning in the SMS's day-to-day functioning.[234] In 1990, the SMS was created out of the Paschim Banga Khet Majdoor Samity (PBKMS) as a separate organisation for women workers.[235] Women agricultural workers can become members of the SMS upon the payment of a membership fee of two rupees per annum; SMS generates its own funding through village-level contributions.[236] The organisation functions through six elected committees at different levels.[237] Through direct political action the SMS has taken up issues such as women's employment, government corruption and minimum wages.[238]

The SMS has successfully organised rallies, agitations and picketing in order to pressurise the government of West Bengal to implement government welfare schemes in a fair and transparent manner.[239] The SMS has successfully lobbied the government to implement an employment generation scheme for agricultural workers during the non-agricultural season in southern districts of West Bengal.[240] The SMS has also initiated an open forum bringing together all stakeholders

---

227 ibid 63.
228 ibid.
229 ibid 65.
230 ibid.
231 ibid 22, 32, 75; The Sramajibee Mahila Samiti (SMS) is a society registered under the Societies Registration Act 1860.
232 Antony (n 212) 22.
233 NCEUS, *Definitional and Statistical Issues* (n 92) 44.
234 Antony (n 212) 22.
235 ibid 75.
236 ibid 22.
237 ibid.
238 ibid 75, 78–80.
239 ibid 77.
240 ibid 77–78.

involved in the development of local areas in the four districts of the SMS's operation.[241] The SMS mobilises local people to participate in such forums along with representatives of political parties and civil society.[242]

Although predominantly political, the SMS's activities are not limited to direct political mobilisation. The SMS undertakes a range of socio-economic programmes. The voluntary organisation Jan Sangati Kendra (JSK) that promoted PBKMS (SMS's parent organisation) has established a dairy farm, a training centre, residential villas, a mess and a child care facility.[243] The SMS separately owns land where full-time workers live in a community.[244] SMS members have access to the JSK facilities. Members of the community draw from the community according to their needs.[245] Community living is devised to ensure stakeholder participation in management (workers' participation in management is a constitutional right).[246] While the JSK provides for food, education (of children) and health needs, the SMS organises training of new members, imparts social education and promotes self-help groups.[247] The SMS has also promoted village-level arbitration by organising *salishi* sessions in matters such as divorce, compensation etc.[248] The SMS undertakes development works such as road repair by successfully establishing relations with the government.[249] The SMS is part of a network of 40 women's organisations named Maitri.

In direct contrast to the SMS's orientation, the Annapurna Mahila Mandal (AMM) is more concerned with informal workers' socio-economic betterment, rather than their political empowerment. The AMM is a charitable trust and society registered in Mumbai.[250] The AMM has more than 200,000 members in the state of Maharashtra.[251] AMM membership is not subscription-based membership – membership is granted while workers avail themselves of credit from the organisation.[252] The AMM's members engage in a variety of informal economic activities such as cooking and serving food; selling fruits, vegetables, fish, flowers, bangles and grain; stitching; and beading.[253] The AMM's principal activity is its micro-credit programme for these informal workers.[254]

However, apart from the micro-credit programme, the AMM undertakes a range of socio-economic initiatives for informal women workers. The AMM imparts leadership and vocational training to its members; the society also sensitises

241   ibid 78.
242   ibid.
243   ibid 76.
244   ibid.
245   ibid.
246   ibid; Constitution of India pt IV art 43A.
247   Antony (n 212) 76–77.
248   ibid 78–79.
249   ibid 79.
250   ibid 91.
251   ibid 92.
252   ibid 27.
253   ibid 92.
254   ibid 28, 91–93.

its members on matters such as health, sanitation, family planning, domestic violence, child marriage, access to electricity and access to water and gas.[255] The society also educates and trains its members' daughters, and encourages them to join the society.[256]

The society has established food-processing units such as a catering unit, a fast-food counter and a department store, where it engages women workers in these enterprises.[257] The department store sells products prepared by the AMM members in their homes.[258] Apart from income-generating programmes for its members, the AMM houses destitute women, such as victims of domestic violence and physically and mentally disabled persons, in its rehabilitation centre at Vashi Nagar in Navi Mumbai.[259] The society also provides medical and legal aid to its members, and mediates in domestic disputes.[260] The AMM runs a crèche for its members' children; it also bears the cost of their education and sometimes arranges their marriages.[261] Apart from running a hostel for working women with government collaboration, the AMM has established two cooperative housing societies in Mumbai.[262] The secretary of the AMM, Prema Purao, is an influential organiser who represents the AMM in various government and non-governmental bodies.[263]

A final form of organising of self-employed informal workers that I want to discuss is a cooperative society, the Sakti Mahila Vikas Swavlambi Co-operative Society (SMVSS), registered in the state of Bihar.[264] The SMVSS was established by an NGO called the Sakti Mahila Vikas Swavlambi Sarkari Samiti (SMVSSS).[265] Members of the cooperative society are engaged in creative activities such as traditional Maithili painting, appliqué work, manufacturing of paper toys and carpet manufacturing.[266] The SMVSS has established fruitful relations with the government agency Housing and Urban Development Corporation (HUDCO).[267] HUDCO promotes the work done by the members of the cooperative by providing them with loans, offering them training and marketing their work.[268]

Although the SMVSS's initiatives are limited to the economic sphere, the parent NGO (ie the SMVSSS) undertakes a range of social empowerment strategies.[269] By collaborating with the government, the NGO avails itself of

255   ibid 92–95.
256   ibid 93.
257   ibid 94.
258   ibid.
259   ibid.
260   ibid 94–95.
261   ibid 95.
262   ibid.
263   ibid 95–96.
264   ibid 89.
265   ibid.
266   ibid.
267   ibid.
268   ibid.
269   ibid 89–90.

government welfare schemes for the cooperative members; it undertakes awareness programmes on health and nutrition, specifically focused on children; it conducts awareness drives to promote female children's education and prevents child marriage.[270] The SMVSS networks with government agencies and NGOs in order to enhance its visibility and strengthen its voice.[271]

I have provided a brief overview of five organisational initiatives amongst self-employed informal workers. Most of these organisations are organisations of women informal workers. In selecting organisational initiatives of informal workers, I wanted to identify the range of legal status of these organisations. Amongst the above-mentioned organisations, while SEWA and KKPKP are trade unions, SMS is a society, AMM is a charitable trust and SMVSS is a cooperative. Thus, there is a great diversity of legal status amongst the different organisations of informal workers. However, despite this diversity within the informal workers' organisations, functionally the organisations are strikingly similar. The organisations undertake a range of socio-economic-political activities with the active involvement of their members.[272] Many of the programmes undertaken by these organisations are different from programmes traditionally associated with trade unions.

Traditionally, trade unions have primarily undertaken political mobilisation through direct political action.[273] The principal purpose of trade unions has been to redress the power imbalance between workers and employer(s). Such balancing of (bargaining) power is the result of trade union activity mainly in the formal industry-based framework characterised by employment relationships. Employment relationships are, however, conspicuous by their absence in informal economic activities in India. Waged workers receiving wages from an employer constitute only a small section of informal workers. Moreover, there exists high mobility of informal workers between one activity and another. Accordingly, organisations of informal workers cannot function in the same manner as traditional trade unions do with a reasonably fixed number of members employed in the same job for a long period of time. Therefore, economic support and protection become central to informal workers' organisations.

Organisations of self-employed informal workers in India provide comprehensive services to their members. Amongst economic services, informal self-employed workers' organisations provide credit opportunities to their members, which have been acknowledged as central in the development of informal self-employed workers in India.[274] By organising themselves into trade or service-specific cooperatives, informal workers bargain with the government and other private agencies in order to attain security and continuity in their respective works.

---

270   ibid.
271   ibid 90.
272   Kapoor (n 170) 561–65.
273   ibid 561–62.
274   NCEUS, 'Conditions of work' (n 96) 54–55, 62–63, 66, 68, 74, 135–39; Chikarmane and Narayan, 'Organising' (n 213); Jhabvala, 'Participatory approaches' (n 135) 35; Subrahmanya, 'Support' (n 133) 59–62.

Cooperative business and financial entities ensure that cooperative members have uninterrupted access to resources and places that are essential for the performance of their work.

Another important (economic) security-enhancing factor is group insurance for informal workers that the membership-based informal workers' organisations promote. At a minimum, such insurance schemes cover disability and death. These organisations also provide for health care, child care and sometimes low-cost housing services for their members. Some organisations provide legal services to their members.

Amongst social empowerment services, informal workers' organisations attach central importance to awareness promotion initiatives. Members of these organisations are not only made aware of the government and non-government support programmes that are available to them, they are also sensitised about the significance of their work and its value to society. Most informal workers suffer from an inferiority complex and undervalue their contribution to society. They do not consider their activity as valuable work.[275] Therefore, one of the primary responsibilities of informal workers' organisations is to inculcate amongst members a sense of dignity and their relevance to society.[276] Members are also sensitised on social issues such as child labour, domestic violence, child marriage etc. Additionally, organisations impart vocational training to their members. The organisations undertake sustained educational and training drives amongst their members' children. Informal workers' organisations also impart health education and legal awareness amongst their members.

Direct political actions such as rallies, picketing, demonstrations and strikes are also strategic to some of the informal workers' organisations. Some of the informal workers' organisations have also been successful in lobbying local administrative bodies and governments to secure improvements in the lives of informal workers. There are instances where governments, under pressure from informal workers' organisations, have enacted beneficial legislation for informal workers. Informal workers' organisations in India, therefore, organise workers in furtherance of political participation, social empowerment and economic security. By providing for a range of comprehensive resources and services, these organisations promote informal workers' dignified life.

In Chapter 6, based on a fieldwork in Kolkata (Calcutta), India, I report on working conditions and living standards of the specific group of self-employed informal waste pickers, who, at the beginning of the study, did not belong to any membership-based organisation. Although waste pickers belong to membership-based organisations in Indian cities such as Pune, Ahmedabad and Delhi, they were not organised in Kolkata. Waste pickers' organisations in these other cities have been able to secure better working conditions and living standards for informal waste pickers. Accordingly, in the next section, I briefly discuss some of

---

275 Hill, *Worker Identity* (n 172) 61–72, 103–107.
276 ibid 103–107, 109, 116–17, 119.

the initiatives undertaken by waste pickers' organisations in different parts of India. On the one hand, the next section will demonstrate how organisation initiatives can improve working and living conditions of specific groups of informal workers and, on the other hand, it will also help me contextualise my case study of waste pickers in Kolkata.

2.4.1 Waste picker activism in India

In this section, I document organisation initiatives of waste pickers by analysing four organisations promoting waste pickers' interests. I have already introduced SEWA and KKPKP, two of the four organisations that I will discuss in this section. The other two organisations are CHINTAN Environmental Research and Action Group (Chintan) and Nidan, registered societies organising waste pickers. In this section, my purpose is to show how organisations of waste pickers (whether trade unions or not) are making improvements in the lives of waste pickers by intervening in their work arrangements, their relationship with society and their interactions with government(s) at different levels (local, provincial, federal). I propose to link this discussion on waste-picker activism and organisation initiatives in India to the report from my fieldwork in Kolkata in Chapter 6.

The KKPKP is a remarkable instance of waste pickers' activism in India. The KKPKP has been able significantly to improve working and living conditions for its members through its multi-dimensional initiatives.[277] The KKPKP campaigned for segregation of waste at its source for recycling purposes; arranged for identity cards to be issued to its members;[278] arranged for credit facilities and education; and advocated child labour issues.[279] The union successfully lobbied with the Pune Municipality and the Pimpri Chinchwad Municipality to recognise and register waste pickers, and endorse their identity cards.[280] Such official recognition and registration helped promote unhindered collection of waste by waste pickers in the respective cities.[281] Pune Municipality became the first municipality in India to institutionalise a medical insurance scheme for registered waste pickers.[282] The KKPKP has also been able to influence policy on solid waste management of the country by contributing to an expert committee on solid waste management constituted by the Supreme Court of India.[283]

The KKPKP's door-to-door collection mechanism is a remarkable achievement where municipal authorities and municipal residents are made participants in the promotion of waste pickers' livelihoods. With the endorsement of the Pune Municipal Corporation, the KKPKP has arranged door-to-door waste collection

---

277   Shekar, 'Suman more' (n 216) 11–13.
278   Chikarmane and Narayan, 'Organising' (n 213) 2.
279   ibid 8.
280   ibid 16.
281   ibid.
282   ibid 17.
283   ibid 18.

by its members from residential and commercial complexes.[284] The added benefit of such an arrangement is that waste pickers receive payment from the apartment complexes in addition to the money they earn by selling their collections. The KKPKP initiative is extraordinary in this regard: although some NGOs in some parts of the country have door-to-door collection arrangements, they do not involve waste pickers in such activities.[285] The KKPKP also mobilises its members around political agendas, such as legislative and social protection of waste pickers.[286]

During its early years of operation, the SEWA contracted with textile mills in Ahmedabad city so as to enable the union's waste picker members to undertake mill-to-mill collection of paper waste.[287] Over the years, the mill-to-mill collection of waste fell short of the increasing demand of the SEWA waste picker members for productive work.[288] The SEWA then established waste pickers' cooperatives that diversified the waste recycling business into waste collection, waste segregation and sale; waste collection negotiation and contract; and weaving and waste recycling.[289] The SEWA engaged their waste picker members in these cooperatives.[290] The SEWA currently operates three cooperatives of waste picker members.[291] The SEWA cooperatives have contracted with the Vejalpur Nagarpalika (Vejalpur Municipality) to provide door-to-door waste collection services to 46,842 households.[292] The SEWA has also successfully mobilised waste pickers in order to secure government-issued identity cards, medical assistance, skills training, tool kits, and financial benefits for its members.[293]

Similarly an NGO named Chintan,[294] based in Delhi, has arranged for door-to-door waste collection by waste pickers in Delhi.[295] Chintan has collaborated with municipal authorities in order to contract waste-picking services on behalf of waste pickers.[296] Another NGO, named Nidan, which is itself a registered society, established and registered a company, the NIDAN Swachdhara Private Limited Company of waste pickers.[297] Run by waste pickers themselves, the company has

---

284 ibid 18–20.
285 ibid 20.
286 ibid 23, 42–43.
287 Dave, Shah and Parikh (n 185) 28–29.
288 ibid.
289 ibid 29–30.
290 ibid.
291 ibid 30.
292 ibid.
293 ibid 30–32.
294 Chintan is a registered society under the Societies Registration Act 1860.
295 See 'Scavengers to managers', available at http://www.chintan-india.org/initiatives_scavengers_ to_managers.htm (last visited 16 January 2012); Bharati Chaturvedi, 'Santraj Maurya and Lipi in India: tales of two waste pickers in Delhi, India' in Samson (n 185) 8.
296 'Scavengers to managers' (n 295).
297 Nidan, 'Activities, empowering the informal workers and children', available at http://www. nidan.in/otherpage.php?page_code_no=3 (last visited 16 January 2012); Arbind Singh, Rakesh Saran, 'NIDAN Swachdhara Private Ltd forming a company with waste pickers in India' in Samson (n 185) 17 at 18.

successfully contracted for the delivery of door-to-door waste collection services to 68,000 households in three municipalities.[298] The company's contracts with three municipalities also include provisions for weekly leave, health check-ups, and health, accidental and death insurance for waste pickers.[299]

Both the membership-based organisations (such as the KKPKP and the SEWA) and the NGOs (such as the Chintan and the Nidan) adopt a two-pronged approach in promoting a dignified life for waste pickers in India. At one level, these organisations negotiate with local administration (ie municipalities) in furtherance of the recognition of waste pickers and facilitation of waste collection.[300] At another level, these organisations provide for social security and skills training for waste pickers either by themselves or in collaboration with the government. Formal integration of waste pickers into the government waste-management system follows different patterns.[301] In Delhi, through an understanding between Chintan and the New Delhi Municipal Council (NDMC), waste pickers provide door-to-door waste collection services.[302] Waste pickers are directly paid by the households for their services.[303] The NDMC supports the waste collection by providing for segregation spaces and vehicles for waste collection and removal.[304]

In Pune, under pressure from the KKPKP, the Pune Municipal Corporation has abandoned the contract model of waste disposal, and has instead left door-to-door waste collection to the waste pickers' cooperative.[305] The waste pickers' cooperative in Pune is an autonomous body working independently, and is accountable to the households directly.[306] Neither the municipality nor the KKPKP has any ownership over the cooperative and its functioning.[307] The municipality has also determined the rate of pay, to be paid by households directly to the cooperative for the services rendered.[308] However, for the door-to-door waste collection service provided in slums, the municipality takes the responsibility for payment to the cooperative.[309] The municipality has also provided segregation space and other support to the cooperative.[310] While the cooperative is supported by the municipality, it is controlled by its members.[311]

In 2005 a group of eight waste pickers' organisations from the states of Bihar, Delhi, Gujarat, Karnataka, Madhya Pradesh and Maharashtra forged an alliance

---

298 Singh and Saran, 'NIDAN' (n 298) at 18.
299 ibid 18–19.
300 'Municipal and organizational arrangements' (n 160).
301 Melanie Samson, 'Formal integration into municipal waste management systems' in Samson (n 185) ch 4 at 50; Melanie Samson, 'Using the law' in Samson (n 185) ch 5 60 at 72–74.
302 Samson, 'Formal integration' (n 185) ch 4 at 50–51.
303 ibid 50.
304 ibid 52.
305 ibid 50, 57–59; Samson, 'Using the law' (n 301) ch 5 72.
306 Samson, 'Formal integration' (n 185) ch 4 58–59.
307 ibid.
308 ibid.
309 ibid.
310 ibid 59.
311 ibid 50.

called SWACHH.[312] The KKPKP functions as the secretariat for the alliance.[313] SWACHH currently has 24 organisations working with issues involving waste pickers.[314] The alliance developed a national policy on solid waste management and proposes to lobby with government(s) in order to implement their policy proposal.[315] Agendas such as gender discrimination, door-to-door waste collection, mode of waste pickers' organisation, organisational assistance and networking in furtherance of common purposes are central to the alliance's mandate.[316] Thus, waste pickers are increasingly becoming a visible group amongst informal workers in India. Both membership-based and NGO-based waste picker movements are spreading around the country. However, despite this activism and visibility of waste pickers in some pockets in India, a large section of waste pickers around the country live at the margins of society.

Waste pickers in the city of Kolkata are one such group (which I will document in Chapter 6). Organising waste pickers is not an easy task, and such effort is fraught with significant problems.[317] However, the above examples show that some organisations are facilitating waste pickers' access to a range of resources, from credit and insurance to municipal contracts. This is true not only for waste pickers but also for other informal workers who are part of an organisation.

Thus, as Hill notes, informal workers' organisations have a multi-dimensional impact on workers.[318] These organisations do not only provide socio-economic resources, they are also responsible for the development of agency amongst informal workers. Agency emanating from the moral condition of psychological wellbeing,[319] along with socio-economic provisions, enables informal workers to lead a life of dignity, a celebrated constitutional goal in India.[320] A dignified life is a fundamental right under the Constitution of India.[321] The right to life under the

312 KKPKP Central Secretariat, 'The SWACHH National Alliance of Waste Pickers, India' in Samson (n 185) 37 at 38.

313 ibid.

314 ibid.

315 ibid.

316 ibid 38–39.

317 Gill, *Of Poverty and Plastic* (n 168) 25.

318 Hill, *Worker Identity* (n 172) 117–25.

319 ibid 104–12, 119–25.

320 Justice Bhagwati in *Francis Coralie* (n 28); *Bandhua Mukti Morcha* (n 56) para 14; *Indra Sawhney v Union of India* [1992] MANU 0665 (SC) paras 1–4, 262, 412–17, 565; *Akhil Bharatiya Soshit Karamchari Sangh (Railway) v Union of India* [1980] MANU 0058 (SC) paras 16, 134; *Mrs Maneka Gandhi v Union of India* [1978] MANU 0133 (SC) paras 13, 53, 79–80, 125; *Minerva Mills v Union of India* [1980] MANU 0075 (SC) paras 62, 109, 118; *Miss Mohini Jain v State of Karnataka* [1992] MANU 0357 (SC) paras 8–13; *Municipal Corporation of the City of Ahmedabad v Jan Mohammed Usmanbhai* [1986] MANU 0099 (SC) para 19; *P Rathinam v Union of India* [1994] MANU 0433 (SC) para 27; *Prem Shankar Shukla v Delhi Administration* [1980] MANU 0084 (SC) paras 1, 11, 23–25; *People's Union for Democratic Rights v Union of India* [1982] MANU 0038 (SC) paras 10, 12, 14, 16, 19; *Sheela Barse v State of Maharashtra* [1987] MANU 0139 (SC); *Sunil Batra v Delhi Administration* [1978] MANU 0184 (SC) paras 57, 266; *Vikram Deo Singh Tomar v State of Bihar* [1988] MANU 0572 (SC) para 2.

321 ibid.

Constitution of India[322] does not mean mere animal existence; it guarantees a dignified life with freedom and entitlements.[323]

Although the state has failed to secure a dignified life for the majority of the Indian working class who toil in informal economic activities, this void is being increasingly filled by trade unions and organisations such as SEWA, KKPKP, SMS, AMM and Chintan. These organisations are attempting to secure institutional guarantees for the exercise of fundamental rights, together with the wellbeing contemplated under the directive principles of the constitution in order to promote the dignified life of informal workers in India.

The Supreme Court of India reflected that a dignified life requires resources (or factors) such as adequate nutrition, clothing, shelter, education, socialisation, socio-political participation, freedom of movement and economic development.[324] By providing for these comprehensive resources informal workers' organisations are seeking to promote a dignified life for informal workers.

However, development economist and philosopher Amartya Sen argues that these resources alone cannot ensure human development, and therefore a dignified life.[325] The value and importance of resources, Sen notes, lie on what resources 'can do for people'.[326] Goods and services are important for people only when they use such goods and services in furtherance of their development.[327] Accordingly, people not only need to exercise command over resources,[328] but they also need the ability to use such resources for their development.[329] According to Sen, human development signifies *freedom of people to choose* the kind of life that they value.[330] The following section briefly looks at the idea of human development as freedom in the context of the present chapter.

2.5 A dignified life for informal workers through human development

In this section, I establish a conceptual link between the ideas of *dignified life* as propounded by the Supreme Court of India and *human development* as conceptualised by Sen. The Supreme Court of India envisaged a dignified life as emanating from a diverse range of civil-political rights and socio-economic resources. Through its concept of dignified life, the Supreme Court sought to deprioritise civil-political rights over socio-economic resources and strike a balance between these two generations of rights. Sen develops this agenda further. He argues that human

322 ibid.
323 ibid.
324 *Francis Coralie* (n 28).
325 Amartya Sen, *Resources, Values and Development* (Cambridge, MA: Harvard University Press, 1984) 510–11.
326 ibid 510.
327 ibid 30–31, 495–504.
328 ibid 30–31, 516.
329 ibid 316–17, 510–11.
330 Amartya Sen, *Development as Freedom* (New York: Alfred A. Knopf, 1999) 18.

development cannot be ensured only through the availability of rights and provision of resources. Sen's focus is on the actual outcome of rights and resources on individual human beings. Based on Sen's conceptualisation, I briefly outline how human development can be the determining factor for a dignified life.

Sen notes that human development ensues through the combination of an individual's command over resources and the individual's ability to use such resources beneficially.[331] The ability to convert resources into human development depends on a number of factors such as 'age, sex, health, social relations, class background, education, ideology, and a variety of other interrelated factors'.[332] Informal workers' organisations in India are seeking to provide for both of these conditions in furtherance of promoting workers' development. These organisations provide for resources such as loans, raw materials, insurance, provision for medical services, provision for child care services, provision for legal services and low-cost housing.

The organisations also promote their members' ability to convert resources into human development. Initiatives such as imparting child and adult education, vocational training, social awareness programmes (eg on child labour or domestic violence), health education and legal awareness etc develop the members' individual and collective character. Political agendas pursued by these organisations (through rallies, demonstrations etc) also inculcate individual and collective identity amongst the members. Direct political action undertaken by these organisations helps overcome their members' fear, insecurity and hesitation; members develop a sense of *right*; they bargain with the government and employers; they make demands of the state. Political action, therefore, promotes psychological development of members, which contributes to the overall personality development of members.

Thus, informal workers' organisations in India are instrumental in promoting *individual abilities* that can convert *resources* into human development. These organisations also make *resources* (such as credit or housing services) available to their members. What follows is that informal workers' organisations in India facilitate social-economic-political conditions in which their members convert their *command over resources* into their *development* in furtherance of a dignified life.

The Constitution of India envisages socio-economic-political conditions in which human development and dignified life can flourish. However, the constitution enumerates factors providing for such socio-economic-political conditions in terms of *rights* and *directives*. Although fundamental in the governance of the country,[333] *directives* of the constitution are not enforceable by the judiciary, except to a limited degree through the interpretation of Part III rights. Therefore, while civil and political rights enumerated in Part III of the constitution are guaranteed, social and economic rights enumerated in Part IV of the constitution are not.

---

331   Sen, *Resources* (n 325) 316–17, 510–11, 516; Amartya Sen, *Commodities and Capabilities* (Amsterdam & New York: North Holland, 1985).
332   Sen, *Resources* (n 325) 511.
333   Constitution of India art 37.

This constitutional hierarchy is reflected in the absence of socio-economic provisioning for informal workers in India. Governments cannot be taken to court even if they are unable to provide living wages or humane conditions of work for informal workers.

The problem is that this hierarchy of rights misses the central point: human development needs both *resources* as well as *appropriate personal characteristics*. The Constitution of India promotes personal characteristics to a great extent in the sense that civil and political rights are enforceable in the court. The constitution, however, fails to guarantee resources in the sense that economic rights cannot be enforced in a court of law. A human development-based understanding of factors responsible for appropriate socio-economic-political conditions provides for a better analytical and strategic framework of informal workers' development. A human development-based analytical framework makes it evident that both resources and appropriate personal characteristics are central in human development.

Provision for *only* resources or *only* conversion factors cannot promote the development of marginalised and vulnerable informal workers in India in any meaningful sense. A human development-based understanding, in the sense Sen conceptualises it, shows that there cannot be any prioritisation between fundamental rights and directive principles in the development of informal workers – such prioritisation would only stunt the development of informal workers. Appreciating this multi-dimensional framework for human development, informal workers' organisations have devised their multi-dimensional agenda.

Moreover, whatever economic and social security guarantees are envisaged under the constitution, such guarantees are subject to the economic capacity of the governments.[334] Such conditionality attached to social and economic protection makes it difficult to question the governments' – central and state – inability to improve conditions of informal workers. Informal workers' organisations fill this void by strategically building a multi-dimensional framework of services (and resources) around their constituencies. Thus, private entities in the nature of trade unions, cooperatives, trusts or societies are in effect providing for constitutional guarantees to informal workers in India. Such guarantees are important, however, for the survival and continuous relevance of membership-based informal workers' organisations.

If informal workers' organisations lobby the government and launch rallies, demonstrations and picketing, and if the government still refuses to grant any tangible benefits to informal workers, then it would be difficult to maintain the momentum of any membership-based informal workers' organisation. If membership-based organisations are unable to secure better working conditions and living standards for their members, there is an imminent possibility that members would

---

334 Constitution of India art 41: 'The State shall, within the limits of its economic capacity and development, make effective provision for securing the right to work, to education and to public assistance in cases of unemployment, old age, sickness and disablement, and in other cases of undeserved want.'

soon become disillusioned with their organisations. In view of these practical and strategic considerations, informal workers' organisations directly provide a range of socio-economic resources and services for their members.

In this chapter, I have primarily discussed self-employed informal workers' organisations. Unfortunately, although a significant number of informal workers are engaged in self-employment, their representative organisations are very few in number. The majority of self-employed informal workers in India are still unrepresented, and do not belong to any membership-based organisation.

2.6 Conclusion

In this chapter, I documented the range of initiatives undertaken by different membership-based and non-membership organisations for the development of informal workers in India. I located the range of socio-economic-political initiatives of these organisations in the backdrop of the constitutional and legislative guarantees for workers in India. While the Constitution of India provides for comprehensive civil-political and social-economic guarantees, most of these guarantees (especially on the social-economic front) remain unavailable to informal workers.

It is only recently that informal workers have begun to receive the benefits of social protection statutes. The large-scale exclusion of informal workers from government policy-making contributes to the marginalisation of informal workers. Private entities (such as unions, cooperatives etc) seek to fill this void in government policy-making. While these entities are doing commendable work, in view of the enormous numbers of informal workers in India, much remains to be done. I also introduced a concept of human development through which a dignified life for informal workers could be realised. In the next chapter I will elaborate upon the idea of human *development as freedom* of people to choose the kind of life that they value.

3 Freedom as human development

3.1 Introduction

The worst fault of the working classes is telling their children they're not going to succeed, saying: 'There is life, but it's not for you.'

John Mortimer *The Daily Mail* (31 May 1988)[1]

In Chapter 2, I analysed the role played by informal workers' organisations in India in promoting a dignified life for informal workers. I show that informal workers' organisations provide a range of social and economic resources for informal workers. These organisations also enable informal workers effectively to exercise their civil and political rights. By providing for socio-economic resources and enabling conditions for the exercise of civil-political rights, informal workers' organisations promote the overall development of informal workers.

Such a development strategy finds support in Amartya Sen's capability approach, which analyses the significance of resources on individual lives, rather than the significance of resources per se. In this chapter, I analyse the nuances of Sen's capability approach. Sen's approach is important for the evaluation of human development; his capability approach can also offer valuable insights in furtherance of a normative goal for informal workers. In order to evaluate the effectiveness of Sen's approach for the formulation of a labour law framework for informal workers in India, I discuss the principal tenets of the capability approach.

In section 3.2 of this chapter, I describe the basic idea of human development formulated by Sen. According to Sen, development policy should aim to create enabling conditions in which individuals are free to do what they want; development should remove unfreedoms suffered by individuals. I analyse how

---

1 This John Mortimer quotation dramatically phrases the risk of 'adaptive preference' against which Amartya Sen revolts in his work on development and welfare. See Amartya Sen, *Development as Freedom* (New York: Alfred A. Knopf, 1999) 62–63. 'Adaptive preferences' are adjusted preferences that people accept in accordance with the realities of their practical situations. 'Adaptive preferences' are shaped by a person's social environment and institutions that influence her life. See also John Alexander, *Capabilities and Social Justice: the Political Philosophy of Amartya Sen and Martha Nussbaum* (Farnham & Burlington: Ashgate, 2008) 14. Some parts of this chapter have appeared previously as an article, see Supriya Rouch, 'Developing human capabilities through law: is Indian law failing?' (2012) 3(1) *Asian Journal of Law and Economics* 1.

the capability approach came into existence as an alternative to the existing dominant development approaches, prominent amongst which is the utilitarian theory.

In section 3.3 of the chapter, I analyse the fundamental tenets of Sen's approach. Sen asserts that development means freedom of individuals to lead their lives as they wish. Instead of focusing on resources per se, Sen looks at what resources do to enhance individual freedom. In this respect his theory diverges from the social justice theories of John Rawls and Ronald Dworkin, whose emphasis is on resources, rather than the effect of resources on individual lives.

In section 3.4, I discuss Sen's conceptualisation of freedom. Sen articulates a concept of positive freedom, which not only signifies an individual's wellbeing, but is also concerned with the exercise of agency by an individual. In this section I also ascertain the link between the idea of human rights and the concept of freedom as envisaged by Sen. Democratic participation and the different institutions of the democratic society attain central significance in Sen's theory.

In section 3.5, I discuss Sen's idea of integrated institutions, a concept of multiple institutions that interact amongst themselves in order to promote individual freedom. Although Sen's theory is not an institution-centric theory, multiple institutions in a democratic society play a major role in his conceptualisation.

In section 3.6, I briefly compare Sen's conceptualisation of the capability approach and Martha Nussbaum's idea of capabilities. While Sen is happy to leave the determination of desirable capabilities to the democratic dialogue process, Nussbaum thinks it useful to delineate a minimum list of desirable capabilities for all societies. Their conceptual divergence pertains to their theoretical focus: while Sen's focus is on the evaluation of human development, Nussbaum proposes the capability approach to provide a social basis of constitutional guarantees.

The contrast between Sen and Nussbaum is significant for the purpose of my study. In the specific context of informal economic activities, while Sen's concept would allow direct participation of informal workers in the determination of their capability-enhancing factors, Nussbaum's conceptualisation will lead towards a decision a priori on such factors. I conclude this chapter with a roadmap for the next chapter.

3.2 Sen's idea of human development

Amartya Sen's theory of *development as freedom* has revolutionised the way development is seen and analysed in economic and philosophical circles.[2] According to Sen's theory of development as freedom, the principal purpose of development is the creation of enabling conditions in which human lives can flourish.[3] Sen traces

---

2 G A Cohen has described Sen as a revolutionary thinker in the context of reformulation of the development philosophy. See G A Cohen, 'Equality of what? On welfare, goods and capabilities' in Martha C Nussbaum, Amartya Sen (eds), *The Quality of Life* (Oxford: Clarendon, 1993) 9 at 10.

3 Sen, *Development* (n 1) 3–4; Amartya Sen, *Inequality Reexamined* (New York: Russell Sage Foundation/ Cambridge, MA: Harvard University Press, 1992) 39–41, in particular at 41 n 8.

his idea of human development to Aristotle's formulation of meaningful human life (what it is to live like human beings).[4] To Sen, the purpose of development is the facilitation of the freedom of individuals so that they can choose the kind of life for themselves that they have reason to value.[5] He conceptualises development in the following words: 'Development consists of the removal of various types of unfreedoms that leave people with little choice and little opportunity of exercising their reasoned agency. The removal of substantial unfreedoms, it is argued here, is constitutive of development.'[6]

Instead of being an institution-centric idea of development, Sen's conception makes human agency central. Institutions are important in Sen's theory only so far as such institutions guarantee enabling circumstances in which individuals can freely exercise their agency or initiative according to their choosing.

Sen's concept of development as freedom is expressed in terms of the concepts of *capability* and *functionings*. Capability is the freedom to choose[7] and functionings are the achievement that an individual actually attains.[8] Capability is, therefore, the freedom available to individuals to choose the functionings that they want to attain. Sen's theory of development as freedom is based on three principal premises: first, the idea of development in terms of freedom; secondly, a positive concept of freedom; thirdly, the role of institutions in promoting development as freedom.[9] These are the constitutive elements of Sen's theory.

Sen's theory of development as freedom was conceptualised as an alternative to the mainstream theories of development and wellbeing.[10] In his 1979 Tanner lecture, where he first introduced his concept, he criticised and rejected the

4   Sen, *Development* (n 1) 14–15, 24, 73; Martha Nussbaum, 'Nature, function and capability: Aristotle on political distribution' (1987) WIDER Working Papers 31 (December 1987) World Institute for Development Economics Research of the United Nations University.
5   Sen, *Development* (n 1) 18.
6   ibid xii.
7   Sen explains 'capability' in the following words: 'A person's capability refers to the alternative combinations of functionings that are feasible for her to achieve. Capability is thus a kind of freedom: the substantive freedom to achieve alternative functioning combinations (or, less formally put, the freedom to achieve various lifestyles). For example, an affluent person who fasts may have the same functioning achievement in terms of eating or nourishment as a destitute person who is forced to starve, but the first person does have a different "capability set" than the second (the first can choose to eat well and be well nourished in a way the second cannot).' Sen, *Development* (n 1) 75.
8   Sen explains 'functionings' in the following terms: 'The concept of "functionings" which has distinctly Aristotelian roots, reflects the various things a person may value doing or being [footnote omitted]. The valued functionings may vary from elementary ones, such as being adequately nourished and being free from avoidable disease [footnote omitted], to very complex activities or personal states, such as being able to take part in the life of the community and having self-respect.' Sen, *Development* (n 1) 75.
9   See Sen, *Development* (n 1) 3–11.
10   See Amartya Sen, 'Equality of what?' The Tanner Lectures on Human Values, delivered at Stanford University (22 May 1979) in *The Tanner Lectures on Human Values, vol. I* (Salt Lake City: University of Utah Press/Cambridge, London, Melbourne and Sydney: Cambridge University Press, 1980).

welfarist concept of social good in terms of utility and Rawlsian concepts of equality of primary goods[11] as incomplete theories of social wellbeing.[12] A welfarist concept measures individual wellbeing in terms of happiness – if an individual is happy, she is well off. The Rawlsian concept measures individual wellbeing in terms of possession of primary goods – an individual is well off if she possesses primary goods. Rejecting the dominant ideas of development and social justice of the time, Sen introduced his concept of 'basic capability equality'.[13] He argued that the social framework should aim to equalise the 'basic capabilities' of individuals, wherein basic capabilities are a person's ability to do certain basic things.[14]

Refining his views over the years, Sen now argues that development should promote freedom of individuals with freedom expressed in terms of capability. He defined capability as the actual freedom available to people to be and do what they have reason to value.[15] The ends of wellbeing, justice and development need to be evaluated in terms of capabilities to function.[16] Thus, over the years Sen has emphasised the term 'freedom' rather than the technical coinage 'capability'.[17] I now take each one of the constitutive elements of Sen's theory to explain the nature and implications of his theory of development.

3.3 Human development in terms of freedom

Sen asserts that the other dominant theories of development, such as utilitarianism and Rawlsianism, concentrate on the means to development rather than on the ends of development in order to analyse the mechanism and purpose of development.[18] He observes:

> If freedom is what development advances, then there is a major argument for concentrating on the overarching objective, rather than on some particular means, or some specially chosen list of instruments. Viewing development in terms of expanding substantive freedoms directs attention to the ends that make development important, rather than merely to some of the means that, *inter alia*, play a prominent part in the process.[19]

11 To which he has later added the Dworkinian concept of 'equality of resources'. See Sen, *Inequality* (n 3) 42.
12 See Sen, 'Equality' (n 10).
13 ibid 217–18.
14 ibid 218.
15 Sen, *Development* (n 1) 18; also see the examples at 5–6.
16 Ingrid Robeyns, 'The capability approach: a theoretical survey' (2005) 6(1) *Journal of Human Development* 93 at 95–96.
17 In his Tanner Lectures in 1979 he introduces the term 'capability' as a technical terminology, and in his book *Development as Freedom* in 1999 he focuses on the concept of 'freedom'. However, both the coinages have the same orientation signifying freedom of choice.
18 Sen, *Development* (n 1) 54–74.
19 ibid 3.

Utilitarianism dominates development policy circles. The question that utilitarianism asks of individuals is whether individuals are *happy* in their plight, or whether their *desires* are fulfilled.[20] Utilitarianism (or at a general level, welfarism) focuses on the mental state of the individual in order to ascertain development. Sen argues that utilitarianism, while important, fails to assess development or wellbeing on an objective basis because it focuses on the subjective criterion of happiness or desire fulfilment.[21] He contends that utilitarianism fails to appreciate the diversity of human beings.[22] He argues that because of the diversity of human beings the extent (and measurement) of happiness or desire-fulfilment cannot be an objective basis of determination of wellbeing or development.[23]

Since happiness and desire-fulfilment are mental states, it is possible that an individual who has had a terrible life might be made happy by some meagre act of mercy, or she has adjusted her desires to be commensurate with the practical state she is in – Sen terms this adjustment *adaptive preference*.[24] On the other hand, someone who is born with a silver spoon in her mouth might not be happy with all the comforts of life, or her desires might be very difficult to satisfy.[25]

Therefore, measuring only the mental state of an individual, without regard to the diversity of individuals, does not provide an objective, appropriate, and adequate version of development, because mental state is subjective, and hence, the measurement runs the risk of documenting the adaptive preference of individuals. Moreover, Sen argues that the analytical focus of the utilitarian idea of development is the end-product of development ('welfarism . . . combined with consequentialism'), i.e. happiness in achievement.[26] Utilitarianism does not attach any significance to the opportunities actually available to the people in their achievement.[27]

Sen commends John Rawls for filling this void left by utilitarianism.[28] Rawls's analytical focus is opportunities available to people[29] rather than the end-result (of happiness or desire fulfilment).[30] Rawls's theory of social justice is the most significant one outside the utilitarian tradition.[31] Rawls moved away from

---

20   See Sen, 'Equality' (n 10); Sen, *Development* (n 1) 56–63.
21   See Sen, 'Equality' (n 10) 211–12; Sen, *Development* (n 1) 56–63.
22   Sen, *Development* (n 1) 67–71; Sen, 'Equality' (n 10) 202, 215.
23   Sen, *Development* (n 1) 70–72, 74–81; Sen, 'Equality' (n 10).
24   Sen, *Development* (n 1) 62–63, 67.
25   See Sen, 'Equality' (n 10) 203.
26   Sen, *Development* (n 1) 58–59.
27   ibid 63.
28   See Sen, 'Equality' (n 10) 214–15.
29   See John Rawls, *A Theory of Justice* (Cambridge, MA: Harvard University Press, 1971) 62, 93–95, 395–96, 399–404.
30   But see Sen *Development* (n 1) 72–73; Sen, 'Equality' (n 10) 215.
31   Sen *Development* (n 1) 63. With respect to Rawls's contribution to the theory of justice, Robert Nozick observes: 'A *Theory of Justice* is a powerful, deep, subtle, wide-ranging, systematic work in political and moral philosophy which has not seen its like since the writings of John Stuart Mill, if then. . . . Political philosophers now must either work within Rawls's theory or explain why not.' See Robert Nozick, *Anarchy, State, and Utopia* (New York: Basic Books, 1974) 183.

utilitarianism's focus on mental states and devised an objective basis for the analysis of social good and human development.[32] Rawls devised a list of *primary goods*,[33] and argued that equality of primary goods serves the social good.[34] Rawls's argument is that it is the duty of society to ensure that every individual in the society has equal access to the primary goods (the list of goods that is valued by all).[35] Individual development is to be judged objectively by the number of primary goods that an individual has access to.[36] His theory shifted the focus of development from the measurement of mental state (the utilitarian principle) to the objective ascertainment of the presence or absence of primary goods.[37]

Ronald Dworkin provided the other non-utilitarian objective basis for the determination of social good.[38] Dworkin argues that society should strive to provide equality of resources (rather than welfare) to the people: 'Equality of resources supposes that the resources devoted to each person's life should be equal.'[39] Equality of resources will be achieved when no person should envy the bundle of resources privately owned by any other person in the society.[40] His theory of distribution of resources is based on an initial hypothetical equality of means to purchase resources.[41] Delineating the limits on equal distribution of resources Dworkin observes:

> [A] political community should aim to erase or mitigate differences between people in their personal resources [personal resources are health, strength, and talent] – should aim to improve the position of people who are physically handicapped or otherwise unable to earn a satisfactory income, for example – but should not aim to mitigate or compensate for differences in personality [personality includes character, convictions, preferences, motives, tastes, and ambitions] – for differences traceable to the fact that some people's tastes and ambitions are expensive and other people's cheap, for instance.[42]

Dworkin's agenda is to enable people to have equal social resources throughout their lives.[43]

---

32 See Rawls (n 29) 90–92, 95; Sen 'Equality' (n 10).
33 The chief categories of primary goods for Rawls are rights and liberties, powers and opportunities, income and wealth, and self-respect. He also includes 'natural goods' such as health and vigour, intelligence and imagination as primary goods. See Rawls, *A Theory of Justice* (n 29) 62, 92.
34 See Rawls, *A Theory of Justice* (n 29) 62, 93–95, 395–96, 399–404; Sen, 'Equality' (n 10) 213–214.
35 See Rawls, *A Theory of Justice* (n 29) 62; Sen, 'Equality' (n 10) 214.
36 See Rawls, *A Theory of Justice* (n 29) 62, 92–93; Amartya Sen, *The Idea of Justice* (Cambridge, MA: Harvard University Press, 2009) 60, 63.
37 See Rawls, *A Theory of Justice* (n 29) 90–92; Sen, 'Equality' (n 10).
38 See Ronald Dworkin, 'What is equality? Part 2: equality of resources' (1981) 10(4) *Philosophy and Public Affairs* 283.
39 ibid 289.
40 ibid 285.
41 ibid 286–87.
42 ibid 286.
43 ibid 289–90, 295.

While commending the shift in Rawls's theory (from mental state or end-result as proposed by utilitarianism to objective analysis of availability of primary goods), Sen criticises Rawls for not allowing room for human diversity in his theory.[44] Sen argues that even if individuals have equal access to primary goods that access will not result in equal opportunity for all individuals because of the differences among individuals.[45] He gives the examples of a disabled person *vis-à-vis* a healthy human being and a woman *vis-à-vis* a man to argue his case that the same set of primary goods would result in different opportunities for different individuals.[46]

Sen's case is that a disabled person or a woman might need more resources or primary goods to come to the same level of opportunity that is enjoyed by a healthy human being or a man.[47] Hence, Sen alleges that Rawls suffers from commodity fetishism that might result in opportunity deprivation rather than actual development of individuals.[48] Thus, while Sen commends the scope of objective analysis that Rawls's theory provides for, he asserts that primary goods are only a *means* to achieve the *end* of development.[49] Likewise, Sen rejects Dworkin's theory of equal access to resources on identical grounds.[50] Sen offers a multidimensional view of development,[51] which includes both wellbeing freedom and agency freedom (discussed below).[52]

3.4 The concept of freedom

Elizabeth S. Anderson observes that Sen offers a rich way to understand freedom.[53] Sen's concept of freedom has distinct Aristotelian roots.[54] Aristotle saw human functioning in terms of being able to choose and live a 'flourishing living (*eudaimonia*)'.[55] According to Aristotle the mere availability of wealth, goods or

---

44 See Sen, 'Equality' (n 10) 215–16; Sen, *Development* (n 1) 72–73.

45 Sen, 'Equality' (n 10); Sen, *Development* (n 1) 72–73.

46 Sen, 'Equality' (n 10) 203, 215, 217–18.

47 ibid 203, 215, 218.

48 ibid 216, 218–19.

49 ibid 218–19.

50 Sen, *Inequality* (n 3) 42; Amartya Sen, 'Capability and well-being' in Nussbaum and Sen, *The Quality of Life* (n 2) 30 at 33.

51 Sen, *Development* (n 1) 3–4, 18–19, 33–40, 74–86; Sabina Alkire, 'Dimensions of human development' (2002) 30(2) *World Development* 181 at 182–84.

52 Amartya Sen, 'Well-being, agency and freedom: the Dewey Lectures 1984' (1985) 82(4) *Journal of Philosophy* 169 at 208; Sen, *Development* (n 1) 3, 36, 74–75.

53 Elizabeth S Anderson, 'What is the point of equality?' (1999) 109(2) *Ethics* 287 at 316.

54 Sen, *Development* (n 1) 14–15, 24, 73, 75; Nussbaum, 'Nature' (n 4).

55 Nussbaum (n 4) 3; Aristotle, *Nicomachean Ethics, Book I* (2nd edn trans by Terence Irwin) (Indianapolis/Cambridge, MA: Hackett Publishing, 1999) 4–5, 7–11; also see *Translator's Introduction*, Aristotle, ibid xvii–xviii, xxiii–xxv. Aristotle notes: '[W]e intuitively believe that the good is something of our own and hard to take from us. . . . Further, each type of person finds pleasure in whatever he is called a lover of; a horse, for instance, pleases the horse-lover, a spectacle the lover of spectacles. Similarly, what is just pleases the lover of justice, and in general what accords with virtue pleases the lover of virtue.'

resources is not sufficient for a flourishing living or a good human life.[56] Likewise, Sen distances himself from the narrowly defined notion of opportunity through the availability of primary goods or resources and takes a multidimensional view of freedom.[57]

According to Sen an individual has real freedom[58] when she is able to choose the kind of life that she wants to lead.[59] Sen terms this freedom capability.[60] Sen defines capability as a functioning-set that an individual can choose to achieve.[61] Functionings are what individuals actually achieve in their lives.[62] A functioning-set consists of number of functionings that an individual values amongst the different other functionings.[63] Thus, capability is the capacity (or freedom) of an individual to choose one set of functioning amongst the different functioning-sets available to her.[64] Sen proposes to see freedom as the freedom or capacity to choose. However, the capacity to choose need not reside together with the capacity to control.[65] Choice is central to Sen's conceptualisation of freedom, even if control over such choice is exercised by others.[66] Instead of wellbeing, the achievement of functionings, or the availability of goods or resources, Sen argues that this freedom (to choose) is the appropriate measurement of development.[67]

Sen's notion of freedom is far from a negative notion of freedom that is equivalent to non-interference by the state.[68] His notion of freedom is a sub-stantive notion of positive freedom that enables an individual to achieve in life what she wants. It is his focus on *freedom to* (*do* or *be*) that is captured by the use of the term 'capability'.[69] Sen's notion of freedom has two principal dimensions: first, the socio-economic dimension that creates appropriate conditions for individuals to exercise their choice; and, secondly, the individuals' own initiative

56 Nussbaum (n 4) 7, 9–10.
57 See Sen, 'Equality' (n 10); Amartya Sen, *Commodities and Capabilities* (Amsterdam & New York: North Holland, 1985).
58 Sen, *Development* (n 1) p 3, 36; Sabina Alkire, 'Why the capability approach?' (2005) 6(1) *Journal of Human Development* 115 at 121.
59 Sen, *Development* (n 1) 74–75.
60 Sen, 'Capability and well-being' (n 50); Sen, *Development* (n 1) 74–75.
61 Sen, *Development* (n 1) 75.
62 ibid.
63 ibid 75–76.
64 ibid 75.
65 Alkire, 'Capability approach?' (n 58) 121–22.
66 ibid.
67 Sen, *Development* (n 1) 74–76; Nussbaum offers some challenge to Sen's perspective of seeing development as 'freedom'. She asks whether 'promoting freedom can be seen as a coherent political project'. She asserts that 'freedom' conceptualised by Sen needs clarification, because there are freedoms that are sometimes conflicting in nature. See Martha C Nussbaum, 'Capabilities as fundamental entitlements: Sen and social justice' (2003) 9(2/3) *Feminist Economics* 33 at 44–45.
68 Sen, *Development* (n 1) xii, 63–67.
69 Sabina Alkire, *Valuing Freedoms: Sen's Capability Approach and Poverty Reduction* (Oxford: Oxford University Press, 2002) 6.

or agency to lead the kind of life she has chosen.[70] In Sen's own words: 'The capability of a person depends on a variety of factors, including personal characteristics and social arrangements.'[71] Accordingly, Sen breaks down his idea of freedom into *wellbeing freedom* and *agency freedom*.[72]

3.4.1 Wellbeing and agency

Wellbeing is defined as the measurement or extent of how well or comfortable an individual is in her life.[73] Sen argues 'that the well-being that a person actually enjoys is often more closely related to . . . functioning achievements'.[74] Accordingly, Sen asserts that the wellbeing of an individual 'leads to a particular concept of freedom'.[75] Sen calls this the wellbeing freedom.[76] He observes that '[t]his view relates to the idea that the good life is inter alia also a life of freedom'.[77] This freedom is an individual's capability to choose and enjoy definite functioning-sets.[78] Thus, wellbeing achievements are achieved functionings and wellbeing freedom is an individual's capability set.[79] Sen distinguishes this wellbeing freedom from agency freedom.[80]

According to Sen, agency freedom is the freedom of an individual to achieve something that she decides to achieve as a responsible agent.[81] He reasons that, while wellbeing freedom is a particular type of freedom to attain definite wellbeing, agency freedom is the general type of freedom that enables an individual to achieve whatever she decides to achieve.[82] Agency freedom need not be limited to achievement of wellbeing only; there may be occasions when an individual may choose to achieve something that is detrimental to her own wellbeing, but nonetheless of some value to her.[83] Thus, Sen observes: 'A person's agency aspect cannot be understood without taking note of his or her aims, objectives,

---

70   Sen, *Development* (n 1) 10, 17–19, 31; Sen, 'Capability and well-being' (n 50) 39; Sen, 'Well-being' (n 52).
71   Sen, 'Capability and well-being' (n 50).
72   Sen, 'Well-being' (n 52) 169, 203–204, 208; Sen, 'Capability and well-being' (n 50) 35, 39 (especially footnote 23 at 39); John M Alexander, 'Capabilities, human rights and moral pluralism' (2004) 8(4) *International Journal of Human Rights* 451 at 457.
73   Sen, 'Well-being' (n 52) 202.
74   ibid.
75   ibid 202–203.
76   ibid.
77   Sen, 'Well-being' (n 52).
78   ibid 203–204.
79   Robeyns (n 16) 103.
80   Sen, 'Well-being' (n 52).
81   ibid 78.
82   ibid.
83   ibid 208–12. Sen gives examples of an individual eating on the bank of a river while another person is dying from drowning in the river. The individual on the bank enjoying her meal may derive wellbeing from her meal, but in pursuance of her 'agency freedom' she may decide to sacrifice her meal and save the drowning individual. Thus, if the individual decides to save the drowning individual in accordance with her 'agency freedom', she chooses something other than her own wellbeing.

allegiances, obligations and, in a broad sense, the person's conception of the good'.[84]

Therefore, while wellbeing is associated with the idea of wellness, comfort or a good life for all people, the agency aspect is extremely subjective since it is shaped by each individual's prudence and conscience. Sen captures these two dimensions of freedom in the following words:

> Although the agency aspect and the well-being aspect both are important, they are important for quite different reasons. In one perspective, a person is seen as a doer and a judge, whereas in the other the same person is seen as a beneficiary whose interests and advantages have to be considered. There is no way of reducing this plural-information base into a monist one without losing something of importance.[85]

Sen argues that all these aspects of freedom are valuable (and no one of these factors could be prioritised) and each needs to be kept in mind in an evaluation of development as freedom. Thus, there is an internal plurality in Sen's concept of freedom.[86] In facilitating the freedom of choosing by an individual, Sen argues that both the wellbeing freedom and the agency freedom are equally valuable, and one cannot be reduced to the other.

3.4.2 Positive freedom and negative freedom

Based on his analysis of the wellbeing and the agency aspects of freedom, Sen reasons that analysing development (achievement) in terms only of wellbeing would take us in one direction; analysing development (achievement) in terms only of an individual's overall goals and agency would take us in a different direction.[87] Both of these kinds of achievement would in turn differ from the 'freedom to achieve' measurement of development.[88] Sen argues in favour of measurement of development in terms of freedom to achieve rather than actual achievement (of wellbeing or agency objective).[89] He reasons that it is with respect to freedom to achieve that an individual can lay claim on society – there cannot be any claim with respect to the actual achievements attained by an individual.[90] Despite having the same level of freedom to achieve if an individual achieves less, she cannot complain against social arrangements.[91]

---

84   Sen, 'Well-being' (n 52).
85   ibid 208.
86   Alkire, 'Capability approach?' (n 58) 122.
87   Sen, 'Capability and well-being' (n 50) 35.
88   ibid.
89   ibid 39–40.
90   ibid.
91   ibid. Sen here can be seen to be promoting the idea of equality of capabilities, rather than enhancement of capabilities, although the two concepts are not totally devoid of each other. See Alkire, *Valuing Freedoms* (n 69) 177.

John Alexander notes: 'Freedom [according to capability theorists] is not merely the absence of interference, but also the possession of different capabilities to achieve valuable human functionings.'[92] Sen is not content with the idea of non-interference[93] – his is a concept of positive freedom.[94] Benedetta Giovanola asserts that Sen's conceptualisation of freedom 'allows us to think of human beings in a *dynamic* frame in which they are constantly involved in the process of "becoming" themselves and realizing themselves'.[95] His conception of freedom – as constitutive of wellbeing freedom and agency freedom – is a positive conception of freedom, to be actively pursued by individuals, with appropriate social provisioning being provided by integrated institutions, a term that Sen uses to suggest multiplicity of institutions working together.[96]

Based on Aristotle and Karl Marx, Sen holds that individual freedom has intrinsic value.[97] It is this intrinsic value of freedom that every good society should promote as social good.[98] The intrinsic value of freedom is 'significant in itself for the person's overall freedom'.[99] Sen notes that intrinsic freedom is not only important as a valuable social good, it is also 'important in fostering the person's opportunity to have valuable outcomes'.[100] In this sense, freedom is instrumental in attaining other valuable things in the society.[101] It is in this instrumental sense that freedom is a precondition to either wellbeing achievement or agency achievement of an individual. Freedom in its instrumental sense is

92   Alexander, *Amartya Sen and Martha Nussbaum* (n 1) 4. Taking a leaf from Sen's argument Alexander further notes: 'A person who is poor, uneducated, unemployed, afflicted by a preventable disease or socially excluded might encounter no interference from the state or fellow citizens, but he or she certainly lacks the required capacities and opportunities to live a life of freedom. This being the stark reality in most of our contemporary capitalist liberal democracies, it is important to emphasize the idea that a society fails to treat some of its members as equals not only when it restricts or interferes with them, but also when it permits them to grow up in poverty and suffer serious forms of capability shortfalls and deprivation. Hence, the capability theorists, as it is argued here, are not against interferences *per se*. It is well within the spirit of the capability approach to tolerate certain qualified forms of "interferences" for distributive purposes and for the provision of public goods so that maximum conditions for basic capabilities can be realized for all citizens. Particularly when these interventions are capabilities-promoting for everyone and are stipulated to take place under the purview of a fair rule of law and in compliance with human rights, they can hardly be considered as interferences in the negative sense of the term.'
93   Anderson (n 53) 316–18.
94   Amartya Sen, 'Freedom of choice: concepts and content' (1988) 32 *European Economic Review* 269 at 272; Sen also contends that the idea of freedom that is implicit in Rawls's work is also a notion of positive freedom; see Sen, *Idea of Justice* (n 3) 64–65; Alexander, *Amartya Sen and Martha Nussbaum* (n 1) 149–52, 155.
95   Benedetta Giovanola, 'Personhood and human richness: good and well-being in the capability approach and beyond' (2005) 63(2) *Review of Social Economy* 249 at 252.
96   Alexander, 'Moral pluralism' (n 72) 457.
97   Sen, *Inequality* (n 3) 41; Sen, *Development* (n 1) 18; Alexander, 'Moral pluralism' (n 72) 455.
98   Sen, *Inequality* (n 3).
99   Sen, *Development* (n 1) 18.
100   ibid 18, xii.
101   Sen, *Inequality* (n 97); Alexander, 'Moral pluralism' (n 72).
102   Sen, *Inequality* (n 3).

important 'in judging how good a "deal" a person has in the society'.[102] Social development, therefore, needs to be judged on the basis of freedom in both its intrinsic as well as its instrumental senses.[103]

Sen's idea of freedom as positive entitlements and agency initiatives stands in sharp contrast to that of 'negative rights' ('what one is not prevented from doing').[104] In Sen's proposition of freedom as determinant of development public policy has a significant role to play.[105] According to Sen, freedom 'in terms of the choice of functionings' is a combination of an individual's command over resources (individual entitlements) and the individual's personal *conversion factors* (an individual's personal characteristics and ability to convert those characteristics into functionings with her command over resources).[106] Therefore, public policy needs to ensure the appropriate availability of resources (entitlements) that could help in individual conversion of characteristics into respective functionings.[107] The concept of a conversion factor is important in the capability approach.

A conversion factor is a *combination* of factors/characteristics that generates such *conditions* (not the individual factors/characteristics *per se*) in which an individual can have the freedom to do or to be. Conversion factors can be personal (that is, combined personal characteristics giving rise to conditions in which an individual can choose her life); social (that is, combined social characteristics giving rise to conditions in which an individual is free to choose her life); and environmental (that is, combined environmental characteristics giving rise to conditions in which an individual is free to choose her life). What is important to note is that conversion factors are not *per se* resources or characteristics (including liberty and rights etc). Conversion factors are an *intangible combination of circumstances* that facilitate freedom to choose (capabilities). Each of these definite categories of conversion factors (that is, personal, social or environmental) converts the characteristics of other categories (*inter se*) into functionings.

Sen asserts that freedom from hunger and from malaria enhances the possibility of living as one chooses to live.[108] These freedoms could be secured by public action.[109] In this sense these public policy-induced freedoms are instrumental for the overall capability development of an individual. Public policy-induced freedoms are not, however, conclusive in themselves. The entitlement freedom (that is, freedom of access to resources) has to be converted to functionings by the 'active choice' of an individual.[110] Thus, development as freedom has two axes: freedom to entitlements and entitlement-induced freedom, which is ensured by public action, and the freedom of individual agency.[111]

103 Sen, *Development* (n 1) 18.
104 Sen, *Inequality* (n 3) see footnote 8).
105 Sen, 'Capability and well-being' (n 50) 44.
106 Sen, *Commodities* (n 57) 13; Robeyns (n 16) 99; Sen, *Development* (n 1) 74.
107 Sen, 'Capability and well-being' (n 105); Robeyns (n 16).
108 Sen, 'Capability and well-being' (n 50).
109 ibid.
110 ibid.
111 ibid.

Despite charting a positive discourse of individual freedom, however, Sen does not deny the significance of negative freedoms in terms of civil and political rights.[112] Sen's view of democracy and public participation in the determination of the priorities for social action and prioritisation of functionings (with respect to individual societies) is based on the pillars of civil and political rights.[113] It is useful in this context to compare the language of human rights to that of the capability approach.

3.4.3 Human rights and the concept of freedom

The capability approach shares the substantive basis of the human rights approach, which is the dignity of human beings.[114] However, the two concepts also differ in specific ways.[115] While mention of definite capabilities could be found in Sen's theory only as examples, Martha Nussbaum, the other prominent pioneer of the capability approach, provides us with a universal list of desirable capabilities in a society.[116] The capabilities Sen refers to in his work and the list of capabilities provided by Nussbaum are to a great extent human rights goals.[117] However, Nussbaum points out the problems with the human rights discourse in the following words:

> People differ about what the *basis* of a rights claim is: rationality, sentience, and mere life have all had their defenders. They differ, too, about whether rights are prepolitical or artefacts of laws and institutions. They differ about whether rights belong only to individual persons, or also to groups . . . They differ, again, about the relationship between rights and duties . . . They differ, finally, what rights are to be understood as *rights to*. Are human rights primarily *rights to* be treated in certain ways? *Rights to* a certain level of achieved well-being? *Rights to* resources with which one may pursue one's life plan? *Rights to* certain opportunities and capacities with which one may make choices about one's life plan?[118]

Nussbaum argues that the capability approach has answers to these questions in the context of each specific purpose wherein the approach is applied.[119] Quoting Bernard Williams, Nussbaum argues that given the confusing nature of the basic

112   Sen, *Development* (n 1) 3, 63–67.
113   ibid 31–32, 36–40, 51–53, 123, 147–48, 152–55; Alexander, 'Moral pluralism' (n 72) 458.
114   Nussbaum, 'Capabilities as fundamental entitlements' (n 67) 36–37; Amartya Sen, 'Human rights and capabilities' (2005) 6(2) *Journal of Human Development* 151 at 152.
115   Sen, 'Human rights and capabilities' (n 114).
116   See Martha C Nussbaum, *Women and Human Development: the Capabilities Approach* (Cambridge: Cambridge University Press, 2000).
117   See Nussbaum, 'Capabilities as fundamental entitlements' (n 67) 36–37; Alexander, 'Moral pluralism' (n 72) 455, 457–58.
118   Nussbaum, *Women* (n 116) 97.
119   ibid.

human rights discourse it might be useful to see human rights as combined capabilities.[120] Nussbaum's idea of combined capabilities expresses an individual's innate powers and the social opportunities available to her.[121] Alexander argues that combined capabilities are, therefore, a better way of addressing issues of social justice.[122] Nussbaum, however, is not in favour of discarding the human rights language altogether.[123]

Sen, too, argues in favour of retaining the rights discourse because of its entrenched nature in the development domain.[124] He further observes that rights discourse is useful because it frames individual entitlements in succinct and concrete language as a 'universal ethical demand'.[125] Both Nussbaum and Sen emphasise the role of political liberties in seeing development as freedom.[126] However, they do not prioritise specific rights or liberties.

While Sen himself prioritised social and economic rights (namely freedom from hunger) under certain circumstances,[127] equally he emphasised the importance of civil and political rights and democratic dialogue in other situations.[128] Thus, one of the virtues of the capability approach (over human rights language) is that the capability approach successfully avoids the tendency to hierarchise capabilities (and exerts substantial emphasis on social and economic rights), thereby avoiding the politics associated with the hierarchisation of rights.[129]

While the list of capabilities generated by Nussbaum incorporates both the so-called first and second generations of human rights (civil and political rights, and economic and social rights respectively),[130] Sen leaves it to the democratic

---

120   ibid 97–98. Nussbaum subdivides 'capabilities' into 'basic capabilities', 'internal capabilities' and 'combined capabilities' in her work. She contends that human beings have certain 'basic capabilities', including speech, love, practical reason etc; the 'basic capabilities' require appropriate external conditions for their development as 'internal capabilities'; 'internal capabilities' could then be used to choose and fulfil 'functionings' – it is at this stage of choosing and realising functionings that 'internal capabilities' becomes 'combined capabilities'. 'Combined capabilities' are therefore manifestation of an individual's 'internal capabilities' and external opportunities; Alexander, 'Moral pluralism' (n 72) 459; David A Clark, 'The capability approach: its development, critiques and recent advances', GPRG-WPS-032, Global Poverty Research Group at 9, available at http://www.gprg.org/pubs/workingpapers/pdfs/gprg-wps-032.pdf (last visited 26 December 2010).

121   Alexander, 'Moral pluralism' (n 72); Clark 'The capability approach' (n 120).

122   Alexander, 'Moral pluralism' (n 72).

123   Nussbaum, 'Capabilities as fundamental entitlements' (n 67) 39–40.

124   Sen, *Development* (n 1) 229–34, 246–47.

125   Sen, *Idea of Justice* (n 36) 373–76.

126   Sen, *Development* (n 1) 31–32, 36–40, 51–53, 123, 147–48, 152–55 (where he discusses the importance of Rawls's political liberties); Nussbaum, *Women* (n 116) 12.

127   See Amartya Sen, *Hunger and Entitlements* (Helsinki: World Institute for Development Economics Research, 1987); Sen, *Idea of Justice* (n 36) 379–85, where he argues that the social and economic rights cannot be left outside the human rights domain keeping civil and political rights as the only prerogative of the rights' language.

128   Sen, *Development* (n 1) 31–32, 36–40, 51–53, 123, 147–48, 152–55.

129   Alexander, 'Moral pluralism' (n 72).

130   Nussbaum, *Women* (n 118); Nussbaum, 'Capabilities as fundamental entitlements' (n 67) 36–37.

deliberation process to decide what a society would value as capabilities.[131] Both of them, however, defend human rights in terms of some fundamental capabilities that are sensitive to socio-cultural contexts.[132] In this sense, Alexander observes that both Sen's and Nussbaum's conception of human rights are compatible with moral pluralism.[133] Thus, the capability approach effectively reduces the tension associated with the human rights language by positioning human diversity in the centre of the human rights debate.[134]

It is important in Sen's view of freedom that the state and other institutions ensure appropriate conditions for the democratic deliberative process through the promotion of civil and political rights that are themselves instrumental in ensuring development of capability of an individual. Thus, what is important in the notion of development as freedom is the active role of institutions in ensuring basic entitlements in the society and creating appropriate conditions for the exercise of civil and political rights by the citizens, which promotes the individual conversion factors that can convert characteristics into capabilities.[135] Accordingly, Alexander observes that the relation between an individual's capabilities and non-individualised social goods is central to the capability approach.[136] In this relation, the institutional framework becomes important in facilitating individual capabilities (or freedom).[137] The next section looks at the role of institutions in promoting freedom of individuals.

3.5 Role of institutions

Sen observes that: '[s]ociety might accept some responsibility for a person's wellbeing, especially when that is in some danger of being particularly low.'[138] He argues that, with respect to public goods,[139] it is the duty of society to ensure the minimum wellbeing of its people.[140] This claim, however, does not mean that society is to be responsible for the agency aspect of an individual in society as well.[141] Society's role is important with respect to matters (public goods) such as social security, poverty alleviation, removal of gross economic inequality, pursuit of social justice,[142] education, health, nutrition, civil liberties etc.[143] Thus, the conversion

---

131   Sen, *Development* (n 1) 31–32, 36–40, 51–53, 123, 147–48, 152–55; Sen, *Idea of Justice* (n 36) 91, 324–27, 392; Sen, 'Human rights' (n 114) 157–58.
132   Alexander, 'Moral pluralism' (n 72) 461.
133   ibid 461–62.
134   ibid; see also Nussbaum, 'Capabilities as fundamental entitlements' (n 67) 39.
135   Robeyns (n 16) 99–100.
136   Alexander, 'Moral pluralism' (n 72) 465–66.
137   ibid.
138   Sen, *Inequality* (n 3) 71.
139   Sen, *Development* (n 1) 128.
140   Sen, *Inequality* (n 138).
141   ibid.
142   ibid.
143   Jean Drèze, Amartya Sen, *India Development and Participation* (New Delhi: Oxford University Press, 2002) 6–7.

of 'commodity-characteristics' into individual functionings does not depend only on individual agency; it is also conditional upon social factors.[144]

Sen also observes that: '[f]reedom is central to the process of development for two distinct reasons: (1) the evaluative reason: assessment of progress has to be done primarily in terms of whether the freedoms that people have are enhanced; (2) the effectiveness reason: achievement of development is thoroughly dependent on the free agency of people'.[145]

Thus, for evaluative purposes of social development it is important to analyse the role of institutions from the point of view of their ability to enhance the freedoms that people have.

Pointing to the importance of evaluating institutions for an analysis of development as freedom Sen notes that:

> Individuals live and operate in a world of institutions. Our opportunities and prospects depend crucially on what institutions exist and how they function. Not only do institutions contribute to our freedoms, their roles can be sensibly evaluated in the light of their contributions to our freedom. To see development as freedom provides a perspective in which institutional assessment can systematically occur.
>
> Even though different commentators have chosen to focus on particular institutions (such as the market, or the democratic system, or the media or the public distribution system), we have to view them together, to be able to see what they can or cannot do in combination with other institutions. It is in this integrated perspective that the different institutions can be reasonably assessed and examined.[146]

Thus, Sen takes an 'institutionally integrated approach'[147] that takes into account the role of multiple institutions such as the government, the market, the legal system, the judicial system, political parties, public services, the media, public interest groups and public discussion forums etc.[148]

Although Sen values the institution of the free market[149] (his support for the market arises from his perception of the market as one of the most significant domains for the exercise of freedom and the market's capacity for economic development), his adherence to the virtues of the free market is far from being unconditional.[150] Sen holds the role of social provisioning of public goods as being

---

144 Sen, *Commodities* (n 57) 25–26.
145 Sen, *Development* (n 1) 4. The effectiveness reason Sen provides seeks to answer the question of whether people are able to convert their 'enhanced' freedom through their 'agency' in furtherance of achieving what they want.
146 ibid 142.
147 Drèze and Sen (n 143) 20.
148 Sen, *Development* (n 1) xii–xiii.
149 ibid 112–19.
150 ibid 45–49, 120–29; Sen, *Idea of Justice* (n 36) 83.

of the utmost importance for the promotion of basic capabilities of individuals.[151] He argues that social provisioning needs to supplement the free market.[152] However, although the government is given a pre-eminent position in social provisioning, there are adequate reasons not to expect the government to be a benevolent public good provider: 'The implicit faith in the goodness and the good sense of the government that underlies much reasoning in favour [of] government-led economic development cannot, frequently, stand up to scrutiny.'[153]

Thus, the role of the executive component of the government needs to be mediated by the parliament, the legal system, the judiciary, opposition parties, the electoral process, the media and so on, all of which together constitute the concept of the democratic polity.[154] The concept of state is much broader than that of government.[155] Thus, a debate in terms of either the free market-led development or the government-led development is incomplete at best since both of these perspectives depend on a number of other factors, including *inter alia* the extent of competition in the market, openness of entry, scope of manipulability, the nature of the government, power of the ruling political groups, political system of the state, legal system, political freedom and treatment of opposition, and value of dissent.[156]

It is not merely the presence of institutions that matters for a freedom-centric idea of development. What is important for the concept of development as freedom is to ascertain what the institutions characterise and the role the institutions play in promoting freedom and wellbeing.[157] In his book *The Idea of Justice*[158] Sen criticises theories of justice that give pre-eminence to institutions themselves as 'manifestations of justice'.[159] He criticises David Gauthier,[160] Robert Nozick[161] and John Rawls[162] for emphasising the socially agreed installation of institutions as conditions sufficient for social justice.[163] Sen's view is that, even if institutions are installed by social agreement, these institutions may fail to deliver the results for which they were established.[164] It would be a mistake to see the establishment of institutions as an end in itself in furthering social conditions for individual wellbeing and freedom.[165] Institutions need to be evaluated on the basis of actual consequences generated by such institutions.[166]

151   Sen, *Development* (n 1) 127–29.
152   ibid 142–45.
153   Drèze and Sen (n 143) 45.
154   ibid.
155   ibid.
156   ibid 46.
157   Sen, *Idea of Justice* (n 36) 75–86.
158   ibid (n 36).
159   ibid 82.
160   ibid 83–84.
161   ibid 84–85.
162   ibid 79–80, 85.
163   ibid 83–84.
164   ibid 81, 83.
165   ibid 81.
166   ibid 82–83.

What is implied by Sen in this argument is that institutions are important if they facilitate actual freedom and wellbeing and, thereby, development. Institutions are able to facilitate freedom if they institutionalise certain characteristics with a view to having desired (and targeted) consequences that promote social provisioning for the guarantees of freedom (capability). What is important in Sen's view is the institutionalisation of definite characteristics in furtherance of definite consequences.[167]

In this idea, institutions by themselves are not important. They are important for what they characterise and what they ensure. An institution may have been established in furtherance of some consequences, but at a later point in time it may turn out that such an institution has failed to deliver the results for which it was established.[168] Under such circumstances, Sen argues, such an institution would have outlived its requirement.[169] There is a need, therefore, to undertake constant evaluation of institutions to ascertain whether they are able to generate the consequences for which they were established.[170] Sen, therefore, notes: '[t]o ask how things are going and whether they can be improved is a constant and inescapable part of the pursuit of justice.'[171]

What follows from Sen's analysis of the role of institutions in promoting wellbeing and capability is that there need not be any prioritisation of one institution over another. Institutions need not be limited to either the government or the market. A society should choose institutions that promote development as freedom in accordance with the necessities of the particular society. No institution is final or conclusive; instead, institutions must be continuously evaluated, and then either continued or discarded based on their performance.

There is, thus, no restriction on the creation of new institutions or the institutionalisation of new characteristics that promote individual conversion factors in turning commodity-characteristics into functionings. Sen points to the necessity of multiple institutions in a society to ensure that these institutions exercise countervailing power over each other, thereby balancing power in society by preventing one institution from becoming too powerful.[172] It is in these respects, therefore, that democracy and public participation become very important in Sen's idea of development as freedom.[173]

---

167   Sen's idea of consequences is far removed from the utility-based consequentialism that is dependent on 'happiness' or 'desire-fulfilment' evaluation. Sen's evaluation of consequences is based on the capability-evaluation of an individual. His approach is a 'broad consequentialist' approach to social ethics. See Alexander, *Amartya Sen and Martha Nussbaum* (n 1) 17–21.
168   Sen, *Idea of Justice* (n 36) 85–86.
169   ibid.
170   ibid 85.
171   ibid 86.
172   ibid 81.
173   ibid 345–46.

3.5.1 *Role of democracy in development as freedom*

According to Sen and Drèze, 'the interactions between the state, the public and the market have to be seen in a larger framework, with influences operating in different directions'.[174] They further observe: 'In emphasising the role of non-market institutions in successful development, it is extremely important to see the different institutions in an integrated way, and here the practice of democracy – in the fullest sense – can be critically important.'[175] The practice of democracy is central in Sen's theory,[176] especially if the *integrated institutional* approach is to be pursued. What Sen means by democracy in the fullest sense becomes clear when he links democracy to his idea of development:

> Developing and strengthening a democratic system is an essential component of the process of development. The significance of democracy lies . . . in three distinct virtues: (1) its intrinsic importance, (2) its instrumental contributions, and (3) its constructive role in the creation of values and norms. No evaluation of the democratic form of governance can be complete without considering each.[177]

In its intrinsic importance democracy is itself constitutive of development. Democracy promotes individual freedom by ensuring and protecting political freedom and civil rights.[178] In its instrumental role, democracy is the means to achieve other freedoms – economic and social.[179] In its constructive role, democracy helps to create social norms: it is this constructive role of democracy that Sen depends on for the ascertainment of capabilities and functionings that every society would value.[180] He leaves the prioritisation of functionings in a particular society to the democratic deliberative process practised in that particular society.

The focus of Sen's idea of democracy is public participation and democratic deliberation.[181] Sen asserts that the mere presence of democratic institutions (the integrated institutions of government, market, legal system, judiciary, media etc) does not suffice for an idea of development as freedom.[182] Formal democracy, in the sense of public balloting[183] is of little use in Sen's theory.[184] What is required

---

174   Drèze and Sen (n 143) 21.
175   ibid 24.
176   Sen, *Idea of Justice* (n 36) 345–54.
177   Sen, *Development* (n 1) 157–58.
178   ibid 147–48, 154–55.
179   ibid 147, 152–53.
180   ibid 153–54.
181   ibid 155–57; Sen, *Idea of Justice* (n 36) 91, 324–27, 392. It is not totally irrelevant at this point to note that public participation and democratic deliberation underlie Sen's overall conceptualisation of the idea of justice. Instead of providing a substantive basis of 'justice', Sen argues for an idea of justice that is indeterminate in substance and is shaped by a participatory process in a democratic polity. See Sen, *Idea of Justice* (n 36) 388–415.
182   Sen, *Development* (n 1) 155–57; Sen, *Idea of Justice* (n 36) 81, 83, 354.
183   Sen, *Idea of Justice* (n 36) 324.
184   ibid 354.

for the concept of democracy in Sen's theory is actual participation of the people. Sen conceptualises democracy in its substantive sense. The essence of democracy, in his view, lies in public discussion.[185] In this view of democracy, free speech, access to information and freedom of dissent is prioritised over balloting.[186] Sen gives centrality to the collective decision-making process in a society. Such a process requires the continuous practice of democracy rather than only the establishment of democratic institutions. This distinction relates back to Sen's idea of the role of institutions in promoting freedom. He proposes a continuous evaluative process that social institutions should be subjected to with a view to justifying their effectiveness at all times. Such an evaluation should be based on the process of democratic dialogue and social participation. The democratic process is a dynamic one that involves participation and continuity.

Thus, from the capability point of view the democratic deliberative process has two central functions: first, prioritisation of values as functionings (and corresponding capabilities) for every society; and, secondly, the institutionalisation of characteristics with a view to ensuring social provisioning for the realisation and promotion of capabilities. It is here that Sen's conceptualisation of capabilities differs from that of Martha Nussbaum's capabilities framework.[187] While Sen thinks that the formulation and prioritisation of capabilities and functionings should be left to the democratic deliberation process of respective societies, Nussbaum provides a general list of capabilities that every society needs to value. Moreover, while the question of institutionalisation remains implicit in Sen's theory, it is central to Nussbaum's project.[188] It is, therefore, worthwhile to note the divergences between the conceptualisation of capability in Sen and Nussbaum's theories.

3.6 Sen and Nussbaum

Although both Sen and Nussbaum are the pioneers of the capability approach, their theories have different goals.[189] Sen's project is evaluative and comparative.[190] His idea of development as freedom is based on the evaluation of social provisioning to determine whether people's freedom has been enhanced.[191] The Human Development Report of the United Nations Development Programme (UNDP), which is based on the capability approach developed by Sen,[192] uses capabilities to compare development amongst countries. In contrast, the principal focus of

---

185 Sen, *Development* (n 1) 9.
186 Sen, *Idea of Justice* (n 36) 327, 335–37.
187 See Nussbaum, *Women* (n 116).
188 ibid; see also Nussbaum, 'Capabilities as fundamental entitlements' (n 67) 55–56.
189 Robeyns (n 16) 103.
190 Nussbaum, *Women* (n 116) 12; Nussbaum, 'Capabilities as fundamental entitlements' (n 67) 35; Robeyns (n 16) 94, 96.
191 Sen, *Development* (n 1) 4.
192 The UNDP describes the concept of human development in the following terms: 'Human Development is a development paradigm that is about much more than the rise or fall of national incomes. It is about creating an environment in which people can develop their full potential and

Nussbaum's project is the institutionalisation of characteristics that enhances capabilities of individuals.[193]

Nussbaum proposes such institutionalisation through constitutional incorporation of the social basis[194] of the desired capabilities.[195] Synthesising the capability approach offered by Sen and Nussbaum in his own terms, Alexander asserts that the capability approach can offer a theory of social justice that aims at the 'realization of basic capabilities for all' by the creation of 'greatest possible condition' through appropriate designing of a 'society's economic and political institutions'.[196] Alexander, while not committing himself to the constitutional incorporation of listed capabilities, nonetheless endorses the idea of institutionalisation of basic capabilities.

In Sen's project, the process of institutionalisation is implicit, and he does not provide any specific direction in that regard. Nussbaum, on the other hand, provides a general list of capabilities that is to be achieved through the institutionalisation process.[197] The general list of capabilities that she provides consists of: life; bodily health; bodily integrity; senses, imagination and thought; emotions; practical reason; affiliation; living together and concern for other species; play; and control over one's environment.[198] Nussbaum mentions that her list is 'open-ended and humble; it can always be contested and remade',[199] and that the list is culturally sensitive.[200] In line with Nussbaum, Anderson too thinks that there needs to be some minimum list of capabilities.[201] She identifies three spheres of capability that should constitute core human capabilities: capabilities as a human being; capabilities as a participant in a system of cooperative production; and capabilities as a citizen of a democratic state.[202] Even if Sen himself does not provide any list of desired capabilities, he thinks that it is a useful endeavour to pursue such a list.[203]

---

lead productive, creative lives in accord with their needs and interests. People are the real wealth of nations. Development is thus about expanding the choices people have to lead lives that they value. And it is thus about much more than economic growth, which is only a means – if a very important one – of enlarging people's choices. Fundamental to enlarging these choices is building human capabilities – the range of things that people can do or be in life. The most basic capabilities for human development are to lead long and healthy lives, to be knowledgeable, to have access to the resources needed for a decent standard of living and to be able to participate in the life of the community. Without these, many choices are simply not available, and many opportunities in life remain inaccessible.' http://hdr.undp.org/en/humandev/ (last visited 24 September 2010).

193 Nussbaum, *Women* (n 116) 6, 12, 34–35, 70–71, 74–75; Nussbaum, 'Capabilities as fundamental entitlements' (n 67) 55–56; Alexander, 'Moral pluralism' (n 72) 457–58.
194 Nussbaum, *Women* (n 116) 12, 81–82.
195 ibid 12, 70–71; Robeyns (n 16) 103.
196 Alexander, *Amartya Sen and Martha Nussbaum* (n 1) 1–2.
197 Nussbaum, *Women* (n 116) 77–80; Nussbaum, 'Capabilities as fundamental entitlements' (n 67) 40.
198 Nussbaum, *Women* (n 116) 78–80.
199 ibid 77; Nussbaum, 'Capabilities as fundamental entitlements' (n 67) 40–42.
200 Nussbaum, *Women* (n 116) 77, 96; Nussbaum, 'Capabilities as fundamental entitlements' (n 67) 42.
201 Anderson (n 53) 317–18.
202 ibid.

Sen himself, however, prefers to leave it to the democratic deliberation process to decide on the desired capabilities for individual societies.[204] Although he gives examples of desired capabilities[205] and uses some basic capabilities index in the Indian context to chart a development discourse,[206] he refrains from providing a list in his works. Sen argues for omitting a list that:

> The problem is not with listing important capabilities, but with insisting on one pre-determined canonical list of capabilities, chosen by theorists without any general social discussion or public reasoning. To have such a fixed list, emanating entirely from pure theory, is to deny the possibility of fruitful public participation on what should be included and why.[207]

Supporting Sen's stand on a list of capabilities, Sabina Alkire argues that, since Sen's theory is a general theory capable of application to specific evaluations, a list will always depend on (and differ on the basis of) the nature of the specific evaluation (application) undertaken.[208] Nussbaum, however, argues that in the absence of a list of desired capabilities Sen's theory lacks normative power.[209] She further asserts that, in the absence of a list of freedoms (or capabilities), Sen's development as freedom perspective suffers from some inherent flaws.[210] She argues that if the goal of development is to promote freedom for all, there is a genuine problem that the freedom of some people will be an impediment in the realisation of freedom for other people.[211] In this debate Alexander, however, takes a mediatory position by asserting that Anderson's spheres of capabilities concept is a mid-way point between Sen's lack of list and Nussbaum's elaborate list in providing a capabilities concept of social justice.[212] In view of the nature of Sen's objection to the list of capabilities, there is scope to construe Nussbaum's list with Sen's objections in a harmonious manner, because Nussbaum categorically asserts that her list is open-ended and leaves room for democratic deliberation on the list of capabilities.[213]

203 See Sen, 'Human rights' (n 114) 159–60.
204 Note 131; Sen, 'Human rights (n 114) 158–63.
205 Sen, 'Human rights' (n 114) 158.
206 See Drèze and Sen (n 143) 143–274. The basic capabilities that Sen and Drèze analyse in the Indian context are basic education, health and environment, and gender equality.
207 Note 205.
208 Alkire, 'Capability approach?' (n 58) 115–17, 119.
209 See Nussbaum, 'Capabilities as fundamental entitlements' (n 67) 35, 46–48.
210 ibid 44–47.
211 ibid. Sen replied to these objections by observing that 'freedom' per se is good, but it might be used for bad purposes (Sen's response to Nussbaum's paper at the Zentrum für interdiziplinarische Forschung in Bielefeld at which it was first presented in July 2001, cited in Nussbaum, 'Capabilities as fundamental entitlements' (n 67) 46).
212 Alexander, *Amartya Sen and Martha Nussbaum* (n 1) 70–71.
213 See Sen, 'Human rights' (n 114) 158–60; Nussbaum, 'Capabilities as fundamental entitlements' (n 67) 40–42.

3.7 Conclusion

The capabilities approach developed by Sen and Nussbaum thus provides an alternative theoretical framework that is concerned with aspirations of individuals in their lives. Sen's conceptualisation of development as freedom (where freedom is synonymous with capabilities) is particularly useful in public policy studies. Sen has himself (along with Jean Drèze) applied the concept of freedom to reconceptualise development in the Indian context. From a feminist perspective, Nussbaum has also applied the concept to the Indian context to analyse gender development. There are other studies that use the development as freedom framework to analyse freedom as a normative basis of development, prominent amongst which is the comparative Human Development Report prepared annually by the UNDP. These studies have shown that it is possible to invoke the capability approach for evaluative and normative purposes to a diverse range of issues.

Use of the capability approach for normative policy purposes is to be mediated by public participation and democratic dialogue processes. Although the capability approach is primarily an individual-centric concept, in addition to agency, individual capabilities are dependent on social, economic, political, environmental and cultural factors, which are determined through public policy. Since the capability approach envisioned by Sen is non-paternalistic, individuals in a society are themselves able to decide the desirable capabilities and consequent public policy through participation and democratic deliberation. Effective democratic deliberation is central to Sen's conceptualisation of the capability approach. Although Nussbaum offers a list of desirable capabilities, she leaves space for democratic deliberation in furtherance of modification of her list. Thus, democratic dialogue with active participation of social partners is central to the capability approach.

The ILO advocates a strategy of democratic dialogue in the furtherance of promoting a dignified life for workers. While tripartite participants – government representatives, workers' representatives and employers' representatives – and democratic dialogue are central to the ILO's decision-making process, the organisation mandates its member states to promote the social dialogue process in their respective jurisdictions. In furtherance of the ILO's mandate of social dialogue, it developed the 1998 Declaration on Fundamental Principles and Rights at Work mandating the recognition of collective bargaining. In 1999 the ILO made social dialogue a constitutive principle of the organisation's thematic agenda – Decent Work (DW). The DW agenda, which is now the ILO's motto, was specifically created in order to account for informal and atypical economic activities (as I explain in the next chapter). These developments at the ILO show that the organisation has positioned democratic dialogue at the centre of policy-making for informal workers. The ILO strategy is an example of how a democratic dialogue mechanism could be employed in a specific policy context.

The capability approach, along with the social dialogue strategy of the ILO, provides an appropriate theoretical basis for an analysis of informal economic activities and informal workers. Informal workers encounter working and living conditions that are very different from industry-based formal workers. Moreover, informal economic activities are heterogeneous in nature. Accordingly, in order to understand the problems of informal workers their own perspective and participation is necessary. Any policy initiative must understand what informal workers need in their lives in order to fulfil their aspirations. The capability approach provides the basis for such an aspiration-centric analysis of informal workers' working conditions and living standards. My discussion of the capability approach in this chapter will contribute towards the theoretical underpinning for my study.

In the next chapter, I discuss the developments at the ILO that culminated in the DW agenda. The DW agenda is based on four strategic principles: productive employment, rights at work, social protection and social dialogue. I specifically focus on the social dialogue strategy and analyse how far the strategy can integrate multiple stakeholders engaged in and related to informal economic activities in the furtherance of policy-making. My larger purpose is to ascertain whether the ILO social dialogue strategy is adequate for enhancing capabilities for informal workers through a democratic process. I also aim to find out whether the ILO social dialogue strategy can help institutionalise capability-enhancing factors for informal workers. My next chapter is a stepping stone towards these goals.

4 Social dialogue in promoting decent work

4.1 Introduction

In Chapter 3, I discussed the nuances of the capability approach as a human development framework. The essence of the capability approach is that it takes freedom to choose as the determinant of development and analyses the role of resources in the promotion of capabilities. Resources per se are not important for the capability approach; the evaluative reference point of the capability approach is what resources do for the enhancement of capabilities. In a capability approach framework, although individuals would determine which capabilities are desirable to them, for policy purposes it becomes important to ascertain desirable capabilities for the society as a whole (ie which capabilities are deemed desirable by individuals in a society/community). As I discussed in Chapter 3, Martha Nussbaum provides a generic list of capabilities that she deems desirable for all societies situated in any developmental stage, albeit with a caveat that her list is only indicative, not exhaustive.

Amartya Sen, on the other hand, refrains from providing a list of desirable capabilities. According to Sen, specific societies or communities need to decide the desirable capabilities for those particular societies or communities through a democratic dialogue process. The dialogue process Sen envisages needs to be broad-based, with effective participation of concerned social partners. Sen's abstract formulation of social dialogue could be found in strategic policy elaboration in the work of the ILO.

The ILO is a specialised agency of the United Nations (UN),[1] which is concerned with the welfare of workers and fair competition around the globe.[2] The ILO seeks to achieve these goals through the promulgation and supervision of labour standards,[3] and through technical cooperation.[4] The ILO presently has 183

---

1 See United Nations, 'Structure and organization', available at http://www.un.org/en/aboutun/structure/index.shtml (last visited 22 April 2012). For an account of how the ILO became a part of the United Nations, see David A Morse, *The Origin and Evolution of the I.L.O. and Its Role in the World Community* (New York: Cornell University, 1969) 30–32.
2 See ILO, 'Mission and objectives', available at http://www.ilo.org/global/about-the-ilo/mission-and-objectives/lang--en/index.htm (last visited 22 April 2012).
3 See ILO, 'About the ILO', available at http://www.ilo.org/global/about-the-ilo/lang--en/index.htm (last visited 4 January 2013).
4 See ILO, 'Programmes and projects', available at http://www.ilo.org/global/programmes-and-projects/lang--en/index.htm (last visited 22 April 2012).

member states, and each member state participates in the ILO decision-making process through tripartite representation: government representatives, employer representatives and worker representatives.[5] Accordingly, social dialogue through tripartite participation is the functional basis of the ILO.

The ILO defines social dialogue as: 'all types of negotiation, consultation and exchange of information between, or among, representatives of governments, employers and workers, on issues of common interest'.[6] The social dialogue strategy of the ILO is a constitutive pillar of the ILO's thematic goal – the Decent Work (DW) Agenda. The DW Agenda is expressed as a fourfold strategy of employment, rights at work, social protection and social dialogue, which operate simultaneously without prioritisation of any one strategy over another. These strategies are also known as the pillars of the DW Agenda. The novelty of the DW Agenda lies in the fact that the agenda is targeted at informal economic activities and all four pillars are intended for all workers, including informal workers.[7]

The DW Agenda is a flexible concept wherein the content of each of the four constitutive pillars is to be determined by the ILO member states themselves. This flexibility in realising the goal of DW allows ILO member states leeway to devise their labour welfare regimes suited to their respective socio-economic-political conditions. The flexibility in the DW Agenda creates scope for policy space in favour of informal workers. The social dialogue pillar of the DW Agenda acts as a check and balance device against a flexible principle-based international regime to counter member states' flexibility in acting upon the DW Agenda.

In this chapter, I analyse the DW pillar of social dialogue and discuss the pillar's efficacy in the context of informal workers. The strategy of social dialogue, conceptualised in the context of informal economic activities, could facilitate informal workers' voice in policy circles.[8] An innovative social dialogue mechanism especially crafted for informal economic activities could also shed light on the operationalisation of other pillars of the DW Agenda, such as rights at work and social protection. Therefore, in this chapter, I consider the scope and role of the social dialogue pillar of the DW Agenda in enhancing capabilities for informal workers. I argue that, if the social dialogue strategy is to be effective in the context of informal workers, such strategy needs to transcend the tripartite structure of social dialogue promoted by the ILO. Social dialogue for informal economic activities needs to be multipartite, involving as many concerned social partners as possible.

In the next section of the chapter (4.2), I briefly explain the function and *modus operandi* of the ILO. In this section I point out that the ILO was established to cater to the needs of developed countries. However, in order to address

---

5 Morse (n 1) 8–9.
6 ILO, 'Social dialogue', available at http://www.ilo.org/global/about-the-ilo/decent-work-agenda/social-dialogue/lang--en/index.htm (last visited 20 May 2012); ILO, *Decent Work*, Report of the Director-General, International Labour Conference, 87th Session, June 1999 (Geneva: ILO, 1999) 38–39, 42–43.
7 See ILO, *Decent Work* (n 3) 3–4.
8 See Ela R Bhat, *We Are Poor But So Many: the Story of Self-Employed Women in India* (New York: Oxford University Press, 2006).

developing country concerns the organisation has modified its approach over the decades. In section 4.3, I analyse the genesis of the DW Agenda. I look into the shift in the ILO strategy from promulgation of conventions and recommendations to the facilitation of statement of principles. I look at the contribution of the DW Agenda to the overall ILO policy. In this section, I also discuss the four pillars that the DW Agenda promotes (4.3.1). I discuss how the 2008 ILO Declaration on Social Justice for a Fair Globalization adds significance to the principle of DW (4.3.2).

In section 4.4 of the chapter, I analyse the social dialogue pillar of the DW Agenda and look into its efficacy in the context of informal economic activities. I argue that the pillar of social dialogue offers a democratic way to decide on the nature and level of protection afforded to informal workers with active participation of stakeholders and social partners. I discuss the role that integrated institutions could play in promoting social dialogue for informal workers (4.4.1 and 4.4.2). Having discussed the efficacy of the DW Agenda and the social dialogue pillar, I compare the DW Agenda as an analytical framework with the capability approach in the next section of the chapter (4.5). This discussion is necessary because I will be using one of these two analytical frameworks to analyse my case study of informal waste pickers in Kolkata, India, in Chapter 6.

4.2 The ILO: what it is and how it works

The most significant role of the ILO is 'drawing up and overseeing international labour standards'.[9] Therefore, the ILO works through the creation and supervision of conventions, recommendations and declarations.[10] While conventions are binding on ILO member states upon ratification,[11] recommendations have only persuasive significance.[12] Declarations are statements of principles that inspire policy.[13]

The ILO was founded on the principle of social justice, both in its initial version as Part XIII of the Treaty of Versailles,[14] and in its later incarnation as a specialised

---

9   See ILO, 'About the ILO' (n 3); Morse (n 1) 9.

10   Constitution of the International Labour Organisation art 19, available at http://www.ilo.org/ ilolex/english/constq.htm (last visited 22 April 2012).

11   ibid arts 19, 20; Charter of the United Nations 1945 art 102, available at http://treaties.un.org/ doc/Publication/CTC/uncharter.pdf (last visited 22 April 2012).

12   Constitution of the International Labour Organisation art 19 (n 10); see Nicolas Valticos, 'Fifty years of standard-setting activities by the International Labour Organisation' (1996) 135(3–4) *International Labour Review* 393 at 404–405 for a discussion of the utilities of ILO conventions and recommendations.

13   See ILO, 'Declaration concerning the aims and purposes of the International Labour Organisation', available at http://www.ilo.org/ilolex/english/constq.htm (last visited 22 April 2012).

14   Part XIII of the Treaty of Versailles begins by declaring: '[w]hereas the League of Nations has for its object the establishment of universal peace, and such a peace can be established only if it is based upon social justice'. See Treaty of Versailles, 1919 s I pt III, Official Bulletin, International Labour Office (Geneva: ILO, 1923), available at http://www.ilo.org/public/english/bureau/ leg/download/partxiii-treaty.pdf (last visited 14 September 2011).

agency of the United Nations (UN).[15] The official ILO history explains the three main motivations for the establishment of the ILO.[16] The motivations are: humanitarian, in so far as injustice and exploitation are meted out to the ever-increasing number of workers in the increasingly industrialised world;[17] political, in so far as workers in precarious conditions could cause social unrest and revolt;[18] and economic, in so far as low labour conditions in one country would allow it to have competitive advantage in trade over its competitors by reducing the cost of production.[19]

Principally, the ILO was to provide 'equality of trade conditions'[20] among nations by establishing 'a social framework for economic exchange'.[21] The organisation provides for a space wherein employers, workers and governments can meet and discuss in order to find a non-conflicting middle ground of cooperative coexistence.[22] Although this tripartism gives legitimacy to the ILO, as I will explore later in this chapter, the tripartite structure sometimes restricts the organisation's effort in ameliorating the conditions of workers around the globe.[23]

The ILO was established in 1919. In the first few years the ILO was busy in setting a minimum floor through detailed conventions and recommendations to ward off the competitive advantage that a country might enjoy because of its low labour standards, a constitutional goal 'designed to reconcile the requirements

15 The ILO Constitution, in its preamble, reiterates its objective: '[w]hereas universal and lasting peace can be established only if it is based upon social justice'. See Constitution of the ILO (n 10) preamble.

16 See ILO, 'ILO history', available at http://www.ilo.org/public/english/about/history.htm (last visited 14 September 2011); Morse (n 1) 6; Nigel Haworth, Stephen Hughes, 'Trade and international labour standards: issues and debates over a social clause' (1997) 39(2) *Journal of Industrial Relations* 179 at 182; Robert W Cox, 'The idea of international labour regulation' (1953) 67 *International Labour Review* 191 at 191–94.

17 See ILO, 'ILO history' (n 16).

18 See Gerry Rodgers and others, *The International Labour Organization and the Quest for Social Justice, 1919–2009* (Geneva: ILO, 2009) 2; Guy Standing, 'The ILO: an agency for globalization?' (2008) 39(3) *Development and Change* 355 at 357; Steve Hughes, Nigel Haworth, *The International Labour Organisation (ILO)* (New York: Routledge, 2011) xvi; Cox, 'The idea' (n 16) 191–94; Robert W Cox, 'Labor and hegemony' (1977) 31(3) *International Organization* 385 at 387.

19 Karl Polanyi noted that the International Labour Office was instituted 'partly in order to equalize conditions of competition amongst the nations'. See Karl Polanyi, *The Great Transformation* (Boston: Beacon Press, 1957) 26.; Alfred Wisskirchen, 'The standard-setting and monitoring activity of the ILO: legal questions and practical experience' (2005) 144(3) *International Labour Review* 253 at 255; Haworth and Hughes, 'Trade and international' (n 16) 182; Cox, 'The idea' (n 16) 195.

20 Asserted by Woodrow Wilson, as quoted in Rodgers and others, *1919–2009* (n 18) 6.

21 ibid 6.

22 ibid 2.

23 The tripartite ILO framework is problematic so far as representation of informal workers are concerned. Informal workers mostly do not have unions. Some NGOs work with informal workers, and therefore claim to be representative of informal workers. However, ILO employer and employee constituents object to NGO representation in the ILO (sometimes rightly so) on the ground that NGOs are non-democratic and non-representative. See ibid 17–18.

of social justice with the realities of international competition'.[24] Since the ILO was created by Western nations, the ILO has principally been concerned with the labour problems of industrialised developed countries.[25] This bias is evident from the nature of issues and labour standards that the organisation was concerned with until the 1950s and 1960s.[26] However, after the 1950s the ILO gradually and incrementally began to address labour problems of developing countries.[27] In recent decades the ILO has focused on principles rather than specific labour standards in order to integrate informal workers in developing countries into its policy fold. The latest of such initiatives is the DW Agenda, which I discuss in the following sections.

4.3 Genesis of the decent work (DW) agenda

The approach of promulgating detailed trade and industry-specific conventions, and getting member states to ratify those conventions, has worked well for the organisation and its member states for some time. The ILO's survival through the Second World War was dependent to a large extent on the success of the 'reformist vision of social justice' (as distinct from a revolutionary vision, as I discuss presently), which the organisation was furthering through its conventions and recommendations.[28] During this phase of the organisation, the support of the United States of America (USA) was also central for its survival.[29] Scholars assert that the Cold War era after the Second World War was a 'golden age' for the ILO's standard-setting function.[30] This was because the world had two versions of social justice at that time: the reformist vision and the revolutionary vision of social justice.[31] The ILO's standard-setting succeeded during this period because the

---

24 Francis Maupain, 'New foundation or new façade? The ILO and the 2008 Declaration on Social Justice for a Fair Globalization' (2009) 20(3) *EJIL* 823 at 825.

25 See Morse (n 1) 18–23; Bob Hepple, *Labour Laws and Global Trade* (Oxford and Portland: Hart, 2005) 28–29; Rodgers and others, *1919–2009* (n 18) 41, 178, 183; Standing, 'The ILO' (n 18) 356–57; Hughes and Haworth, *International Labour Organisation* (n 18) xvi, 7–8, 16; Daniel Maul, *Human Rights, Development and Decolonization: the International Labour Organization, 1940–70* (Basingstoke: Palgrave Macmillan & Geneva: ILO, 2012) 114–15; Jasmien van Daele notes that the ILO's Eurocentrism also has a deep impact on the literature involving the organisation. See Jasmien van Daele, 'The International Labour Organization (ILO) in past and present research' (2008) 53 *International Review of Social History* 485 at 491, 509; Cox, 'Labor' (n 18) 409–10.

26 See Morse (n 1) 43, 64–68, wherein the then Director-General of the ILO, Morse, describes the industry-based understanding of labour problems, which was significantly a developed industrialised country phenomenon; Rodgers and others (n 18) 41, 178, 183; Valticos (n 12) 398–99.

27 See Maul (n 25) 64, 70, 77–78, 105, 111–18, 121, 124–39, 160–84, 192–214, 220–23, 227–58; Morse (n 1) 45–56; Rodgers and others (n 18) 180–85; Hepple, *Labour Laws* (n 25) 34; Hughes and Haworth, *International Labour Organisation* (n 18) 14–15, 29; Valticos (n 12) 399–401.

28 Maupain (n 24) 825–26.

29 See Rodgers and others, *1919–2009* (n 18) 29.

30 See Haworth and Hughes, 'Trade and international' (n 16) 184; Hughes and Haworth, *International Labour Organisation* (n 18) 15–16; Maupain (n 24) 826.

31 Maupain (n 24) 826; Hepple, *Labour Laws* (n 25) 34–35.

organisation's reformist vision of social justice drew sympathy and support from capitalist industrialised countries and their workers.[32]

The ILO was a model that was antithetical to the revolutionary model of social justice[33] and capitalist developed countries could project the ILO model as an alternative to the revolutionary model of social justice in order to discourage workers from revolting against capitalism. Unprecedented expansion of international trade and commerce[34] also contributed to the ILO's success during this period.[35] However, some observers note that the connection between ILO standards and economic and commercial growth during this time was much less evident than in the pre-Second World War period.[36]

In its quest to promulgate industrial model-based detailed labour standards, the ILO failed to pay enough attention to the realities of non-industrial developing and least developed member states. As early as 1947, the ILO was told that ILO conventions need to be tailored to local conditions in Asian countries.[37] India's first Prime Minister, Jawaharlal Nehru, urged the ILO to work with informal agricultural workers in India (which engaged, and still engages the majority of the Indian workforce) during the first ILO Asian Regional Conference in Delhi in 1947.[38] However, these proposals did not resonate with the ILO, because at that time the ILO's priority was to universalise labour standards globally within a frame of industrial establishments;[39] the organisation had no intention to attune its activities to local conditions.[40]

Bob Hepple expresses serious doubts about the relevance of ILO standards for the majority of workers around the world, especially in developing countries.[41] He is also sceptical of the actual implementation of ratified ILO standards in developing countries.[42] Moreover, Hepple attributes non-ratification and non-implementation of ILO standards, especially by developing countries, to the perception of competitive advantage on labour that developing countries (believe they) enjoy.[43] He notes that developing countries perceive that adoption and compliance with

---

32 Maupain (n 24); Cox, 'Labor' (n 18) 387.
33 Maupain (n 24).
34 Competitive concern about international trade and commerce, and the need to set a minimum platform of labour standards in furtherance of such competitive concern, is well articulated in the preamble of the constitution of the ILO. See ILO Constitution (n 10).
35 Maupain (n 24) 826.
36 See Rodgers and others, *1919–2009* (n 18) 209–10.
37 See Maul (n 25) 117.
38 ibid 116–17.
39 See Cox, 'Labor' (n 18) 409–10.
40 See Maul (n 25) 118, 132; van Daele (n 25) 501.
41 See Bob Hepple, *Labour Law, Inequality and Global Trade* Sinzheimer Lecture 2002 (Amsterdam: Hugo Sinzheimer Instituut, 2002) 25, 27; Hepple, *Labour Laws* (n 25) 39–47; Simon Deakin, 'The contribution of labour law to economic and human development' in Guy Davidov, Brian Langille (eds), *The Idea of Labour Law* (New York: Oxford University Press, 2011) 156 at 163; Standing, 'The ILO' (n 18) 375–76.
42 Hepple, *Labour Law, Inequality* (n 41) 19–20, 25; Hepple, *Labour Laws* (n 25) 47.
43 Hepple, *Labour Law, Inequality* (n 41) 28.

ILO standards would put them in a disadvantageous position as far as the cost of labour is concerned.[44] Thus, developing countries allege that developed countries are guilty of social imperialism whenever there is talk of linking trade to labour standards.[45] Because of such a stand adopted by developing countries there is a disparity between developed and developing countries in adopting and implementing ILO standards.[46] According to Hepple, these developments question the very legitimacy and survival of the ILO.[47]

Additionally, the ILO was also suffering from internal incoherence during the post-Second World War period. During the post-Second World War era, because of its engagement with a range of issues, for example, from working time to social insurance, the ILO was internally pursuing fragmented policy approaches, apparently unconnected to each other.[48] Even if these ILO policies were connected, connections between them were difficult to discern, by insiders as well as by outsiders.[49] Moreover, the ILO's initial plan of shaping global development policies was discarded by the ILO Governing Body.[50]

Externally, after 1989 and during the post-Cold War period, the ILO's standard-setting function faced serious challenge.[51] After the disintegration of support for the revolutionary vision of social justice, the need to have a counterview of reformative social justice subsided. Therefore, production of labour standards by the ILO was perceived to be politically redundant.[52] The ILO standards were also perceived to be economically inefficient because over-regulation of labour was perceived to be an obstacle in foreign direct investment.[53] Additionally, the ILO standards were found to be failing to provide a universal 'level playing field' (so far as labour standards were concerned) because member states were free to ratify standards or reject them.[54] With the erosion of trade union membership and bargaining power, labour unions could not influence governments to ratify ILO standards.[55] Moreover, Francis Maupain identifies 'standards fatigue' as another reason for the decreasing popularity of ILO standards,[56] by which he means that

---

44 ibid 27–28.
45 ibid.
46 ibid 28.
47 ibid.
48 See Rodgers and others, *1919–2009* (n 18) 207–209.
49 ibid.
50 ibid 210.
51 Maupain (n 24) 826–29.
52 ibid 826–27.
53 ibid 826–27. Maupain, however, does not agree with this economic view. He cites an ILO inquiry report in 1996 and an OECD study of 1996 to argue that this economic argument is not supported by reality. See footnote 10 at 826–27.
54 ibid 827.
55 ibid 827; Hughes and Haworth, *International Labour Organisation* (n 18) 47–51.
56 Maupain (n 24) 827.
57 This is evident from the list of conventions and recommendations that the ILO has promulgated so far. ILO conventions and recommendations address topics as varied as Unemployment Indemnity (Shipwreck) Convention 1920 to Labour Statistics Recommendation 1985. For the list of ILO conventions see http://www.ilo.org/ilolex/english/conventions.pdf (last visited

the ILO instruments have covered almost all aspects of labour issues,[57] and hence, fewer issues remain wherein the ILO can promulgate an instrument.[58] Maupain reasons that these factors in the post-Cold War era slowed down the ratification rate of ILO instruments, resulting in an existential crisis of the ILO.[59]

Observers point out other causes of the ILO's existential crisis. During the post-Cold War period, the ILO's internal weaknesses and external survival prospects were aggravated by political pressures from major economic powers and funding concerns for the organisation's programmes.[60] When the major economic powers, such as the United States and the United Kingdom, pushed for a neo-liberal global trading regime led by the Bretton Woods institutions,[61] they did not encourage ideologically alternative policies from the ILO.[62] These developments sidelined the legitimacy and significance of the ILO as an organisation having valid concern in trade and labour debates.

The 1998 ILO Declaration on Fundamental Principles and Rights at Work marked the culmination of the developments in the preceding decades that first threatened the survival of the ILO and then presented the organisation with new opportunities in view of the re-emergence of the trade and labour standards debate.[63] The 1998 Declaration provided for a social floor of labour standards, without requiring member states to ratify any convention in that regard.[64] In principle, the declaration mandated adherence to the identified core labour standards by ILO member states. The labour standards identified by the declaration are: 'freedom of association and the effective recognition of the right to collective bargaining'; 'elimination of all forms of forced or compulsory labour'; 'effective abolition of child labour'; and 'elimination of discrimination in respect of employment and occupation'.[65]

16 September 2011); for the list of ILO recommendations see http://www.ilo.org/ilolex/english/recommendations.pdf (last visited 16 September 2011).

58 Maupain (n 24) 827.

59 ibid; Laurence R Helfer, 'Understanding change in international organizations: globalization and innovation in the ILO' (2006) 59 *Vanderbilt Law Review* 649; Hepple, *Labour Laws* (n 25) 35–37; Wisskirchen (n 19) 261–65, 268.

60 Rodgers and others, *1919–2009* (n 18) 197.

61 See David Harvey, 'From globalization to the new imperialism' in Richard P Appelbaum, William I Robinson (eds), *Critical Globalization Studies* (New York: Routledge, 2005) 91 at 98–100; Fred Halliday, 'The pertinence of imperialism' in Mark Rupert, Hazel Smith (eds), *Historical Materialism and Globalization* (London: Routledge, 2002) 75 at 83–84, 86–87.

62 See Rodgers and others, *1919–2009* (n 18) 197–98; Hughes and Haworth, *International Labour Organisation* (n 18) 35–36.

63 Hepple, *Labour Laws* (n 25) 35–59; Helfer (n 59).

64 A declaration is not a one-way tool imposed by an organisation (in this case, the ILO) over the member states to accept (or reject); a declaration is an expression of joint commitment shared by an organisation and its member states issued on rare occasions of long-term significance. See ILO Report VII, 'Consideration of a possible declaration of principles of the International Labour Organization concerning fundamental rights and its appropriate follow-up mechanism' 86th Session, Geneva (June 1998), available at http://www.ilo.org/public/english/standards/relm/ilc/ilc86/rep-vii.htm (last visited 20 September 2011); Maupain (n 24) 831–32.

65 Declaration on the Fundamental Principles and Rights at Work 1998, available at http://www.ilo.org/declaration/thedeclaration/textdeclaration/lang--en/index.htm (last visited 20 August 2010).

The declaration, which is a joint expression of commitment by the ILO and its member states, forms the core labour standards, as distinguished from cash standards (that have direct financial implications on the part of employers or the government).[66] The core standards identified in the 1998 Declaration do not necessarily have financial implications that cash standards might have. Member states do not need substantial spending to ensure freedom of association, abolition of forced or child labour, or non-discrimination.[67] Ensuring these conditions would therefore not make labour more costly or deny the comparative advantage that developing countries might have in global trade.[68]

However, Philip Alston argues that by providing for *core* labour standards the 1998 Declaration has envisaged a hierarchy of labour rights, thereby transforming the international labour rights regime.[69] He notes that the 1998 Declaration aims at addressing the trade–labour linkage,[70] and does little to protect and promote workers' rights.[71] Moreover, the declaration is not binding[72] and hence cannot mandate member states to adhere to the so-called core rights.[73]

As pointed out by Alston, the declaration does not include cash standards or economic guarantees, such as maternity benefits or health insurance, within its scheme. However, as I discussed in Chapter 2, for the overall development of workers and the promotion of their dignified life, cost standards or economic provisioning are immensely important. This absence of cost standards in the 1998 Declaration was addressed through the DW Agenda envisaged by the ILO in 1999.[74]

In 1999, under the leadership of the Director-General Juan Somavia, the ILO arranged the entire organisation's work around the concept of DW.[75] The DW

---

66 See Brian A Langille, 'Core labour rights: the true story (Reply to Alston)' (2005) 16(3) *European Journal of International Law* 409 at 413–17, 418–20, 423, 425–26; Maupain (n 24) 442, 444–45, 447, 453–55, 459–63; Supriya Routh, 'Globalizing labor standards: the developed–developing divide' (2010) 2(1) *Jindal Global Law Review* 153.

67 There might, however, be costs to ensure appropriate conditions in which freedom of association or abolition of child labour can become a reality. These costs are mostly inherent in the administration of the (primarily democratic) member states, and do not require additional budgetary allocation under separate heads of expenses.

68 See Leah Vosko, '"Decent Work": the shifting role of the ILO and the struggle for global social justice' (2002) 19(2) *Global Social Policy* 19 at 27–29, 31–32.

69 Philip Alston, '"Core labour standards" and the transformation of the international labour rights regime' (2004) 15(3) *European Journal of International Law* 457 at 458.

70 ibid 460–517; Hepple, *Labour Laws* (n 25) 59; Vosko (n 68) 20, 27–28, 31.

71 Alston (n 69) 461.

72 The 1998 Declaration is not binding in the sense that the ILO member states are not required to ratify the underlying conventions of the declaration. Since the member states are not required to ratify these conventions, they are not obligated to adhere to the conventions.

73 Alston (n 69) 461, 465, 518–20.

74 Civil and political rights converge with social and economic goals in the DW Agenda. See Adelle Blackett, 'Situated reflections on international labour law, capabilities, and decent work: the case of centre *Mariachi* Eugene Guineas' (2007) *Revue québécoise de droit international (Hors-série)* 223 at 224–26, 242–43.

75 See ILO, *Decent Work* (n 6).

Agenda consists of four strategic pillars: 'fundamental principles and rights at work'; 'employment'; 'social protection'; and 'social dialogue'.[76] Thus, over the years, the ILO's preambulary goal of social justice is expressed through different strategies, initially through the promulgation of definite labour standards and presently through the expression of principles through the 1998 Declaration and the 1999 DW Agenda.

The DW Agenda offers a new integrated and proactive ILO approach.[77] It is an integrated approach because it is a non-controversial synthesis of a range of ILO instruments, where member states are free to decide the content of each pillar.[78] It is a proactive approach because the ILO moved from a strategy of negative safeguards to a policy of positive promotion,[79] which is evident in the shift in the ILO policy: from *prevention of unemployment* in the 1919 Constitution to *creation and development of work* in the 2008 Declaration.[80] Another example of this shift is from 'protecting tripartism', following the constitution to 'promoting social dialogue' in the DW Agenda and the 2008 Declaration.[81]

However, there is another way of looking at the DW Agenda. The DW Agenda can also be seen as a compromise by the ILO under pressure from its member states. Countries such as the United States claim to provide a right to association and collective bargaining in their domestic legislation, even if they have not ratified ILO conventions on these issues.[82] Non-ratifying member states such as the United States contend that, since they already provide these guarantees in their domestic legislation and since some of the ILO standards are in conflict with their *law and practice*, they are unable to ratify ILO instruments.[83]

On the other hand, there are ILO member states such as India who contend that if they are required to ratify some ILO conventions, they will not have any flexibility in exempting certain categories of workers (such as government servants, otherwise known as public sector employees) from the scope of the guarantees specified under those conventions.[84] Now that the ILO has adopted the DW Agenda, which specifies that, even if member states do not ratify ILO instruments,

---

76 ibid v, 3.
77 Maupain (n 24) 834–39.
78 ibid 837–39.
79 ibid 834–37.
80 See ILO Declaration on Social Justice for a Fair Globalisation, available at http://www.ilo.org/public/english/bureau/dgo/download/dg_announce_en.pdf (last visited 20 September 2011).
81 Maupain (n 24) 834–35.
82 See 'Reich urges adherence to "core" labor standards (Reconciliation of trade, labor rules needed)', available at http://www.usembassy-israel.org.il/publish/press/labor/archive/june/dl1_6-12.htm (last visited 30 March 2012); United States Council for International Business, 'Issue analysis: US ratification of ILO core labor standards' (April 2007), available at http://www.uscib.org/docs/US_Ratification_of_ILO_Core_Conventions.pdf (last visited 30 March 2012); Bureau of International Labor Affairs, 'United States Department of Labor, ILO standards', available at http://www.dol.gov/ilab/programs/oir/PC-ILO-page2.htm (last visited 30 March 2012).
83 See Bureau of International Labor Affairs (n 82).
84 See Government of India, 'India and the ILO', available at http://labour.nic.in/ilas/indiaandilo.htm (last visited 30 March 2012).

they are bound by it, and countries such as the US or India do not need to ratify these ILO instruments any longer. In this sense, the DW Agenda is a compromise that holds the diverse ILO membership together.[85]

From a positive point of view, the DW Agenda supplements and transcends the 1998 ILO Declaration.[86] Through the 1998 Declaration, the ILO mandated adherence to *core* labour standards by its member states. As previously noted, *cash* standards such as old age or maternity benefits, unemployment benefits, insurance against occupational accidents etc were not made part of the 1998 Declaration. The DW Agenda, by providing for pillars such as productive employment and social protection, incorporates cash standards as an inseparable part of the agenda.

Incorporation of core standards as well as cash standards as part of the DW Agenda was possible in part because the agenda did not mandate definite legal obligations (on ILO member states) and because the agenda was vaguely stated and couched in aspirational terms. Since member states were free to decide on the level of cash standards that are suited to their developmental level, the DW Agenda received support from all ILO constituents. The 2008 ILO Declaration on Social Justice for a Fair Globalization eventually gives legal meaning to the DW Agenda as I discuss later. In the following section I discuss the content of the DW Agenda in detail.

4.3.1 The decent work agenda

The DW Agenda was aimed at improving the relevance of the ILO in the international community in the 21st century by capturing the disparate ILO functions within a single theme.[87] Addressing varied concerns of the tripartite constituency, ILO programmes were dealing with a wide range of issues such as rights at work, employment, enterprise growth, security and protection, development and dialogue etc.[88] These programmes were executed as independent distinct programmes.[89]

The DW Agenda signified a new regime at the ILO. In his 1999 report[90] to the International Labour Conference, identifying the priorities of the ILO, the Director-General Juan Somavia stated that:[91]

---

85   The ILO does not have an impeccable record of commanding allegiance from its members. The United States withdrew from the organisation in 1975. The US withdrawal not only had symbolic and strategic significance, it was also important for the funding of the organisation. Some scholars note that the ILO never fully recovered from the shock of US withdrawal from the organisation. See Standing, 'The ILO' (n 18) 359–62; Hughes and Haworth, *International Labour Organisation* (n 18) 17; Cox, 'Labor' (n 18) 401–402, 404, 422.

86   Gary S Fields, 'Decent work and development policies' (2003) 142(2) *International Labour Review* 239 at 239, 252; Hepple, *Labour Laws* (n 25) 22; Amartya Sen, 'Work and rights' (2000) 139(2) *International Labour Review* 119 at 123–24.

87   See Rodgers and others, *1919–2009* (n 18) 222, in particular the interview with the Director-General.

88   ibid 223.

89   ILO, *Decent Work* (n 6) 2–3.

90   ibid.

91   ibid 3.

The primary goal of the ILO today is to promote opportunities for women and men to obtain decent and productive work, in conditions of freedom, equity, security and human dignity.

He noted that the DW Agenda is the converging focus of the ILO's strategic objectives and must shape the organisation's policies and sketch its international role.[92] This shift in ILO policy, he observed, was mandated by the changes in socio-economic conditions worldwide brought about by globalisation in the previous two decades.[93] The DW Agenda was envisaged to overcome two distinct ILO problems: first, the problem of multiple distinct ILO programmes without any clear overall agenda; and, secondly, the weakening of a sense of purpose amongst the ILO constituents resulting in diminishing external influence of the organisation.[94]

The DW Agenda sought to provide synergy between different ILO programmes and the different departments of the ILO.[95] The DW Agenda is a substantive, political and management strategy of the ILO.[96] It provides for substantive rights of the workers; it promotes a smooth and unified management system within the ILO; and politically, it bridges the concerns of developed and developing countries without mandating ratification of specific standards.[97] The DW Agenda envisages a *comprehensive approach* to ILO work.[98] The agenda merges legal rights with social goals.[99]

Politically, one of the significant achievements of the DW Agenda is that the agenda seeks to bridge the gap between formal and informal workers so far as the promotion of decent work is concerned.[100] The ILO's traditional focus has been wage workers in industrialised countries, ie workers who are part of an employment relationship.[101] One of the reasons for the ILO's diminishing influence internationally was the organisation's inability to address the problems of informal workers.[102] The DW Agenda was seen as a tool to promote decent working conditions for all workers, formal or informal, taking account of the diverse

92   ibid.
93   ibid 1.
94   ibid 2–3, 11.
95   See ILO, 'Reducing the decent work deficit: a global challenge', Report of the Director-General, International Labour Conference, 89th Session 2001 (Geneva: ILO, 2001) 33–40, available at http://www.ilo.org/public/portugue/region/eurpro/lisbon/pdf/rep-i-a.pdf (last visited 20 May 2012); Rodgers and others, *1919–2009* (n 18) 223.
96   Rodgers and others (n 18) 223.
97   ibid 223.
98   Sen, 'Work and rights' (n 86) 120; Gerry Rodgers, 'The goal of decent work' (2008) 39(2) *IDS Bulletin* 63 at 66; Ignacy Sachs, 'Inclusive development and decent work for all' (2004) 143(1–2) *International Labour Review* 161; Wisskirchen (n 19) 266–69.
99   Sen, 'Work and rights' (n 86) at 123, 127; Amartya Sen, 'Human rights and the limits of law' (2006) 27 *Cardozo Law Review* 2913 at 2916, 2924.
100 ILO, *Decent Work* (n 6) 3–4; Hepple, *Labour Laws* (n 25) 64; Sen, 'Work and rights' (n 86) 120; Vosko (n 68) 20–21, 26, 32.
101 ILO, *Decent Work* (n 6) 3; Standing, 'The ILO' (n 18) 357–59.
102 As many scholars have speculated, this might be one of the factors that hindered ratification of ILO conventions by member states. See Hepple, *Labour Law, Inequality* (n 41) 25–28; Langille, 'Core labour rights' (n 66) 414, 420, 423; Vosko (n 68) 20.

regional needs for worker welfare.[103] It is necessary to look at the four pillars of the DW Agenda to understand the capacity of the agenda to fulfil its promises. I briefly look into the founding pillars of the DW Agenda: employment; rights at work; social protection; and social dialogue.

4.3.1.1 Employment

The pillar of productive employment is central to the concept of DW. Employment is a 'source of dignity, satisfaction and fulfilment' for workers[104] and it inculcates a sense of participation amongst workers, which is conducive to democracy and political stability.[105] The concept of productive employment suggests that the ILO is concerned not only about employment of any kind; the organisation seeks to promote quality employment for all workers.[106]

In furtherance of its goal of full and productive employment, the ILO has pursued a three-pronged policy: first, employment promoting macro-economic policies; secondly, an enterprise strategy for employment growth; and, thirdly, a labour market strategy to promote equality and access to employment.[107] One of the determinants of productive employment is that workers must be able to develop their skills and capabilities through their employment.[108] The 1999 report of the Director-General pledged to improve the conditions of informal workers through the promotion of employment and productivity in the informal sector.[109] The employment pillar in the DW Agenda refers to all kinds of employment, including waged employment, self-employment, working from home and unpaid work done by men and women.[110]

4.3.1.2 Rights at work

Rights at work constitute the very heart of the concept of DW. Labour rights emanate from ideas of social justice[111] and thus provide the 'ethical and legal framework' in the furtherance of dignity, equality and freedom of workers.[112] The Director-General's 1999 report identifies the 1998 Declaration on Fundamental Principles and Rights at Work as providing the substantive content of the pillar of rights at work.[113]

---

103 ILO, *Decent Work* (n 6) 3–5, 9.
104 Dharam Ghai, 'Decent work: universality and diversity' in Dharam Ghai (ed), *Decent Work: Objectives and Strategies* (Geneva: IILS, ILO, 2006) 11.
105 ILO, *Decent Work* (n 6) 11.
106 ibid 21, 25.
107 ibid 22.
108 ibid 26.
109 ibid 24. The report notes that the organisation will focus on enterprises in order to promote employment for informal workers.
110 Ghai, 'Universality and diversity' (n 104) 10.
111 Bob Hepple, 'Rights at work' in Ghai (ed), *Decent Work* (n 104), 33.
112 Ghai, 'Universality and diversity' (n 104) 7; Hepple (n 111) at 33.
113 ILO, *Decent Work* (n 6) 14–17.

As part of the DW, workers should have freedom of association and recognition of their right to collective bargaining, freedom from forced work, freedom against child labour and non-discriminatory treatment at work in furtherance of their overall claim to decent work.[114] Through the DW Agenda, the ILO seeks to promote its labour standards and analyse the compatibility of its labour standards with the informal economy, in order to promote overall rights at work.[115] The ILO-identified rights at work are principally procedural rights (civil and political in nature) through which substantive rights could be achieved.[116]

However, a limiting factor with the ILO's conceptualisation of rights at work is that it is principally based on the employer–employee model of industrialised developed countries.[117] In this respect, Hepple notes that in the modern economy, much of which involves services and production chains, rights at work can only be realised if the traditional way of conceptualising them is abandoned, which means that such rights have to be conceptualised beyond the employer–employee relationship.[118] If rights at work could not be conceptualised outside the domain of the employment relationship, informal workers not part of an employment contract would perpetually remain outside the scope of such rights.

4.3.1.3 Social protection

Social protection is the third pillar of the DW Agenda, the aim of which is to safeguard workers from insecurity in relation to a range of contingencies and vulnerabilities.[119] Social protection, if achieved, would significantly enhance workers' capabilities.[120] Calling for reform of social protection systems, the Director-General's Decent Work Report noted that in developing countries the problem is an *inadequate* level of protection available to workers, whereas in industrialised developed countries the concern is the *expensive* social protection system that provides extensive protection to workers.[121] The report proposed a flexible social protection framework attuned to the necessities and capacities of individual countries and specific trades, including informal economic activities.[122]

---

114 ibid 14–17.
115 ibid 17–20.
116 Hepple, 'Rights at work' (n 111) 34, 43.
117 ibid 38.
118 ibid 63–67.
119 Ghai, 'Universality and diversity' (n 104) 14–15.
120 ibid 14–15.
121 ILO, *Decent Work* (n 6) 30–32. The report observes that in most developing countries the traditional system of social protection applies to less than 20 per cent of the total workforce; and in sub-Saharan Africa social protection is available to only less than 10 per cent of the population. Additionally, there are persistent problems regarding the implementation of social protection schemes. Such an observation also points towards the inadequacy of the rights-based/resource-specific protection that labour law guarantees without regard to the consequence of such rights or protections. See ibid 32–33.
122 ibid 31–33.

Adopting a pluralistic approach, the report called upon the developing countries to ensure health, safety and insurance against incapacity or death of its workers, and the developed countries to ensure income security for old age and related protections for their workforce.[123] The report noted that *healthcare coverage, unemployment insurance* and *occupational health and safety* are fundamental in allowing workers to enjoy productive employment and decent work.[124] An important aspect of the pluralistic nature of social protection envisaged by the Director-General is social dialogue.[125] The DW Agenda envisages social dialogue as the *modus operandi* in deciding the level and nature of protection that a country can provide.[126] In fact, the pillar of social dialogue runs as a cross-cutting theme through the DW Agenda. Social dialogue is necessary in ensuring productive employment, providing rights at work and deciding the level of social protection.

4.3.1.4 Social dialogue

The idea of social dialogue is not limited to collective bargaining; social dialogue suggests consultation, sharing of information, negotiation and discussion amongst social partners. The pillar of social dialogue, an important constituent of the DW Agenda, provides a mechanism to arrive at a consensus, or at least a compromise, through democratic deliberation between the stakeholders in the world of work.[127] Social dialogue provides a mechanism to balance bargaining power in the market.[128] The ILO has a tripartite constituency – employers, governments and workers. Social dialogue within the organisation engages this tripartite structure in deciding the policies and priorities of the organisation.[129] However, while elaborating upon the social dialogue pillar, the Director-General's report calls upon the member states to engage 'other groups' in addition to employers, governments and workers in policy deliberations and decisions.[130]

The report notes that the ILO would benefit from the contributions of civil society, particularly from groups and people engaged in the informal sector.[131] Thus, the ILO proposes moving beyond the traditional tripartite dialogue process to incorporate newer and diverse stakeholders and social partners. In view of the complexities of the modern world of work, the Director-General's report also calls for innovative trade unionism through the expansion of services rendered by trade unions and through effective collaboration with civil society,[132] something that resonates with the realities of Indian informal workers' organisations

---

123 ibid 32–33, 35–37.
124 ibid 35–37.
125 ibid 31–32.
126 ibid.
127 ibid 38–39.
128 Ghai, 'Universality and diversity' (n 104) 18.
129 ibid 18–19.
130 ILO, *Decent Work* (n 6) 39.
131 ibid 39; Ghai, 'Universality and diversity' (n 104) 19–21.
132 ILO, *Decent Work* (n 6) 41.

(discussed in Chapter 2). The ILO's goal is to facilitate social dialogue through advocating for the social dialogue pillar, strengthening the capacity of social partners, forging links with civil society and showcasing successful social dialogue initiatives.[133]

4.3.2 ILO Declaration on Social Justice for a Fair Globalization and Decent Work 2008

The 2008 ILO Declaration 'imparts legal meaning to the concept of "DW" within the ILO'.[134] Before the 2008 Declaration, the DW Agenda was *only* a policy goal, a principle or an aspirational agenda. At least formally, the 2008 Declaration, by recognising the DW Agenda, gave legal force to the concept. The DW Agenda has now become an expression of commitment shared by the ILO and by governments, workers and employers of the ILO member states. By virtue of being part of the declaration, the ILO member states commit themselves to adhere to both the core and the cash standards as set out in the DW Agenda. It is in this sense that the DW Agenda is an addition and a supplement to the 1998 Declaration.

However, as innovative, influential and politically successful[135] as the DW Agenda may be, doubts have been expressed as to the exact nature of the DW Agenda.[136] Stakeholders are not sure of the substantive contents of the different DW pillars.[137] Existing statistical systems do not provide adequate data through which DW could be empirically measured.[138] All this contributes to the vagueness of the DW Agenda.[139]

Senior ILO officials and policy-makers are themselves not sure of the appropriate import of the DW Agenda.[140] While ILO officials sympathetic to the DW Agenda hold the view that the actual import of the DW Agenda is to be determined by respective member states and societies that are working with the DW Agenda,[141] ILO officials critical of the DW Agenda hold the view that the DW Agenda is, at best, political rhetoric, devoid of any practical meaning.[142]

---

133   ibid 42.
134   Maupain (n 24) 832; Hughes and Haworth, *International Labour Organisation* (n 18) 80.
135   Hughes and Haworth, *International Labour Organisation* (n 18) 30, 84; Rodgers and others, *1919–2009* (n 18) 225–32.
136   See Rodgers and others, *1919–2009* (n 18) 233–35; Fields (n 86) 239.
137   See Rodgers and others (n 18) 233–35; Fields (n 86) 239.
138   See Rodgers and others (n 18).
139   ibid.
140   This observation and the following assertions are based on my interviews with retired and senior ILO officials who were and are directly involved in the policy-making process within the ILO. I had interviewed ILO officials in New Delhi and Geneva from April to October 2011.
141   The 2008 Declaration leaves it to the ILO member states to develop appropriate indicators to determine the substantive import of DW in their countries and, if necessary, seek ILO assistance in this regard. See ILO Declaration on Social Justice 2008 (n 80) para C pt I: Scope and Principles; para A, pt II: Method of Implementation.
142   Interview with senior ILO official at the ILO, Geneva on 10 October 2011.

The official ILO position is that: 'Decent work is not defined in terms of any fixed standard or monetary level. It varies from country to country. But everybody, everywhere, has a sense of what decent work means . . .'[143]

Commentators point out that this flexibility might instigate trade-offs between different DW pillars, which might adversely affect workers' interests. Rodgers and others identify an important conceptual dilemma of the DW Agenda:[144]

> [T]he extent to which there are trade-offs between different DW goals needs to be better explored. . . . [M]ore social protection can be at the expense of employment, if it is not designed with the interrelationships in mind.

Although the DW Agenda suffers from vagueness and allows leeway to member states to determine the nature and scope of protection afforded to workers, the convention-based international labour standards regime is ill-suited for workers engaged in informal economic activities.[145] ILO conventions are primarily targeted towards formal workers employed in an industry. Accordingly, the 1998 Declaration and the DW Agenda allow flexibility for governments of member states to promote informal workers' interests. While this flexibility has the risk of allowing member states to escape responsibility and accountability internationally, such flexibility can be beneficially used by stakeholders in the domestic context of the ILO member states.[146]

In this sense, Sen argues that the DW Agenda signifies the beginning of a truly global approach[147] to labour regulation that concerns people, rather than an international approach that concerns nations.[148] The pillars of the DW Agenda are particularly enabling in the furtherance of improving conditions of informal workers. The DW Agenda encourages informal workers themselves to become active participants in the improvement of their working conditions and living standards.[149] The social dialogue pillar of the DW Agenda envisages participation of stakeholders in the policy-making process, and promotes responsibility and accountability of governments to domestic stakeholders (instead of the international community). Hepple indicates that the framework of rights established through social dialogue is an appropriate substitute for harmonisation of labour law.[150]

---

143 Juan Somavia, 'Decent work in the global economy' Vigyan Bhawan (New Delhi 18 February 2000), available at http://www.ilo.org/public/english/bureau/dgo/speeches/somavia/2000/delhi.htm (last visited 25 March 2012); Rodgers, 'The goal' (n 98) 66–67; Juan Somavia, 'Promoting the MDGs: the role of employment and decent work' (2007) 4 *UN Chronicle* 28 at 30.
144 See Rodgers and others, *1919–2009* (n 18) 234; Rodgers, 'The goal' (n 98) 67.
145 Rodgers and others, *1919–2009* (n 18) 16.
146 See Blackett (n 74) 230, 243–44; Rodgers, 'The goal' (n 98) 67.
147 Sen, 'Work and rights' (n 86) 127. In the same vein, Leah Vosko notes that the DW Agenda opens up a transnational space, which could be beneficially used to challenge the ILO's hegemonic practices. See Vosko (n 68) 20.
148 Sen (n 86) 120, 127–28; Sachs (n 98) 180.
149 Blackett (n 74) 230, 243–44.
150 Hepple, *Labour Laws* (n 25) xii–xiii; Sen, 'Human rights' (n 99) 2925, 2927; Deakin, 'The contribution' (n 41) 172–73.

While the DW Agenda provides a flexible approach that could be beneficial for informal workers, the danger of trade-offs inherent in the Agenda (pointed out by Rodgers and others) could not be totally ignored.[151] However, the DW Agenda has an inbuilt mechanism that restricts the governments of the member states from having a free rein on labour standards. The social dialogue pillar provides for the inbuilt checks and balances system in the DW Agenda.[152] The social dialogue mechanism is capable of determining the content of the otherwise flexible DW Agenda.[153] The social dialogue pillar of the DW Agenda envisages a much broader democratic agenda than the traditional ILO tripartite dialogue process.[154] In the following section, I analyse the social dialogue pillar and ascertain its relevance in enhancing capabilities of informal workers.

4.4 Social dialogue pillar and integrated institutions

The concept of social dialogue is central for the achievement of *decency* in work.[155] Sarosh Kuruvilla asserts that the ILO's conceptualisation of social dialogue is rooted in the traditional bipartite and tripartite frameworks.[156] Kuruvilla identifies four limitations of the social dialogue framework promoted by the ILO. First, he argues that the bipartite and tripartite social dialogue mechanisms exclude all other actors (such as civil society) in the dialogue process except the representatives of employers, employees and the government.[157] Secondly, the collective bargaining envisaged by the ILO might not be able to influence policies at the national political level.[158] Thirdly, a representative focus on social dialogue is a limiting factor because a significant number of workers (and some employers) are never represented in social dialogue mechanisms.[159] Finally, the implied assumption that an employment relationship is necessary for social dialogue to operate excludes workers (mostly informal workers) who do not have an explicit employment relationship.[160]

---

151 Gary S Fields notes that one of the principal operational goals of the DW Agenda needs to be the resolution of the trade-off between quantity and quality of employment by appropriate policy mechanisms. See Fields (n 86) 244–46.
152 ILO, *Decent Work* (n 6) 7.
153 Vosko (n 68) 26.
154 See Maupain (n 24) 835–39.
155 See Jean-Michel Servais, 'Globalization and decent work policy: reflections upon a new legal approach' (2004) 143(1–2) *International Labour Review* 185 at 186; Sen, 'Work and rights' (n 86) 125–26; Sen, 'Human rights' (n 99) 2925, 2927; Tayo Fashoyin, 'Tripartite cooperation, social dialogue and national development' (2004) 143(4) *International Labour Review* 341 at 341–42, 344; Sachs (n 98) 180–81; Rodgers, 'The goal' (n 98) 67; Somavia, 'Promoting the MDGs' (n 143) 30; Guy Standing, *Beyond the New Paternalism: Basic Security as Equality* (London & New York: Verso, 2002) 264.
156 Sarosh Kuruvilla, 'Social dialogue for decent work' in Ghai *Decent Work* (n 104), 175 at 175–80; Fashoyin (n 155) 341, 343–45, 362; Hepple, *Labour Laws* (n 25) 53; 'Perspectives: towards a policy framework for decent work' (2002) 141(1–2) *International Labour Review* 161 at 173.
157 Kuruvilla (n 156) 175–76, 180–83.
158 ibid.
159 ibid.
160 ibid; Cox, 'Labor' (n 18) 422–23.

Although Kuruvilla identifies some limitations with the ILO's social dialogue framework, such as the limited scope of dialogue and the involvement of social partners, he fails to mention some positive aspects of the social dialogue pillar promoted by the ILO. The ILO at least formally recognises some of the problems with the social dialogue concept and seeks to address them. In a leaflet published by the Social Dialogue Sector of the organisation,[161] the ILO identifies the purposes of social dialogue: consultation, negotiation, collective bargaining, employment, equality and inclusion.[162]

Although consultation, negotiation and collective bargaining remain the core of the ILO's conceptualisation of social dialogue, the organisation also envisages equality and inclusion in the dialogue process. Thus, at least formally, the ILO recognises dialogue to be conversation or discourse, which are wider concepts than negotiation or collective bargaining. Moreover, the 1999 report of the Director-General[163] notes that: '[t]he State has an important role in enabling and fostering all forms of social dialogue. It needs to create an affirming environment in which the contributions of employers, workers and other groups are solicited and valued'.[164] Thus, the ILO does recognise the significance of *civil society* and *other groups*[165] as participants in the social dialogue process, in addition to governments, employers and workers. However, at its very core the ILO remains a tripartite organisation.[166]

Although the ILO boasts of its tripartite composition,[167] tripartism is also a weakness of the organisation, especially in the context of informal workers.[168] Informal workers do not fit within the tripartite ILO framework because workers engaged in informal economic activities are mostly unorganised.[169] Because of the ILO's (tripartite) structural limitation, informal workers are not represented in ILO policy-making.[170] Although the organisation is trying to improve this situation by reaching out to NGOs,[171] the constituents of the organisation object to ceding representation space to civil society or NGOs.[172] Workers' and employers' representatives argue that NGOs are non-representative and unaccountable organisations and, therefore, incapable of representing informal workers in the ILO.[173]

161   ILO, *InFocus Programme on Strengthening Social Dialogue* Social Dialogue Sector (Geneva: ILO, undated).
162   ibid; Fashoyin (n 155) 344, 346–47.
163   ILO, *Decent Work* (n 6).
164   ibid 39.
165   ibid 39–40.
166   See ILO, 'Social dialogue' (n 6).
167   See Morse (n 1) 40–41; Hughes and Haworth, *International Labour Organisation* (n 18) xvi, 3, 5, 21–23, 41; Van Daele (n 25) 485–86.
168   See Hepple, *Labour Laws* (n 25) 53–54; Rodgers and others, *1919–2009* (n 18) 17; Van Daele (n 25) 507.
169   See Hepple (n 25) 11, 53; Rodgers and others (n 18).
170   Hepple (n 25); Rodgers and others (n 18).
171   See Rodgers and others (n 18) 17–18.
172   ibid; Standing, 'The ILO' (n 18) 373.
173   Rodgers and others (n 18); Hepple, *Labour Laws* (n 25) 53–54.

As a result of pressure exerted on the ILO by its member states, the 2008 ILO Declaration categorically frames social dialogue as a tripartite affair between the representatives of governments, employers and workers.[174] The ILO website further points out that a social dialogue framework is a country-specific matter and can be either informal or institutional, or a combination of both, which can be practised at the enterprise, regional or national levels.[175] However, in all its versions, it is a process that involves either tripartism or bipartism.[176] Social dialogue, seen in such a way, raises serious problems of participation and democracy amongst the stakeholders related to informal economic activities. To make social dialogue a participatory democratic process for informal workers, it must be envisaged in such a manner that allows participation beyond the tripartite structure and outside the enterprise model.[177] Next, I discuss a multiple (integrated) institutional framework to help achieve this purpose.

4.4.1 Integrated institutions in furthering social dialogue

The ILO has occasionally resorted to ad hoc tripartism-plus social dialogue mechanisms.[178] In its official publications the organisation also showcases successful tripartism-plus social dialogue mechanisms practised in its member states. In one of the ILO publications relating to the InFocus Programme on social dialogue, Lajos Héthy describes the social dialogue process practised in Hungary after its transition from communism to democracy.[179]

The Interest Reconciliation Council (IRC), established by the last communist government, constituted the country's tripartite framework, wherein workers, employers and the government would discuss and negotiate labour relations, drafts of labour laws and other economic and social issues of national significance.[180] However, Héthy notes that after 1998 the tripartite dialogue mechanism has increasingly failed to represent the diversity of interests that exist in Hungary in the post-communist era.[181]

Accordingly, during this time the socialist-liberal government of the country began conducting a wide range of informal consultations outside the tripartite framework.[182] A wide range of participants was consulted in the informal dialogue process, which included the Council for the Elderly, the Council for Children

---

174 ILO Declaration on Social Justice (n 80) preface, preamble and para A (iii) pt I: Scope and Principles.
175 ILO, 'Social dialogue' (n 6).
176 ibid.
177 Servais (n 155) 186.
178 See Vosko (n 68) 24, 34–36, 38–39.
179 L Héthy, *Hungary: Social Dialogue Within and Outside of the Framework of Tripartism* InFocus programme on strengthening social dialogue WP 4 (Geneva: ILO, 2000).
180 ibid 2, 9.
181 ibid 1, 17–18.
182 ibid 18–20.

and Young People,[183] a Social Council,[184] groups of differently abled people, unemployed persons' groups and women's organisations etc.[185] The tripartite-plus consultation complemented the existing tripartite dialogue mechanism.[186] In recent decades, the government of the country has established new institutions to provide tripartism-plus dialogue processes.[187]

Tripartism-plus initiatives for social dialogue together with collective action are increasingly practised in other parts of Europe too. European trade unions are building alliances with NGOs and community organisations in the furtherance of atypical workers' interests.[188] French trade unions collaborated with NGOs and student organisations in their campaign against the government.[189] Likewise, trade unions in the Netherlands, the UK and Germany are engaging with NGOs and community organisations in their struggle for workers' interests.[190] Outside Europe, the tripartism-plus social dialogue mechanism is practised in Panama, for example.[191]

However, the informal tripartism-plus-discussions approach drew accusations of being undemocratic and non-representative, because the entities involved in the process were not always public or democratic in nature.[192] While it may be true that private groups such as the NGOs and other community organisations may not be democratic in character, it is also true that some of these groups do actually represent substantial numbers of workers (mainly informal or atypical) that remain outside the tripartite (or bipartite) social dialogue process.[193] It is also widely observed that the trade unions, in their present disposition, do not represent a large section of informal workers.[194] In the absence of a tripartism-plus social dialogue process, the interests of these informal workers are never adequately represented in policy circles.

Such non-representation in policy formulation not only goes against the democratic ethos of industrial (production) relations, but it seriously and perpetually hinders development and equality of the capabilities of workers engaged in the

---

183 Interestingly enough these councils were set up and chaired by the Prime Minister of Hungary. See Héthy (n 179) 20.

184 The Social Council is operated by the Ministry of Public Welfare. See Héthy (n 179) 20.

185 ibid 20.

186 ibid 18–20.

187 ibid 22–23.

188 Rebecca Gumbrell-McCormick, 'European trade unions and "atypical" workers' (2011) 42(3) *Industrial Relations Journal* 293 at 305.

189 ibid.

190 ibid 305–307.

191 Fashoyin (n 155) 357–60.

192 See Gumbrell-McCormick (n 188) 293–310; Héthy (n 179); ICFTU, *Building Workers' Human Rights into the Global Trading System* (Geneva: ICFTU, 1999); Natacha David, *Worlds Apart: Women and the Global Economy* (Geneva: ICFTU, 1996).

193 The Self Employed Women's Association (SEWA) in India has 1,256,944 members (2009 membership) across India. See http://www.sewa.org/ (last visited 20 May 2012); The Chintan Environmental Research and Action Group, available at http://www.chintan-india.org/ (last visited 20 May 2012); Kagad Kach Patra Kashtakari Panchayat (KKPKP), available at http://www.wastepickerscollective.org/ (last visited 20 May 2012).

194 Fashoyin (n 155) 361–62, 365–66.

economy. Enhancement of capability for workers entails that workers are free to be (or to do) what they choose to be (or to do). Capability enhancement would therefore require that appropriate circumstances are created so that workers can exercise their choices. Thus, any mechanism proposing to enhance capabilities for informal workers (or, for that matter, for all workers) should allow participation by the workers at various levels of dialogue. Hence, it is not surprising that Hepple advocates 'a wide range of methods of participation including consultation rights' for workers.[195] It is because of the connection between development of capabilities and social dialogue that Sen holds *democratic participation* central to his idea of enhancement of capabilities.[196]

Democratic participation in the social dialogue process must be actual, rather than formal. An actual social dialogue process in the world of work needs to take account of all stakeholders involved.[197] What this would mean in the context of informal economic activities is that all informal workers, irrespective of their employment status or union membership, must be part of the social dialogue process. This is merely the minimum requirement for a successful social dialogue process for informal economic activities. Social dialogue for informal economic activities also needs to involve a plethora of other social actors in the dialogue process.[198]

Realising that for informal workers there are serious problems of participation in social dialogue through the tripartite framework, the 1999 ILO report calls upon the state to take a central role in facilitating social dialogue.[199] It is not clear from the ILO report whether the term 'state' is used as synonymous with government. However, state means more than the government – government is only a part of the state.[200] On the other hand, civil society includes more groups than simply trade unions. Based on Drèze and Sen's reflection, as I discussed in Chapter 3, a democratic society would consist of the institutions of government, council of ministers, Members of Parliament and legislative assemblies, judiciary, legislature, opposition parties, media, political parties, law enforcement machinery, trade unions and NGOs.[201]

While some of these institutions are part of the state, others are institutions that interact with state institutions. It is important to note that these institutions of a democratic society exercise countervailing power over each other, thereby balancing the state machinery in a democratic polity. In the tripartism-plus experience in Hungary, the government takes a proactive role in identifying and incorporating a variety of representative bodies in the social dialogue framework.

195 Bob Hepple, 'The future of labour law' (1995) 24(4) *Industrial Law Journal* 303 at 321; Servais (n 155) 188; Fashoyin (n 155) 362, 365–68.

196 Amartya Sen, *Development as Freedom* (New York: Alfred A. Knopf, 1999) 148, 152–59; Amartya Sen, *The Idea of Justice* (Cambridge, MA: Harvard University Press, 2009) 327, 335–37, 345–48.

197 See Servais (n 155) 189, 196.

198 ibid 189–91, 202–204.

199 ILO, *Decent Work* (n 6) 39.

200 See Jean Drèze, Amartya Sen, *India Development and Participation* (New Delhi: Oxford University Press, 2002) 20. I have discussed this aspect in ch 3.

201 ibid.

The focus in the Hungarian example is on representative bodies. Since informal workers are not always part of a representative body, the challenge remains as to how to integrate unorganised informal workers into the social dialogue process. I address this issue in the next section.

4.4.2 Social dialogue for unorganised informal workers

As noted earlier, there are problems with social dialogue for informal economic activities if only representative bodies (such as trade unions or NGOs) are allowed to become part of the social dialogue framework. A significant number of informal workers (either because of the nature of their activities, or because of their ignorance) are not part of a group or organisation. If social dialogue were to be the prerogative only of representative bodies, informal workers without representation would be excluded from such frameworks. Thus, to formulate a successful social dialogue framework, the idea of representation needs rethinking.

In an ideal situation, informal workers should participate in the social dialogue process through their membership-based representative organisation. No other representation mechanism could, perhaps, substitute representation through a membership-based organisation. However, in the absence of membership-based organisations of informal workers, I propose an alternative mechanism for integrating informal workers into the social dialogue process. I propose this mechanism as an alternative to, but not as a substitute for, membership-based organisations of informal workers.

Although informal workers (mostly self-employed informal workers) are outside the trade union-based representative system, they are not outside the economy or society. These workers extensively take part in the socio-economic-political life of the community. As part of their regular day-to-day activities, informal workers interact with a number of different institutions in a democratic society. Some of the institutions of a democratic society with which informal workers are in regular interaction are law enforcement officials, media, local politicians, local administration (of a municipality etc) and NGOs. Many of these institutions could be of vital importance in reaching out to informal workers who do not have appropriate representation.

Thus, in situations of non-representation and under-representation of informal workers in the social dialogue framework, the *integrated institutions*[202] of the democratic society should be brought into action. Governments and legislature(s) need to involve any or all institutions in the social dialogue process that have an interface with informal workers.[203] In India, there have been at least two instances

---

202 Integrated institutions mean multiple institutions that constitute a democratic society. A democratic society includes a government, and many more institutions such as political parties, opposition, media, judiciary and NGOs. See Sen, *Development* (n 196) xii–xiii; John Alexander, *Capabilities and Social Justice: the Political Philosophy of Amartya Sen and Martha Nussbaum* (Farnham & Burlington: Ashgate, 2008) 457.

203 See Servais (n 155) 191.

where university professors have organised informal workers.[204] Accordingly, universities or research institutions could also be thought of as social partners in the dialogue process.

Law enforcement officials are sometimes the source of harassment and threat for informal workers.[205] However, as I will discuss in Chapters 6 and 7, there is immense potential for law enforcement officials to become partners of informal workers in the social dialogue process. For this potential to be realised it might, however, require some legislative initiatives to ensure that work by informal workers is not criminalised or ethically degraded. Then there are NGOs who work with one group of informal workers or another in different dimensions: NGOs working with the homeless necessarily work with rickshaw-pullers or waste pickers; NGOs working with children necessarily work with child labour in street vending; NGOs working with environmental issues interface with waste pickers. Moreover, informal workers are participants in the political process of the democratic polity – they regularly interact with local politicians and administrators. Thus, although informal workers may not be organised in the traditional sense, they could be effectively reached through proactive policies because these workers are not hidden from the economy or the polity.

The state needs to institute a policy, backed up by legislative guarantees, that facilitates social dialogue amongst all stakeholders engaged in informal economic activities. Such legislative guarantees should enable any institution of a democratic society to initiate and promote social dialogue, provided that the interests of the informal workers are involved.

Integrated institutions, such as NGOs, the media, Members of Parliament, Members of the Legislative Assembly, local politicians, or activists, including university professors, can exert pressure on the government of the day to engage in the dialogue process with an open mind and with a view to providing entitlements to workers. It can be a complex process that needs subtle planning and honest execution. However, if an effective social dialogue mechanism involving informal workers is to be achieved, such a framework needs to be a legally guaranteed, broad-based one. Accordingly, labour law for informal economic activities needs to emanate from the broad-based social dialogue process involving integrated institutions capable of promoting capabilities of informal workers, something that I discuss in subsequent chapters.

What are the substantive aspects of an effective legally guaranteed social dialogue process? Or, to put it slightly differently, what must be the subject-matter of the dialogue process? As I have pointed out earlier, social dialogue involving informal economic activities needs to take place at different levels. At the first level, dialogue should aim to find out what informal workers want, which means that members of integrated institutions should interrogate the valuable capabilities of informal

---

204   The KKPKP in Pune organised waste pickers, and the BPSSS in Kolkata organised waste pickers.
205   Almost all waste pickers I interviewed in Kolkata either had had an unpleasant experience with law enforcement officials, or were apprehensive of the role of these officials. Informal workers identify police as responsible for much of their harassment and eviction.

workers, ie what do informal workers want to do or to be? Once the valuable capabilities of informal workers are identified, the next level of dialogue needs to consider how informal workers can be enabled to achieve the identified capabilities. This level would require appropriate institutional frameworks that ensure social, economic, political and cultural circumstances aimed at helping convert characteristics into capabilities for workers.[206]

In Chapter 5, I will chart a labour law framework for the informal economic activity of waste picking, using the background of social dialogue and conceptualising capabilities within the *space* of *participants in the system of cooperative production*.[207] I will use the informal economic activity of waste picking to demonstrate the nature of a new labour law, because waste picking is one of the most marginalised of all informal economic activities. It is also performed at the edges of legality. It is generally undertaken by the most unskilled of all workers and is mostly devoid of any choice on the part of the workers. Therefore, if a new labour law framework could be conceptualised for waste pickers, it is possible that such a framework might work for other informal workers too.

Chapter 6 is based on my fieldwork on waste pickers, conducted during the months of March 2011 to July 2011 in Kolkata (Calcutta) in India. Before moving on to that chapter it is necessary to determine an analytical framework with reference to which the case study will be analysed. There are two frameworks through which my case study of waste pickers could be analysed within the scope of my overall study: the analytical framework of the DW Agenda and the capability approach framework. I discuss the efficacy of each of these frameworks in the following section.

4.5 Choice of framework for the analysis of work-lives of waste pickers in Kolkata: Decent Work Agenda or the capability approach framework

The DW Agenda is set at a highly ambitious conceptual level of productive employment, rights at work, social protection and social dialogue. Accordingly, an analysis of decent work deficit needs to determine the deficit in terms of these DW pillars. The informal activity of waste picking, on the other hand, is one of the most precarious and exploitative of all economic activities.

Waste pickers are the most vulnerable of all workers; waste picking is a matter of subsistence for these workers. Therefore, the DW pillars, as they are articulated at the conceptual level, are a real stretch for waste pickers. The productive nature of employment, the rights available at the workplace or the social protection arising

---

206 Sen, *Development* (n 196) 74; Amartya Sen, 'Capability and well-being' in Martha Nussbaum, Amartya Sen (eds), *The Quality of Life* (Oxford: Oxford University Press, 1993) 30 at 44; Jude Browne, Simon Deakin and Frank Wilkinson, 'Capabilities, social rights and European market integration' in Robert Salais, Robert Villeneuve (eds), *Europe and the Politics of Capabilities* (Cambridge: Cambridge University Press, 2004) 211.

207 Elizabeth S Anderson, 'What is the point of equality?' (1999) 109(2) *Ethics* 287 at 317–18.

from their status as workers are a far cry in concrete terms for waste pickers. Concerns at the level of informal economic activities such as waste picking relate more to basic capabilities and resources, rather than pillars associated with the DW Agenda.

As I have discussed earlier in this chapter, the DW Agenda is a highly flexible agenda, capable of many interpretations. Similarly, the capability approach is also a flexible concept (as discussed in Chapter 3). The objective of the DW Agenda is to promote 'people's well-being'.[208] DW 'can pave the way for broader social and economic advancement, strengthening individuals, their families and communities'.[209] The agenda seeks to further 'aspirations of people in their working lives'.[210] The capability approach, on the other hand, provides a sophisticated understanding of individual wellbeing and agency.[211]

According to Sen, individual development and wellbeing could be measured in terms of actual freedom that an individual has to choose the kind of life she wants to lead.[212] In this sense of individual development, which permeates social, economic and individual advancement (which is also the objective of the DW Agenda), the DW pillars need to promote conditions in which workers can choose the kind of life they want to lead. Since the DW Agenda seeks to further aspirations of people in their working lives, the agenda also furthers the same choice-based normative goal that underlies the capability approach. Therefore, the pillars of the DW Agenda could be seen as the sources of conversion factors,[213] which help convert individual characteristics into capabilities of workers.

However, despite the compatibility of the DW Agenda and the capability approach, the major difference between the two concepts lies in their respective scope. While the normative goal of the DW Agenda is promotion of aspirations of people in their *working lives*, the capability approach seeks to promote capabilities of individuals beyond their working lives. In promoting the aspirations of people, the DW Agenda aims to secure the four pillars in their working lives. The capability approach, on the other hand, takes account of all factors (resources, environment, culture, individual physical features, social conditions and political structure) in promoting individual capabilities. In this comparative backdrop of the two concepts it is useful to take stock of the analytical and measurement indices developed under the two concepts in order to ascertain the appropriate framework for the analysis of working conditions and living standards of waste pickers in India. I begin with the discussion of the DW indicators.

---

208 See ILO, 'Decent work agenda: promoting decent work for all', available at http://www.ilo.org/global/about-the-ilo/decent-work-agenda/lang--en/index.htm (last visited 11 August 2012).
209 ibid.
210 ibid.
211 Sen, *Development* (n 196) 74–75.
212 ibid 18, 74–75.
213 See Amartya Sen, *Commodities and Capabilities* (Amsterdam & New York: North Holland, 1985) 13; Ingrid Robeyns, 'The capability approach: a theoretical survey' (2005) 6(1) *Journal of Human Development* 93 at 99; Sen, *Development* (n 196) 74.

The ILO's DW measurement indicators are divided into groups of main indicators, additional indicators, economic and social context indicators, and legal framework indicators.[214] The list[215] is also open to future indicators to be developed by the ILO.[216] The ILO official list closely resembles the list of indicators developed by Anker and others.[217] The ILO DW index is principally based on rates, ratios and available quantitative data.[218] However, the ILO claims that indicators measuring social dialogue are based on qualitative data and method.[219] However, one fails to understand how indicators such as union density rate, enterprises belonging to employer organisations, collective bargaining coverage rate, number of strikes and lockouts or the rate of days not worked etc,[220] which are all measurements of social dialogue, could qualify to be qualitative indicators! Such emphasis on quantitative indicators also characterises the DW measurement indicators developed by other scholars.[221]

Thus, the ILO's DW measurement indicators suffer from serious shortcomings so far as measuring the aspirations and deprivations of informal workers are concerned. The indicators are primarily based on quantitative data that are officially available. Quantitative measurement of existing data excludes informal workers from its scope because informal workers are not documented in most jurisdictions (as discussed in earlier chapters).

Moreover, a quantitative method forbids a DW Agenda-based analysis of the work-life situation of workers engaged in informal economic activities. Measuring DW only on the basis of quantitative data misses the subtle range of insecurities that creep into everyday work-life experiences of workers. DW measurements are also biased towards formal work relations characterised by employment contracts. Therefore, because of methodological limitations and preconceived biases (towards

---

214   See 'Revised office proposal for the measurement of decent work based on guidance received at the TME on the measurement of decent work' (to be read in conjunction with the Discussion Paper and the detailed comments made by experts as reflected in the chairperson's report), available at http://www.ilo.org/wcmsp5/groups/public/---dgreports/---integration/documents/meetingdocument/wcms_115402.pdf (last visited 19 November 2011).

215   ibid. Some of the indicators in the ILO list are: employment-to-population ratio; unemployment rate; unemployment insurance; low pay rate; statutory minimum wage; child labour; occupational segregation by sex; anti-discrimination law based on sex of worker; occupational injury rate; union density rate etc.

216   ibid.

217   See Richard Anker and others, 'Measuring decent work with statistical indicators' (2003) 142(2) *International Labour Review* 147 at 151–52.

218   ibid 154–68.

219   See ILO, 'Measurement of decent work' Discussion Paper for the Tripartite Meeting of Experts on the Measurement of Decent Work (8–10 September 2008) TMEMDW/2008 at para 12 at 4 (Geneva: ILO, 2008), available at http://www.ilo.org/wcmsp5/groups/public/---dgreports/---stat/documents/meetingdocument/wcms_100335.pdf (last visited 19 November 2011).

220   See 'Revised office proposal' (n 214) 3.

221   Florence Bonnet, Jose B Figueiredo and Guy Standing, 'A family of decent work indexes' (2003) 142(2) *International Labour Review* 213; Guy Standing, 'From people's security surveys to a decent work index' (2002) 141(4) *International Labour Review* 441.

employment relationship-based work), DW measurement tools would fail to answer questions relevant to informal workers, such as what conditions necessitated a waste picker (informal worker) to resort to his present work, or what are the problems associated with work-site access for waste pickers. The quantitative method is designed to answer questions such as how many waste pickers there are in a country, or how many government schemes are applicable to waste pickers.

However, the Chairperson's Report on the Tripartite Meeting of Experts on the Measurement of Decent Work in 2008 specifies that the ILO DW index needs to be read along with the Discussion Paper prepared for the Tripartite Meeting.[222] The Discussion Paper provides *inter alia* that, apart from work and workplace-related indicators, the DW Agenda must be concerned with income, medical care, nutrition, housing, child welfare, education, recreation, culture and overall development-related indicators.[223] These indicators, along with other strictly work-related indicators (discussed above), shift the focus of the DW Agenda from a work-centred strategic concept to a developmental policy mechanism.

With this shift from a strictly work-related concept to a development paradigm, the DW Agenda moves closer to the capability approach. According to the ILO, labour productivity, inflation, education and income inequality are all part of the DW indicators.[224] These indicators would reflect wage increases, capability promotion, enterprise development and economic growth of a society.[225] The above-mentioned indicators could very well be part of the capability approach if those promote individual capabilities. In fact, the United Nations Development Programme's (UNDP) Human Development Index, which is based on the capability approach, evaluates country-level human development in terms of some of the indicators, such as education and income pointed out by the ILO.[226]

Many of the criticisms levelled against the different indicators seeking to measure DW could also be levelled against the UNDP's Human Development Indicators. The Human Development Index is primarily based on four indicators: *life expectancy at birth*, *mean years of schooling*, *expected years of schooling* and *gross national income per capita*.[227] Thus, the Human Development Index too is based on quantitative indicators for the purpose of country-level comparisons of human development.[228]

---

222 ILO, Tripartite Meeting of Experts (n 219) 28 (Appendix 1), available at http://www.ilo.org/wcmsp5/groups/public/---dgreports/---integration/documents/meetingdocument/wcms_099764.pdf (last visited 19 November 2011); ILO, 'Measurement of decent work' (n 219).

223 ILO, 'Measurement of decent work' (n 219) 9–10.

224 ibid 10.

225 ibid. Also see Iftikhar Ahmed, 'Decent work and human development' (2003) 142(2) *International Labour Review* 263.

226 See UNDP, 'Human Development Index', available at http://hdr.undp.org/en/statistics/hdi/ (last visited 11 August 2012).

227 ibid; Mark McGillivray, Howard White, 'Measuring development? The UNDP's Human Development Index' (1993) 5(2) *Journal of International Development* 183.

228 Commentators who criticise the Human Development Index as incomplete also offer quantitative indicators for a more comprehensive country-level analysis of human development. See Gustav Ranis, Frances Stewart and Emma Samman, 'Human development: beyond the Human Development Index' (2006) 7(3) *Journal of Human Development* 323 at 333–42; Linda Low, T C Aw

Although the indicators constituting the Human Development Index have undergone substantial evolution since its birth, many of the principal indicators remain unchanged.[229] However, the purpose of the Human Development Index is to compare countries on the basis of development that is not limited to economic or income measures only.[230] As shorthand for such a comparison the UNDP employs quantitative indicators, where choice of indicators is sometimes constrained by the availability of data across countries.[231]

Since the purpose of the Human Development Index is a comparison between countries, the constitutive indicators need to be quantitative because of data availability and for better comparison. Similarly, for a country-level comparison of the DW Agenda, it might be useful to devise quantitative indicators to measure DW. However, quantitative indicators are inadequate to measure work-life deprivations of informal workers. Accordingly, for a micro-level evaluation of capability deprivation in waste pickers' work-lives in India, existing quantitative indicators developed both under the DW Agenda and the capability approach discussed above are inadequate.[232]

However, it would be a mistake to conflate ideas with indicators.[233] Although existing indicators are inadequate for a micro-level analysis of waste picking, the ideas – the capability approach and the DW Agenda – could very well provide the evaluative basis of waste pickers' work-lives. By work-life I mean the intertwined nature of informal workers' work and their family lives and the related situation of physical proximity of their work and their slums. For informal workers, their work-life situation needs to be analysed in order to form a clear idea of their deprivations.[234] The everyday balance between work and family lives constitutes the overall experience of informal workers. It is difficult neatly to conceive of the working lives of informal workers as distinct from their family lives. There is also a merger between their worksites and their homes; informal workers such as waste

'The Human Development Index revisited' (1997) *Singapore Management Review* 1; Farhad Noorbakhsh, 'The Human Development Index: some technical issues and alternative indices' (1998) 10 *Journal of International Development* 589; Bojana Radovanovic, 'The Human Development Index as a measure of human development' (2011) *FilozofijaiDrustvo* 193 at 201–202.

229 See Low and Aw (n 228) 2, 5–6; Radovanovic (n 228) 199–200. For a current list of human development indicators see UNDP, 'International Human Development Indicators', available at http://hdrstats.undp.org/en/indicators/default.html (last visited 11 August) 2012.

230 See Ranis, Stewart and Samman (n 228) 324; Radovanovic (n 228).

231 See Ranis, Stewart and Samman (n 228) 324, 328–30, 333–42; Radovanovic (n 228) 205.

232 A note is in order here. The Human Development Index does not envisage evaluating informal economic activities, which is my concern in this study. Therefore, it would be wrong to assume that the human development indicators could offer indicators for the analysis of the informal economic activity of waste picking. On the other hand, DW indicators are devised *inter alia* for the purpose of the analysis of informal economic activities. However, as I argue, while the DW indicators might be able to compare decency of work amongst countries, such indicators are inadequate for a micro-level analysis of work-lives of informal workers.

233 See Ranis, Stewart and Samman (n 228); Radovanovic (n 228).

234 Elizabeth Hill, *Worker Identity, Agency and Economic Development: Women's Empowerment in the Indian Informal Economy* (London & New York: Routledge, 2010) 3–5.

pickers effectively use their homes in furtherance of their work.[235] Noting the convergence of informal workers' work and their living,[236] Kalyan Sanyal and Rajesh Bhattacharya observe:

> Slums are more than poor people's settlements – each slum literally is a production hub by itself. . . . The convergence of the home and the workshop takes place at the level of entire 'townships' which is what the mega-slums already are in urban metropolises. . . . [Slums] can function both as the site of production of commodities and reproduction of life. [citation omitted][237]

In similar vein, for the informal activity of waste picking, work experience and life experience cannot be distinguished in a categorical manner.[238] Their work and their lives are woven in a seamless web.[239] Working conditions and living situations overlap each other – they work in close proximity to their slums.[240] They have to balance their family responsibilities with their work obligations simultaneously.[241] They work from home while managing family responsibilities; and they care for their families even while working outside the home.[242]

235 See Bhat (n 8) 47–58; Poornima Chikarmane, Lakshmi Narayan, *Rising from the Waste: Organising Wastepickers in India, Thailand and the Philippines* (Bangkok: Committee for Asian Women, 2009) 13, 17, 26.

236 See Kalyan Sanyal, Rajesh Bhattacharya, 'Beyond the factory: globalization, informalization of production and the changing locations of labour' in Paul Bowles, John Harriss (eds), *Globalization and Labour in China and India: Impacts and Responses* (New York: Palgrave Macmillan, 2010) 151 at 160–63.

237 ibid 162–63. For an account of the significance of slums for waste pickers, especially as a storage and sorting place, see Bhat (n 8) 52; Kaveri Gill, *Of Poverty and Plastic: Scavenging and Scrap Trading Entrepreneurs in India's Urban Informal Economy* (New Delhi: Oxford University Press, 2010) 99–100, 138–39.

238 This is something that I had observed during my fieldwork in Kolkata, India, from March to July 2011. While I will document my fieldwork in ch 6, this is a good opportunity to note the work-life relation of waste pickers. See also Martin Medina, 'Waste pickers cooperatives in developing countries' (Paper prepared for WIEGO/Cornell/SEWA Conference on Membership-based Organizations of the poor, Ahmedabad, India, January 2005) 1–36, available at http://wiego.org/publications/waste picker-cooperatives-developing-countries (last visited 18 May 2012); Marijk Huysman, 'Waste picking as a survival strategy for women in Indian cities' (1994) 6(2) *Environment and Urbanization* 155.

239 Huysman (n 238) 159, 169.

240 David C Wilson, Costas Velis and Chris Cheeseman, 'Role of informal sector recycling in waste management in developing countries' (2006) 30 *Habitat International* 797 at 803; Michael Yhdego, 'Scavenging solid wastes in Dar es Salaam, Tanzania' (1991) 9 *Waste Management and Research* 259 at 263; Daniel T Sicular, 'Pockets of peasants in Indonesian cities: the case of scavengers' (1991) 19(2/3) *World Development* 137 at 143, 145, 153; Poornima Chikarmane, Medha Deshpande and Lakshmi Narayan, 'Untitled' 13, 17, 27, available at http://ilo-mirror.library.cornell.edu/public/english/region/asro/newdelhi/download/puneabst.pdf (last visited 20 May 2012).

241 See Bhat (n 8) 47–58; Chikarmane and Narayan, *Rising from the Waste* (n 235) 32; Huysman (n 238) 157, 159, 161, 163, 165–66, 168, 170; Sicular (n 240) 147, 153; Chikarmane, Deshpande and Narayan (n 240) 16.

242 Ela Bhat provides a fascinating account of waste pickers' work-life experiences: A rag picker's day begins at the crack of dawn. She picks up her large *thela* and sets off on her daily beat, her

Considering the juxtaposition of work experiences and life experiences of waste pickers, the capability approach provides a suitable framework for a capability-based development analysis. Instead of a narrower work-based analysis envisaged by the DW Agenda, it would be far more useful to analyse capability deprivation of these waste pickers. The decent work deficit is principally an analysis of work-related aspects, whereas capability deficiency is a larger concept encompassing any aspect of a person's life that is considered valuable by that person. Although the present study is principally concerned with work and workers, the nature of the informal work of waste picking makes it necessary to go beyond the limited notion of work and take work-life as the term of reference. The capability framework helps in the identification of functionings attained by waste pickers. Functionings go on to point out the capability deprivation of the waste pickers, which in turn helps in identifying resources that are required for the promotion of capabilities of such workers.

Functioning deficiencies and capability deprivations of waste pickers (or informal workers in general) result from the absence of resources (and thereby, conversion factors) that go beyond the four pillars identified by the DW Agenda. For example, lack of *basic education* and *cultural mindset* (of not showing any particular urge to send children to school, even if such schooling is accessible) substantially limit the choice of a worker to decide the kind of work she wants to do (or lead the kind of life she prefers). Under such circumstances, a capability (deprivation) analysis would be helpful in identifying the capability-inhibiting factors (resources, such as availability of primary education, or cultural awareness initiatives) that are not necessarily limited to the right to association, safety at work or unemployment insurance etc. The capability framework helps in moving beyond the limited notion of work and the workplace and helps conceptualise work in the larger context of work-lives.

In view of some of the myriad forms of unfreedoms encountered by informal workers it is necessary to undertake a qualitative method-based analysis of their work-lives so that their lived experiences can form the basis of such analysis. Although it is possible to develop a qualitative method-based analysis of DW for informal economic activities, it is more useful to employ the capability framework in such analysis for the reasons discussed above. Qualitative methods are perfectly suited for a choice-based development analysis, which is the crux of the capability

---

quick, trained eyes scouring the roads and sidewalks for marketable waste. She bends to pick it up with her right hand and drops it in the *thela* hanging over her left shoulder. She walks, she sees, she bends, she picks, she throws in her bag and walks on. She is home by nine o'clock in the morning, just as the morning rush begins. She quickly cooks lunch, feeds the family, and returns to the streets once again. At midday, she spreads the collection on the floor, sorts the various items into separate bags, and delivers the haul to a dealer. The dealer gives her cash – the price for each of the various categories she collects is different. . . . Back home, she lifts her *thela* and is off on her beat once again. She is home before dark. On the way home, she buys groceries for the evening meal from the cash she earned that day – flour, rice, salt, onions and a few spoonfuls of oil. She cooks the supper, feeds her family the evening meal and, if she is not too tired, she will sort the waste collected in the afternoon. If there is some water left over in the bucket, she will take a bath and then go to sleep. See Bhat (n 8) 47–48.

approach.[243] There are two manners in which capability deprivation of waste pickers could be analysed: tracing deprivation of capabilities by analysing achieved functionings and directly identifying deprivation of capabilities. The relation between capabilities and functionings can sometimes be confusing. Capability means freedom to choose, while functionings signify the actual achievements of individuals.

Functionings could be valuable resources available to an individual to exercise her capabilities. Functionings attained at one level can act as a conversion factor at another level. For example, education is an extremely valuable functioning, important by itself (ie promotes intrinsic freedom). Education, on the other hand, is also an immensely important conversion factor (ie promotes instrumental freedom) for the attainment of other functionings. In the context of the present analysis, education, a functioning, is also a resource which expands capabilities of workers by enabling them to decide whether they want to work as an office clerk or labourer, or they would prefer to work as a waste picker (both of these professional attainments are also functionings).

Thus, there are two levels at which development of waste pickers in terms of freedom could be examined. First, by analysing their achieved functionings, waste pickers' capabilities could be traced back.[244] This method is easier because achieved functionings could actually be observed by a researcher, whose findings could then be linked to possible capability sets available to waste pickers. Secondly, a more difficult approach, capabilities of waste pickers could be directly analysed through probing questions about their choices in their work-lives.[245]

The problem with the second approach is that there is no tangible evidence for a researcher to observe. A researcher would have to depend totally on the version expressed by research participants. Such interpretative dependence might not be a problem for other kinds of research, but for capability analysis it would be a problem because the researcher needs to know the set of choices available to her participants. In a direct analysis of capability deprivation, a researcher would have to depend on the participant's understanding of alternative capability sets from which the participant has chosen the present functioning set.[246]

Most of the empirical research conducted within the capability framework has analysed achieved functionings as a proxy to capability achievement.[247] To a great extent, this is a result of the complications associated with direct analysis of available capability – practicality and data availability are reasons why most researchers

---

243 For a discussion on the usefulness of qualitative methods in poverty and capability development analysis of informal workers in India see Jan Breman, *The Making and Unmaking of an Industrial Working Class: Sliding Down the Labour Hierarchy in Ahmedabad, India* (New Delhi: Oxford University Press, 2004) 271–78.

244 Ruhi Saith, 'Capabilities: the concept and its operationalization' (2001) Working Paper No 66 QEH Working Paper Series (University of Oxford) 1 at 11–12, available at http://www3.qeh. ox.ac.uk/pdf/qehwp/qehwps66.pdf (last visited 11 June 2012).

245 ibid.

246 ibid 12–13.

247 ibid 10, 12, 19–20.

choose to look into achieved functionings in order to identify available capabilities.[248] In an analysis of one of the most precarious forms of informal economic
activity (waste picking) in a developing country context, the difference between
the two approaches (ie functioning analysis and direct capability analysis) is hardly
a matter of concern. Waste pickers in India suffer from educational deprivation,
nutritional deprivation, health deprivation, all basic functionings identified by
capability scholars.[249] It is improbable (if not impossible) to think that if waste
pickers had any *real choice* in their lives they would voluntarily choose to deprive
themselves of these functionings.[250]

Accordingly, in determining capability deficiency in the context of the present
study (of waste pickers), it will be useful to uncover achieved functionings of the
waste pickers in Kolkata, India. Although a functioning analysis is a sufficient
pointer towards capability deprivation of the participant waste pickers in Kolkata,
I also devised some *why* questions to see if they had any choice over their work-
lives. Although some scholars think that probing freedom to choose or *refined
functionings* might not be a meaningful exercise in the context of developing
countries,[251] I undertook such an exercise for the limited purpose of seeing whether
the waste pickers had made *any choice* in their work-lives, however minuscule in
nature, from amongst the narrow range of capability sets available to them.

The guiding questionnaire for the qualitative interviews probes refined
functionings using a two-pronged logic. First, a waste picker's exercise of choice,
howsoever limited in nature, is suggestive of some amount of capability available
to a waste picker.[252] Secondly, it is only when the waste pickers have already
exercised choice in their work-lives that they would be able to identify future
valuable capabilities and functionings. This future orientation, which is more
prescriptive, is an important part of my study's scope.

4.6 Conclusion

In this chapter, I have discussed the shift in the ILO approach from a specific labour
standards-based system to a principle-based framework. I briefly mentioned the
reasons that propelled the ILO to shift its focus from an instrument-based system
to a principle-based system without discarding its standard-setting function.
Recognising that needs and necessities of labour vary globally, first with the 1998
Declaration, and then through its 1999 DW Agenda, the ILO shifted from a
uniform system to a flexible system of operation. Both its 1998 Declaration and
its DW Agenda are devised in such a manner that they allow enough scope to

---

248 ibid 12.
249 ibid 13–22.
250 ibid 13.
251 ibid 28.
252 However surprising it might sound for capability studies, the majority of waste pickers who were
      interviewed did exercise some choice in their work-lives. A significant number of the 75 waste
      pickers interviewed chose to be waste pickers rather than domestic worker, rickshaw-puller or
      construction worker.

address the concerns of formal as well as informal workers. While the pillars of the DW Agenda are flexible enough to allow domestic jurisdictions to decide the nature and extent of protection that could be afforded to workers, the social dialogue pillar of the agenda works as a safety-valve against precarious treatment of workers.

The ILO envisages a tripartite social dialogue framework. However, in the context of informal workers, domestic jurisdictions need to devise a tripartite-plus social dialogue framework. The majority of informal workers are not part of a representative organisation. However, NGOs and a plurality of democratic institutions interact with informal workers at different levels. In order to install a successful framework for the improvement of informal workers, it is incumbent on domestic jurisdictions to include all these diverse bodies (stakeholders) in an institutionalised social dialogue framework.

In this chapter, I have also compared the DW framework with the capability approach in order to select an analytical framework for the analysis of my case study of informal workers in Kolkata, India (Chapter 6). Having compared the two frameworks, I propose to analyse my case study on the basis of the capability approach framework because the capability approach provides an encompassing framework which can be used to analyse the work-life conditions of informal waste pickers in India.

In Chapter 3, I discussed the nuances of the capability approach. The analytical reference point of the capability approach is human development in terms of freedom. According to the capability approach, several institutions of a democratic society should aim at creating conditions in which social, economic, environmental and personal factors can help to convert (social, economic, environmental and personal) characteristics into individual capabilities. Promotion of capabilities is an ongoing process, which requires continuous and effective evaluation of public policies and democratic participation. In the context of informal workers, the ILO envisages participation and involvement of stakeholders through its social dialogue strategy. I contend that in order effectively to integrate informal workers in the social dialogue process, such a process needs to transcend the traditional tripartite framework.

In the next chapter, I offer a theoretical framework through which labour law for informal economic activities could be conceptualised. I invoke the capability approach in order to develop such a framework. Although I use the capability approach – which, as I have argued, extends beyond the scope of work – in invoking it to conceptualise labour law I shall be concerned with only those capabilities that are valuable for informal workers in their working lives. The social dialogue strategy through the involvement of integrated institutions attains centre stage in the labour law framework that I propose. I supplement the capability approach and the social dialogue strategy with other theoretical conceptualisations in order to develop a labour law framework for informal workers.

5 A capability approach to labour law

5.1 Introduction

In Chapter 3, I discussed the human development theory known as the capability approach offered by Amartya Sen. The capability approach emerges as a non-dogmatic approach, which does not dictate a definite goal as an objective of development. The capability approach is also a non-hierarchical theoretical framework in so far as it does not rank specific rights (such as civil-political and socio-economic rights). The capability approach envisages a theoretical framework that promotes a dignified life for individuals in the sense that it enables individuals both to decide what a dignified and meaningful life would mean to them and to pursue such a life.

The capability approach advocates the promotion of social, economic, physical, cultural and environmental factors that can help individuals convert characteristics into capabilities. Democratic dialogue through public participation is central to the capability approach since democratic dialogue provides the mechanism to decide upon the desirable capabilities for a society and determine the necessary factors for the promotion of such capabilities.

The ILO adopts a strategy of democratic dialogue in order to improve the working conditions and living standards of informal workers. In Chapter 4, I discussed how the ILO strategy of social dialogue might promote decent work for informal workers. I argued that, if the social dialogue strategy of the ILO is to be effective for informal workers, it needs to integrate multiple institutions in the sense that Drèze and Sen conceptualise, in the dialogue process (discussed in Chapter 3). Drèze and Sen's concept of integrated institutions is, accordingly, central for a democratically developed framework for the enhancement of capabilities for informal workers.

Developing from my discussions in Chapters 3 and 4, in this chapter I undertake the task of formulating a theoretical approach to labour law to address the problems of informal work and workers. My purpose is to devise an approach to labour law that can improve the conditions of work and living standards of informal workers. As I discussed in earlier chapters, traditionally labour law is based on the juridical concept of employment relationship and one of the central normative goals of labour law is striking a balance in bargaining power between employers and employees.

In this chapter, I advocate a new normative goal, which labour law should pursue in the context of informal economic activities. I also advocate a new juridical basis of labour law that is attuned to informal economic activities. If labour law needs to be sensitive to informal economic activities, its normative focus needs to shift from *balancing bargaining power* to something else that is not based on an a priori assumption of the existence of two entities – employers and employees. Labour law needs to focus somewhere else in order to build a theoretical basis that is attentive to informal economic activities. In this respect the capability approach can provide valuable insights into developing a theoretical basis for labour law.

In imagining labour law for informal economic activities, I invoke the capability approach developed by Amartya Sen and Martha Nussbaum. The capability approach, with its associated concepts, can provide a rich theoretical basis in formulating labour law for informal workers. In this chapter, I chart a capability approach-based theoretical conception to argue for a renewed labour law framework for informal economic activities.

My conceptual initiative draws upon the existing theoretical positions that take the capability approach as their point of departure. Building on the works of Elizabeth Anderson, Amartya Sen and Jean Drèze, I will supplement the capability approach with the concepts of *democratic equality* and *integrated institutions* to develop a capability approach-based labour law. Recently, labour law scholars have shown interest in the capability approach in reconceptualising labour law and I build on their attempts to use the capability approach in order to reconceptualise labour law.[1]

This chapter is divided into six main sections apart from the introduction and the conclusion. In section 5.2 of this chapter, I discuss the traditional basis of labour law that developed in the common law countries, of which India is one. I discuss how far the traditional basis of labour law applies to informal workers. As I discussed in earlier chapters, the heterogeneous informal activities do not always conform to an employment relationship model. Because of this hetero-geneous nature of informal economic activities, labour law that seeks to strike a

---

1 Judy Fudge has specifically titled her article 'Reconceptualizing labour law'. See Judy Fudge, 'Labour as a "fictive commodity": radically reconceptualizing labour law' in Guy Davidov, Brian Langille (eds), *The Idea of Labour Law* (New York: Oxford University Press, 2011) 120. Other scholars who employed the capability approach are Jude Browne, Simon Deakin and Frank Wilkinson, 'Capabilities, social rights and European market integration' in Robert Salais, Robert Villeneuve (eds), *Europe and the Politics of Capabilities* (New York: Cambridge University Press, 2004) 205; Simon Deakin, 'The contribution of labour law to economic and human development' in Langille and Davidov, *The Idea of Labour Law*, (ibid) 156; Brian A Langille, 'Core labour rights: the true story (Reply to Alston)' (2005) 16(3) *European Journal of International Law* 409; Judy Fudge, 'The new discourse of labor rights' (2007) 29 *Comparative Labor Law and Policy Journal* 29; Brian Langille, 'Labour law's theory of justice' in Langille and Davidov, *The Idea of Labour Law* (ibid) 101; Kevin Kolben, 'A development approach to trade and labor regimes' (2010) 45(2) *Wake Forest Law Review* 355; Adelle Blackett, 'Situated reflections on international labour, capabilities, and decent work: the case of centre *Maraicher* Eugène Guinois' (2007) *Revue québécoise de droit international* 223; Adelle Blackett, 'Emancipation in the idea of labour law' in Langille and Davidov, *The Idea of Labour Law* (ibid) 420.

balance of bargaining power between employers and employees remains irrelevant for informal economic activities.

In section 5.3, I briefly review the literature that reconceptualises labour law using the capability approach. The capability approach has lately received attention from labour law scholars who employ it to chart a new normative basis of labour law. While these scholars provide a direction in which labour law can be steered, they have focused on developed industrial economies and not on informal economic activities in developing countries. There are, however, social scientists who are interested in a capability analysis of informal economic activities. In section 5.4 of the chapter, I review some of the literature that analyses informal economic activities from the perspective of the capability approach. Examining specific categories of informal economic activities these scholars show that by making small interventions in the lives of the most marginalised population their capabilities could be substantially enhanced. I draw on the insights from these two streams of literature to discuss a capability approach to labour law for informal workers.

In my attempt to chart a capability approach-based concept of labour law for informal economic activities, in section 5.5 I argue that the normative goal of labour law should be the enhancement and equality of capabilities of workers. Based on the idea of democratic equality offered by Elizabeth Anderson, in section 5.6 I argue that the enhancement and equal distribution of capabilities amongst informal workers is grounded on the idea that these workers are equal participants in a cooperative production process.[2]

In section 5.7 of the chapter I analyse how the concept of integrated institutions might help develop labour law for informal workers. I argue that, in order to develop a democratically grounded labour law framework that engages informal workers themselves in the development of the law, multiple institutions of a democratic society need to be integrated in the law-making process. In this context I discuss how norms for informal economic activities emerge out of different institutions such as family, kinship, caste and neighbourhood. I end this chapter with a brief conclusion.

5.2 Labour law and informal economic activities

Traditionally, the normative goal of labour law has been the protection of workers[3] by equalising their bargaining power with that of employers[4] and the juridical basis

---

2   Elizabeth S Anderson, 'What is the point of equality?' (1999) 109(2) *Ethics* 287 at 317–18, 321–22.

3   Hugo Sinzheimer, 'The development of labour law and the task of legal theory' ('Die Fortentwicklung des Arbeitsrechts und die Aufgabe der Rechtslehre') (1910–11) 20 *Soziale Praxis* 1237 ff, as cited in Bob Hepple, 'Introduction' in Bob Hepple (ed), *The Making of Labour Law in Europe: a Comparative Study of Nine Countries up to 1945* (London: Mansell, 1986) 1 at 8–9; Ruth Dukes, 'Hugo Sinzheimer and the constitutional function of labour law' in Langille and Davidov, *The Idea of Labour Law* (n 1) 57; Thilo Ramm, 'Epilogue: the new ordering of labour law 1918–45' in Hepple, *A Comparative Study of Nine Countries* (n 3) 277 at 278.

4   Otto Kahn-Freund, *Labour and the Law* (2nd edn London: Stevens & Sons, 1972) 1, 4–5, 8–9, 11–15; Guy Davidov, 'The (changing?) idea of labour law' (2007) 146(3–4) *International Labour*

of labour law has been seen as the employment relationship or, more specifically, the employment contract.[5] However, scholars increasingly regard the traditional model of labour law, which seeks to strike a balance of power[6] between employers and employees, as inadequate to deal with modern social, economic and political realities. In fact, Bob Hepple has asked 'Have we reached the "end" of labour law?'[7] As Hepple observes, labour law that is specifically concerned with dependent workers necessarily excludes the independent and self-employed workforce from its purview.[8] This orientation was, however, not perceived to undermine labour law because of the predominant nature of the employer–employee relationship in developed Western societies.[9] In the last two decades, however, the changing nature of work (and employment relationships) and worker protection has challenged the traditional scope of labour law. Labour law scholars are increasingly engaged in the search for new labour law realities.[10]

In the standard employment relationship-based model it is assumed that a worker is employed in a stable employment relationship throughout his life. However, the traditional model of the male breadwinner, working throughout his life for one or two employers in a definite workplace and earning security for

Review 311, 312, 314–15; Manfred Weiss, 'Re-inventing labour law?' in Langille and Davidov, *The Idea of Labour Law* (n 1) 43 at 44; Hepple (n 3) 32; Harry Arthurs, 'Labour law after labour' in Langille and Davidov, *The Idea of Labour Law* (n 1) 13 at 17–18; Dukes (n 3) 60, 63.

5 Kahn-Freund, *Labour and the Law* (n 4) 4, 6; Paul Davies, Mark Freedland, *Labour Law: Text and Materials* (London: Weidenfeld and Nicolson, 1984) 1–2; Arthurs (n 4) 18; Judy Fudge, Eric Tucker and Leah Vosko, *The Legal Concepts of Employment: Marginalizing Workers* (Ottawa, Ontario: Law Commission of Canada, 2002) 1–4, 8–12; Hepple, 'Introduction' (n 3) 11; Simon Deakin, Gillian S Morris, *Labour Law* (4th edn Portland: Hart Publishing, 2005) 1, 4; Sinzheimer, 'The development of labour law' (n 3); Weiss, 'Re-inventing' (n 4) 44–46.

6 Anne Trebilcock, 'Using development approaches to address the challenge of the informal economy for labour law' in Guy Davidov, Brian Langille (eds), *Boundaries and Frontiers of Labour Law* (Oxford: Hart Publishing, 2006) 63 at 63, 66; Davidov, 'The (changing?) idea' (n 4) 312, 314–15.

7 Bob Hepple, 'The future of labour law' (1995) 24(4) *Industrial Law Journal* 303.

8 Hepple, 'Introduction' (n 3) 11.

9 See Adrian Goldin, 'Global conceptualizations and local constructions of the idea of labour law' in Langille and Davidov, *The Idea of Labour Law* (n 1) 69 at 75–76. Goldin notes that, although atypical and informal workers always existed alongside formal subordinated employees, because of the predominant nature of dependent employment labour law has historically ignored atypical workers.

10 Recently 29 scholars from around the globe published their essays in a collected volume called *The Idea of Labour Law*, in their quest to find new ideas of labour law. See Langille and Davidov, *The Idea of Labour Law* (n 1); Hepple, 'Future of labour law' (n 7); Bob Hepple, *Labour Laws and Global Trade* (Oxford: Hart Publishing, 2005); Alain Supiot and others, *Beyond Employment Changes in Work and the Future of Labour Law in Europe* (New York: Oxford University Press, 2001); Richard Mitchell (ed), *Redefining Labour Law: New Perspectives on the Future of Teaching and Research*, University of Melbourne Law School, Occasional Monograph Series No 3 (Melbourne: Centre for Employment and Labour Relations Law, 1995); Joanne Conaghan, Richard Michael Fischl and Karl Klare (eds), *Labour Law in an Era of Globalization: Transformative Practices and Possibilities* (Oxford & New York: Oxford University Press, 2002); Catherine Barnard, Simon Deakin and Gillian Morris (eds), *The Future of Labour Law: Liber amicorum Sir Bob Hepple QC* (Portland, OR: Hart Publishing, 2004); Katherine V W Stone, *From Widgets to Digits: Employment Regulation for the Changing*

his family,[11] is increasingly giving way to non-standard work, the feminisation of the workforce,[12] insecurity at work and unemployment.[13] Because of these challenges scholars are reconceptualising labour law.[14] What has been absent in the reconceptualisation,[15] and generally from the labour law narrative, is the perspective of developing countries on labour protection.[16]

It is only recently that the protection of workers in developing countries has received attention.[17] Such attention is inevitable because globalisation has induced integration of domestic markets with the larger world market. Workers engaged in outsourced and sub-contracted activities, informal wage earners and self-employed workers in developing countries are now part of the larger world market and are vulnerable because of the nature of their work and the absence of any

Workplace (New York: Cambridge University Press, 2004); Hugh Collins, 'Justifications and techniques of legal regulation of the employment relation' in Hugh Collins, M Davies and Roger Rideout (eds), *Legal Regulation of the Employment Relation* (London: Kluwer Law International, 2003) 3; Brian Langille, 'Labour law's back pages' in Davidov and Langille (eds), *Boundaries and Frontiers* (n 6) 13; Alan Hyde, 'What is labour law?' in Davidov and Langille (eds), *Boundaries and Frontiers* (ibid) 37; Christopher Arup and others (eds), *Labour Law and Labour Market Regulation: Essays on the Construction, Constitution and Regulation of Labour Markets* (Sydney: Federation Press, 2006); Horacio Spector, 'Philosophical foundations of labor law' (2006) 33 *Florida State University Law Review* 1119; Davidov, 'The (changing?) idea' (n 4); Ruth Dukes, 'Constitutionalizing employment relations: Sinzheimer, Kahn-Freund, and the role of labour law' (2008) 35 *Journal of Law and Society* 341.

11   Weiss, 'Re-inventing' (n 4) 45–47; Alan Hyde, 'The idea of the idea of labour law: a parable' in Langille and Davidov, *The Idea of Labour Law* (n 1) 88; Tzehainesh Tekle, 'Labour law and worker protection in the south: an evolving tension between models and reality' in Tzehainesh Tekle (ed), *Labour Law and Worker Protection in Developing Countries* (Oxford and Portland, OR: Hart; Geneva: ILO, 2010) 3 3–4; Supiot and others, *Beyond Employment* (n 10) 24–25, 52.

12   I use the term feminisation to suggest an exponential increase of women in the workforce and the degradation of conditions in previously male-dominated work, in the sense used by Lourdes Beneria. See Lourdes Beneria, *Changing Employment Patterns and the Informalization of Jobs: General Trends and Gender Dimensions* (Geneva: ILO, 2001) 1; Richard Anker, *Gender and Jobs: Sex Segregation of Occupations in the World* (Geneva: ILO, 1998) 3, 7, 329–36, 357–59, 367–69, 411–15, for an analysis of the large increase of participation of women in the workforce around the world.

13   Weiss, 'Re-inventing' (n 4) 45–46, 48–49; Tekle, 'Labour law and worker protection' (n 11) 4–5; Hyde, 'The idea of the idea' (n 11) 92–93; Supiot and others, *Beyond Employment* (n 10).

14   See note 1 and note 10 above (list of scholars working on reconceptualisation of labour law). In particular Blackett, 'Emancipation' (n 1); Browne, Deakin and Wilkinson, 'European market integration' (n 1); Fudge, 'Labour as a "fictive commodity"' (n 1); Langille, 'Core labour rights' (n 1); Fudge, 'The new discourse' (n 1); Langille, 'Labour law's theory' (n 1) 101; Hyde, 'The idea of the idea' (n 11) 88.

15   Scholars who are active in the reconceptualisation project of labour law are from developed countries. Their academic interests and careers are concerned more with the developed country problems and issues. See ibid for the list and works of scholars who are working on conceptualising labour law.

16   Tekle, 'Labour law and worker protection' (n 11) 8.

17   Tekle, *Developing Countries* (n 11); Nicola Smit, Elmarie Fourie, 'Extending protection to atypical workers, including workers in the informal economy, in developing countries' (2010) 26(1) *International Journal of Comparative Labor Law & Industrial Relations* 43; Rene Ofreneo, *Informal Sector: Labour Laws and Industrial Relations, Interdepartmental Project on the Urban Informal Sector: Philippines*, Assessment Report Series No 6 (Manila: ILO, 1994).

protection or security in their work.[18] The absence of legal protection for informal economic activities has prompted Peruvian economist Hernando de Soto to observe that law and legal institutions have lost social relevance in the sphere of informal economic activities.[19]

Such lack of protection can be attributed to a great extent to the mismatch between labour law regimes and social, economic and political realities in developing countries.[20] Labour law in the global South has either been transplanted from Europe, or has been deeply influenced by European labour law.[21] This is true for South Asia,[22] Africa[23] and Latin America.[24] Moreover, labour laws in these jurisdictions have influenced each other.[25]

Labour laws in South Asia (ie the Indian subcontinent, including India, Pakistan, Bangladesh and Sri Lanka) have distinct British roots that derive from the law of master and servant.[26] Because of this influence, the labour laws of this region are predominantly based on the employer–employee model in the context of industry.[27] African labour laws were also shaped by European colonisers and ILO standards.[28]

---

18 Tekle, 'Labour law and worker protection' (n 11) 9, 13–17, 20–28, 32–36, 40–42; Kamala Sankaran, 'Informal employment and the challenges for labour law' in Langille and Davidov, *The Idea of Labour Law* (n 1) 223.

19 Hernando de Soto, *The Other Path: the Invisible Revolution in the Third World* (New York: Harper & Row, 1989) 11–12, 231–33.

20 Tekle, 'Labour law and worker protection' (n 11) 3–4, 9, 12–13; Goldin, 'Global conceptualizations' (n 9) 81; Deakin, 'The contribution of labour law' (n 1) 168; Shelley Marshall (undated), 'Main findings concerning the role of labour law in promoting decent work' in *Promoting Decent Work: the Role of Labour Law* (on file with author).

21 Tekle (n 11) 9–11.

22 ibid 17; Kamala Sankaran, 'Labour laws in South Asia: the need for an inclusive approach' in Tekle, *Developing Countries* (n 11) 225.

23 Tekle, 'Labour law and worker protection' (n 11) 17–18; Colin Fenwick, Evance Kalula and Ingrid Landau, 'Labour law: a southern African perspective' in Tekle, *Developing Countries* (n 11) 175.

24 Tekle, 'Labour law and worker protection' (n 11) 18–19; Graciela Bensusan, 'Labour law in Latin America: the gap between norms and reality' in Tekle, *Developing Countries* (n 11) 135.

25 Tekle, 'Labour law and worker protection' (n 11) 19; Fenwick, Kalula and Landau, 'African perspective' (n 23) 185.

26 Sankaran, 'South Asia' (n 22) 225–26. See Michael Anderson, 'India 1858–1930: the illusion of free labour' in Douglas Hay, Paul Craven (eds), *Masters, Servants, and Magistrates in Britain and the Empire, 1562–1955* (Chapel Hill & London: The University of North Carolina Press, 2004) 422, wherein Anderson describes how the British master and servant law established itself in India, and found expression in Indian laws and judicial decisions regulating indentured labour for different industrial and plantation ventures in the country and other parts of the British empire. Also see Prabhu P Mohapatra, 'Assam and the West Indies, 1860–1920: immobilizing plantation labour' in Hay and Craven (ibid) 455, where Mohapatra documents the plight of the workers employed in plantations in the West Indies and the Assam state in India. He shows that, although separated by thousands of kilometres in distance, labour laws in both of these regions (West Indies and Assam) were shaped by the master and servant laws characterised by the compulsory nature of employment contract enforced by penal sanctions. Also see Sankaran (n 22) 226.

27 Sankaran, 'South Asia' (n 22) 229–35.

28 Fenwick, Kalula and Landau, 'African perspective' (n 23) 175, 178–80, 183–84; see Martin Chanock, 'South Africa, 1841–1924: race, contract, and coercion' in Hay and Craven (n 26) 338 for a discussion on how the master and servant laws were used as an instrument in South

The labour laws of Latin America are based on the Spanish inspection model, which itself was influenced by the French model of inspection.[29] Because of labour laws' fundamental assumption of employment relationships in industrial settings in the European context and consequent influence of such labour law, atypical informal workers are excluded from the protection of labour laws in Asia, Africa and Latin America.[30]

Informal workers constitute the majority of workers around the globe[31] – in some of the countries in the South, such as India, atypical workers constitute more than 90 per cent of the workforce.[32] An ILO report of 2002, *Women and Men in the Informal Economy: a Statistical Picture*, notes that informal employment constitutes 93 per cent of total employment in India, 62 per cent of total employment in Mexico and 34 per cent of total employment in South Africa.[33] Informal employment, excluding agricultural employment, constitutes 48 per cent of total employment in North Africa; 72 per cent in sub-Saharan Africa; 51 per cent in Latin America; and 65 per cent in Asia.[34] The report also observes that atypical work, such as self-employment, part-time work and temporary work, constitutes 30 per cent of total work in 15 European countries, and 25 per cent of total work in the United States.[35] Self-employment constitutes a significant proportion of atypical or informal work; other categories of informal work are informal waged employment (in developing countries) and non-standard waged employment (in developed countries).[36]

Labour law, which is based on the juridical concept of the employment relationship, fails to address the concerns of these informal workers who constitute the majority of workers around the globe. Since labour law has traditionally relied on the Fordist model of mass production as a frame of reference, it is not applicable to informal work arrangements (self-employment or waged work on a small

---

Africa to bind labour to an employer, and to control and discipline such labour. See Richard Rathbone, 'West Africa, 1874–1948: employment legislation in a nonsettler peasant economy' in Hay and Craven (n 26) 481 at 492, where the author notes that the purpose of the colonial master and servant law was 'to erode slavery by compelling "masters" to forego ideas of "ownership" of labor in favor of contract'. Employers 'could not use the courts to recall "deserters" without proof of contract'. See David M Anderson, 'Kenya, 1895–1939: registration and rough justice' in Hay and Craven (n 26) 498 at 500–501 for a discussion on how the master and servant law was promulgated in Kenya and other parts of East Africa after they were abolished in England to 'protect the contractual interests of the employer', so that the employers could control the workers and punish their desertion.

29 Bensusan, 'Latin America' (n 24) 149.
30 Sankaran, 'South Asia' (n 22) 229–35; Fenwick, Kalula and Landau, 'African perspective' (n 23) 176–77, 198–205; Bensusan (n 24) 142–46.
31 See ILO, *Women and Men in the Informal Economy: a Statistical Picture* (Geneva: ILO, 2002).
32 NCEUS, *Report on Definitional and Statistical Issues Relating to Informal Economy*, November 2008 (New Delhi: NCEUS, 2008) 44.
33 ILO, *Women and Men* (n 31) 7.
34 ibid. The report also noted that '[i]f data were available for additional countries in Southern Asia, the regional average for Asia would likely be much higher'.
35 ibid. The report, however, makes it clear that all atypical workers in European countries and the United States are not necessarily informally employed, but very few of them receive work- or employment-related benefits.
36 ibid 7–8.

scale).[37] Moreover, because of ineffective administration of labour laws most of the informal workers remain outside the scope and protection of labour laws.[38] Mindful of these realities, Hepple asks:[39]

> What is the use of labour law if it is at best a law for an elite of workers in the industrialized states, while alongside this there is not only widespread poverty and powerlessness in the developing countries but also relative poverty and inequality in the developed countries?

Against this backdrop, what is required is a reformulation of labour laws that is attuned to the needs of informal work and workers so that conditions of work and living standards of workers engaged in informal work can be improved. In the next section, I will look at some of the attempts at reformulation of labour law that invoke the capability approach.

5.3 Capability approach in conceptualising labour law

In this section, I discuss how labour law scholars invoke the capability approach in order to offer a normative goal of labour law, which can help conceptualise labour law outside its traditional frame of reference. Being a human development approach, the capability approach is free from the narrow employment relationship-based conceptualisation of labour law. Since the capability approach is concerned with an individual's opportunity aspect of freedom (in addition to an individual's agency), it is seen as offering a normative goal that can mediate the different frameworks of labour and social law as varied as the corporate codes of conduct and the ILO standards. From a capability approach point of view the purpose of labour law and social rights could be seen as the promotion of freedom of workers. Since the capability approach is non-paternalistic, both procedural rights and substantive guarantees could be conceptualised in terms of capabilities. Moreover, since the capability approach offers a basis of social justice, which is non-dogmatic, the approach is equally attractive in both a market and a non-market set-up.

Hepple argues that in the modern globalised era the central purpose of labour law should be to promote equality of capabilities for workers.[40] He notes that equality of capabilities can successfully negotiate the many emerging strands of labour law,[41] such as the European Community Social and Employment Charter,

---

37 Tekle, 'Labour law and worker protection' (n 11) 3, 9, 17; Rachid Filali Meknassi, 'The effectiveness of labour law and decent work aspirations in the developing countries: a framework for analysis' in Tekle, *Developing Countries* (n 11) 51 at 54–57, 59–63, 65–66; Sankaran, 'South Asia' (n 22) 229–35; Smit and Fourie, 'Atypical workers' (n 17); Ofreneo, *Informal Sector* (n 17).

38 See Tekle, 'Labour law and worker protection' (n 11) 5–8, 12–17, 32–36; Bensusan, 'Latin America' (n 24) 139, 147–61; Fenwick, Kalula and Landau, 'African perspective' (n 23) 212–13; Sankaran, 'South Asia' (n 22) 229–35, 249–52; Smit and Fourie (n 17); Ofreneo (n 17).

39 See Bob Hepple, *Labour Law, Inequality and Global Trade*, Sinzheimer Lecture 2002 (Amsterdam: Hugo Sinzheimer Instituut, 2002) 6–7; Hepple, 'Introduction' (n 3) 11.

40 See Hepple, *Inequality and Global Trade* (n 39) 7, 9–11, 14, 23.

multinational corporations' codes of conduct, empowerment of local stakeholders and ILO-promulgated international labour law.[42]

Simon Deakin, Jude Browne[43] and Frank Wilkinson[44] invoke the capability approach to argue that social rights have a market-enabling role.[45] Defending the provisions on social rights in the Charter of Fundamental Rights of the European Union as market supportive, Deakin and Browne rebut the proposition of T H Marshall and F A Hayek that social rights have a market-distorting role.[46] Deakin, Browne and Wilkinson note that social rights and labour laws can provide social and economic guarantees that could create conditions leading to the enhancement of an individual's capability, thereby enabling that individual to exercise her choice.[47] They identify two categories of social rights: first, 'claims to resources' such as unemployment payments and medical insurance; and, secondly, '*procedural* or institutionalized interaction', such as provisions regarding organisation and collective bargaining.[48] Seen in this manner, they argue, social rights provide for financial and social conversion factors[49] in the process of 'institutionalising capabilities'[50] that 'determine the translation of impersonal and transferable resources, such as human and physical resources, into functionings and capabilities'.[51] Conversion factors are factors that help convert personal, social, physical and environmental characteristics into capabilities.[52] Thus, social rights and labour standards provide institutional foundations for individual capabilities.[53] According to Deakin, Browne and Wilkinson, the normative goal of social rights and labour standards is enhancement and equality of capability sets.[54] Their principal aim is to synchronise social rights and existing labour laws[55] with the logic of market freedom.[56]

---

41 ibid 23.

42 ibid 23–25.

43 Simon Deakin, Jude Browne, 'Social rights and market order: adapting the CA' in Tamara K Hervey, Jeff Kenner (eds), *Economic and Social Rights under the EU Charter of Fundamental Rights: a Legal Perspective* (Oxford and Portland, Oregon: Hart, 2003) 27.

44 Simon Deakin, Frank Wilkinson, *The Law of the Labour Market: Industrialization, Employment, and Legal Evolution* (Oxford: Oxford University Press, 2005).

45 ibid 283–84, 291.

46 Deakin and Browne, 'Adapting the CA' (n 43) 27–32, 37–42; Browne, Deakin and Wilkinson, 'European market integration' (n 1) 220.

47 Deakin and Browne, 'Adapting the CA' (n 43) 33–35; Browne, Deakin and Wilkinson, 'European market integration' (n 1) 208; Deakin and Wilkinson, *Law of the Labour Market* (n 44) 290–92.

48 Deakin and Browne, 'Adapting the CA' (n 43) 39.

49 Browne, Deakin and Wilkinson, 'European market integration' (n 1) 211.

50 ibid 210.

51 Deakin and Browne, 'Adapting the CA' (n 43) 38.

52 Browne, Deakin and Wilkinson, 'European market integration' (n 1) 209–10.

53 Deakin and Wilkinson, *Law of the Labour Market* (n 44) 290–91.

54 Deakin and Browne, 'Adapting the CA' (n 43) 39; Browne, Deakin and Wilkinson, 'European market integration' (n 1) 212.

55 Deakin and Wilkinson, *Law of the Labour Market* (n 44) 294–97.

56 Deakin and Browne, 'Adapting the CA' (n 43) 42–43; Browne, Deakin and Wilkinson, 'European market integration' (n 1) 211, 219.

Robert Salais, in a volume dedicated to the role of the capability approach in European Union (EU) social policy, observes that in the EU's social and employment policies focus needs to shift from inequality of resources to inequality of capabilities.[57] To Salais, the capability approach provides a basis of social justice[58] that is grounded on an 'ethics of objectivity'.[59] He asserts that laws and policies should provide institutional guarantees that enable individuals to maximise their individual capabilities depending on their respective personal endowments and their choices.[60] Kevin Kolben too observes that labour law should promote human development by enhancing workers' capabilities.[61]

Thus, Deakin, Browne and Wilkinson agree with Salais that the normative goal of social policies and labour rights in the EU context should be enhancement of capabilities of individuals, which provides an objective basis for evaluation of individual development. Both of these perspectives are concerned with the larger agenda of the integration of the EU market and of asserting the role of social rights in that context. The purpose of these authors in invoking the capability approach is to show that existing social rights and labour standards are compatible with the neo-liberal formulation of the market, which is characterised by unrestricted freedom of contract subject to only the logic of market demand and supply.[62]

Moreover, the use of the capability approach in the EU social rights project is limited to the sphere of EU *social and employment policies*.[63] The social rights project is not concerned with employment, social policy and work scenarios outside Europe, especially not in the developing countries. It is concerned with justifying existing social rights and labour standards in the EU and the United Kingdom as market-enabling policies.[64]

The scholarship of Deakin, Browne and Wilkinson, and Salais, is also limited to the study of labour laws based on employment relations; such laws imagine workers as employees and therefore exclude self-employment, triangular and multilateral employment relationships from their purview.[65] Thus, the implications of the capability approach for social rights and labour laws in developing countries, where there are large numbers of self-employed workers, disguised workers and other informal workers, remain outside their analysis.

---

57 Robert Salais, 'Incorporating the CA into social and employment policies' in Salais and Villeneuve (n 1), 287.
58 ibid 286.
59 ibid 292.
60 ibid 288, 291.
61 Kolben's overall project looks into trade and labour linkages in order to argue that the purpose of such linkages must be the actual development of workers. Kolben (n 1) 355–56, 371, 388.
62 See Deakin and Browne, 'Adapting the CA' (n 43) 27.
63 See Robert Salais and Robert Villeneuve, 'Introduction: Europe and the politics of capabilities' in Salais and Villeneuve (n 1), 1; Salais, 'CA into social and employment policies' (n 57) 283.
64 Deakin and Wilkinson, *Law of the Labour Market* (n 44) 294–353.
65 See Deakin and Wilkinson (n 44) 292–339, wherein the authors chart the evolution of labour law and employment relationships in the UK. The narration makes it clear that even after modification of the nature of work in the UK, compelled by the phenomenon of outsourcing and sub-contracting, the principal requirement for the application of labour laws is the ascertainment of the employer–employee relationship (or the attribution of such relationship by the courts).

While adopting the capability approach, Browne, Deakin and Wilkinson choose to adopt an instrumental view of freedom. Freedom is instrumental when it is used in furtherance of some other purpose.[66] These authors perceive social right-enabled freedom as instrumental in promoting market participation and, thus, as being compatible with the market. The capability framework, however, does not promote freedom only in its instrumental sense. As I discussed earlier (in Chapter 3), the capability approach values freedom foremost in its intrinsic sense.[67] Freedom in its intrinsic value is itself treated as a social good, significant for a person's overall development.[68]

Benedetta Giovanola explains how the capability approach promotes intrinsic freedom. Giovanola delineates an anthropological account of human richness, which she claims to be implicit in the capability approach.[69] She argues that, from an anthropological perspective, the concept of human essence moves beyond the concepts of individual wellbeing and agency to chart a "'universal" feature of human essence' that exceeds the limited concept of individual freedom.[70] Thus, there is nothing in the capability approach *per se* that calls for justifying social justice or capability in terms of its market-enabling role. The danger of ceding moral ground to the market[71] could be avoided by a claim to the philosophical underpinnings of the capability approach that is based on the concept of intrinsic freedom of human lives as charted by Aristotle and Karl Marx, among others.[72]

While Browne, Deakin and Wilkinson reconceptualise social rights as constitutive of claims to resources and institutional conversion factors, Brian Langille invokes the capability approach to provide a hierarchical conceptualisation of core labour rights and non-core substantive standards.[73] According to Langille, Sen's account provides for a concept of freedom that prioritises core labour rights, which are envisaged in the 1998 Declaration of Fundamental Principles and Rights at Work.[74] Langille argues that, by prioritising these core rights, Sen's account of

---

66   Amartya Sen, *Development as Freedom* (New York: Alfred A. Knopf, 1999) 10, 17–18, 35–40; Amartya Sen, *Inequality Reexamined* (New York: Russell Sage & Cambridge, MA: Harvard University Press, 1992) 41; John M Alexander, 'Capabilities, human rights and moral pluralism' (2004) 8(4) *International Journal of Human Rights* 451 at 455. By disguised workers I mean workers who share an employment relationship with an employer or are dependent on an employer in their (the workers') working capacity, but their employment relationship or dependence is disguised under some other garb such as self-employment, family relation, or business relation (not amounting to an employment relationship).

67   Sen, *Inequality* (n 66) 41; Sen, *Development* (n 66) xii, 5, 18, 35–37; Alexander (n 66).

68   Sen, *Inequality* (n 66); Sen, *Development* (n 66) 18, 35–37; Alexander (n 66).

69   See Benedetta Giovanola, 'Personhood and human richness: good and well-being in the capability approach and beyond' (2005) 63(2) *Review of Social Economy* 249.

70   ibid 262.

71   Fudge, 'Labour as a "fictive commodity"' (n 1) 128; Fudge, 'The new discourse' (n 1) 65.

72   Sen, *Development* (n 66) 7, 24–25, 29, 73, 75.

73   See Langille, 'Core labour rights' (n 1).

74   ibid 433–34. The 1998 Declaration of Fundamental Principles and Rights at Work envisages right to association and collective bargaining, elimination of forced labour, abolition of child labour, and prohibition of discrimination at work as fundamental principles.

freedom proposes 'to unleash the power of individuals themselves to pursue their own freedom'.[75]

Langille maintains that there is no inherent tension between core rights and other substantive concerns; rather, there is a positive relationship between the two.[76] He further notes that removing barriers to self-help so that individuals can pursue their own freedom is the concern of labour rights.[77] According to Langille, core rights, which are procedural in nature, are market enabling.[78] In his account, once workers' core rights are ensured they can themselves attain the substantive standards by using their freedom. For this reason, he thinks that prioritisation of core rights is conceptually coherent, normatively appealing and pragmatically useful,[79] and is supported by Sen's conceptualisation of freedom.[80]

Langille asserts that the goal of labour rights is human freedom, which is freedom to lead the life one has reason to value. However, by prioritising core rights over substantive standards, Langille misses the centrality of Sen's approach. Sen's idea of freedom is based not only on negative civil, political or procedural rights, but it also gives equal and adequate weight to social and substantive rights.[81] Judy Fudge points out that, although Langille dismisses the comparison between civil and social rights, his distinction between procedural and substantive rights has the same effect.[82]

Sen's idea of freedom is non-dogmatic[83] and context-specific. Without pre-determining the priority of civil-political or procedural rights over social-economic and substantive rights, Sen argues that promotion of the freedom to choose (capabilities) requires different conditions under different circumstances. For a starving population, freedom of expression holds little value; similarly, in a prosperous totalitarian society, people have little freedom in the absence of freedom of expression. For the latter society, civil rights are a precondition to freedom but, for the former, economic rights are essential for real freedom.

According to Sen, in every society the content of freedom (functionings and corresponding capabilities) is to be determined by participation and deliberation.[84] To make people effectively participate in determining the nature and extent of their freedom, a multiplicity of factors need to interact to shape individual, social and environmental characteristics into individual capabilities.[85] An a priori

---

75   Langille (n 1) 433–34.
76   ibid 435.
77   ibid 433–34.
78   ibid 429–30.
79   ibid 423–24, 427–28.
80   ibid 432–34.
81   See Amartya Sen, *Hunger and Entitlements* (Helsinki: World Institute for Development Economics Research, 1987); Sen, *Development* (n 66) 31–32, 36–40, 51–53, 123, 147–48, 152–55.
82   Fudge, 'The new discourse' (n 1) 60–61.
83   Browne, Deakin and Wilkinson, 'European market integration' (n 1) 205, 212.
84   Sen, *Development* (n 66) xii–xiii, 31, 78–79, 110; Amartya Sen, *The Idea of Justice* (Cambridge, MA: The Belknap Press of Harvard University Press, 2009) 88, 91, 326–28, 346–47, 350–51.
85   Sen, *Development* (n 66) 3–4, 10, 35–41, 43–53, 72–86, 109–110.

hierarchisation of such factors is uncalled for and might fail to remove 'unfreedoms', which is Sen's objective.[86] Thus, Sen's is a complex idea of freedom,[87] which Langille oversimplifies to the extent of rendering it misleading.

Fudge notes that Langille's view of fundamental labour rights is based on a thin conception of the capability approach, whereas Brown, Deakin and Wilkinson's conception of social rights is based on a much more nuanced understanding of the capability approach, because they are attentive to social rights in addition to civil and political rights.[88] She further observes that Langille's version of fundamental labour rights is individualistic in nature.[89] Langille discusses freedom of association and collective bargaining in terms of an individual right rather than a collective right,[90] which might pose problems for the institutions of collective bargaining and organisation.[91]

Fudge commends the capability approach as providing a moral justification for the legal form and normative content of labour and social rights in a market framework.[92] In agreement with Browne, Deakin and Wilkinson, she argues that *capabilities*, as the normative basis of labour and social rights, provide the much-needed support for labour rights[93] in order to 're-institutionalize the employment relationship'[94] in 'developed non-socialist countries'.[95] Cautious of the limitations of the capability approach, Fudge notes that it would be wrong to assume that Sen's approach can provide a ready-made theory of social justice for labour and social rights.[96] It is only by supplementing the capability framework with 'a theory of social choice, deliberative mechanisms and a social theory about power' that we can devise a theory of social justice for workers.[97]

Accordingly, Fudge supplements Sen's capability approach with philosopher Elizabeth Anderson's theory of *democratic equality* to provide a normative goal of law governing the labour market.[98] According to Fudge, the normative goal of law governing the labour market should be democratic equality of capabilities in the labour market.[99] Importantly, Fudge identifies the significance of the capability approach for reconceptualising labour law not only for paid workers, but also for unpaid workers.[100]

---

86 ibid xii, 3–4, 10, 35–41, 43–53, 72–86, 109–110.
87 Fudge, 'The new discourse' (n 1) 61.
88 ibid 58, 64; Kolben (n 1).
89 Fudge, 'The new discourse' (n 1) 62.
90 ibid.
91 ibid.
92 ibid 63, 66.
93 ibid 31–32, 57–58; Fudge, 'Labour as a "fictive commodity"' (n 1) 128–29.
94 Fudge, 'The new discourse' (n 1) 31.
95 ibid.
96 ibid 65.
97 ibid.
98 Fudge, 'Labour as a "fictive commodity"' (n 1) 129, 132–35.
99 ibid 132–35.
100 ibid 134–35.

While Fudge provides us with a nuanced version of the use of the capability approach in labour law, her primary focus remains re-institutionalisation of employment relationships in the context of developed non-socialist countries.[101] Fudge contributes to the debate about reconceptualisation of labour law in a significant way. By invoking Anderson's insight, she uses the capability approach to argue for labour law that can govern workers outside the employment relationship model, which is a significant step towards reconceptualisation of labour law for informal workers.

Thus, from the literature review on the use of the capability approach in labour law reconceptualisation, it is clear that the debate about reconceptualisation of labour law has remained confined to issues in the developed world and is overwhelmingly concerned with the employment relationship model. Although the literature surveyed provides glimpses into the use of the capability approach in the absence of the employment relationship model, such arguments remain underdeveloped. Informal economic activities in developing countries pose particular problems of their own, which cannot be appreciated and addressed by new proposals of labour law if they are not contextual and not set specifically against the backdrop of such problems. In the next section of this chapter, I look into the literature that uses the capability approach in the context of informal economic activities in developing countries.

5.4 Capability approach and informal economic activities

A capability approach-based analysis of working conditions and living standards of informal workers has received the most comprehensive treatment at the hands of Elizabeth Hill.[102] In her book *Worker Identity, Agency and Economic Development*, Hill analyses the relevance of the capability approach as a theoretical justification for the multi-dimensional facilitative programme (developed by the trade union Self Employed Women's Association, or SEWA[103]) for improving the overall conditions of work and life for the informal women workers in India.[104] She observes that the capability approach provides a nuanced framework for the evaluation of deprivation and development of informal workers when compared with the human capital approach.[105] To Hill, the essence of Sen's approach lies in his conceptualisation of conversion factors.[106]

---

101 Fudge, 'The new discourse' (n 1) 31.
102 Elizabeth Hill, *Worker Identity, Agency and Economic Development: Women's Empowerment in the Indian Informal Economy* (London and New York: Routledge, 2010); Elizabeth Hill, 'Women in the Indian informal economy: collective strategies for work life improvement and development' (2001) 15(3) *Work, Employment & Society* 443.
103 SEWA is the abbreviated form of the trade union Self Employed Women's Association.
104 See Hill, *Worker Identity* (n 102).
105 ibid 29, 35.
106 ibid 29.

Rather than celebrating the mere presence of resources, what the emphasis on conversion factors in Sen's theory does is show how resources can become useful in the lives of informal workers.[107] Hill notes that the capability approach, by distinguishing between resources and capabilities, gives us the opportunity to analyse the reasons for and forms of marginalisation, vulnerability, poverty, exclusion and underdevelopment of informal workers.[108]

The capability approach is a tool to analyse 'all sources of human constraint and non-freedom'.[109] Hill shows that, by providing for institutional recognition, respect, work security, worker solidarity, child care and health care, establishment of alternative economic institutions such as cooperatives and banking services, vocational training, information exchange, legal and social support services, lobbying and direct action (agitation), SEWA enhances the capabilities and functionings of its members who are informal women workers.[110] SEWA's provisions help to convert individual, social, economic and political characteristics (resources) into capabilities of informal women workers.[111]

Hill is, however, also critical of the capability approach. She argues that, although the capability approach provides a space to think about constraints and non-freedoms that hinder an individual's capabilities and functionings, it is not concerned with 'why or how' socio-economic and political institutional conversion factors impinge on labour.[112] She is also critical of Sen's delineation of the concept of *agency*:[113] 'Sen has not included the most fundamental issue, which is the internally determined capacity of a person to *be* free to *exercise* freedom and choice, that is, their agency.'[114] She argues that Sen provides an inadequate account of agency in the sense that, instead of looking into the reasons for the absence of agency and how it could be inculcated in individuals, he assumes that each individual possesses agency to convert resources into capabilities.[115]

She also notes that Nussbaum's account of capabilities (and her list of desired capabilities) provides a better approach to analyse agency in marginal women informal workers as an outcome of self-respect and self-esteem, which emanates from the process of affiliation to and reciprocity within an organisation.[116] Hill concludes that social relations of recognition and respect have both intrinsic and

---

107 ibid 29, 32, 34.
108 ibid 35.
109 ibid.
110 ibid 46–47, 73–95; Hill, 'Indian informal economy' (n 102) 450–62.
111 Hill, *Worker Identity* (n 102) 96–114.
112 ibid 35, 36–45. Hill resorts to a Marxist account of labour in the informal economy to address the questions of 'why or how'. She develops a Marxist account of social reproduction of labour and relations of power in the informal economy to analyse why socio-economic and political institutional conversion factors hinder labour's productivity, capability and functionings.
113 ibid 126–31.
114 ibid 128.
115 ibid 126–30.
116 ibid 130–31. The list of capabilities offered by Nussbaum includes *capability of affiliation*, and *capability to exercise political and material control over one's environment*. See Martha Nussbaum, *Women and Human Development: the Capabilities Approach* (Cambridge: Cambridge University Press, 2000) 79–80.

instrumental value that is necessary for the creation of agency as a personal characteristic.[117] Agency, in turn, is a prerequisite for economic development and capability enhancement.[118]

Hill provides a very useful study of informal women workers in India within the theoretical framework of the capability approach. However, there are some problems with Hill's understanding of the capability approach. Sen has categorically observed[119] and others have noted[120] that the capability approach does not provide a complete theory of justice. It would therefore be wrong to assume that the capability approach will provide a complete theory of social justice including perspectives on power relations in society, and subtle socio-economic and political influences that are responsible for perpetual deprivation of marginalised people (ie the 'why or how' questions, in Hill's terms).[121] Hence, Sen's theoretical framework needs to be supplemented by other theoretical frameworks to answer 'why or how' questions, as Hill herself does by using the Marxist approach.[122]

Moreover, Hill's critique of Sen's theorising of *agency* sinks into quicksand. Agency in Sen's theory refers to individual preference and initiative,[123] which are the result of family values, education, socialisation, environment, culture, physical capacity and a range of other factors. These factors are resources as well as *conversion factors* (for other resources). Thus, agency as a functioning (and a capability for other functionings) is created or enhanced by means of different conversion factors. Hill has herself argued that agency amongst informal women workers in India is created through social relations of recognition and respect.[124] While Sen might have given less attention to theorising agency, there is enough space in the capability approach (both Sen's and Nussbaum's versions) to account for agency in marginal workers.

Sabina Alkire shows how the capability approach could be used to analyse the multi-dimensional capability improvement of marginalised people in Pakistan.[125] Alkire discusses three case studies of Oxfam-funded small-scale projects in Pakistan

---

117   Hill, *Worker Identity* (n 102) 131.
118   ibid 131–32.
119   Amartya Sen, 'The place of capability in a theory of justice' in Harry Brighouse, Ingrid Robeyns (eds), *Measuring Justice Primary Goods and Capabilities* (Cambridge: Cambridge University Press, 2010) 239 at 242–43, 249–50.
120   Fudge, 'The new discourse' (n 1) 62; Elizabeth Anderson, 'Justifying the capabilities approach to justice' in Brighouse and Robeyns (n 119) 81 at 81–84.
121   Fudge (n 1) 62.
122   Ingrid Robeyns notes that different results will be obtained by supplementing Sen's capability approach with a diverse range of theoretical frameworks. See Ingrid Robeyns, 'Sen's capability approach and gender inequality: selecting relevant capabilities' (2003) 9(2–3) *Feminist Economics* 61 at 67.
123   Sen, *Development* (n 66) xi, 18–19.
124   Hill, *Worker Identity* (n 102) 131.
125   Sabina Alkire, *Valuing Freedoms: Sen's CA and Poverty Reduction* (New York: Oxford University Press, 2002).

and analyses how these 'local participatory activities'[126] have been able to enhance multiple capabilities of the project participants.[127] Local participatory activities discussed by Alkire are goat rearing, rose cultivation and literacy enhancement.[128] While goat rearing and rose cultivation are directly linked to income generation, the literacy project is aimed at empowering women participants.[129]

Based on the outcome of these projects, Alkire notes that '[e]mpowerment indicated their [participants'] awareness of what they themselves could do and be'.[130] This observation resonates very closely with what Hill describes as the process of building agency in marginalised people.[131] Improvement of capabilities through the three projects has been made possible because of initial access to resources such as money, participation, mobilisation and social organisation,[132] which acted as conversion factors in improving the overall capability sets of the participants.

Alkire's study is important in reflecting about the improvement of working conditions and living standards of informal workers. Her operational definition of capability provides us with a plan, which can be used in an institutionalisation programme that targets improvement of working conditions and living standards of informal workers. Her identification of the basic functionings (such as money, participation) required for long-term capability improvement in marginalised and deprived communities in Pakistan is also a significant indicator of what needs to be done in order to improve conditions of informal workers in developing countries.

Pointing out the necessity of reconceptualising labour law for informal economic activities in developing countries,[133] Anne Trebilcock offers three development approaches for reconceptualising labour law. She does not, however, provide details about any one of these alternative frameworks. Her limited purpose is only to indicate how different development-related theoretical frameworks might be useful in meeting the challenge of crafting good legislation that can administer labour beyond the formal sector.[134] Identifying that the problems with informal economic activities are the precariousness and insecurity of workers,[135] she offers the sustainable livelihoods approach, the human capability perspective and the empowerment approach as possible ways for thinking about labour law that are capable of addressing the problems associated with informal economic activities.[136]

126   ibid 205.
127   ibid 233–96.
128   ibid.
129   ibid.
130   ibid 266.
131   Hill, *Worker Identity* (n 102) 131–32.
132   Alkire, *Valuing Freedoms* (n 125) 235–36.
133   Trebilcock, 'Using development approaches' (n 6) 63–64, 66–67.
134   ibid 68–69, 86.
135   ibid 67.
136   ibid 76–86.

According to Trebilcock, the sustainable livelihoods approach is concerned with providing or improving livelihood assets, such as skills, knowledge, health, infrastructure, natural resources (eg water, biodiversity), savings, credit, social assets (eg networks, associations) for the target population.[137] Since this approach builds on 'people's strengths, promote[s] links between policies and institutions that operate at the macro and the micro levels, encourages broad partnering from the public and private sectors and aims at long-term sustainability', it can provide a theoretical basis for labour law for informal economic activities.[138]

Trebilcock further notes that, since the human capability perspective theorises the relevance of *human capabilities* as an intrinsic factor in people's wellbeing and freedom and is an instrumental factor influencing social change and economic production, it can also be a possible candidate for theorising labour law for informal economic activities.[139]

Finally, her enthusiasm for the empowerment approach seems to have arisen from the fact that, while the sustainable livelihood approach and the human capability approach take the individual as their point of analysis, the empowerment approach (the World Bank's approach) takes the collective as its analytical basis.[140] The empowerment approach argues that an effective institution (eg the institution of *law*) needs to combine the elements of empowerment – information, inclusion/participation, accountability and local organisational capacity – that will enable people to move out of poverty.[141]

Amongst the alternative development frameworks suggested by Trebilcock, the sustainable livelihood approach argues for the provision of resources to encounter deprivations of vulnerable and marginalised sections of the population.[142] Such a theoretical framework resonates well with the Rawlsian and Dworkinian concepts of *primary goods* and *resources*[143] (discussed in Chapter 3). However, by not concentrating on the outcome of using such resources, the sustainable livelihoods approach attracts the same criticism that resources alone cannot guarantee development; what is important is looking into the consequences of using such resources.[144] The World Bank's empowerment approach, on the other hand, provides for collective empowerment in addition to provision for resources and opportunity (or capability).[145]

However, what is problematic in the World Bank approach is that empowerment has to happen according to the Bank's terms and conditions.[146] Trebilcock

---

137 ibid 76–77.
138 ibid 77.
139 ibid 79–81.
140 ibid 81–83.
141 ibid 81.
142 ibid 77.
143 See John Rawls, *A Theory of Justice* (Cambridge, MA: Harvard University Press, 1971) 62, 92, 93–95, 395–96, 399–404; Ronald Dworkin, 'What is equality? Part 2: Equality of resources' (1981) 10(4) *Philosophy and Public Affairs* 283 at 289.
144 Sen, *Development* (n 66) 58–76.
145 Trebilcock, 'Using development approaches' (n 6) 81.
146 ibid 82–84.

identifies serious limitations of the collective empowerment proposal of the World Bank.[147] The third approach suggested by Trebilcock is the consequentialist approach of capabilities, which looks into the role of resources in enhancing the capability and functionings of individuals.[148] Although Trebilcock notes that the individual (not collective) is the reference point for the capability approach,[149] Ingrid Robeyns points out that such individualism is only a commitment to ethical individualism.[150] Ethical individualism means that the analytical unit for the capability approach is the individual and not collective.[151] Thus, the evaluation of an individual's capabilities is not subsumed into the evaluation of a group's capability to which an individual might belong.[152]

In the context of the capability approach, ethical individualism means that, although for evaluative purposes individual capabilities are analysed, such individual capabilities may be influenced by (or dependent on) collective initiatives (of groups/associations).[153] There is, therefore, nothing in the capability approach that hinders collective effort or association by individuals in furtherance of their capabilities.[154]

Taking Trebilcock's proposal forward, I now conceptualise labour law for informal economic activities based on the capability approach. Deakin and Wilkinson, in their reconceptualisation project, note that: 'the capability concept can be understood as an answer, or perhaps the beginning of an answer'.[155] It is in this spirit that I attempt to take the 'beginning of an answer'[156] forward by arguing for a labour law conceptualisation that is attentive to the requirements of informal workers principally in the global South.

In line with Sen, Browne, Deakin, Wilkinson and Hepple, I begin the following section by arguing that the normative goal of new labour law must be enhancement and equality of capability of all workers. I then discuss the basis of the claim to enhancement and equality of capability. Following Fudge, I draw on Elizabeth Anderson's theory of *democratic equality* to argue for the basis of distribution of capabilities. Finally, I draw on Sen and Jean Drèze's formulation of integrated institutions to argue for a framework that can formulate the new labour law in informal economic activity settings.

---

147   ibid.
148   ibid 78–81. I discussed this aspect of the capability approach in detail in ch 3.
149   ibid 81.
150   Robeyns, 'Sen's capability approach' (n 122) 65; Ingrid Robeyns, 'The capability approach: a theoretical survey' (2005) 6(1) *Journal of Human Development* 93 at 107–109.
151   Robeyns, 'Sen's capability approach' (n 122); Robeyns, 'Theoretical survey' (n 150).
152   Robeyns, 'Sen's capability approach' (n 122); Robeyns, 'Theoretical survey' (n 150).
153   Robeyns, 'Theoretical survey' (n 150) 109–10.
154   Peter Evans, 'Collective capabilities, culture, and Amartya Sen's development as freedom' (2002) 37(2) *Studies in Comparative International Development* 54; Sen, 'Capability in a theory of justice' (n 119) 249–50.
155   Deakin and Wilkinson, *Law of the Labour Market* (n 44) 348.
156   ibid.

5.5 Claim to a new normative goal of labour law

Since the post-Second World War era, one of labour law's goals has been to address the power imbalance between employers and employees[157] by providing minimum labour standards, provident funds, medical benefits, the right to contract and the right to participate in trade unions and collective bargaining. While these guarantees are primarily viewed as disjunctive stand-alone rights, the capability approach offers a lens through which to look at labour rights in a goal-based consequentialist manner[158] from a human development perspective.

Browne, Deakin and Wilkinson suggest that, instead of viewing labour rights merely as resources available to workers, such rights could be viewed as conversion factors in the process of 'institutionalizing capabilities' whereby resources are converted to capabilities.[159] Labour rights, in this sense, provide institutional foundations for enhancement of capabilities.[160] Thus, labour rights could also be understood as providing for social conditions for capabilities or freedom.

Sen has argued that institutional guarantees by themselves are not sufficient conditions for social justice.[161] What is needed is constant evaluation of institutional guarantees to examine their effects on targeted populations.[162] Therefore, even if labour rights are viewed as institutional foundations for conversion of resources to capabilities, such rights need to justify themselves on a consequentialist examination. Labour rights, as they exist today, fail to address the concerns of the large number of informal workers across the globe who continue to remain outside the purview of labour law.[163] Thus, from a consequentialist analysis, the institutional foundations of labour law in its present form fail to justify its relevance for the majority of workers worldwide.

Moreover, labour rights, as they exist today, constitute a given list of entitlements (resources or options) that are available to workers. However, the problem with this given list of options, which are reasonably fixed (such as maternity benefits, provident funds), is that workers cannot have access to other social conditions of freedom that might be necessary for their human development in terms of

---

157 Kahn-Freund, *Labour and the Law* (n 4) 1, 4–5, 8–9, 11–15; Trebilcock, 'Using development approaches' (n 6) 66; Davidov, 'The (changing?) idea' (n 4) 312, 314–15.

158 See John Alexander, *Capabilities and Social Justice: the Political Philosophy of Amartya Sen and Martha Nussbaum* (Farnham & Burlington: Ashgate, 2008) 17–21 (discussed in ch 3).

159 Browne, Deakin and Wilkinson, 'European market integration' (n 1) 210–11; Deakin and Browne, 'Adapting the CA' (n 43) 38.

160 Deakin and Wilkinson, *Law of the Labour Market* (n 44) 290–91.

161 Sen, *Idea of Justice* (n 84) 81–86.

162 ibid.

163 See ch 2. Also see Tekle, 'Labour law and worker protection' (n 11) 3–5, 8–9, 12–28, 32–36. It is in this context that scholars have proposed viewing labour law as 'the law of labour market regulation', or 'the law based on the labour force membership status' to do away with the employment-specific dispensation of labour law. See Richard Mitchell, Christopher Arup, 'Labour law and labour market regulation' in Arup and others, *Labour Law* (n 10) 3; Supiot and others, *Beyond Employment* (n 10) 52, 54–55; Fudge, 'Labour as a "Fictive commodity"' (n 1), 120–36.

capabilities related to their work. Against this backdrop, the capability approach offers the advantage of looking at all social conditions of freedom that are necessary for capability enhancement of workers, even if some of such social conditions do not attain the status of labour rights.

Thus, on a rights-based labour law conceptualisation the content of labour law becomes more or less fixed. This fixed and determinate content of labour rights is an obstacle for new and innovative labour guarantees (or social conditions of freedom), which might be necessary for informal workers. The capability approach, by taking account of a range of factors necessary for human development of workers (not necessarily limited to labour rights) can also overcome the fixed and rigid terrain of a rights-based approach. Thus, there are valid reasons for pursuing the capability approach as a normative goal of labour law. However, one must be careful not to embrace all social conditions of freedom as part of a labour law conceptualisation. For example, the capability approach might require that informal workers have access to housing and education, but it does not follow that these extremely valuable resources necessary for informal workers should be assimilated into labour law. For informal workers, conceptualisation of labour law should be context specific.

According to Sen, expansion (enhancement) of freedom or capability,[164] and equality in the space of capability,[165] should be the aim of public policy. This conceptualisation of freedom allows labour law to be reframed in terms of its ability to enhance 'freedom' of workers.[166] According to Hepple,[167] Browne, Deakin and Wilkinson, the normative goal of labour law should be enhancement and equality of capability sets.[168]

The advantage of envisioning enhancement and equality of capability as a normative goal of labour law for informal economic activities is that, in such a scenario, labour law could be freed from its dependence on an employer–employee relationship. Enhancement and equality of capabilities of workers are independent of the employment relationship model of labour law that operates at the workplace. The normative goal of enhancement and equality of capabilities of workers could be formulated irrespective of the nature of work, the employment relationship or the place of work. Such a normative goal is therefore valid for both formal and informal workers.

---

164   Sen, *Development* (n 66) 4; Sen, *Idea of Justice* (n 84) 232, 298.
165   Amartya Sen, 'Equality of what?' The Tanner Lectures on Human Values, delivered at Stanford University, on 22 May 1979 in *The Tanner Lectures on Human Values, vol I* (Salt Lake City: University of Utah Press/Cambridge, London, Melbourne and Sydney: Cambridge University Press, 1980) 217–18; also Browne, Deakin and Wilkinson, 'European market integration' (n 1) 209, 211–12; Sen, *Idea of Justice* (n 84) 298. However, it must be noted that Sen is quite aware of the dangers of mooting for absolute *equality of capability*, because such claim to equality might conflict with other important equality claims. See Sen, *Idea of Justice* (n 84) 232, 295–98.
166   Browne, Deakin and Wilkinson, 'European market integration' (n 1) 208–209, 213.
167   See Hepple, *Inequality and Global Trade* (n 39) 7, 9–11, 23.
168   Deakin and Browne, 'Adapting the CA' (n 43) 39; Browne, Deakin and Wilkinson, 'European market integration' (n 1) 212.

While Sen's idea of freedom is apt for reconceptualising labour law, I want to add further clarifications to his idea of freedom in conceiving labour law for informal economic activities. The normative goal of freedom in terms of capabilities has to be content-independent as well as permit-independent.[169] Freedom is content-independent when an individual is assured of appropriate circumstances wherein she can (subject, of course, to the exercise of her *agency*) achieve whatever she chooses to achieve, rather than choosing from a given list of options that society might offer.[170]

For example, a society might offer an individual a choice between options A and B. The choice an individual prefers under these circumstances means that her freedom is nonetheless content-dependent. In the alternative, if an individual chooses option Z (ie neither option A nor B) and social arrangements could ensure the achievement of such option, an individual has content-independent freedom. In this sense a rights-based approach to labour law could only enable an individual (a worker) to realise a content-dependent freedom, but a capability approach-based conceptualisation can take into account any factor (ie where options are not limited) necessary for individual development in addition to entitlements that have attained the status of rights. Freedom is permit-independent when such freedom is enjoyed on an equal basis without an individual having to negotiate with the power or domination of others.[171] For example, when an individual has freedom to choose but such freedom can only be exercised as a favour through sycophancy or other kinds of negotiation, such freedom becomes permit-dependent.[172]

Freedom in this content-independent and permit-independent sense has two dimensions: individual agency and social arrangements. Sen calls for the evaluation of institutional arrangements on the basis of their ability to promote freedom.[173] Accordingly, a normative reconceptualisation of labour law has to be premised on its ability to promote individual and social development in terms of *freedom*. What follows from the reconceptualisation of the normative basis of labour law is the shift in its analytical focus from mere existence of goods, provisions and resources (including individual and collective rights) or institutional foundations, to the role of such goods, provisions and resources in ensuring *real freedom* for workers.[174]

What this would mean for labour law is that, instead of focusing on goods and resources (or factors[175]) such as rights to association, collective bargaining, unemployment insurance, maternity benefits, pensions etc, one needs to look to the extent to which such factors have been able to promote improved freedom in terms of

---

169 Philip Petit, 'Freedom in the spirit of Sen' in Christopher W Morris (ed), *Amartya Sen* (New York: Cambridge University Press, 2010) 91 at 97–98.
170 ibid.
171 ibid 98–100.
172 ibid.
173 ibid 103.
174 Browne, Deakin and Wilkinson, 'European market integration' (n 1) 209–13; Sen, *Development* (n 66) 3, 36; Sabina Alkire, 'Why the capability approach?' (2005) 6(1) *Journal of Human Development* 115 at 121.
175 I will use the phrases *goods and resources* and *factors* interchangeably.

actual choice for workers. For example, the right to association would be meaningless if the structure of the political economy makes it impossible for workers to organise. Informal workers, such as domestic workers or waste pickers, tend to work on their own and not with other workers. Very seldom do they come into contact with each other to exchange views or cooperate in furtherance of some common purpose. These workers are mostly uneducated; they are unaware of any rights associated with work or citizenship. Under these circumstances, if the structural and social constraints to the right to association are not removed, mere availability of the right to association cannot promote freedom of these workers in terms of capabilities.

Similarly, the mere availability of workplace bargaining rights would only be a formal notional guarantee for workers (principally informal workers) who do not have a workplace or who are uneducated and so cannot appreciate the issues for which they need to bargain. Unemployment insurance is another factor that may have little value if there is no provision for skill development or education for workers. The mere availability of resources or goods, thus, is not sufficient for promoting capabilities of workers. A definite kind of good or resource (such as the right to association) could provide social conditions in which certain categories of workers could enhance their capabilities; but the same resource might not be able to promote capabilities for some other categories of workers.

Therefore, in thinking about legislative guarantees for informal workers, the typical socio-economic-cultural-political situations in which informal economic activities are performed need to be understood appropriately. Factors hindering capability development of such workers need to be identified. It is only from an appropriate understanding of these factors that legislative guarantees can be made, which could promote capabilities of informal workers by removing the obstacles to the development of such workers' capabilities.

The proposal of a normative goal of labour law that is based on a claim to enhancement and equality (of capability) in the context of work needs to specify the basis of such a claim. The problem with the capability approach is that while it envisages the opportunity aspect of freedom[176] it is not concerned with the process aspect of freedom.[177] Sen acknowledges that the capability approach does not provide a complete theory of justice.[178] Sen's approach is not concerned with the distributive aspects of freedom (ie how to determine distribution).[179] He does not deal with the basis of claims to entitlements or equality of capabilities.[180] To make the capability approach operational as a theory of social justice it needs to be supplemented by a theory of distribution. In the following section of the chapter, I examine the basis of the normative claim to enhancement and equality of capability of workers on the basis of a theory of distribution.

176   Sen, *Idea of Justice* (n 84) 232, 295.
177   ibid 296.
178   Sen, 'Capability in a theory of justice' (n 119) 232–33, 242–43, 249–50.
179   ibid 248–49.
180   ibid 248; Anderson, 'Justifying the capabilities approach to justice' (n 120) 81–83.

Anderson has theorised a worker-centric idea of equality that takes the capability approach as its reference point. Fudge has invoked Anderson's concept of *democratic equality* to supplement Sen's approach.[181] Following Fudge, I adopt Anderson's concept of democratic equality to supplement Sen's approach. I will be using Anderson's conceptualisation of democratic equality to argue for equality amongst participants in the cooperative production process as a starting point for the distribution of capabilities.[182] Fudge envisages democratic equality as the normative goal of labour law.[183] I will argue, instead, that the concept of democratic equality can act as a basis of 'a claim to a capability set'[184] for workers engaged in a cooperative production process. My premise is that because workers are equal democratic participants in production processes they can lay their claim to equality and enhancement of capabilities. Thus, I use the concept of democratic equality as *a premise* of equality in a production process, rather than as a normative goal of labour law.

5.6 What is the basis of the normative claim (to enhancement and equality of capability)?

A theory of social justice needs to have certain components. First, it needs to have a metric, which characterises the type of good that is the subject of the demands of justice.[185] Secondly, there has to be a rule, which specifies the basis of distribution of the metric.[186] I adopt a social justice approach to labour law. The metric I adopt is that of the capabilities metric, which is an objective metric (rather than the subjective metric of happiness or desire fulfilment). I propose that distribution of the metric be based on the principle of democratic equality.

Fudge observes that Anderson's political concept of equality can be a good supplement to Sen's capability approach in conceptualising labour law.[187] Anderson justifies the claim to equality of capabilities on the basis of what she terms *democratic equality*.[188] Her concept of democratic equality proposes recognition of persons as equals in a society in the matters of democratic participation and collective self-determination.[189] Her idea of democratic equality 'guarantees all law-abiding citizens equal and effective access to the social conditions of their freedom at all times'.[190] She elaborates on the richness of her conception of democratic equality:

---

181 Fudge, 'Labour as a "fictive commodity"' (n 1) 132–36.
182 This aspect has received specific treatment from Anderson, who conceptualises equality amongst workers in the globalised production system. See Anderson, 'What is the point of equality?' (n 2) 321.
183 Fudge, 'Labour as a "fictive commodity"' (n 1) 129, 132–33.
184 Anderson, 'Justifying the capabilities approach to justice' (n 120) 83.
185 ibid 81–82.
186 ibid.
187 Fudge, 'Labour as a "fictive commodity"' (n 1) 132–33.
188 Anderson, 'What is the point of equality?' (n 2) 316–21.
189 ibid 313.
190 ibid 289.

Democracy is here understood as collective self-determination by means of open discussion among equals, in accordance with rules acceptable to all. To stand as an equal before others in discussion means that one is entitled to participate, that others recognize an obligation to listen respectfully and respond to one's arguments, that no one need bow and scrape before others or represent themselves as inferior to others as a condition of having their claim heard. [footnote omitted][191]

Anderson's idea of democratic equality can be traced back to Rawls's conceptualisation of democratic equality.[192] According to Rawls, moral personality is the basis of democratic equality.[193] Rawls notes:

[P]rinciple of (equal) participation . . . requires that all citizens are to have an equal right to take part in, and to determine the outcome of, the constitutional process that establishes the laws with which they are to comply.[194]

However, unlike Anderson's conceptualisation, Rawls's conceptualisation of equal citizenship is available only in the original position[195] (and later transferred to constitutional rule-making) when, behind the veil of ignorance, equal citizens decide the basic structure of society.[196] It is in this sense that Rawls's democratic equality is a starting-gate theory.

According to Anderson, on the other hand, democratic equality is a relational theory of equality.[197] It calls for the removal of socially created relations of oppression, violence, marginalisation, domination, exploitation and cultural imperialism.[198] Although the theory of democratic equality acknowledges the important role played by distribution of goods and resources in abolishing the social relations of oppression, it is far from advocating distribution of goods and resources as the principal mechanism of ensuring democratic equality.[199] The theory synthesises the requirement of equal recognition and equal distribution by asserting that the pattern of distribution might be a precondition to equal recognition.[200]

---

191   ibid 313.
192   Rawls, *Theory of Justice* (n 143) 66.
193   ibid 75, 504f.
194   ibid 221–22.
195   Rawls describes original position as a hypothetical position of initial equality in which autonomous people enjoying equal status decide 'the principles of justice for the basic structure of society'. In this hypothetical situation of equality participants are unaware of their class positions, social status, economic capacities, physical and mental strength, and even their conception of good. See Rawls, *Theory of Justice* (n 143) 11–12, 17–19.
196   ibid 96–97, 221–22.
197   Anderson, 'What is the point of equality?' (n 2) 313–14.
198   ibid 313, 315.
199   ibid 288–89, 313–14.
200   ibid 313–14.

In line with Sen, Anderson claims that the *raison d'être* of the creation of the state is to secure citizens' freedom in it; the promotion of freedom is the purpose of the state.[201] Anderson observes that democratic equality is based on the fundamental principle of equal respect for others, which is the determinant of social conditions of freedom.[202] According to this concept, a *free life* is one in which relationships are based on equality.[203] Anderson claims that, while democratic equality allows individuals to enter into contractual relationships on an equal basis, it prohibits individuals from voluntarily giving up their freedom in pursuance of such contracts.[204] Thus, she asserts that democratic equality provides for the basis of lifetime equality rather than a starting-gate equality ensured by equality of fortune or resources.[205]

Anderson's conception of equality is non-paternalistic.[206] It does not propose to guide people's behaviour.[207] The concept envisages equality in the creation of opportunities without directing people to use their opportunities in a particular way.[208] The concept of freedom and equality is based not on an individual's subjective interests but on the obligations of other citizens in the society and the state.[209] The purpose of democratic equality is to remove the social basis of inequality in order to achieve effective citizenship.[210] Accordingly, institutional arrangements should promote the social basis of equality so that everyone can exercise effective citizenship rights instead of attempting to provide equality of fortune or resources.[211]

According to Anderson, the appropriate objective metrics for democratic equality are capabilities.[212] She identifies three spaces of capabilities: capabilities as human beings, capabilities as democratic citizens and capabilities as participants in cooperative production.[213] Amongst the three spheres that she mentions, she theorises the equality of capabilities in the sphere of democratic citizenship. Although Anderson does not provide a list of capabilities, she argues that for effective equal democratic citizenship there need to be some minimum capabilities that people must have, such as health, nutrition and education.[214]

Anderson maintains that '[d]emocratic equality thus aims for equality across a wide range of capabilities. But it does not support comprehensive equality in the

201   ibid 289.
202   ibid 315.
203   ibid 314–15.
204   ibid 319.
205   ibid.
206   ibid 288–319.
207   ibid 288–89.
208   ibid.
209   ibid 319.
210   ibid 288, 291.
211   ibid 308–309.
212   See Anderson, 'Justifying the capabilities approach to justice' (n 120) 81–82.
213   Anderson, 'What is the point of equality?' (n 2) 317–18.
214   Anderson, 'Justifying the capabilities approach to justice' (n 120) 83–84.

space of capabilities'.[215] Democratic equality aims to achieve equality of those capabilities that are necessary in order to perform as an equal citizen in the polity.[216] The claim of equality of capabilities is dependent on the obligation of equal respect of individuals towards each other in a democratic society, rather than on the inferiority of some.[217] What follows from Anderson's model of democratic equality (within the metric of capabilities) is that the selection of specific capabilities would depend on the purpose for which the metric of capabilities is claimed. Thus, if the purpose of the claim of the capability metric is *respect as human beings*, the specific capabilities might be different (although some specific capabilities would be overlapping) from those which are necessary for equal democratic citizenship.

This flexibility is something that Sen values in his approach and Anderson maintains in her theory. Commending Anderson for her conceptualisation of capabilities in the context of democratic equality, Sen notes that Anderson's conceptualisation provides for 'greater flexibility and with much more room for accommodating different demands of distributional reasoning'.[218] Sen leaves his capability approach open-ended, so that it can be supplemented by different distributive patterns. Sen's own conceptualisation of capabilities concedes a great deal of ground to democratic participation and deliberation.[219]

In his *Idea of Justice*,[220] Sen provides a 'comparative' approach[221] to justice, as distinct from a transcendental theory of justice.[222] Transcendental theories of justice provide for *ideal social arrangements* in furtherance of a just society.[223] Sen's comparative idea of justice, on the other hand, proposes the ranking of alternative social arrangements on a scale of 'more just' to 'less just'.[224] Sen is not concerned with the *ideal* just society. He is concerned with removing injustices[225] (or removing *unfreedoms*[226]) from society. Public discussion and democratic deliberation are central to Sen's comparative idea of justice. It is through democratic deliberation that the ordering of alternative social arrangements is to be executed.[227] As a prerequisite to ranking alternative social arrangements, public discussion and democratic deliberation is pre-eminent in determining functionings that are important for society and deciding the capabilities necessary for such functionings. From this dual perspective, democratic deliberation is central in Sen's theory.

---

215   Anderson, 'What is the point of equality?' (n 2) 317.
216   ibid.
217   ibid 289.
218   Sen, 'Capability in a theory of justice' (n 119) 249.
219   Sen, *Development* (n 66) 148, 152–59; Sen, *Idea of Justice* (n 84) 327, 335–37, 345–48. I have elaborated on this aspect of Sen's theory in ch 3.
220   Sen, *Idea of Justice* (n 84).
221   Sen, 'Capability in a theory of justice' (n 119) 243–45.
222   ibid 243–46.
223   ibid 243–45.
224   ibid 244.
225   ibid.
226   Sen, *Development* (n 66) xii, 3–4.
227   ibid 153–55; Sen, *Idea of Justice* (n 84) 17, 97, 102, 106–107.

Anderson's version of democratic equality is also based on the principle of equality of citizens to participate in national democratic processes. One of the three spheres of democratic equality proposed by Anderson is the *equality as participants in the system of cooperative production*.[228] In following Anderson, I advocate for the rule of (recognition of workers and) distribution of capabilities determined by democratic equality within the sphere of the system of cooperative production. Such equality in the system of cooperative production would mean equality between workers and employers, and amongst workers themselves. Hugo Sinzheimer visualised labour law as promoting such 'vertical' equality between workers and employers, and 'horizontal' equality amongst workers in employment relationships.[229] The premise of democratic equality as a starting point might help us realise such a vision of labour law.

The idea of democratic equality is central in conceptualising labour law for informal economic activities. Anderson's democratic equality mandates that all participants in the democratic process must enjoy actual (as distinct from formal) equality. Every participant in a democratic deliberative process is duty-bound to respect and recognise the value of contributions made by all other participants in the democratic process. Democratic equality's ultimate aim is 'collective self-determination'.[230] In the context of labour law for informal economic activities, democratic equality and consequently collective self-determination, would mean two things: first, informal workers are equal participants in the democratic deliberation process; and, secondly, informal workers as responsible agents of the democratic process have the right to self-determination. At a concrete level, these two ideas signify that legal policy-making needs to take into account perspectives from informal workers themselves.

As I have pointed out earlier, legal policy-making needs to ascertain factors hindering capability development of informal workers. It is essential, for both Sen's capability perspective and Anderson's democratic equality formulation, that informal workers themselves identify what they want to do or what they want to become in their lives. Accordingly, they would be the best judges of the capabilities required for the attainment of goals in their lives. It follows that informal workers can not only identify the factors inhibiting their capability enhancement, but they can also propose mechanisms through which the capability-inhibiting factors could be removed. Thus, consideration of the reflections of informal workers themselves needs to inform labour law for informal economic activities.

Anderson acknowledges that her political conceptualisation of the capability approach does not provide a comprehensive theory of justice.[231] She observes that her theory of democratic equality only specifies the role and extent of equality in a theory of justice for democratic societies.[232] To convert her theory of democratic

---

228 Anderson, 'What is the point of equality?' (n 2) 317–18.
229 See Hepple, *Inequality and Global Trade* (n 39) 3.
230 Anderson, 'What is the point of equality?' (n 2) 313.
231 ibid 84.
232 ibid.

equality into a full theory of justice, she suggests that her theory needs to be supplemented by addressing issues of taxation and issues involving people who are inherently incapable of standing equally and exercising agency.[233] However, it is my contention that Anderson's theory, although it is incomplete in some respects, provides a strong substantive basis for reconceptualisation of labour law.

The capability approach provides a novel insight into the reconceptualisation project of labour law so far as the role of institutions is concerned. In the next section, I discuss the concept and role of integrated institutions (as conceptualised by capability theorists) in the reconceptualisation of labour law.

5.7 Integrated institutions and labour law

So far, I have argued that the normative goal of labour law should be capability enhancement and equality of positive freedom for informal workers. I have also argued that the claim to enhancement of real freedom and equality of capabilities should be based on the idea of democratic equality of workers as participants in the cooperative production system. In this section of the chapter, I analyse the role of institutions in operationalising the approach to labour law that I argue for.

Sen and Drèze chart the need to take an integrated look at the multiple institutions in furtherance of freedom in terms of capabilities.[234] In Sen's *Idea of Justice* the concept of integrated institutions enjoys centre stage.[235] Sen argues that institutions by themselves cannot be manifestations of justice.[236] While analysing the necessity and efficacy of institutions we need to look at the characteristics of the institutions and analyse how such characteristics facilitate individual capabilities.[237]

Sen is against an *institutionally fundamentalist* view of justice.[238] An institutionally fundamentalist view of justice is concerned only with the establishment of just institutions – it does not concern itself with the actual performance of the established institutions. Integrated institutions are important in Sen's idea from a three-pronged perspective: first, as a practically realisable concept of institutions, which is attuned to the complexities of modern society (in distinction to that of an idealised society with assumed behavioural patterns);[239] secondly, as a multiple-institutions concept, wherein institutions exercise countervailing power over each other to balance the overall power equilibrium of society;[240] and, thirdly, constant evaluation of results delivered by institutions and, in turn, institutional changes made as a consequence of such evaluation.[241]

---

233 ibid.
234 Jean Drèze, Amartya Sen, *India Development and Participation* (New Delhi: Oxford University Press, 2002) 20–25.
235 Sen, *Idea of Justice* (n 84) 75–86.
236 ibid 82.
237 ibid 82–86.
238 ibid.
239 ibid 79–81.
240 ibid 81–82.
241 ibid 82–86.

Sen's reason for proposing the concept of integrated institutions, public participation and a comparative approach to justice (rather than a transcendental theory of justice) is his belief that a transcendental theory of justice is not able to address justice issues posed by diverse social problems in different societies.[242] People of a given society may not agree on any one view of (transcendental) justice and its corresponding institutions. There may be different views of justice prevailing in a society. An idea of justice, therefore, needs to choose from among the different conceptions of justice that are appropriate to specific societies. In similar vein, there need not be predetermined institutions only capable of facilitating justice. Institutions have to justify their existence by the results they deliver. If predetermined institutions fail to achieve their intended results, they must be replaced by newer institutions.

Democracy is central in Sen's idea of integrated institutions.[243] The essence of Sen's idea of democracy lies in actual participation and democratic dialogue of people in establishing and evaluating multiple institutions that further justice.[244] Sen argues that the institutions of media, political parties, government, opposition, judiciary, legislature and NGOs can exercise countervailing power over one another in generating social discourse based on the democratic deliberation process.[245]

While Sen's concept of institutions suggests that he thinks of institutions as organised bodies, Rawls conceptualises institutions as 'practices and rules that structure relationships and interactions among agents'.[246] It is in both these senses of institutions that the concept of integrated institutions is extremely important for reconceptualisation of labour law, especially for informal workers.

The present labour law dispensation emphasises contracts between employers and employees. For a new conceptualisation of labour law that is sensitive to the problems of informal workers, the role of social institutions such as families, kinship relationships, work-related organisations, legal systems and property rights needs to be taken into account. However, whilst rules and practices generated by these institutions are important for labour law for informal workers, all of these institutions cannot be subsumed into labour law. It is also important to engage multiple institutions such as NGOs, political parties, media and government in the making of a reconceptualised labour law. Collective capabilities emanating from collective organisations[247] would be an important institution in conceptualising the new labour law. The institution of collective organisation needs to be integrated with the overall functional role of multiple institutions.

242   ibid ix–x, 7, 9–11, 15–16, 18, 20–21, 25–27, 90, 100; Sen, 'Capability in a theory of justice' (n 119) 243–46.
243   Sen, *Idea of Justice* (n 84) 91, 324–27, 388–415; Sen, *Development* (n 66) 148–59; Drèze and Sen (n 234) 20–25, 347–52.
244   Sen, *Idea of Justice* (n 84) 327, 335–37, 345–46, 388–415; Sen, *Development* (n 66) 153–59.
245   Sen, *Development* (n 66) xii–xiii; Drèze and Sen (n 234) 20.
246   Thomas Pogge, *John Rawls* (New York: Oxford University Press, 2007) 28; Sen, *Idea of Justice* (n 84) 78.
247   Evans (n 154).

What follows from Sen and Drèze's conceptualisation of institutions is that we need to establish and evaluate institutions with an eye to the objective that is to be attained. If attainment of any objective requires multiple institutions, we have to establish those institutions. If attainment of an objective requires changes in the character of some institutions, we need to make those changes. Institutions need not be seen as inviolable and fixed entities – they must be viewed as instruments that need constant adjustments.

What this implies for labour law regulating informal work is that the purpose of such multiple institutions is enhancement of capabilities of informal workers. Institutions are instruments that need to create conditions wherein workers can convert their personal characteristics into capabilities with the help of institutionally created social conversion factors. Institutions can justify their existence only by the creation of appropriate conditions that facilitate capabilities of workers. To create such enabling conditions for workers engaged in informal economic activities, more than one institution is required. Therefore, in addition to conceptualising labour law in terms of claims to resources and institutional (social) conversion factors, it is necessary to recognise the role of integrated institutions in the making of labour law, especially with reference to informal work. Efficacy of labour law for informal workers would depend on these integrated institutions to a large extent.

Barbara Harriss-White notes that the informal labour market is embedded in social institutions such as caste, language, ethnicity, religion and gender.[248] Much of the exploitation of informal workers is, therefore, attributable to these social institutions.[249] However, these social institutions also structure workers' entitlements,[250] such as providing help in time of need and making specific allocations for particular occasions.[251] For example, workers' rights at work, and their social and physical security, are informally mediated through institutions of gang-masters (at work), grocers or food retailers and local mafia.[252] NGOs and new civil society organisations are increasingly providing social security and social provisioning of health and education (as I discussed in Chapter 2).[253] Informal work is regulated by non-state local regulatory mechanisms devised by social institutions.[254] Some of these institutions need not necessarily have democratic underpinnings.[255] Harriss-White observes that the social institutions regulating India's informal economy express both identity and class.[256]

---

248 Barbara Harriss-White, 'Work and wellbeing in informal economies: the regulative roles of institutions of identity and the state' (2010) 38(2) *World Development* 170 at 172.
249 ibid 172–74.
250 ibid 173.
251 ibid 173–74; Barbara Harriss-White, 'Globalization, the financial crisis and petty production in India's socially regulated informal economy' (2010) 1(1) *Global Labour Journal* 152 at 153.
252 Harriss-White, 'Work and wellbeing' (n 248) 174.
253 ibid 176–77.
254 ibid 176, 178; Harriss-White, 'Globalization' (n 251) 156–57, 162–63.
255 Harriss-White, 'Work and wellbeing' (n 248) 176–77.
256 Harriss-White, 'Globalization' (n 251) 152.

Charting the depth of regulation of informal businesses by social institutions, Harriss-White notes:

> Age/generation, gender, caste, ethnicity, religion and place constitute regulative forces all of which play a role in – and disguise, delay, but do not halt – class formation. Ethnicity and caste, for instance, persistently structure recruitment and occupation. Caste and ethnicity lie behind the guild-like business associations – which are obstacles to the mobility of capital and labour and which were also confidently predicted to disappear with modern market forces. These small units of accountability and of collective action may police entry, organize apprenticeships, calibrate weights and measures, regulate derived markets (labour, porters, transport), adjudicate disputes, guarantee livelihoods, respond to individual or collective misfortune and accumulate the funds necessary to represent the interests of market actors, shape the way policy is implemented and collectively evade tax. [Footnotes omitted][257]

She also notes that, despite the extensive social regulation of informal economic activities, the interests of labour are often overlooked.[258]

While Harriss-White observes social regulation with respect to South Asia (India, in particular) and Africa, the World Bank report *Informality: Exit and Exclusion*[259] notes a regulatory preference for local institutions based on trust and reciprocity rather than on state institutions in informal economic activities in Latin America and the Caribbean.[260] Local institutions are capable of being tailored as a response to market failure, thereby providing better safeguards in time of need.[261] Informal safety nets based on relations of trust and reciprocity, such as memberships in community, religious and neighbourhood organisations, provide better insurance against adverse shocks to informal workers and their families.[262]

Similarly, Hernando de Soto documents that, instead of complying with state laws, informal entrepreneurs (and workers) comply with the laws and practices they themselves have developed,[263] some of which are 'illegal'.[264] De Soto notes that not all informal economic activities are totally informal – they are generally partly formal and partly informal.[265] Informal entrepreneurs (and workers) regulate their informal activities to their advantage by manoeuvring their localised practices and institutions. What this practice reveals is that laws regulating informal economic

---

257 ibid 156–57.
258 ibid 157, 162–63.
259 See Guillermo E Perry and others (eds), *Informality: Exit and Exclusion* (Washington DC: The World Bank, 2007).
260 ibid 24–25.
261 ibid.
262 ibid 24–25, 190–91.
263 de Soto (n 19) 151–72.
264 ibid 131–72.
265 ibid.

activities in general and labour laws regulating such activities in particular, need to be sensitive to actual local-level social situations and to engage local social institutions.

Sen's concept of integrated institutions is vital in this context. What it means for labour law to take an institutionally integrated approach is to take note of the social and political institutions that are in operation in informal economic activities. Institutions adversely and beneficially affecting informal workers need to be distinguished. In the next stage, social and political institutions that promote informal workers' capabilities need to be made part of the labour law dispensation.

It is useful here to consider how integrated institutions could be involved in reconceptualising labour law for informal economic activities. As I have argued earlier in this chapter, the normative goal of labour law must be enhancement of informal workers' capabilities. In this process, it is necessary to ascertain what the valuable capabilities are for specific groups of informal workers (ie workers engaged in similar activities and sharing identical or similar socio-economic-political conditions). In the process of identifying valuable capabilities, the theory of democratic equality mandates that informal workers are engaged to identify valuable capabilities for themselves. However, in the process of identification of valuable capabilities, informal workers might suffer from what Sen calls adaptive preference.[266]

Adaptive preference results from lack of education, health, nutrition, awareness and a plethora of other factors that are responsible for the perpetual marginalisation of informal workers. In this respect, the role of integrated institutions is extremely important. Integrated institutions including political parties, media and NGOs, by getting involved in the democratic (social) dialogue process, have the capacity to ward off the danger of adaptive preference by contributing to the process of determining and institutionalising valuable capabilities. Additionally, once desirable capabilities are identified by informal workers, integrated institutions can help to determine factors (resources and social conditions) necessary for the promotion of desirable capabilities.

Moreover, integrated institutions can also contribute to the representation of informal workers. Informal workers can organise themselves only under specific political-economic and socio-cultural contingencies, as I have documented in Chapter 2. However, the majority of informal workers are non-unionised. In the absence of trade unions (or other organisations), it is difficult for informal workers to participate in a representative democratic deliberation process. Integrated institutions may also become important by giving voice to informal workers in the democratic deliberation process. Institutions such as the media, political parties,

---

266 Amartya Sen defines adaptive preference thus: 'our desires and pleasure-taking abilities adjust to circumstances, especially to make life bearable in adverse situations. . . . [F]or example, the usual underdogs in stratified societies, perennially oppressed minorities in intolerant communities, traditionally precarious sharecroppers living in a world of uncertainty, routinely overworked sweatshop employees in exploitative economic arrangements, hopelessly subdued housewives in severely sexist cultures. The deprived people tend to come to terms with their deprivation because of the sheer necessity of survival, and they may, as a result, lack the courage to demand any radical change, and may even adjust their desires and expectations to what they unambitiously see as feasible.' [footnote omitted] See Sen, *Development* (n 66) 62–63.

local Members of Parliament, opposition party leaders and NGOs can ensure participation of informal workers in policy-making in the absence of unions for informal workers.

Thus, during the process of ascertaining the capability deprivation of informal workers and envisaging appropriate institutional frameworks for the promotion of capabilities of informal workers, integrated institutions of a democratic society can attain immense significance. It is through the participation of integrated institutions along with informal workers in the legal policy-making process that labour law for informal economic activities could take a definite shape. Once informal workers (with the assistance of integrated institutions) decide on the conditions that are necessary for their capability enhancement, their decision (arrived at through social dialogue) needs to be institutionalised through law, thereby integrating democratic law-making in production relations, which Otto Kahn-Freund noted as lacking in labour law.[267]

However, what is theoretically possible might be difficult to implement. The biggest challenge for labour law in adopting an institutionally integrated approach to the effective administration of informal economic activities is to find the right balance of institutions that enhance workers' capabilities. This approach will require an appropriate understanding of the way informal economic activities function and identify the effective institutions; it will also need to restrict the role of adversarial institutions. One of the principal purposes of this equation is to strike a balance of power that underlies informal economic activities. I am proposing a more comprehensive conceptualisation of labour law that is attentive to the problems of informal workers.

What follows from Sen's idea of comparative justice and integrated institutions is that labour law needs to take account of specific informal activities (instead of providing a transcendental formula) to address the deprivation of capabilities of the workers engaged in these activities. To do this, labour law needs to recognise the multiple institutions that interact amongst themselves in promoting workers' capabilities. Thus, the normative goal of a reconceptualised labour law focused on the enhancement of capabilities needs to be supplemented by a mechanism that takes integrated institutions into account.

However, in order to make labour law compatible with informal economic activities the juridical notion of employment relationship needs to be transcended. As I discussed in Chapter 1, the employment relationship is not a universal phenomenon for informal economic activities. Accordingly, in order to address

---

267 Kahn-Freund notes: 'The central problem how to adjust managerial power and the co-ordinated power of labour and management appears to the legal mind as a problem of the relation between the collective agreement and the contract of employment, made between the individual worker with his employer. In fact the worker does not participate in the making of the rules which govern his work, any more than the citizen, as a citizen, participates in the making of the laws he has to obey. Nor does "democracy" mean that those who have to obey rules have an active share in making them, and this is true of political as well as of "industrial" democracy. In both spheres–the political and the industrial–democracy means that those who obey the rules have a right (and a moral duty) to select those who represent them in making the rules.' See Kahn-Freund, *Labour and the Law* (n 4) 14–15.

the diverse range of self-employed and wage-employed informal workers labour law must be based on the concept of *work* rather than any *employment relationship*.[268] If the conceptual basis of labour law is work, then the idea can integrate both formal and informal workers into it.

5.8 Conclusion

In this chapter, I have charted a regulatory logic for the improvement of living standards and service conditions of informal workers. I have sought to advocate a normative goal of regulation. I also proposed a framework compatible with my regulatory proposal. Based on Sen's theorisation, I have argued that capability development and equality of capabilities should be the normative goal for regulation of informal workers. I proposed that Anderson's idea of democratic equality should become the distributive basis of capabilities. I have also argued (based on Sen's proposition) that formulation and administration of a regulatory regime involving informal workers needs to engage integrated institutions of a democratic society. This chapter offers a theoretical basis in furtherance of a labour law framework for informal economic activities with a view to improving the conditions of informal workers. Its contribution lies in its systematic presentation of a capability approach-based comprehensive conceptualisation of labour law for informal economic activities.

Operationalising the proposed theoretical model of labour law might differ from one category of informal economic activity to another in view of the heterogeneity of informal economic activities. Given the wide variety of informal economic activities, it is necessary to analyse concrete implications of the theoretical approach for specific informal economic activities.

In the following chapters of the book, I look at how the proposed theoretical framework of labour law (for informal economic activities) might work in the concrete context of the specific informal waste-picking activity in India. In the following chapter (Chapter 6), based on my fieldwork in Kolkata, India, I seek to ascertain working conditions and living standards of waste pickers in Kolkata. Employing semi-structured interviewing and participant observation methods, I discuss an interpretative account (ie research participant's account) of waste pickers' experiences.

Based on waste pickers' own accounts of their working conditions and living standards, my purpose is to determine the desirable capabilities that waste pickers deem valuable for themselves. Using these reflections from the waste pickers themselves, in Chapter 7, I draw a concrete account of a labour law framework for the informal economic activity of waste picking in India. I test my theoretical framework of labour law with reference to specific informal economic activity in a specific democratic society.

268 Judy Fudge, 'Blurring legal boundaries' in Judy Fudge, Shae McCrystal and Kamala Sankaran (eds), *Challenging the Legal Boundaries of Work Regulation* (Oxford & Portland, OR: Hart Publishing, 2012) 1; Supiot and others, *Beyond Employment* (n 10).

6 Capability deprivations of waste pickers in India

If I were literate I would have got a job at Bangur [Government Hospital]. Since I could not sign my name, I could not get the job at Bangur. Would I have ever done this [waste picking]? I would have been an Aaya [midwife/hospital personnel assisting patients – but not trained nurse] at Bangur. Since I knew [traditional] first aid stuff doctors and nurses would love me. But my thumb impression was not sufficient for the government service.

Kangali Roy[1] (Woman waste picker aged 66
in Golfgreen area, Kolkata, India)

6.1 Introduction

Kangali Roy's is not an isolated experience. She is one of the thousands of waste pickers crowding the garbage dumps in and around the city of Kolkata in order to earn a living. Her inability to sign her name forced her to make a constrained choice of becoming a waste picker. However, the 66-year-old fragile Kangali has also found a special niche as a waste picker. In order to avoid competition from much younger and able-bodied waste pickers, Kangali works at night. She goes to work at around 11 pm at night and comes back home with her collect at about 3 in the morning; she sleeps from 3 am to 7 am and then carries on with her daily routine (which includes a weekly or bi-weekly visit to the *intermediary* to sell her collect).

Kangali came to Kolkata when she got married, about 45 years ago. After her husband's accidental death, when her son refused to look after her, she began to work as a waste picker. It was her daughter who took care of Kangali and Kangali is delighted to acknowledge that: 'my daughter is my everything'. Kangali lives in a slum with her daughter and her grandchildren at the edges of what is one

---

1 Interview conducted on 30 April 2011 in the Golfgreen area of Kolkata, India. I have used pseudonyms for all my waste picker and intermediary (middlemen and middle women) informants throughout this chapter, and in other chapters. I have also mentioned 'areas' of my interviews instead of exact locations (of waste pickers). However, I have used real names for my organiser, elected representative and government official informants, except when I have been advised not to do so.

of the posh localities in Kolkata. Shanty slums are scattered all around the city of Kolkata and coexist with residential and office buildings.[2] Kangali lives in a small bamboo-thatched shanty beside a high-rise residential complex.

Most of the migrant workers (interstate migrants, as well as undocumented international migrants) in Kolkata live in these slums scattered around the city. To contextualise the informal economic activity of waste picking and understand the work-lives[3] of the waste pickers in Kolkata, it is necessary to reflect on the socio-economic-political profile of the city.

As Kangali Roy's story suggests, this chapter is based on my case study in Kolkata. In Chapter 5, I offered a capability approach-based theoretical conceptualisation of labour law. In order to see how such labour law might take shape in the specific context of definite informal economic activity, I analysed the informal activity of waste picking in Kolkata. In this chapter, my purpose is to understand the working conditions and living standards of informal waste pickers with a view to identifying their existing capabilities (or the lack of them) and ascertain their future desirable capabilities. I use my case study to identify factors that might be able to promote desirable capabilities of waste pickers in Kolkata. In the next chapter, I propose institutionalisation of these identified factors through a social dialogue process in order to develop a labour law framework for the concrete situation of waste pickers in Kolkata, India.

This chapter is divided into five main sections, excluding the introduction and the conclusion. In the following section (section 6.2) of the chapter I chart a socio-economic-political profile of the city of Kolkata. After delineating a brief profile of the city of Kolkata, I look into the left-wing politics in the state of West Bengal and the city of Kolkata and note how such left-wing politics have influenced rural and urban development in the state (section 6.3). Against the backdrop of the long Left Front governance in the state, I describe the institutional protections afforded to informal workers in West Bengal in section 6.4.

In section 6.5, I discuss the methodology employed (and its limitations) for the case study of informal waste pickers in Kolkata. In section 6.6, based on my fieldwork in Kolkata, I analyse the working conditions and living standards of waste pickers in Kolkata, with specific emphasis on their capability deprivations. My discussion in this section is based on the reflections of the waste pickers interviewed: I draw the different subheadings for this section of the chapter on the basis of my research participants' identification of desirable factors necessary for their capability-enhancement.

6.2 A profile of the city of Kolkata

Kolkata, the British India capital until 1911, is today the seventh largest city (in area and population) of India and the capital of the state of West Bengal (WB),

---

2 Ananya Roy, *City Requiem, Calcutta: Gender and the Politics of Poverty* (Minneapolis & London: University of Minnesota Press, 2003) 35–40, 48–49.
3 I have elaborated my use of the term work-life in ch 4.

with an area of 1480 square kilometres (of which 185 square kilometres is within the Kolkata Municipal Corporation area) and a population of 4,486,679[4] (2011 census).[5] The population density is 24,252 per square kilometre, with 899 females for every 1000 males (2011 census).[6] Poverty and precariousness in Kolkata is well documented, both in the research literature[7] and in popular literature.[8] Because of rapid urbanisation and migration, Kolkata has developed haphazardly from its early days, resulting in a large number of slums and squatter settlements with extremely inefficient civic amenities.[9] Urban growth in WB is characterised by 'poor development of employment generating activities'[10] – a significantly large number of families in Kolkata do not have regular jobs.[11] The majority of these families live in abject poverty in slums or squatter settlements, and are homeless (living on streets and railway platforms).[12] Kolkata's poorest eke out their living by working in informal economic activities, including waste picking.[13]

The birthplace of Indian nationalism and the independence movement, scholars also identify Bengal (which included the present-day Bangladesh and WB state in India until 1947) as the centre of Indian renaissance.[14] Consistent with such identification, social status in Bengal and in Kolkata (being at the centre of such renaissance) was dependent on education, learning, professional excellence and culture, rather than on birth or wealth.[15] Hence caste (which is determined by birth) never became central in WB's political discourse.[16]

4   Government of India, 'Statement 1, Ranking of districts by population size in 2001 and 2011' Provisional Population Totals for West Bengal, *Census of India 2011*, available at http://www.censusindia.gov.in/2011-prov-results/prov_data_products_wb.html (last visited 3 February 2012).
5   Kolkata Municipal Corporation (KMC), *Basic Statistics of Kolkata*, available at https://www.kmcgov.in/KMCPortal/jsp/KolkataStatistics.jsp (last visited 10 December 2011).
6   Government of India, 'Area, population, decennial growth rate and density for 2001 and 2011 at a glance for West Bengal and the districts' Provisional Population Totals for West Bengal *Census of India 2011* (n 4).
7   See Geoffrey Moorhouse, *Calcutta: the City Revealed* (New York: Penguin Books, 1984).
8   See Dominique Lapierre, *The City of Joy* (New York: Warner Books, 1986).
9   See Ashis Sarkar, *Urban System, Urban Growth and Urbanisation in the 20th Century West Bengal* (Delhi: New Academic Publishers, 1998) 15–16, 85–88, 131–34.
10 ibid 130.
11 See Pranab Bardhan, 'Poverty and employment characteristics of urban households in West Bengal' (1987) 22(35) *Economic and Political Weekly* 1496.
12 Atul Kohli, *Democracy and Discontent: India's Growing Crisis of Governability* (Cambridge: Cambridge University Press, 1990) 123.
13 Roy, *City Requiem* (n 2) 12, 80–84, 88, 94–97; Ishita Mukhopadhyay, 'Calcutta's informal sector: changing pattern of labour use' (1998) 33(47/48) *Economic and Political Weekly* 3075 at 3078–80.
14 See Partha Chatterjee, *The Present History of West Bengal: Essays in Political Criticism* (Delhi: Oxford University Press, 1997) 14–25; Atul Kohli, *Democracy and Development in India* (New Delhi: Oxford University Press, 2009) 333–35; Kheya Bag, 'Red Bengal's rise and fall' (2011) 70 *New Left Review* 69 at 71.
15 Chatterjee (n 14) 24; Kohli, *Democracy and Development* (n 12) 322–23, 333–34, 350.
16 Chatterjee (n 14) 21–24, 69–71; Kohli, *Democracy and Development* (n 12) 316, 319, 323–24, 344–46; Rina Agarwala, 'From work to welfare: informal worker's organizations and the State in India' (unpublished PhD Thesis, Faculty of Princeton University 2006) 113, 118–19.

The combination of urbanism and radicalism, influenced largely by European intellectual thought, gave WB its left ideological orientation in politics.[17] Bengal's radicalism and nationalism threatened the British, so much so that they deployed partition as a strategy to divide Bengal in 1905.[18] Although the partition plan of 1905 was not executed,[19] Bengal was finally partitioned in 1947 when India became independent.[20] The partition of 1947 saw *en masse* migration of the Hindu population from East Pakistan (today's Bangladesh) to WB and the Muslim population from WB to East Pakistan.[21] The cross-flow of migration may have resulted in the largest migration into Kolkata; however, this was not the last time people migrated to WB and Kolkata in great numbers. Kolkata was always and still is a city of migrants.[22]

Migrants mostly constitute the underclass of the city of Kolkata, engaging in low-paid and insecure activities such as rickshaw-pulling, waste picking, labouring in brick-kilns, street vending, domestic work, tailoring, umbrella-repairing and prostitution.[23] Migrants are important in the city's and the state's politics insofar as Bengali migrants (those who migrated from today's Bangladesh) living in slums have been identified as traditional vote banks for the left parties.[24]

Kolkata is one of the most politically active cities in India.[25] From 1977 the state of WB has experienced a democratically elected Left Front government led by the Communist Party of India (Marxist) (CPM) for 34 consecutive years that only ended in 2011.[26] However, post-independence, because of the state's overall left orientation and its ideological and strategic distance from the dominant political class of India (the Union Government), the state of WB has been systematically marginalised from investment for development purposes, especially in the last few

17 Chatterjee (n 14) 14–23; Kohli, *Democracy and Development* (n 12) 336–37, 341–43; Kohli, *Democracy and Discontent* (n 12) 269–72.
18 Chatterjee (n 14) 27–28. British administrators perceived united Bengal as a threatening power; and hence wanted to split and weaken that power so that opponents of the British rule *pull in different ways*.
19 Chatterjee (n 14) 28–29; Kohli, *Democracy and Development* (n 14) 337.
20 Chatterjee (n 14) 37–43.
21 Ranabir Samaddar, *The Marginal Nation: Transborder Migration from Bangladesh to West Bengal* (New Delhi: Sage, 1999) 29–30; Chatterjee (n 14) 43–45, 186–87; Pranati Datta, 'Push–pull factors of undocumented migration from Bangladesh to West Bengal: a perception study' (2004) 9(2) *The Qualitative Report* 335 at 336–39.
22 Samaddar (n 21) 17–18, 29–30; Kohli, *Democracy and Discontent* (n 12) 124; Chatterjee (n 14) 187; Nitai Kundu, 'The case of Kolkata, India' 2, 4, available at http://www.ucl.ac.uk/dpu-projects/Global_Report/pdfs/Kolkata.pdf (last visited 11 June 2012); Sarkar, *Urban System* (n 9) 16, 131–34; Roy, *City Requiem* (n 2) 29–30, 34, 55, 57; Arjan de Haan, 'Calcutta's labour migrants: encounters with modernity' (2003) 37 *Contributions to Indian Sociology* 189 at 192–96; Geetanjali Gangoli, 'Sex work, poverty and migration in Eastern India' in Sadhna Arya, Anupama Roy (eds), *Poverty, Gender and Migration* (New Delhi, Thousand Oaks & London: Sage Publications, 2006) 214; Shutapa Paul, 'East Bengal in West Bengal', *India Today* (24 January 2011).
23 Samaddar (n 21) 25–26, 30, 36–39, 141–45.
24 Kohli, *Democracy and Discontent* (n 12) 140–41.
25 ibid 183.
26 See Bag (n 14) 69.

decades.[27] It is not surprising, therefore, that the capital of the state (Kolkata) has earned the title of being a *neglected city*.[28] However, neglect cannot alone explain the comparative industrial stagnation and unemployment in WB.[29] Partha Chatterjee sums up modern day Kolkata thus:

> Property developers and speculators have turned the centre of the city into a high-rise slum for the affluent, while small savings, provident fund loans and co-operative housing societies are quietly changing the squalid chaos of the refugee colonies into havens of middle-class respectability. The poor, whose labour and enterprise provide the lifeblood for all productive activities and services in the city, are being rapidly banished to a still more distant periphery from where they commute daily to earn their livelihood in factories, trading centres, on the pavements and in the sweatshops of the 'informal sector'. It is this sector that sustains the economic life of a metropolis which has seen virtually no industrial growth in two decades.[30]

I use Chatterjee's observation as a starting point for the discussion of left-wing politics in the state of West Bengal and contextualise informal workers in the backdrop of such politics.

6.3 Left-wing politics and urban informal workers in Kolkata

Although informal workers in the state of WB do receive some legislative and executive protections from the state, Rina Agarwala has shown that benefits received by informal workers in WB are less than those received by informal workers in some other Indian states such as Tamil Nadu[31] and the benefits in WB are not consistent across different informal economic activities.[32] Agarwala argued that the relative apathy of the CPM-led Government of WB in providing benefits for informal workers in the state results from the fact that the CPM's operational principle of *democratic centralism*,[33] coupled with lack of interest in neo-liberal

---

27 See Sarkar, *Urban System* (n 9) 12; Chatterjee (n 14) 25, 30; Bag (n 14) 72, 81, 83.

28 Kohli, *Democracy and Discontent* (n 12) 123.

29 Agarwala (n 16) 113–39; Roy, *City Requiem* (n 2) 89–94.

30 Chatterjee (n 14) 191–92.

31 Agarwala (n 16) 80–112, 113–39.

32 ibid 113.

33 Democratic centralism (DC) is the operational policy of the CPM that led the Government of WB for 34 years from 1977 to 2011. While DC encourages a democratic dialogue process within the party structure, it is ultimately the decision of the party top brass that is binding on the entire party structure. Kohli argues that CPM's operational policy became the government's operational policy because of the long and entrenched nature of the CPM-led rule in the state of WB. See Kohli, *Democracy and Development* (n 14) 320, 366, 370–71; Kohli, *Democracy and Discontent* (n 12) 137–38; Prakash Karat, 'On democratic centralism' (2010) 26(1) *The Marxist* 3; Party Constitution art XIII, available at http://www.cpim.org/content/party-constitution#Principles%20of%20Democratic%20Centralism (last visited 12 June 2012).

market policies make it difficult for workers' unions to exert pressures on the government for populist policies.[34] Democratic centralism entails decision-making at the highest level of the Party (CPM) leadership,[35] rather than at the grassroots level. Agarwala argued that such a top-down approach has not worked well for the grassroots demands of informal workers in the state.[36]

WB is an exceptional state in Indian politics.[37] Compared with many states in India, WB has been governed well by the Left Front.[38] Communist parties leading the Left Front were in reality *social democratic* in nature.[39] Despite radicalism and nationalism characterising the politics in Bengal since the early decades of the 20th century,[40] it was not until 1967 that the state had any form of a left government.[41] The Indian National Congress Party (Congress-I) that gained popularity during the Indian independence movement governed India continuously for about four decades after the country's independence.[42] However, the Congress-I never gained much popularity and did not establish a good foothold in WB.[43] Primarily a party led by upper-caste Hindus, lower-caste Hindus and Muslims in WB were never attracted to the Congress-I.[44] Congress-I also did not receive much support from the upper-caste Hindus in WB, who were drawn towards radical political ideals.[45] Congress-I ruled WB from 1947 (the year of independence) until 1967.[46] In 1967 an alliance of 14 left parties, known as the United Front (UF), defeated the Congress-I Party in WB.[47]

---

34 Agarwala (n 16) 113, 120–21.
35 For an understanding of the tight-knit organisational framework of the CPM see Atul Kohli, *The State and Poverty in India: the Politics of Reform* (Cambridge: Cambridge University Press, 1987) 96–108.
36 Agarwala (n 16) 113, 120–21.
37 Kohli, *Democracy and Discontent* (n 12) 267; Kohli, *Democracy and Development* (n 14) 315, 361.
38 Kohli, *Democracy and Discontent* (n 12) 267–68, 294.
39 ibid 267.
40 Kohli, *Democracy and Development* (n 14) 315–16, 351.
41 Chatterjee (n 14) 14–23.
42 Agarwala (n 16) 117; Kohli, *Democracy and Development* (n 14) 356.
43 Kohli, *Democracy and Development* (n 12) 315, 339–41, 355–59; Kohli, *Democracy and Discontent* (n 12) 273; Agarwala (n 16) 117; Kheya Bag notes why Congress fell out of favour in pre-independence Bengal: 'In 1937, at the urging of the millionaire magnate G. D. Birla, then based in Calcutta, the Congress High Command under Nehru, taking orders from [Mohandas] Gandhi, forbade the provincial Congress to form a joint ministry with the pro-peasant, predominantly Muslim Krishak Praja Party [KPP] in the Bengal legislature. This sectarian decision, foreshadowing the Hindu chauvinism of its later years, sidelined Congress over the next decade, forcing the KPP into a coalition with the Muslim League, a landlord organisation in Bengal, thereby helping to popularize the League and turn the KPP from socio-economic to communal issues. Any rapprochement between the Bengali Congress and the peasant movement was ruled out when Gandhi mounted a putsch against Subhas Bose, who had been democratically elected president of Congress in 1939, and had him expelled from the party in best authoritarian fashion.' See Bag (n 14) 71–72.
44 Kohli, *Democracy and Development* (n 12) 361–62; Agarwala (n 16).
45 Kohli, *Democracy and Development* (n 12) 350, 355; Agarwala (n 16) 117–19.
46 Agarwala (n 16) 119.
47 Kohli, *Democracy and Discontent* (n 12) 126; Agarwala (n 16) 119–20.

Radicalism characterised the UF rule in WB for the first few years after 1967, so much so that the police were instructed not to interfere in workers' unlawful and violent agitations against employers.[48] After a period of political turmoil in the state,[49] Congress-I returned to power in WB through a violence-marred and rigged state-legislative election in 1972.[50] From 1972 until 1977 the Congress-I Government ruled the state with an iron fist, suppressing all dissenting voices against the government.[51] Incidentally, the Congress-I rule in WB ran simultaneously with the infamous state of emergency declared by the Indira Gandhi Government (by Congress-I) over the Indian Union (during which civil and political rights were suppressed in the country).[52] In 1977, amidst much excitement, the CPM-led Left Front defeated the Congress-I Government to claim power in West Bengal.[53] Since 1977 the Left Front has won state-legislative-assembly elections consecutively until 2011, when it comprehensively lost the election to a right-of-centre political alliance (that included the Congress-I).[54]

6.3.1 The Left Front and agricultural and rural development

The Left Front's principal constituencies are in the rural parts of WB. Left Front partners such as the CPM, the Communist Party of India (CPI), the Revolutionary Socialist Party (RSP) and the Forward Block (FB) have been mobilising peasants in rural West Bengal from their (the parties') early days.[55] Amongst the Left Front partners, CPM adopted a much more radical approach in their early days of peasant struggles.[56] However, ever since coming to power in 1977 the CPM has discarded much of its radicalism and pursued a reformist agenda.[57] The Left Front's goal was rural poverty alleviation;[58] some of the most successful policies pursued by the Left Front in rural WB are land distribution and tenancy

48 Kohli, *Democracy and Discontent* (n 12) 126–27; Agarwala (n 16) 120.
49 Chatterjee (n 14) 190–91.
50 Biplab Dasgupta, 'The 1972 election in West Bengal' (1972) 7(16) *Economic and Political Weekly* 804 at 804–805; Kohli, *Democracy and Discontent* (n 12) 132–33, 136, 139, 283, 287.
51 Kohli, *Democracy and Discontent* (n 12) 131, 134, 137, 144, 147, 274–77, 282–84; Kohli, *Democracy and Development* (n 14) 372.
52 Agarwala (n 16) 120.
53 Kohli, *Democracy and Discontent* (n 12) 127; Kohli, *Democracy and Development* (n 14) 360, 371–72.
54 Atul Kohli's prediction that, if the oppositional parties could unite in the *first-past-the-post* electoral system, the Left Front in WB could well be voted out of power seems to have happened in 2011 state assembly elections. See Kohli, *Democracy and Development* (n 12) 360; Bag (n 14); Bidyut Chakrabarty, 'The Left Front's 2009 Lok Sabha poll debacle in West Bengal, India' (2011) 51(2) *Asian Survey* 290 at 307–309. The Left Front Government in West Bengal is the 'world's longest-serving democratically elected communist government'. See Roy, *City Requiem* (n 2) ix.
55 On the relative strengths of the political parties in WB during the first decade of the Left Front Government, see Kohli, *The State and Poverty* (n 35) 106–108.
56 Kohli, *Democracy and Development* (n 14) 352, 360; Agarwala (n 16) 121–22.
57 Agarwala (n 16) 121–23.
58 See Kohli, *Democracy and Development* (n 14) 365, 376–87; a former state labour minister of the Left Front Government observed: 'We have given [rural Bengalis] power, land reform, a decentralized *panchayat*', as cited in Agarwala (n 16) 122.

reform,[59] strengthening the micro-credit system,[60] local self-government (*panchayati* system),[61] and employment and wage schemes.[62] Many commentators believe that the Left Front's rural policies are the reasons for the continuous electoral success of the Left Front.[63]

Small and marginal farmers own 60 per cent of the land in WB.[64] The Left Front's land and agricultural policies are responsible for the success of the state in agriculture. From 1980 to 1990 the state had the highest agricultural growth in India.[65] Currently, WB ranks fourth in agricultural productivity in the country.[66] The Left Front has also been able to reduce rural poverty to a significant extent.[67] Since the Left Front's rural policies have reaped enormous electoral dividends for the left political parties in WB, Agarwala argues that the Left Front has little incentive to revisit its policies in rural WB, especially with respect to the needs of informal workers.[68]

Since Agarwala undertook her study in Kolkata, WB (in 2003), the Left Front has come a long way in recognising the unemployment, underemployment and informal employment problems of the state and has shown a proactive interest in industrialisation (and consequent employment) in the state.[69] However, in its effort to industrialise WB, the Left Front resorted to forcible acquisition of (sometimes

59 For a discussion of the land reform programme undertaken by the Left Front Government in WB see Kohli, *Democracy and Development* (n 12) 377–82.

60 For a discussion of the credit support programme for sharecroppers and small landholders implemented by the Left Front Government in WB see Kohli, *Democracy and Development* (n 12) 382–83.

61 For a detailed discussion of the *panchayati* system in WB, and its political implications for the Left Front and the CPM, see Kohli, *Democracy and Development* (n 12) 327–32, 360, 365, 372–76. The *panchayati* system of local self-government is now mandated by the Constitution of India through the Constitution (Seventy-third Amendment) Act 1992.

62 For a discussion of the Left Front Government implemented employment and wage scheme in WB see Kohli, *Democracy and Development* (n 12) 384–85; Kohli, *The State and Poverty* (n 35) 108–42, for the Left Front's celebrated land reforms and other rural policies.

63 See Bag (n 14) 80; Vikas Rawal, Madhura Swaminathan, 'Changing trajectories: agricultural growth in West Bengal, 1950 to 1996' (1998) 33(40) *Economic and Political Weekly* 2595 at 2598, 2600–2601; Madhusudan Ghosh, 'Agricultural development, agrarian structure and rural poverty in West Bengal' (1998) 33(47/48) *Economic and Political Weekly* 2987; Nikhilesh Bhattacharya, Manabendu Chattopadhyay and Ashok Rudra, 'Changes in level of living in rural West Bengal: perceptions of the people' (1987) 22(48) *Economic and Political Weekly* 2071; Mohan Guruswamy, Kamal Sharma and Jeevan Prakash Mohanty, 'Economic growth and development in West Bengal: reality versus perception' (2005) 40(21) *Economic and Political Weekly* 2151.

64 Agarwala (n 16) 123. For a critical reflection of the land ownership in West Bengal see Roy, *City Requiem* (n 2) 44–48.

65 Agarwala (n 16) 122; Bag (n 14) 80.

66 Agarwala (n 16).

67 ibid.

68 ibid.

69 See Buddhadeb Bhattacharjee, 'On industrialisation in West Bengal' (2007) 23 *The Marxist* 1; Ishita Ayan Dutt, 'CPI(M) toes Buddhadeb line, bats for industrialisation' *Business Standard* Kolkata (4 October 2012); Kalyan Chaudhuri, 'A record in West Bengal: with far-reaching achievements in the fields of agriculture and industry to its credit, the Left Front completes 25

agricultural) land in rural areas, thereby alienating its own constituents (ie the rural population).[70] Such newer Left Front policies of large-scale industrialisation throughout the state (especially in rural areas) and forcible land acquisition resulted in the crushing defeat of the Left Front in the 2011 state-legislative-assembly elections.[71]

6.3.2 The Left Front and industrial and urban development

Observers note that the Left Front has largely failed to address the socio-economic problems of urban Kolkata.[72] The Left Front never enjoyed overwhelming support from the urban population of the state.[73] Accordingly, scholars contend that, because the urban population does not attain enormous significance in the Left Front's ideological or strategic approaches, the Front has ignored industrialisation and urban strategies in WB.[74] The Left Front's industrial policy was always confusing, if not conflicting. On one hand, the Left Front sought to promote small-scale entrepreneurship and the public sector as engines of growth; on the other hand, it invited domestic and foreign investors to make large investments in WB.[75]

After India's liberalisation in 1991, the 1994 Industrial Policy of the state of WB emphasised large investments and joint ventures, domestic or foreign.[76] During the long 34-year rule of the Left Front Government, the percentage of factory production decreased; employment in industries stagnated; and real wages decreased.[77] Some scholars relate the relative failure of industrialisation in WB to the initial years of radical United Front rule (of which the left parties were constituents), when the government instructed police not to interfere in strife between the employers and the workers, which resulted in militant trade unionism.[78] In recent years, whatever employment generation has taken place in the state is in the public sector and informal economic activities.[79]

Scholars contend that the Left Front has failed to address urban poverty alleviation.[80] This failure has increasingly alienated urban voters from the Left

---

years of uninterrupted rule in West Bengal' (2002) 19(14) *Frontline*, available at http://www.front lineonnet.com/fl1914/19140310.htm (last visited 30 December 2012).

70 See Bag (n 14) 90–93; Martha Nussbaum, 'Violence on the left: Nandigram and the communists of West Bengal' (spring 2008) *Dissent* 27.

71 See Bag (n 14) 95–96; Chakrabarty (n 54) 294–300.

72 Kohli, *Democracy and Discontent* (n 12) 144, 150–51, 294; Bag (n 14) 84–85.

73 Agarwala (n 16) 123.

74 Kohli, *Democracy and Discontent* (n 12) 151–52; Agarwala (n 16); Amiya Kumar Bagchi, 'Studies on the economy of West Bengal since Independence' (1998) 33(47/48) *Economic and Political Weekly* 2973 at 2975–77.

75 Agarwala (n 16) 124.

76 Bag (n 14) 87–88; Agarwala (n 16).

77 Agarwala (n 16) 126.

78 Kohli, *Democracy and Discontent* (n 12) 130, 145–46, 284–85, 291; Bag (n 14) 81–82; Bagchi (n 74) 2975–77.

79 Agarwala (n 16) 126; Mukhopadhyay (n 13).

80 Agarwala (n 16).

Front. Slums in urban areas used to be the Left Front vote bank.[81] While in power in the Kolkata Municipal Corporation (KMC) and in the state government, the Left Front legalised slums and provided them with livelihood amenities, infrastructural facilities and recognition.[82] However, more recently, the Left Front attitude towards urban slums has started to change – the Left Front Government attempted to evict slum dwellers and demolish slums.[83] Such policies resulted in the loss of Left Front support in urban slums and amongst informal workers.[84] The Left Front's loss of its support base in urban areas, Kolkata in particular, has been attributed to industrial stagnation, unemployment and inflation.[85]

The Left Front support in Kolkata has thinned so much that it failed to secure more than a single seat from amongst 66 seats in the Kolkata region during the 2011 state-legislative-assembly elections.[86] However, according to the former mayor of Kolkata (his party is presently in power in WB and he is an important minister of the government), it is difficult to imagine that the predicament of the slum dwellers is going to improve in the near future. He observed that, although slum dwellers are good as a vote bank, they are a problem for the corporation (ie the KMC) and the city.[87] What he meant was that even though slum dwellers' votes are important during elections, they exert pressure on municipal resources and services, and illegally occupy municipal land, which adversely affects the efficient functioning of the municipal corporation. Against the backdrop of such a negative attitude towards slum dwellers (who are mainly informal workers), it is useful to look at the treatment received by informal workers in the context of the state government laws and policies. In the following paragraphs, I briefly look into the government assistance programmes for informal workers in West Bengal.

6.4 An appraisal of institutional protection mechanisms for informal workers in West Bengal

The Left Front Government in WB has carved out legislative and executive schemes for the benefit of informal workers in the state. While some of the beneficial guarantees are for specific categories of informal workers engaged in definite activities (such as transport, *bidi* manufacturing, construction),[88] other schemes are targeted towards a range of specified informal activities.[89] In 2001,

---

81   ibid. All of the waste pickers interviewed in Kolkata reside in the slums of Kolkata and in roadside and canal-side squatter settlements.
82   Kohli, *Democracy and Discontent* (n 12) 141; Agarwala (n 16) 126–27.
83   Agarwala (n 16) 127; Bag (n 14) 89–90; Roy, *City Requiem* (n 2) 173–76.
84   Agarwala (n 16).
85   ibid 128; Prasanta Sen Gupta, 'Politics in West Bengal: the Left Front versus the Congress (I)' (1989) 29(9) *Asian Survey* 883.
86   See Bag (n 14) 96.
87   Former mayor of Kolkata, Subrata Mukherjee, who is presently a minister in the Government of WB, as quoted in Agarwala (n 16) 128.
88   See Government of West Bengal, *Labour in West Bengal 2010: Annual Report* (Kolkata: Govt of WB).
89   ibid.

WB became the first state to initiate a provident fund scheme for informal workers, in the absence of any social security guarantee from the Central Government.[90]

The State Assisted Scheme of Provident Fund for Unorganised Workers in West Bengal (SASPFUW)[91] specifies 49 informal enterprises and 15 self-employed activities to be covered within the scope of the scheme.[92] Recognising the heterogeneous and flexible nature of informal economic activities, the scheme maintains eligibility of workers engaged in more than one informal activity.[93] All informal workers engaged in the activities specified under SASPFUW are eligible under the scheme if her/his family monthly income does not exceed 3,500 Indian Rupees, or around 58 US Dollars (approximately 60 Indian Rupees is equal to 1 US Dollar).

In accordance with the SASPFUW, each subscriber needs to contribute a sum of Rs 20 (US$ 0.33) every month in furtherance of the creation of his or her provident fund.[94] The State Government contributes a matching amount every month.[95] The State Government also contributes interest on the balance to the credit of a subscriber at a government declared rate.[96] The fund thus generated is refunded to the workers at the age of 55, or earlier in certain circumstances.[97] Workers can also take out loans against the fund.[98] Subscribing workers are issued with an identity card in order to prove their identity and maintain their provident fund account.[99] Collection of monthly subscription fees from informal workers is undertaken by designated collection agents.[100]

In 2007 the WB Government enacted the West Bengal Unorganised Sector Workers' Welfare Act in order to constitute the West Bengal Unorganised Sector Workers' Welfare Board (WBUSWWB) for the purpose of administering the informal labour-welfare fund created under the Act.[101] The welfare board is to implement the SASPFUW scheme.[102] Additionally, the WBUSWWB is empowered to implement any health insurance scheme, pension scheme, house building loan, educational assistance for workers' children, maternity benefit scheme or any other welfare scheme for informal workers in WB.[103]

---

90 The Parliament recently enacted the social security law in 2008, as discussed in ch 2. The legislative scheme is not yet fully operational in the country. The central and the state governments are to collaborate in the implementation of the law.

91 Introduced in the Labour Department Resolution Nos 180-IR dated 24/01/2001 and 305-IR dated 19/02/2001 of the Government of West Bengal.

92 See List of Industries under Unorganised Sector, Annexure-A cl I of the State Assisted Scheme of Provident Fund for Unorganised Workers in West Bengal (SASPFUW) under Labour Department Resolution No. 180-IR dated 24/01/2001.

93 SASPFUW (n 92) cl 2.

94 ibid cl 4.

95 ibid.

96 ibid.

97 ibid.

98 ibid cl 6.

99 ibid cl 5.

100 ibid cl 7.

101 West Bengal Unorganised Sector Workers' Welfare Act 2007 s 4.

102 See Government of West Bengal, *Labour in West Bengal 2010* (n 88) 74.

103 ibid.

Under a resolution of January 2011, the WB Department of Labour initiated the West Bengal Unorganised Sector Workers' Health Security Scheme (WBUSWHS) with retroactive effect from 17 July 2010.[104] The WBUSWWB (ie the board) is to implement the health scheme, which covers all informal workers who are beneficiaries of the SASPFUW scheme.[105] Workers who are already covered under the Central Government health scheme, the Rashtriya Swastha Bima Yojana (RSBY),[106] the Building and Other Construction Workers Act, 1996, the West Bengal Transport Workers Social Security Scheme, or the Beedi Workers' Welfare Fund Act, 1976, are excluded from the purview of the State Government health scheme WBUSWHS.[107]

A SASPFUW beneficiary who has not defaulted in the last two accounting years is eligible for reimbursement for *hospitalisation, clinical tests* and *costs of medicine* in a government hospital.[108] While clinical tests and costs of medicine are fully reimbursed under the scheme, workers are entitled to partial expenses for daily hospitalisation charges.[109] Workers can receive financial assistance of a maximum amount of Rs 5000 (approximately US$83) per annum under the health scheme.[110] As at March 2011, a total of 2,369,943 informal workers are registered in the SASPFUW scheme and hence can benefit from the health scheme.[111]

Apart from these two social security schemes ensuring provident fund and medical assistance for 61 specified categories of informal workers, the Government of WB has implemented legislative and executive protection for construction workers, *bidi* workers and transport workers of the state.[112] In accordance with the Building and Other Construction Workers' (Regulation of Employment and Conditions of Service) Act 1996 and Rules made thereunder, workers employed in establishments employing 10 or more workers are entitled to accidental and death (financial) assistance, pension benefits, medical expenses, maternity benefits, financial assistance for children's education, house-building loans, funeral expenses, tool and spectacle purchase grants, financial assistance for marriage and bicycle costs.[113] As of March 2011, there are 271,870 registered construction worker-beneficiaries under the legislative scheme.[114]

---

104 West Bengal Unorganised Sector Workers' Health Security Scheme (WBUSWHS), Labour Department, Government of West Bengal Resolution No 34-IR, IR/MISC-06/10 of 5/01/2011.
105 ibid cl 1.
106 The Rashtriya Swastha Bima Yojana (RSBY) is a central government health insurance programme for the below-the-poverty-line (BPL) population. For a detailed description of the scheme see Rashtriya Swastha Bima Yojana website at http://www.rsby.gov.in/index.aspx (last visited 12 June 2012).
107 WBUSWHS (n 104) cl 1.
108 ibid cl 3.
109 ibid.
110 ibid.
111 See Government of West Bengal, *Labour in West Bengal 2010* (n 88) 86.
112 ibid 91–110.
113 ibid 92–94.
114 ibid 97.

In addition to the Revised Integrated Housing Scheme (RIHS) of the Central Government, which provides Rs 40,000 (US$666) to a *bidi* worker in order to assist him or her to build a house, the Government of WB has instituted the West Bengal Beedi Workers' Welfare Scheme (WBBWWS).[115] In accordance with the scheme the government has issued identity cards to 1,427,536 *bidi* workers.[116] Additionally, the WBBWWS provides for electrification of *bidi* workers' houses, house-building subsidies and amenities development grants (eg for water supply, sanitation etc).[117] Significant numbers of *bidi* workers have benefited from these schemes.[118]

The Labour Department of the Government of WB initiated the West Bengal Transport Workers' Social Security Scheme in 2010.[119] Transport workers are entitled to pensions, medical benefits, maternity benefits, disability and death (financial) assistance, assistance for children's education, marriage assistance etc under the 2010 scheme.[120] As of March 2011, 45,697 transport workers have registered under the scheme.[121] The WB Government has introduced this scheme upon the recommendation of the West Bengal State Social Security Board, which is constituted under the Unorganised Workers' Social Security Act 2008 (Central legislation).[122]

It is against the backdrop of these institutional protections that the work-lives of waste pickers in Kolkata need to be contextualised. Waste management in the city of Kolkata is undertaken pursuant to the Municipal Solid Wastes (Management and Handling) Rules 2000 and the Bio-medical Waste (Management and Handling) Rules 1998, both promulgated under the Environment (Protection) Act 1986, which was enacted 'to provide for the protection and improvement of environment and for matters connected therewith'.[123] According to the Municipal Solid Wastes (Management and Handling) Rules 2000, municipal authorities[124] are responsible 'for collection, storage, segregation, transportation, processing and disposal of municipal solid wastes'[125] by establishing waste processing and waste disposal facilities.[126]

It is the responsibility of a municipality (such as the KMC) to prohibit littering of solid waste; organise house-to-house and community-bin waste collection;

---

115 See Labour Department, Government of West Bengal Resolution No 658-LW/2B-02/07 of 23/08/2007.

116 See Government of West Bengal, *Labour in West Bengal 2010* (n 88) 98, 107.

117 ibid 98–100.

118 ibid 101–107.

119 See Labour Department, Government of West Bengal Resolution No 907-IR/EIL/1-A-4/10 of 13/08/2010.

120 See Government of West Bengal, *Labour in West Bengal 2010* (n 88) 108–110.

121 ibid 110.

122 See Labour Department, Government of West Bengal Notification No 1025-IR of 6/11/2009.

123 Environment (Protection) Act 1986 (long title).

124 A municipal authority is a local governing body established under a statute. See Municipal Solid Wastes (Management and Handling) Rules 2000 s 3(xiv).

125 ibid s 4(1). According to s 3(xv), 'municipal solid waste includes commercial and residential wastes generated in a municipal or notified areas in either solid or semi-solid form excluding industrial hazardous wastes but including treated bio-medical wastes'.

126 ibid s 4(2).

arrange for waste collection from slums, squatter areas and slaughter houses; segregate bio-medical and industrial waste from municipal waste; segregate municipal waste for recycling and composting purposes; and minimise the burden on landfill.[127] Bio-medical and hazardous wastes need to be disposed of according to the guidelines under the Bio-medical Wastes (Management and Handling) Rules 1998 and the Hazardous Wastes (Management and Handling) Rules 1989 respectively.[128] Municipal authorities are to collect and transport segregated non-bio-medical wastes and duly-treated bio-medical wastes from hospitals, nursing homes, medical clinics, animal houses etc and dispose of such wastes at municipal dump sites.[129] Municipal dump sites are to be appropriately fenced and kept off limits to unauthorised people and stray animals.[130]

For the city of Kolkata, the Kolkata Municipal Corporation Act 1980 provides for the *modus operandi* of solid waste collection, transportation and disposal.[131] While the KMC has a larger mandate for the collection, segregation, transportation, recycling and composting of waste and management of landfills, waste pickers' activities in relation to waste are limited to segregation, collection and recycling of waste as an economically productive activity. Solid waste is part of waste pickers' livelihoods – waste is central to their work-lives.

So far as solid waste management is concerned, waste pickers' relation to the KMC is complementary rather than competitive. With its existing resources and waste management framework, the KMC is able to segregate and recycle solid waste in only seven of the 141 wards (administrative units) of the KMC.[132] For the rest of the 134 wards, the KMC does not segregate between recyclable, compostable and landfillable solid wastes, thereby violating the mandate of the Municipal Solid Wastes (Management and Handling) Rules 2000.[133] Pragmatically speaking, the KMC is unable to treat and dispose of solid waste in the manner prescribed under the 2000 Rules.[134]

Instead of either recycling or composting, the KMC dumps (landfills) bio-degradable, non-bio-degradable and recyclable solid wastes together, once they are collected from the 134 wards that do not have segregation facilities.

Waste pickers, for their part, segregate a significant amount of solid wastes around all the 141 wards of the KMC, in order to collect recyclable materials such as paper, plastic, glass, cardboard, metal etc. Waste pickers transport recyclable materials to the intermediaries (middlemen or women), who in turn transport these

---

127 ibid Sched II: Management of Municipal Solid Wastes.
128 ibid Sched III: Specifications for Landfill Sites.
129 Bio-medical Waste (Management and Handling) Rules 1998 rr 3(5), 3(7), 4, 6.
130 Municipal Solid Wastes (Management and Handling) Rules 2000 Sched III: Specifications for Landfill Sites.
131 Kolkata Municipal Corporation Act 1980 ch XX: Solid Wastes.
132 Interview with Mr Subhashish Chatterjee, executive engineer, Solid Waste Management Department, Kolkata Municipal Corporation on 19 April 2011 at his office at the Kolkata Municipal Corporation building.
133 Municipal Solid Wastes (Management and Handling) Rules 2000 rr 4, 7 and Sched II.
134 ibid Sched II.

to the recycling industry. Thus, while the KMC could only landfill solid waste generated by the city, waste pickers help in recycling segregated solid waste generated in Kolkata. The complementary nature of the relationship between waste pickers and the KMC is, however, not evident from the work-life analysis of the waste pickers. Waste pickers in Kolkata suffer from serious capability deficiencies in their work-lives. Some of these deficiencies emanate from direct and indirect conflict with the KMC and its laws and policies.

It is in this socio-economic-political context that my case study of waste pickers in Kolkata needs to be located. Typically migrant (both interstate and international) workers, waste pickers in Kolkata live in slums, and roadside and canal-side squatter settlements scattered around the city. While some of these settlements are legal, many are not. Identity, recognition and basic amenities are some of the fundamental challenges faced by the slum dwellers in the city. Although the left political parties have taken the initiative to organise rural landless workers,[135] they have not shown particular interest in organising slum-dwelling urban informal workers in Kolkata.[136] Absence of informal workers' organisation results in invisibility of such workers, which, in turn, is responsible for these workers' marginalisation and exclusion from policy circles.

I attempt to draw out informal workers' own interpretation of their lives. I seek to find issues that informal waste pickers in Kolkata perceive as obstacles in their lives and work. My intention is to ascertain capability deprivations of waste pickers and identification of factors which might be able to enhance waste pickers' capability in Kolkata. I identify these factors from the perspective of the waste pickers in Kolkata. Accordingly, my study is based on multi-method analysis of the informal economic activity of waste picking and waste-recycling in Kolkata, India. Empirical analysis of the study is based on the *semi-structured qualitative interviewing* method along with the *participant observation* method. A brief description of the methodology employed in the study is the subject of the next section.

6.5 Methodology employed in the case study of the informal activity of waste picking in Kolkata, India

The case study of waste pickers in Kolkata has multiple purposes. Since the objective of the larger study is to conceptualise labour law for informal economic activities, the case study helps in such conceptualisation at a concrete level. If the normative goal of labour law for informal economic activities is the promotion of capabilities, it is a useful exercise to identify valuable capabilities for specific informal workers in order to determine sites of legal and regulatory intervention in their work-lives. In furtherance of identification of capabilities of waste pickers, I have employed a *qualitative method* of data collection for the case study.[137]

135 See Kohli, *Democracy and Development* (n 14) 385–87.
136 See Agarwala (n 16) 115, 121, 123, 131–39.
137 Martyn Hammersley, *The Dilemma of Qualitative Method: Herbert Blumer and the Chicago Tradition* (London and New York: Routledge, 1989) 94, 156–57.

The study is principally based on *semi-structured interviews* supplemented by *participant observation*.

A substantial volume of data exists with respect to informal economic activities in India. Most of this data, however, is generated by quantitative methods. Although quantitative methods are extremely useful in charting the larger picture with respect to informal economic activities, they often fall short in seeking out the subtle unfreedoms suffered by the individual workers working informally. A qualitative methodology is especially apt to identify the subtle unfreedoms and thereby development-deprivation, at the individual level of informal workers. In order to ascertain the element of choice and exercise of such choice by waste pickers, individual lived experiences of such waste pickers are central to the analysis.

Thus, my choice of case study methods was dependent on the ontological basis and epistemological considerations of my study. Individual interpretations and experiences of waste pickers, and institutional attitudes towards waste pickers, constitute the ontological basis of my study.[138] While texts and institutional structures are important for my case study, the study is principally dependent on individual workers, social actors and their narratives, experiences, understandings, interpretations and motivations involving waste pickers' work-lives. Accordingly, I devised the qualitative semi-structured interview and participant observation methods for my participants with a view to comprehending underlying justifications for individual interpretations.[139]

The purpose of the case study was the identification of achieved functionings by the waste pickers; identification of capabilities (or capability deficiencies) of waste pickers by directly probing and analysing achieved functionings; and identification of future valuable capabilities and functionings for the waste pickers. These purposes require an analysis of the work-lives of individual waste pickers from their own perspectives, and a close observation of their work and environment. From an epistemological point of view, these perspectives could be obtained through *semi-structured interview* and *participant observation* methods.

6.5.1 Sampling and recruiting

The study was conducted in the urban area of Kolkata during the summer of 2011, from March to July. For the purposes of the study, it was necessary that my analysis be based on multiple perspectives offered by stakeholders directly or indirectly associated with the informal activity of waste picking. Interviewing only waste pickers would have presented one side of the phenomenon, albeit a critical one. Since my purpose was also to find out the sites of legal intervention and remove factors hindering capability development of waste pickers, it was necessary for me to understand the socio-economic-political dynamic involved in the informal economic activity of waste picking.

138 Jennifer Mason, *Qualitative Researching* (London: Sage, 2002) 14–16.
139 ibid 16–17.

Therefore, in order to identify capabilities, or capability deprivation of waste pickers in their work-lives and ascertain capability-enhancing factors, I found it necessary to extend the scope of my interviewing to other stakeholders, such as the *intermediary* (middle-person) to whom waste pickers sell their collect, union leaders and organisers, elected representatives and ministers, government officials and scholars from different disciplines.

I interviewed 75 waste pickers from 11 different locations in Kolkata; six intermediaries; nine government officials of different designations from the Department of Labour, Government of West Bengal; five elected representatives, including incumbent and former Labour Ministers of the Government of West Bengal; eleven union leaders and organisers; seven scholars; and three senior ILO officials as part of the study.

6.5.2 Data collection

Through the case study of waste pickers in Kolkata, I wanted to investigate available capabilities and the extent of choice enjoyed by waste pickers in their work-lives. In order to achieve that goal it was necessary for me to have a clear and cogent idea about their work-lives, in addition to interviewing waste pickers. There are two kinds of waste pickers engaged in the economic activity of waste picking: itinerant buyers and waste scavengers.[140] Both of these categories of waste pickers sell what they collect to an intermediary, who, in turn, buys from these waste pickers and sells the recyclable materials to the recycling industry. The recycling industry uses these recyclables as raw materials for their final product. In this scheme, waste pickers who are informal subsistence workers are linked to the formal establishment – the recycling industry – in a business relationship. Thus, the work-lives of waste pickers need to be contextualised in the interaction between the formal and the informal economic activities in the overall production system.

I was interested in finding out whether an employment relationship exists between the waste pickers and the intermediaries: would they have pseudo-contracts between them? Do the waste pickers receive any benefits from the relationship? Are regular wages paid to waste pickers by the intermediaries? Do the waste pickers receive support from intermediaries during any emergency? Are waste pickers free to change intermediaries? Some of these issues are helpful in identifying economic and social security, and thereby capabilities, enjoyed by waste pickers.

In order to identify the social solidarity and political leverage enjoyed by waste pickers, it was necessary for me to look into the role of trade unions and other

---

140   The Employment of Manual Scavengers and Construction of Dry Latrines (Prohibition) Act 1993 s 2(j) defines *manual scavenger* as 'a person engaged in or employed for manually carrying human excreta'. Accordingly, manual scavenging is the activity of carrying human excreta. However, in the context of my study I use scavenging to mean collection of waste by waste pickers for recycling purposes. Therefore, wherever I use the terms *scavenging* or *scavenger*, it should be understood in connection with waste picking and waste pickers.

organisers such as NGOs in the work-lives of waste pickers. Social solidarity and political power are immensely important factors in promoting capabilities for informal workers (as I discussed in Chapter 2). It was important for me to analyse whether waste pickers were organised or not; whether there were initiatives of organising waste pickers either by trade unions or NGOs; what could be achieved by such organising activities; whether capability development opportunities are forgone because of non-organisation. I interviewed trade unions leaders and NGO organisers to understand some of these issues.

As shown in Chapter 2, recognition and social protection are other significant factors in promoting capabilities of informal workers in general and waste pickers in particular. It was important for me to analyse government documents and initiatives in this regard. However, government documents and initiatives could not have revealed the logic and limitations of recognition and social protection for waste pickers. It was important for the study purposes to interact with government officials and policy-makers in order to understand reasons and justifications for the inclusion or exclusion of waste pickers from government policy consideration. Therefore, I interviewed the incumbent Minister-in-Charge for Labour of the Government of West Bengal, two former Ministers-in-Charge for Labour of the Government of West Bengal and senior government officials in the Department of Labour of the Government of West Bengal.

I also interviewed senior ILO officials in New Delhi and Geneva in order to determine the role of international policy-making in the work-lives of informal workers such as waste pickers in India. Scholars from different disciplines working with informal workers have also been helpful in reflecting on the role of law and policy in promoting capabilities of informal workers in India. I conducted my interviews with waste pickers at their worksites and their residences. I interviewed union leaders and NGO organisers at either their offices or another mutually agreed place. I met government officials, incumbent and former ministers and other elected office-holders at their respective offices. Similarly, I met scholars and ILO officials at their places of business.

One of the limitations of my data collection is the short duration of the study. I conducted my fieldwork in Kolkata, India, from March to July 2011. Qualitative interviewing and participant observation methods require a researcher to spend extended periods in the research universe[141] to have a comprehensive understanding of the research context. This extensive fieldwork was not possible for me because of time and budget constraints during the study. However, since I am an Indian and a Bengali (ie domiciled in West Bengal), I was already familiar with the socio-economic-political-cultural context of my study. Moreover, because of my earlier work with the waste-picking community in Kolkata in 2009, I already had background knowledge before I began my study in 2011. Therefore, I do not think that short duration of my study poses a serious limitation to my research.

---

141   Kathleen M DeWalt, Billie R DeWalt, *Participant Observation: a Guide for Fieldworkers* (Walnut Creek: Altamira, 2002) 4.

Another limitation of my case study is the exclusion of child waste pickers from the scope of the study. Exclusion of child waste pickers was a strategic decision adopted in view of the strict *ethics approval* requirement to interview children. In order to receive ethics approval for interviewing children, I would have had to take written permission from children's parents. Since, I interviewed waste pickers at several places such as dumping sites, slums, an intermediary's business place and at waste-disposal bins around the city of Kolkata, it would have been very difficult for me to obtain access to a child waste picker's parents to seek approval. Moreover, since the significant majority of informal workers (including waste pickers) are illiterate, it would have been impossible for me to take written approval from a child waste pickers' parents. In view of these problems and the short duration of the study, I consciously chose to exclude child waste pickers from the scope of my study.

6.5.3 *Data analysis and use*

As I discussed in Chapters 3 and 4, there is a broad agreement amongst capability scholars that factors such as nutrition, health and education are basic essentials in the enhancement of capabilities of vulnerable and marginalised people. Since the purpose of my fieldwork is to ascertain capability deprivation of waste pickers and identify factors responsible for such deprivation, I analysed waste pickers' interviews in the context of the above-mentioned factors.

My guiding questionnaire reflects these analytical factors (functionings) that I employ for my data analysis. I categorised waste pickers' experiences in functioning categories such as deprivation of health, nutrition and education. Although these widely recognised functionings were the starting point of my analytical framework, I developed, modified and evolved my framework during (and after) my fieldwork in India. In addition to functionings such as health, nutrition and education, which are essential for capability enhancement, there are other functionings that are equally important for waste pickers' capability enhancement. During my fieldwork in Kolkata I found that factors such as recognition as worker, identity cards, physical and mental security at work are fundamental in waste pickers' capability development. Accordingly, I included these factors within the framework of my analysis.

I conducted interviews of my study participants principally in Bengali and in Hindi. I transcribed and translated those interviews into English. Instead of using computer software, I have manually coded my interviews. Having identified the factors capable of promoting waste pickers' capabilities, I categorised my study participants' experiences into 10 factors (or capability aspirations). I had predetermined some of these factors (health, education etc), while other factors (recognition, security at work etc) emerged from my study participants' experiences. Thus, I have charted the stakeholders' experiences through the prism of *factors necessary for the enhancement of capabilities* of informal waste pickers. The present chapter and the next chapter rely upon and incorporate data from my fieldwork.

I have used my fieldwork data sometimes to support my contentions and assertions, and sometimes to supplement or contradict the official position.

My fieldwork is aimed at generating the argument that labour law needs to be reconceptualised for informal economic activities and to show how such labour law could be formulated in the context of a specific informal economic activity. In the next section, I analyse the profile of informal waste pickers in Kolkata.

6.6 A profile of informal workers in West Bengal with specific reference to waste pickers

I have travelled across the Kestopur Khal on many previous occasions on my way to Calcutta airport. Kestopur Khal edges the VIP Road that connects the city of Kolkata with its international airport. The entire stretch of the Kestopur Khal area is unpleasantly distinctive. The canal (*Khal*) carries effluent from the north-eastern part of the city. A foul odour from the canal fills the air around the area. The air is also polluted by sulphur and carbon-monoxide emissions. Business and commuter congestion contributes to the noisy chaos. The filthy water of the canal is covered with a thick green layer of hyacinth plant. Waste pickers have encroached upon part of the canal to build a squatter settlement and a waste-segregation area. Although I had always noticed the squatter settlement, this was the first time I had approached the slum to talk to its inhabitants. I came across Amir Alam and his wife Farida Yasmine while they were segregating waste they had collected.[142]

Amir Alam and Farida Yasmine were both born in Bangladesh. They have been engaged in the activity of waste picking for approximately 23 years and 12 years, respectively. They have two daughters, one four and one six years old, both of whom attend a nearby school. They informed me that there is an *Anganwadi* school (*Anganwadi* schools are government-run pre-schools where children learn to socialise) in their settlement. Amir devotes his entire day to collecting and segregating waste. Farida engages in many different tasks: early in the morning she cooks for the family and sends her children to school; she then works at a nearby house as a domestic help; she returns home at around noon and feeds her children after they come back from school; she then goes on to help her husband with waste-collection and waste-segregation. She has been following this schedule for the last six years. The couple have been maintaining their family without any kind of external support.

When asked, they informed me that they do not receive any government assistance whatsoever, despite the fact that the WB Government has instituted legislative and executive protection for informal workers of the state. In the absence of any assistance from the government, Amir and Farida lead an insecure and uncertain life. Insecurity and uncertainty result from multiple capability deficiencies that characterise informal workers' lives in Kolkata, as I document in the following section. In the following section, I not only analyse the capability deficiencies of waste pickers in Kolkata, I also identify (future) valuable capabilities identified by the waste pickers I interviewed in Kolkata.

---

142 Interview conducted on 13 April 2011 in the Kestopur Khal area, Kolkata, India.

6.6.1 Functionings and capabilities of waste pickers in Kolkata, India

Instead of concentrating on only the work-related issues of waste pickers, my study takes a holistic view of their *work* experiences in the context of their lives. Such an approach was necessary because the informal activity of waste picking is deeply integrated into everyday life; work experience and (family) life experience could not be distinguished in a straight forward manner. Working conditions and living situations are interwoven into each other:

- their worksites are not distant from their homes
- they store and segregate their collect in and around their slums
- flexibility in the nature of work allows them to balance work with family responsibilities
- for women waste pickers (the majority of waste pickers interviewed during the present study are women) the work of waste-collection and segregation can be juxtaposed with their responsibilities of cooking for the family and child-care
- waste-collection, segregation and selling keeps a regular income flow in the waste-picking family, which might not be the case for some other economic activities (such as domestic work, for women) where income generally comes at a monthly interval
- waste picking allows them the freedom to decide how much to work every day
- there are no supervisors in this work.

These are some of the beneficial features of the economic activity of waste picking as perceived by the waste pickers themselves. They identify some of these reasons for which they prefer waste picking to activities such as domestic work or rickshaw-pulling. In the following sections, I discuss some of the valuable capabilities that waste pickers in Kolkata have identified as important to them. These capabilities do not necessarily have a definite order – there is no hierarchy to them. All of these capabilities are necessary to enable waste-workers to lead the lives that they want and attain the functionings they value most.

6.6.1.1 Capability to be able to work: recognition

One of the principal capabilities for the waste pickers is the capability to work and to be recognised as workers. Workers undertake work not only to receive wages; work is a valuable source of self-respect and part of one's personality. While recognition of work or workers might not be an issue for the majority of the workers worldwide, for waste pickers recognition constitutes an immensely important capability in their work-lives. Too often, they are deprived of recognition. Their capability to be recognised as workers is the first step towards the enhancement of their overall capabilities. Although capabilities are a sum of wellbeing and agency, with respect to recognition as workers it is the wellbeing aspect of freedom that is missing. Wellbeing ensured by the recognition as workers could come from institutional conditions that can convert social, economic and political resources into capabilities for these waste pickers.

In accordance with the Kolkata Municipal Corporation Act solid waste generated in the city is the property of the KMC.[143] The KMC has its own team for the collection, transport and disposal of such property. Since waste is the property of the corporation, any unauthorised transaction with such property, legally speaking, will constitute the offence of *theft* under the Indian Penal Code.[144] The non-cooperative and adversarial approach of the law enforcement officials (police) towards waste pickers in Kolkata is in keeping with the juridical notion of waste as property of the corporation. Such a property-based understanding of waste excludes all others from productively using waste, even in the face of the KMC's incapacity to put the waste to productive use. The property-based concept of waste criminalises the informal activity of waste picking, thereby stripping waste pickers of their recognition as workers.

The majority of the waste pickers interviewed in Kolkata have been taken into police custody at least once during the performance of their work.[145] For most of these arrests, the police register *petty cases*[146] against the arrested waste pickers. A petty offence is an offence under the Indian Penal Code that is punishable only with a fine not exceeding Rs 1000.[147] In most cases, the police release the waste pickers after a day or two, after a small amount is paid to the police as a fine (ie when appropriate receipt against such payment is made by the police), or as a bribe.[148]

The vulnerability of waste pickers during the course of their work is not only limited to police harassment. Waste pickers are often harassed by local residents and anti-social elements of a ward during the collection of waste. While waste pickers view these harassments as professional hazards, they are more concerned with harassment meted out by police, because they perceive their interaction with

143   Kolkata Municipal Corporation Act 1980 s 326 provides: 'Solid wastes to be the property of the Corporation: all matters deposited in public receptacles, depots and places provided or appointed by the Corporation and all solid wastes collected shall be the property of the Corporation.'
144   Indian Penal Code 1860 s 378.
145   Interviews conducted with waste pickers in Kolkata, India, from March to July 2011.
146   Even if the waste pickers were not aware of the exact connotation of the phrase *petty offence*, they had a good idea of what it entails. Interviews conducted on 12 May 2011 in the Tala Park area; 9 May 2011 and 11 May 2011 in the Rajabazar area; 30 April 2011 in the Golfgreen area; 12 May 2011 in the BNR area in Kolkata, India.
147   According to s 206(2) of the Code of Criminal Procedure 1973, petty offence means 'any offence punishable only with fine not exceeding one thousand rupees, but does not include any offence so punishable under the Motor Vehicles Act 1939 (4 of 1939) or under any other law which provides for convicting the accused person in his absence on a plea of guilty'.
148   Interviews conducted on 12 May 2011 in the Tala Park area; 9 May 2011 and 11 May 2011 in the Rajabazar area; 30 April 2011 in the Golfgreen area; 12 May 2011 in the BNR area in Kolkata, India.

the police as a necessary part of their work. While waste pickers can secure their release from the police by bribing or paying them, they do not have the same leverage with local residents or touts, who are generally not after the waste pickers' money, and who view waste pickers as thieves and vagrants who should not be allowed to scavenge in their neighbourhood. This approach towards waste pickers in Kolkata (of both the police and civilians) is in keeping with the propertied notion of waste, which is one of the principal hurdles in waste pickers' work-lives.

Moreover, waste pickers are excluded from legislative recognition enjoyed by some of the other informal economic activities. The West Bengal Unorganised Sector Workers' Welfare Act 2007 recognises both self-employed and wage-earning informal workers by providing a list of such activities and enterprises in its schedule.[149] The schedule lists 69 informal enterprises and self-employed activities that are recognised as informal (or unorganised).[150] Waste picking does not feature in the schedule of the 2007 Act. This is an instance of active (conscious) non-recognition and de-legitimisation of the informal activity of waste picking. The SASPFUW scheme also excludes waste pickers from the list of 61 informal activities that are presently under its purview.[151]

However, there is room for argument that the 2007 Act and the SASPFUW scheme implicitly recognise waste picking as an informal activity. Section 3(j) of the Act states: '[u]norganised sector means the Unorganised Sector specified in Part A and Part B of the Schedule and includes any process or branch of work forming a part of such Unorganised Sector.' The schedule of the law lists, and thereby recognises, informal enterprises of *plastic industry* (Entry 28 of the Act and Entry 21 of the scheme), *ceramic industry* (Entry 29), *rubber and rubber products* (Entry 25), *paper board and straw board manufactories* (Entry 43 and Entry 28 of the scheme). The informal activity of waste picking is intricately related to these *recognised* informal enterprises. Therefore, from the wording of section 3(j), it could be argued that waste picking is a *process or branch of work forming a part of the unorganised sector* recognised under the law and therefore waste picking is also a recognised informal activity.

However, the Minister-in-Charge of Labour of the Government of West Bengal and the government officials in the state Labour Department interviewed by me were not convinced by this interpretation. According to them, only an express mention of waste picking would amount to legal recognition of such informal activity. Thus, non-recognition as a worker amounts to a serious capability deprivation for waste pickers. In the following sub-section, I explain why the institutional recognition as a worker constitutes a valuable capability-enhancing measure for informal waste pickers.

---

149   West Bengal Unorganised Sector Workers' Welfare Act 2007 s 3(i), 3(j), 3(k), Sched pts A, B.
150   ibid Sched pts A, B.
151   See Government of West Bengal, *Social Security for the Working Class and Left-Front Government* (*Shramik-shrenir Samajik Suraksha O Bam-Front Sarkar*) (Kolkata: Govt of WB, 2010) 3–4 [English title offered by author].

6.6.1.2 Access to work-sites

As with recognition, problems in access to worksites (or collection sites) comprise an extremely important factor that seriously limits the capability of waste pickers to work as they wish. Limitations on waste pickers' capability to access worksites result from other legal, social, economic and cultural deprivations. Inaccessibility is a unique factor for the activity of waste picking in the sense that workers are not allowed access to their worksites. Waste pickers interviewed in Kolkata have identified access to worksites as one of the valuable capabilities that they lack.[152] Inaccessibility of worksites is the logical outcome of the property concept of waste.

The Kolkata Municipal Corporation Act 1980 declares matters deposited in public receptacles, depots and solid waste dumping places to be KMC property.[153] Therefore, by implication, waste pickers entering these premises to collect waste are trespassing on the corporation's property. According to the directions issued under the Municipal Solid Wastes (Management and Handling) Rules 2000, municipal dumping places or landfill sites are off limits to unauthorised persons.[154] Municipal dumping sites must be fenced and properly monitored to prevent trespassing.[155]

Municipal landfill sites are the biggest repositories of solid waste and therefore the easiest way for waste pickers to find valuable recyclable waste. During my visit to the largest municipal landfill site, Dhapa, on the outskirts of Kolkata, I found about 1000 waste pickers scavenging for valuable recyclable waste.[156] I was informed by one of the attendants of the KMC (Group C employee of the KMC), under conditions of anonymity, that the number of waste pickers at Dhapa varies from 700 to 3000 every day.[157] Legally speaking, all these waste pickers are trespassers on government property. Trespassing is an offence under the Indian Penal Code punishable with three months' imprisonment and/or a fine of Rs 500.[158]

Perhaps mindful of the legal implications, the KMC authorities in charge of the Dhapa landfill site dissuaded me from visiting the site.[159] After repeated attempts and multiple layers of official authorisation, I was allowed to pay an *official visit* to the Dhapa site.

152   Interviews conducted with waste pickers in Kolkata, India, from March to July 2011.
153   Kolkata Municipal Corporation Act 1980 s 326.
154   Municipal Solid Wastes (Management and Handling) Rules 2000 rr 6, 7 and Sched III (Entry 11, 12).
155   ibid.
156   During my fieldwork in Kolkata (March to July 2011), I visited the Dhapa landfill site several times. The first such visit was on 10 April 2011 and the last visit to the site was on 2 June 2011.
157   Interview conducted with the Kolkata Municipal Corporation employee on 2 June 2011 in the the Dhapa landfill site in Kolkata, India.
158   Indian Penal Code 1860 ss 441, 447.
159   When I first approached for permission to visit the Dhapa landfill site on 10 April 2010, I was not only dissuaded from visiting the site, but authorities at the landfill site informed me that in order to visit the site I would need to have written permission from their superior officers. This does not, however, mean that the Dhapa site is inaccessible for outsiders. Thousands of people could access the open landfill site from several unofficial entry-points. Entry through the *official gate* is only restricted and is subject to written permission.

Once at the site it was evident to me that, had I not insisted on paying an official visit, I could have used any one of the multiple inroads to enter the site. These are the same entry-ways that thousands of waste pickers use every day. I was also informed by the KMC attendant accompanying me that during official inspection of the sites (for example, by high-ranking government officials) waste pickers are driven out of the premises by him and other attendants. However sympathetic to the waste pickers he may have been, he admitted that he had to 'follow orders from above and evict waste pickers from the premises'.[160]

Waste pickers in Dhapa as elsewhere, while undertaking their work, are helping the KMC and the environment at large. As I have pointed out earlier, the KMC is only able to segregate waste from seven of the 141 wards. Therefore, waste collected from the majority of the wards in Kolkata is not segregated and is simply dumped into the landfill sites in Dhapa and Garden Reach (Kolkata presently has two landfill sites). Since waste pickers are interested in recyclable waste, they are segregating recyclable waste from non-recyclable and compostable waste at the landfill sites. The KMC has an agreement with a composting company that composts waste generated in Kolkata. The factory of the composting company is located at the premises of the Dhapa landfill site. Waste pickers, by helping in segregation, facilitate work on the composting and waste disposal front. Despite being helpful to the KMC and the environment, waste pickers are often excluded from the very premises that constitute their livelihoods.

Waste pickers in Kolkata are thereby socio-economically marginalised and maligned by the existing legal scheme. While Dhapa stands out as an example for its size, it reflects the exclusion of waste pickers from their worksites that permeates all the wards in Kolkata. Non-access to worksites seriously limits waste pickers' capabilities. Even if waste pickers choose to work in recycling businesses, institutional factors such as laws, policies and social prejudices hinder their choice. Not surprisingly, therefore, waste pickers identify the capability to be able to choose their worksites as a valuable capability in their work-lives.

6.6.1.3 *Identification as a citizen of the country*

Status as a citizen of the country entitles workers to claim certain rights and benefits from the state. Different departments of the state government, including the Food and Public-Distribution Department, the Health and Family Welfare Department, the Labour Department etc, execute hundreds of central and state government welfare schemes that are conditional upon citizenship, or based on the requirement of proof of identity.[161] The absence of identification or citizenship, therefore, seriously limits the capabilities of waste pickers.

---

160 Interview conducted with the Kolkata Municipal Corporation employee on 2 June 2011 at the Dhapa landfill site in Kolkata, India.
161 For a list of the different central and state government schemes executed in West Bengal see Society for Participatory Research in Asia, *People's Autonomy in Government Schemes* (Kolkata: PRIA, 2008).

Proof of citizenship ensures some degree of social, economic and political safeguards for informal workers. In the absence of citizenship identity, waste pickers are deprived of some minimum level of security and remain perpetually vulnerable and marginalised. Their capability sets are significantly limited because of such vulnerability and marginalisation.

The majority of the waste pickers I interviewed in Kolkata were migrants.[162] Most of these migrants were interstate and intrastate migrants. Many waste pickers that I interviewed had migrated from the neighbouring states of Bihar, Orissa and Jharkhand. Some of them had migrated from the Sundarbans area (delta) of the state of WB. I also interviewed waste pickers who had migrated from Bangladesh. A mix of migrant populations, including intrastate, interstate and international migrants, complicate matters related to citizenship and associated rights and privileges.

State government officials argue that they have been unable to provide identification of many of the migrant population in Kolkata who have migrated from different parts of the country because of the complications arising from the risk of issuing identification to illegal immigrants into the country. Many of the migrant waste pickers that I interviewed in Kolkata were second-generation migrants; some of the first-generation migrant waste pickers have been living in Kolkata for about 20 years or more. Despite having lived in the city for more than two decades or a generation, the majority of the waste pickers I interviewed did not possess any identification of citizenship papers such as voter identity cards or ration cards. However, a small minority of waste pickers do possess voter identity cards.

It is very interesting to note the apparent difference of living standards between waste pickers who possess proof of citizenship and those who do not. I interviewed a group of waste pickers in the Rajabazar area of Kolkata.[163] Living by the edge of a canal that carries industrial and non-industrial effluent, the lives of waste pickers in Rajabazar are far from dignified. What is distinctive about waste pickers in this area of Kolkata is that they all had multiple documents proving their citizenship such as voter ID, ration cards, below the poverty line (BPL) cards etc. These workers live in bamboo-thatched houses with the roof covered with tarpaulin sheets or tiles. They have constructed bunks inside the house so that five to six individuals could fit in a tiny house of 5 ft by 10 ft.

What was surprising for me was to note that some of these workers had televisions, video-players and cable television connection in their tiny homes. During my interaction with waste pickers in Rajabazar I was invited into their homes – I was offered tea and snacks – their hospitality and forthcoming nature made up for the foul smell from the canal. Waste pickers here had many complaints against politicians. A few of the waste pickers used to be active members of the

162   Interviews conducted with waste pickers in Kolkata, India, from March to July 2011.
163   Interviews conducted with waste pickers on 9 May 2011 and 11 May 2011 in the Rajabazar area in Kolkata, India.

Communist Party of India (a partner of the Left Front), but had long become inactive, disillusioned with its policies. Waste pickers in Rajabazar complained that politicians come to them only during election time: 'throughout the year we do not see them. If we approach them for some help they have no time for us. But when vote comes [during elections], they are at our doorsteps. [They] tell us: *mashi* [maternal aunt], go and cast your vote soon, don't be late – have your lunch only after casting your vote.'[164]

Such spontaneity was absent when I interviewed waste pickers in the Aajkaal area.[165] Living on the footpath with a tarpaulin sheet or jute sack hanging above their heads, something they call home, these waste pickers were scared to talk to me. They wanted me to talk to their wards' councillor before they could entertain me. However, with much persuasion and help from one of the organisers of the Calcutta Samaritans (NGO), they agreed to talk to me. I learned that the local councillor had destroyed their tarpaulin-covered shanties along with local strongmen on more than one occasion earlier. Since then, these workers have suffered from perpetual insecurity and are scared to talk to strangers.

None of these waste pickers had any citizenship documents. Their lives centre around the footpath where they live and the garbage dumping places where they scavenge, living and working in perpetual fear. Similar insecurities surfaced during my interview with waste pickers in the Kestopur Khal area.[166] Many waste pickers in this area came from Bangladesh. Although they have lived here for decades, they could not secure a citizenship identity card. These waste pickers have been expressly instructed by their local councillor not to talk to strangers. While I was interviewing waste pickers in this area, a local strongman came and mildly threatened me (I use 'mildly' because I was aware of how a fully fledged threat might sound). He wanted me to leave the area immediately and not talk to anyone. Finding me unmoved, he threatened to call the local councillor, but when I insisted that he call the local councillor so that I could talk to her personally, he withdrew.

I am not attributing the difference in living standards (or quality of life) and the interactions of waste pickers with a stranger, *only* to the possession or absence of citizenship identity cards. I am suggesting that there might be a link between citizenship identity and better living standards and security of waste pickers. These workers live in shanties and slums by the side of a canal, or on roadside footpaths or near garbage dumping places. Because of educational, cultural, social, political and economic reasons, these people, more often than not, are not in possession of valid identification documents.

While this absence of documentation prohibits them from seeking any benefits and entitlements from the state, it is much more damaging in terms of perpetually

164 Woman waste picker interviewed on 9 May 2011 in the Rajabazar area in Kolkata, India.
165 Interviews conducted with waste pickers on 1 June 2011 in the Aajkaal area in Kolkata, India.
166 Interviews conducted with waste pickers on 13 April 2011 in the Kestopur Khal area in Kolkata, India.

pushing these workers into ignominy and illegitimacy. Because the waste pickers do not possess valid citizenship documents, they try to hide from state authorities, law enforcement officials and other citizens. They perform their work in a secretive manner and are easily intimidated. Accordingly, identity as a citizen has been enumerated by the waste pickers as an institutional guarantee that is capable of enhancing their capabilities.

6.6.1.4 Shelter or housing

Waste pickers live in slums and squatter settlements spread around the city of Kolkata. Many of these slums and squatter settlements are illegal. The better-off waste pickers would possess a bamboo-thatched hut, in which a space as small as 5 ft by 10 ft would house a family of five people living together. Waste pickers not so well off would spend their lives on railway platforms and footpaths under the shelter of a tarpaulin sheet. In view of their living situations, it was not surprising that almost all of the waste pickers I interviewed have identified shelter as providing them with valuable capability.

Shelter is a source of security, confidence and comfort. Whatever the uncertainties of the informal activity of waste picking may be, shelter provides confidence and satisfaction to the waste pickers. Such confidence and satisfaction is irrespective of the fact that all of the waste pickers I interviewed were occupying shelters that were temporary in nature.[167] The sense of security emanating from the existence of a shelter allows waste pickers to exercise *choice* in their work-lives, however limited in scope.

A shelter is significant for waste pickers not only for their living purposes, it is also valuable for waste pickers' work. Waste pickers' work-lives are spread across different locations around the city. Their work is stretched from the garbage dumping places around the city to their individual shelters. Segregation of solid waste is central to the work of waste pickers. Waste pickers segregate solid waste at two levels: first, while collecting recyclable waste from around the city, waste pickers segregate recyclable plastics, metal, glass, ceramics, paper etc from non-recyclable waste; secondly, once a day's collect has been made, waste pickers segregate their collect into plastic recyclables, glass recyclables, metal recyclables and so on. This second stage of segregation takes place either at or near the shelter of the waste pickers, or a separate designated place (generally in close proximity to the middle-person's business). Accordingly, shelter is not only important for living purposes to these waste pickers; shelter is also an extension of their worksite.

Although there are legal slums and settlements in Kolkata, all the waste pickers I interviewed live in illegal slums, squatter settlements and temporary shanties. Their shelters are actually a manifestation of the marginalised and vulnerable nature of their work. The Kolkata Municipal Corporation Act prohibits construction of any structure over or along any *water-main*, *drain*, or *sewer* without

---

167   Interviews conducted with waste pickers in Kolkata, India, from March to July 2011.

prior permission.[168] Such construction is punishable with a fine of Rs 1000 or six months' imprisonment.[169]

Many of the illegal slums of waste pickers are constructed along drainage canals – the KMC can demolish these slums at any time and punish their owners with imprisonment or fines. The KMC prohibits using residential premises for non-residential purposes.[170] The KMC also prohibits deposit and storage of waste in slums, municipal land and along public highways, violation of which would attract a fine of up to Rs 5000.[171] Moreover, the KMC can order demolition and removal of *huts* and *sheds* if they perceive such shelters as unsanitary[172] and can punish scavenging and waste-carrying as nuisance.[173] Thus, even if waste pickers in Kolkata have temporary shelters, they could be deprived of such shelter anytime under the law.

In view of the legal-institutional arrangements that are prejudicial to their interests, waste pickers in Kolkata have identified *permanent shelter* as an enabling factor towards promotion of their capabilities. However, it was interesting to note the difference amongst different groups of waste pickers in this respect. Those waste pickers who had better shelters than other waste pickers were much more assertive about a permanent shelter. They wanted the government to take proactive measures in offering shelters to them. Waste pickers living in the Golfgreen area of the city went to the extent of showing me a piece of land where they propose the government should build them permanent shelters.[174]

On the other hand, waste pickers who were living in small shanties or living on the footpaths with a tarpaulin cover over their heads did not even bother to talk about a permanent shelter. Such behaviour on the part of the more precarious of the waste pickers is suggestive of their adaptive preference. These migrant waste pickers living on the footpaths and railway platforms have left their aspirations to the mercy of their fate. They have long been subjected to abject poverty and perpetual want and have lost hope in deciding the course of their lives. Irrespective of adaptive preference looming large over many of the waste pickers' psychology, as a group, waste pickers in Kolkata have identified permanent shelter as a capability-enhancing factor.

6.6.1.5 Protection from eviction from resort to temporary shelters

Even when waste pickers have shelter (which are the temporary structures where they live), because of the other deprivations they suffer from (such as educational,

---

168 Kolkata Municipal Corporation Act 1980 s 317.
169 ibid Sched VI.
170 ibid ss 435, 441, and Sched VI.
171 ibid ss 334, 336, 337, 338 and Sched VI.
172 ibid s 493.
173 ibid ss 516, 517, 517A.
174 I visited the waste pickers' squatter settlement in the Golfgreen area on several occasions. On my third visit to the area on 10 May 2011 they showed me this nearby vacant land.

social, political, etc mentioned earlier) and of the illegal nature of such dwellings, they are often evicted. Every so often, law enforcement officials visit the slums, demolish the temporary structures and force the waste pickers to leave, with or without their belongings. Such demolitions are more frequent when these people do not have enough money to bribe the officials.

Tawassum Biwi reflects: 'sometimes they [the police] just come for money. They have no official orders from above, but just come to harass us. If we can give them a 50 [Rs] or 100 [Rs] bill, they leave us in peace.'[175] Waste pickers have pointed out that protection against eviction would be one of the most valuable components towards capability enhancement in their work-lives. All the waste pickers I interviewed in Kolkata, irrespective of their places of residence or area of operation, noted that forced eviction seriously limits their capabilities.

Ameena Bewa has been living in the Tala Park area for the last 35 years since her husband moved to Kolkata in search of work. All of her children were born here and her husband died here. She has experienced many evictions. She describes some of her experiences:

> Police will generally come when we are least prepared to deal with them. They will come and beat our men and young children so that we are scared. They will then smash our shanties. They have kicked out utensils during their raids; they once kicked my bowl full of rice when we were having lunch. Sometimes local people accompany police. The *babus* [local people living in neighbouring residential complexes] don't like us – they call the police to drive us away. When I was young and new here I was very scared during these [police] raids. Now we have our own strategy. We do not argue with or fight police. When they come we simply run away with whatever belongings we can. After things calm down a little we come back and live as usual.[176]

However, law enforcement officials are not always seen in a bad light by the shanty-dwelling waste pickers. Jamina Mahato of Golfgreen is sympathetic:

> We cannot always blame them [the police]. Even they have their limitations – they have to follow orders. What can they do if their bosses pressurise them to demolish our *bustee* [slum] and evict us? Yes, many of them come for money, but not all. There are some good police personnel. Whenever they come to know of a possible eviction and demolition drive, they inform us beforehand. They come during the day and tell us: *mashi* [maternal aunt] be careful for the next few days; there is going to be an eviction drive soon; if possible take your belongings and go somewhere. We are then all prepared when they come to evict us.[177]

---

175   Interview conducted on 10 May 2011 in the Tollygunge area in Kolkata, India.
176   Interview conducted on 12 May 2011 in the Tala Park area, Kolkata, India.
177   Interview conducted on 10 May 2011 in the Tollygunge area, Kolkata, India.

Thus, shelters are a site of regular conflict and a source of insecurity. Challenge, confrontation, struggle and cooperation are performed as everyday activities between the waste pickers and law enforcement officials in particular. It is therefore evident that for a meaningful capability enhancement of waste pickers, protection from eviction needs to be ensured.

6.6.1.6 *Physical and mental security at work-site*

Waste pickers are harassed at their work-sites every day by local touts, hooligans, law enforcement officials, local residents and rodents. Women waste pickers are often sexually and mentally harassed. Accordingly, waste pickers have identified workplace physical and mental security as one of the enabling conditions for enhancing capabilities for their work and lives. For waste pickers, work is spread from dumping grounds to their temporary shelters. It is in this large expanse that waste pickers are concerned about their physical and mental safety and security.

Srikanta Majhi and Indranath Mandal scavenge around the southern fringes of the city.[178] They work together, collecting waste with their hand-pulled cart, which has been loaned to them by a middleman Kuber Mian to whom they sell their collect. Like the majority of waste pickers in Kolkata, both Majhi and Mandal are migrant workers. They have been taken into custody by police several times on varying grounds. Most of the time, police take them into custody without any reasonable proof of theft or vagrancy. However, Majhi and Mandal were never brought before a magistrate;[179] they were always released on bail from the police station.[180] The more outspoken Majhi notes:

> They [the police] have to fulfil a regular quota of arrest per month. They also have to fuel their motorcycles free of charge. Arresting people like us helps them in both of these respects. We are people who know no one [worth knowing] in the city. Therefore we cannot bargain with the police to release us. Either we have to rot in jail for several days or months, or we must pay them [police]. The work we do [ie waste picking] makes it much easier for the police to allege theft against us. We never protest because we have to go back to the same locality for scavenging.[181]

Thus, workplace(s) are sites of constant struggle, where waste pickers find themselves devoid of any power to negotiate their security at work.

---

178   Interview conducted on 30 April 2011 in the Golfgreen area, Kolkata, India.
179   Persons arrested without warrant are to be produced before the nearest competent magistrate within 24 hours of their arrest in accordance with art 22(2) of the Constitution of India, and ss 57 and 76 of the Criminal Procedure Code 1973.
180   Persons arrested without warrant in a bailable offence could be released on bail upon sureties directly from the police station in accordance with ss 50 and 56 of the Criminal Procedure Code 1973.
181   Interview conducted on 30 April 2011 in the Golfgreen area, Kolkata, India.

Law enforcement officials are not the only villains of the story. During the last state assembly elections in 2011, local people in the Tala Park area threatened waste pickers with eviction from their shanties once the election results were out.[182] This threat, although not targeted for the first time, attained significance in the socio-political context of the 2011 assembly elections.

After coming to power in 1977, the Left Front suffered heavy losses in the 2009 parliamentary elections for the first time in 32 years. The right-of-centre opposition began to gain more strength from 2009 onwards. A Left Front loss in the 2011 elections was widely predicted. Traditionally, the right-of-centre opposition has more support in the city of Kolkata than the Left Front. While the Left Front is perceived to be more tolerant of informal workers and their shanties, slums and squatter settlements, opposition forces have always despised these informal workers and their settlements. Therefore, immediately before the elections predicting a heavy Left Front loss, threats from local people from residential complexes of the city held enormous significance.

The right-of-centre government's apparent disapproval of these workers and their living conditions is well captured through the reflections of a Mayor-in-Council of the KMC. Presently, both the KMC and the state government are run by the right-of-centre coalition government (which, incidentally, also runs the central government). The KMC Mayor-in-Council for Parks, Gardens and Sports, Debashish Kumar, reasons:

> Why would the waste pickers live in the city? None of these people are from the city. They have come here from Lakkhikantapur and Canning. They do not belong to the city. They can come and work here but must go back when the day's work is done. They are responsible for the filthy conditions of the city. How can you appreciate people [waste pickers and the like] cooking and reproducing on the footpaths? However, we are not in favour of forcibly evicting them – but they cannot just spoil our city.[183]

While the Mayor-in-Council might be correct in noting that some waste pickers are responsible for polluting and littering the city, he shows a lack of understanding on how the recycling industry (including waste pickers) works. Waste pickers do not have a nine-to-five job. Their collecting hours are varied: some scavenge at midnight, some in the wee hours of the morning, and some in the afternoon. Most of the waste pickers do not sell their collect the same day. After their daily collection, they store their collect in a definite place (generally around their shanties). When they have collected enough to sell, they segregate their collect and sell it to the middle-person.

---

182 Interview conducted on 12 May 2011 in the Tala Park area, Kolkata, India.
183 Interview with Debashish Kumar, Mayor-in-Council, parks, gardens and sports, Kolkata Municipal Corporation on 7 June 2011 at his office at the Kolkata Municipal Corporation building, Kolkata, India.

During their work, therefore, the waste pickers need to be in close proximity to their waste. Moreover, if they had to spend five hours a day commuting, they could not collect enough waste for the activity to be economically viable. Waste pickers also have to negotiate on a regular basis with other waste pickers for the control of designated scavenging areas. If they are absent from the city for chunks of time during a day, they cannot generate enough bargaining power to negotiate with fellow waste pickers for scavenging privileges in a particular area.

Thus, workplace security seriously undermines capabilities of waste pickers to decide when and how to perform their work. These power-based dynamics are not the only source of work-related (physical and mental) insecurity that waste pickers are subjected to. Mundane issues such as absence of protective gear or social security provisions vitiate their work. Waste pickers spend most of their days in garbage dumping places. They sort waste such as metal, glass and ceramics with their bare hands. They are totally ignorant of the risks and dangers posed by handling hazardous materials. A significant number of children waste pickers scavenge with bare hands. They walk barefoot on the landfill areas while scavenging. Almost all waste pickers I interviewed in Kolkata had some cuts or burns that were fresh, suggesting that cuts, burns and scratches are everyday occurrences. They do not even bother to see the doctor for these apparently 'small scratches'.[184]

Social security available to other categories of informal workers such as rickshaw-pullers, *bidi* workers, construction workers, tailors or street hawkers, are not available to waste pickers. All of these factors culminate in depriving waste pickers of their basic capabilities. Waste pickers have therefore identified physical and mental security at work as enabling conditions for capability enhancement.

6.6.1.7 A regular channel to paid labour (or selling their collect)

The informal economic activity of waste picking is dependent to a great extent on relations between people. Such relations are determined by caste, locality, ethnicity etc.[185] Sometimes there are tensions within these relations. Because of these tensions, sometimes it becomes difficult for waste pickers to sell the product of their labour (or collect) on a regular basis to ensure a regular source of income. Therefore, the waste pickers in Kolkata have identified a *regular channel of paid labour* as one of the important factors for the promotion of their capabilities.

Once a waste picker has a problem with an intermediary to whom she usually sells her collect, it becomes difficult for her to find a replacement intermediary. Generally intermediaries are area-specific – in each area there are one or two intermediaries. Therefore, if workers get into trouble with one or both of them, it becomes extremely difficult for them to find an intermediary to whom to sell their collect.

---

184   When asked whether they have seen a doctor for their cuts and burns, this is what all my research participants replied.

185   Barbara Harriss-White, 'Work and wellbeing in informal economies: the regulative roles of institutions of identity and the state' (2010) 38(2) *World Development* 170.

All of the intermediaries I interviewed in Kolkata told me that waste pickers were free to sell their collect to anyone they pleased. Intermediaries do not maintain a contractual employment relationship with the waste pickers. Although sometimes waste pickers accept loans from intermediaries and have to pay back such loans through regular deductions, none of the parties is interested in formalising their relationship. However, the general practice is to sell collect to one specific intermediary, unless something dramatic happens to spoil the relationship. Therefore, although in theory waste pickers are free to sell their collect to anyone, practically speaking, they have to depend on one or two specific intermediaries.

If a waste picker's relationship with an intermediary is irreparably damaged, it is also very difficult for him or her to find replacement work. Ameena Bewa has been living in the Tala Park area for about the last 35 years.[186] She used to work as domestic help in the area when her husband was alive. But after the death of her husband, she could not afford to work as domestic help any more. This is because, as a domestic help, her salary would be due at the end of every month, which is the common payment practice for domestic help in Kolkata and generally in India. Monthly payments make it difficult for her to have a decent income throughout the month, something that she enjoyed when her husband was alive and earning a living. There were times when her salary would be exhausted by the middle of the month and she had to take loans from neighbours.

Waste picking, on the other hand, provided her with a regular source of income throughout the month. She could sell her collect whenever she wanted. She chose to sell her collect twice a week, which provided her with enough resources to look after herself. Although waste picking can generate flexible and regular income, waste picking is physically exerting work, which has taken its toll on Ameena Bewa's health. With age, she was becoming prone to diseases. She would remain sick and bedridden for days, which prohibited her from working and earning regularly.

Because of her deteriorating health and inability to scavenge efficiently, Ameena Bewa decided to return to her earlier work as a domestic help. But this time she could not find work as a domestic help. When she went back to her former client-family, they refused to take her back. She was told that, because she had been working as a waste picker for a long time, she could not work at their house. Her client-family told her that since she scavenged all around the city and worked at the garbage dumping places, she could not maintain the level of cleanliness that is required of domestic staff. They also told her that she was unhygienic and diseased. They did not want her to be around their children or to wash their dishes. With an assurance of helping her in an emergency, they refused to take her back as a domestic help.

She never went back to her client-family's home again. She has met the same fate at other places. She now scavenges from nearby dumps and somehow maintains herself. She told me that she is not scared to work, but if only she could

---

186 Interview conducted on 12 May 2011 in the Tala Park area, Kolkata, India.

have had an assurance of regular income, life would have been much easier for her. A regular source of assured income, therefore, is capable of promoting capabilities for waste pickers.

6.6.1.8 Appropriate payment for their labour/work

Because of their precarious bargaining power that results from their multiple socio-economic-political and cultural deprivations, waste pickers are exploited by the middlemen and middle-women who buy collect from them and sell it to the recyclers. Accordingly, the corresponding capability deprivation identified by the waste pickers in Kolkata was the capability to sell their collect at appropriate market prices to the highest bidder. Their choice to sell the product of their labour to the highest bidder is severely restricted by several factors identified earlier (caste, locality, ethnicity).

For waste pickers in Kolkata, locality-based factors, rather than caste or ethnicity-based factors, seemed to be the biggest obstacle for appropriate payment for labour. The activity of waste picking and consequent selling in Kolkata is arranged in an area-specific manner, which means that both waste pickers and intermediaries operate in an area-specific manner. While localised activities do not pose a problem for waste pickers so far as scavenging is concerned, such limitations have an adverse effect on the selling of waste pickers' collect.

Area-specific scavenging is a practice that waste pickers have themselves devised in order to avoid unhealthy competition amongst themselves. While area-division is not rigid, waste pickers more or less honour such division of areas so far as scavenging is concerned. Division of areas for scavenging does not adversely affect waste pickers because of the availability of recyclable waste all around the city. But because of the area-based operation of intermediaries, the intermediaries enjoy a semi-monopoly in their business.

During my fieldwork in Kolkata, except for the Rajabazar area, I did not find more than one intermediary in or around a waste-picker-inhabited slum. In the Rajabazar area, I found two intermediaries who had specific waste picker clients. This semi-monopolistic situation tends to ensure that prices of collect are unilaterally determined by intermediaries rather than negotiated between intermediaries and waste pickers. There could be an argument that market value determines the price of waste pickers' collect, but such an argument would ignore the monopolistic nature of the transaction that is capable of devaluing waste pickers' labour.

Waste pickers have not thought through the monopolistic nature of their transaction with intermediaries, but they are aware of their limited avenues. Shekhar Seal of the BNR area puts it thus:

> We are not bound to sell our collect only to one person – but then we also do not have a lot of options. I once refused to sell it [his collect] to Maniklal Dam [an intermediary] because he was paying me less than Gangaram Singh [an intermediary of another area]. [But,] if I have to sell to Gangaram [Singh]

I have to go a long way to sell my collect. I segregate my collect here outside my *chala* [hut] – Gangaram's business is an hour's walk from here. I have got back to selling my collect to Dam.[187]

Shyama Das of the Tollygunge area was far more assertive:

They [intermediaries] always cheat us. They keep on telling us that they do not get a good price for these collect and therefore cannot pay us more than what they do. They just need excuses to pay us less. During the rainy season their favourite excuse is that our [waste pickers'] collect have absorbed water and therefore weighs more than it should be. They pay us much less by arbitrarily deducting our [collects'] price.[188]

Shyama reflects that: 'This is something that needs to be corrected if we are to have any say in our business.'[189] Waste pickers' capabilities, therefore, are also dependent on the appropriate valuation of their labour.

6.6.1.9 Provision for emergency fund

Waste pickers interviewed are compelled to take loans from the middle-person to whom they sell their collect. Interest on such loans often becomes burdensome for waste pickers. Often, waste pickers would not understand the nature and extent of the loan and the middle-person would make them work for him almost as bonded workers. When a waste picker borrows from an intermediary, the general practice is that the intermediary would deduct from each day's payment (against the waste picker's collect) to the worker until the loan is fully paid. During the repayment of a loan, the waste pickers are compelled to sell their collect only to the middle-person who has given them the loan. Therefore, the provision of emergency funds has been identified by the workers as a valuable capability-enhancing factor.

The Government of WB has initiated few welfare schemes for informal workers in WB (delineated earlier). The government also executes a few welfare schemes for informal workers that are initiated by the central government. As part of these schemes, the government provides financial assistance for health-related emergencies, housing, electrification, marriage, education, etc to informal workers engaged in a wide range of informal economic activities. However, waste pickers remain outside the scope of all government initiatives in this regard. The Government of WB has not recognised waste picking as an informal economic activity and waste pickers as informal workers (as discussed earlier).

Such non-recognition contributes only towards heightened vulnerability of waste pickers, compared with several other groups of informal workers, such as rickshaw-pullers, street vendors and domestic workers. These other informal

187 Interview conducted on 12 May 2011 in the BNR area, Kolkata, India.
188 Interview conducted on 10 May 2011 in the Tollygunge area, Kolkata, India.
189 ibid.

workers are institutionally recognised and are prospective beneficiaries of government initiatives.

In the light of government non-recognition and exclusion from welfare benefits, waste pickers are compelled to depend on intermediaries and other local money lenders for their emergencies. Because of institutional non-recognition, these waste pickers find it impossible to receive easy loans from banks and other official agencies. Because waste picking is not institutionally recognised as an informal activity while many other informal activities are recognised, it becomes impossible for waste pickers to convince micro-credit organisations of their credit-worthiness. This situation would have been different if none of the informal economic activities were recognised – waste pickers would have been at the same level of vulnerability as other informal workers. But the present situation makes them the most precarious workers amongst other precarious workers. Once waste pickers accept loans from intermediaries, the waste pickers subject themselves to a quasi-debt-bond relationship. Benimadhav Singh of the Sealdah area describes his plight:

> My *mahajan* [intermediary] helps me during my needs. I borrow 100 or 200 rupees from him once in a while. He then gradually deducts around 20 to 30 rupees from each transaction between us. Once I had to borrow some 1000 rupees from him when my child was sick and had to undergo operation. It took me around three years to repay that debt. I do not know accounting or calculation – I cannot even read. Every time I asked [the intermediary] whether my debt was repaid, he kept on telling me it [the loan] is a lot and will take a long time to repay. During all these while I had to sell only to him just to repay my debt.[190]

Evidently, therefore, the lack of institutionalised financial support during emergencies seriously restricts a waste picker's capabilities.

6.6.1.10 Provision for health

Although government hospitals provide treatment with minimal or no payment, medicines have to be bought from outside the hospitals. Many waste pickers are not aware that state hospitals are free. They generally visit the local doctor (sometimes, a crook) for all of their ills, which compels them to borrow money from the middle-person. Unsurprisingly, therefore, provision for health funding (or support for health) has been identified as one of the important factors towards improvement of capabilities of waste pickers. Health provisioning is important for waste pickers from two perspectives.

First, the activity of waste picking is hazardous in nature. Waste pickers spend significant parts of their day amongst waste in different garbage dumping places. They collect waste ranging from metals to plastic. I have come across waste pickers in Dhapa landfill site who burn waste in a drum in order to produce bitumen,

---

190 Interview conducted on 1 June 2011 in the Sealdah area, Kolkata, India.

which fetches them better payment. Hence, because of their work, they are prone to diseases during the course of their work. Secondly, during health emergencies, waste pickers require financial and social support.

Most of the waste pickers I interviewed had given birth to their children in their shanties and huts, without any professional assistance. Although information and registration of birth and death are legally mandated,[191] none of the waste pickers I interviewed have ever registered births or deaths in their families. These workers and their families are not aware of basic health and sanitation safeguards. They often take baths and eat their food in the same place; their cooking area is in close proximity to their toilets. Their living conditions are extremely unhygienic. Therefore, financial provisioning for health alone will not fully address the typical problems waste pickers and their families face. In addition to financial assistance, waste pickers and their families need to be educated and made aware of health- and sanitation-related safeguards and precautions.

Waste pickers are excluded from the institutional health assistance programme WBUSWHS of the state government;[192] they are also excluded from the central government health scheme RSBY. Therefore, waste pickers do not receive assistance for hospitalisation, clinical tests or other medicinal costs that many other informal workers are entitled to. Governmental educational and awareness programmes on health and sanitation are also absent. However, some NGOs occasionally undertake health and sanitation awareness drives in different slums and homeless areas around the city. The effectiveness of these once-in-a-while NGO initiatives is questionable considering the health and sanitary conditions waste pickers and their families live with. In the absence of an institutional health security mechanism, waste pickers' capabilities remain seriously restricted.

Elected representatives at the KMC and at the Government of WB note that many of the proposals (ie the factors identified by waste pickers as promoting their capabilities) could be discussed and brain-stormed at the appropriate level. Although Debabrata Mazumdar, the Mayor-in-Council for Solid Waste Management of KMC pointed out that waste pickers pollute the city by littering and living on footpaths and illegal squatter settlements, he also appreciated that the waste pickers were assisting the KMC by segregating and removing recyclable waste from the city.[193] He informed me that the KMC was executing a workfare programme that provides 100 days of guaranteed work for KMC residents.[194] He thought that the KMC could devise something along similar lines to address some

---

191   Kolkata Municipal Corporation Act 1980 ss 456, 458.
192   See Labour Department, Government of West Bengal Resolution No 34-IR, IR/MISC-06/10 of 05/01/2011.
193   I interviewed Debabrata Mazumdar, Mayor-in-Council, Solid Waste Management, Kolkata Municipality on 4 July 2011 at his office at the Kolkata Municipal Corporation building in Kolkata, India.
194   This KMC programme is modelled on the Mahatma Gandhi National Rural Employment Guarantee Scheme implemented in pursuance of the National Rural Employment Guarantee Act 2005.

of the concerns raised by the waste pickers. Mazumdar noted that the factors identified by waste pickers in Kolkata need to be discussed with the waste pickers before any further progress could be made in promoting their capabilities. However, the problem with such a dialogue with waste pickers, Mazumdar pointed out, was that waste pickers are scattered around the city and they do not have a representative organisation with whom the KMC can speak. He observed that, if the waste pickers could organise themselves and send representatives to the KMC with definite proposals, the KMC could have a social dialogue with waste pickers.

When the KMC proposal was conveyed to waste pickers, they showed enthusiasm and initiative by quickly organising themselves into a trade union. Such enthusiasm was further promoted by the Calcutta Samaritans (NGO), the WB National University of Juridical Sciences (a premier university) and other intellectuals. I describe the trade union formation and its prospective role for waste pickers in Kolkata in the next chapter. Trade union formation by waste pickers in Kolkata, although a remarkable initiative, was not in any way surprising considering the political consciousness of waste pickers in the city.

I had undertaken my fieldwork in Kolkata in the immediate aftermath of the electoral defeat of the Left Front Government in May 2011. In its 34 years in power, the CPM-led Left Front had two chief ministers – Jyoti Basu and Buddhadev Bhattacharya. Basu led the Left Front uninterrupted for 23 years (from 1977), a record period of elected chief ministership. Bhattacharya, Basu's successor, was defeated by the right-of-centre coalition led by Mamata Banerjee in 2011. In the context of this political-administrative shift, Jehadi Bewa reflects:

> CPM Party allowed us to live here [squatter settlement]. Now that these people [the right-of-centre coalition government] have come to power we do not know what they will do. Our Jyoti-Babu [former Left Front Chief Minister], who ruled for twenty-five years,[195] protected all poor, marginalised, and indigent people everywhere around the state. Police used to torture us a lot – police used to take us into custody at will. But he [Basu] would say that my poor brothers can eat and live in their chosen places [without police interference]. But, the future is threatening for us, these people [her co-workers] do not understand; in near future we will be destroyed. The local councillor who died recently used to help us in getting our ration cards.[196] If we have ration card, forget Mamata [present right-of-centre coalition Chief Minister], even Mamata's father [this is a typical Bengali slang, which means *however powerful a person is*] could not evict us from our places. A ration card is very valuable. Do you understand?[197]

---

195 Jyoti Basu actually ruled the state for 23 years.

196 A ration card acts as proof of identification and domicile. Holders of ration cards are entitled to free or subsidised rations from the state through the public distribution system.

197 Interview conducted on 1 June 2011 in the Sealdah area, Kolkata, India.

6.7 Conclusion

In this chapter, I analysed capability deficiencies suffered by waste pickers in Kolkata. Based on reflections of the waste pickers I interviewed in Kolkata, I have also identified desirable capabilities for the promotion of functionings important for waste pickers. I have also shown that waste pickers have identified factors which might be able to enhance their capabilities. For a labour law-based enhancement of capabilities for waste pickers, it would, therefore, be necessary to institutionalise the identified factors into law. However, for a labour law dispensation not all of the valuable capabilities identified by waste pickers need to be promoted through law; a labour law framework needs to promote capabilities that are related to *work* performed by waste pickers.

In the next chapter I will show how the strategy of social dialogue could be used in formulating labour law for informal waste pickers in order to promote their capabilities. I will argue that capability-enhancing factors identified by waste pickers could be institutionalised into labour law through a process of social dialogue that engages multiple institutions in the dialogue process. I will also analyse the unionisation initiative of the waste pickers in Kolkata, which may be instrumental in promoting capabilities of waste pickers in the absence of legal-institutional protection.

7 Proposal for a labour law framework

7.1 Introduction

In Chapter 5, I proposed a labour law framework for informal workers, which is based on the capability approach developed by Amartya Sen and Martha Nussbaum. The theoretical framework that I proposed argues that enhancement and equality of capability should be the normative goal of labour law. It also proposes that labour law conceptualisation should be based on the idea of democratic equality amongst stakeholders involved in the cooperative system of production. The theoretical framework further argues that labour law for informal workers must be developed through a democratic deliberation process involving all stakeholders engaged in, or related to, a specific informal economic activity.

In Chapter 4, I discussed the significance of the social dialogue pillar of the Decent Work Agenda as a strategy in the development of labour law for informal workers. In Chapter 6, charting an account of informal waste pickers in Kolkata, India, I described necessary factors identified by waste pickers in the development of their desirable capabilities. In this chapter, I propose to offer a labour law approach for waste pickers in India by merging theoretical insights from Chapter 5 and strategic principles from Chapter 4, with the concrete situation of waste pickers' work-lives described in Chapter 6.

In this chapter, I propose to show how a labour law approach might work for the informal economic activity of waste picking. The labour law framework developed in Chapter 5 is a theoretical exercise. From the theoretical exercise it is not clear how such a conception of labour law might work in a concrete situation involving informal workers. By using the different components of the theoretical framework developed in Chapter 5, I show how they might work for developing a labour law for waste pickers. I discuss the development of labour law for waste pickers in different stages, largely following the stages described in the theoretical model developed in Chapter 5.

Since I am concerned with the enhancement and equality of capabilities of informal workers, in this chapter I propose ways in which capability-enhancing factors could be institutionalised through law. I propose pluralistic ways for the institutionalisation of capability-enhancing factors with active and direct participation of informal workers. I argue that institutionalisation effort requires collective action, wherein stakeholders engaged in a specific informal economic activity need to be integrated.

In the context of informal waste pickers in Kolkata, I argue that collective action towards institutionalisation could be undertaken through two principal mechanisms – the unionisation or organisation of informal workers and the involvement of other integrated institutions. Using specific examples involving waste pickers in Kolkata, I discuss the role of integrated institutions including trade unions and other membership-based organisations to indicate how an institutionalisation process needs to be devised for informal workers.

In my proposed scheme, social dialogue is central to the development of a labour law framework for informal workers in general and waste pickers in particular. I conceive of two situations for an effective social dialogue process: first, when waste pickers have a representative organisation; and, secondly, when waste pickers (like most other informal workers) do not have their own organisation. I discuss the significance of unionisation for an effective and productive social dialogue process. As a backdrop to this discussion of the significance of unionisation, I describe the unionisation initiative of waste pickers in Kolkata, which began during the course of my fieldwork. I then argue that in the absence of representative organisation of waste pickers, integrated institutions of a democratic society can integrate waste pickers into the social dialogue process.

In section 7.2, I discuss the significance of unionisation for social dialogue. Referring back to some of the earlier chapters of the book, I argue that informal workers' organisations play a three-pronged role in the lives of their members: the promotion of capabilities of members as an intrinsic factor; the provision for socio-economic resources; and the negotiation with government. By drawing on my fieldwork in Kolkata, I also discuss why it is necessary for waste pickers to organise themselves into a union.

In section 7.3, I describe the unionisation initiative of waste pickers in Kolkata. In sections 7.4 and 7.5, I discuss how integrated institutions can promote social dialogue through the integration of waste pickers into the dialogue process in the absence of a workers' organisation initiative. I use specific examples in order to point out how multiple institutions in Kolkata can integrate waste pickers into a social dialogue process. In section 7.6, I also consider a concrete implication of the idea of democratic equality in the context of labour law for informal economic activities.

7.2 Role of unionisation in social dialogue

Unionisation has multiple benefits for workers and for the society as a whole. In their book *What do Unions Do?*,[1] Richard B Freeman and James L Medoff articulate that first and foremost labour unions enable workers to have a *collective voice* in the sense that workers can directly communicate in order to 'bring actual

---

1 See Richard B Freeman, James L Medoff, *What do Unions Do?* (New York: Basic Books, 1984).

and desired conditions closer together'.[2] Unions are constitutive units of a democratic polity.[3] By enabling political voice and political participation[4] labour unions influence outcomes in a democratic polity.[5] In this sense labour unions are important institutions of social dialogue in the democratic deliberation process. Unions are not only important institutions of social dialogue in the political process; they also inculcate the culture of democratic dialogue internally amongst their members,[6] something that Hill documents through her study of informal workers of the trade union Self Employed Women's Association (SEWA).[7]

Analysing the larger social role played by the unions, Tito Boeri and others show how unions have been able to negotiate socio-economic benefits not only for union members, but also for non-members and society as a whole.[8] Unions historically were crucial in the development of the welfare state.[9] In some regions, unions had developed significant political clout that shaped the political discourse of nations and stabilised societies.[10] Considering the enormity and marginalisation of informal workers in India and the role that unions are capable of performing in a democratic polity, there is an urgent need for unions in India to organise informal workers in order to ensure basic minimum conditions of a dignified life for them. Unionisation ensures the visibility of informal workers,[11] which is an essential requirement for an effective process of social dialogue.

However, as the 2007 National Commission for Enterprises in the Unorganised Sector (NCEUS) report notes, informal workers in India remain largely invisible to policy circles,[12] a fact confirmed during my fieldwork in Kolkata, India. Informal workers' organisations generally adopt a three-pronged strategy in improving the conditions of specific groups of informal workers. As I discussed earlier, they enable workers to take advantage of the existing beneficial guarantees; they negotiate with government in extracting benefits for workers; and they directly provide for social and economic benefits for workers. The following is a brief description of the relation between informal workers' organisations and enhancement of capabilities of informal workers in India.

---

2 ibid 8; Ela R Bhat, *We Are Poor But So Many: the Story of Self-employed Women in India* (New York: Oxford University Press, 2006).
3 See Freeman and Medoff (n 1) 18.
4 ibid 17.
5 ibid 192–206.
6 ibid 10.
7 See Elizabeth Hill, *Worker Identity, Agency and Economic Development: Women's Empowerment in the Indian Informal Economy* (New York: Routledge, 2010) 104–14.
8 Tito Boeri and others, *The Role of Unions in the Twenty-first Century: a Report for the Fondazione Rodolfo Debenedetti* (New York: Oxford University Press, 2001) 17–19, 159–62, 196–204.
9 ibid 163–71.
10 See Gregory M Luebbert, *Liberalism, Fascism, or Social Democracy* (New York: Oxford University Press, 1991) 159–84, 175–77, 183–86.
11 See Bhat (n 2).
12 NCEUS, *Report on conditions of work and promotion of livelihoods in the unorganised sector* August 2007 (New Delhi: NCEUS, 2007) 37, 50, 75–76, 79–80, 165, 196, 356.

7.2.1 Empowering informal workers

During my fieldwork in India, ILO officials emphasised the indispensability of a union to enhance visibility of waste pickers in policy-circles and promote bargaining with the government. Coen Kompier, a senior specialist on international labour standards at the ILO Country Office for India, noted:[13]

> The first element would be organising, you know. [It] creates some kind of a platform for them to raise their voice. There are different kinds of small [trade] unions. For instance, here in Gurgaon informal garment workers are part of many small trade unions. The first problem that many run into is that the Labour Commissioner [. . .] refuses to register [these small trade unions]. This is a symptom of a larger disease . . . there are these powers of exclusion . . . certain categories of workers cannot organise on the basis of definitional deficiencies.[14]

Kompier identifies initiatives to organise informal workers as a central requirement in furtherance of empowering such workers so that they can pursue their goals.

In Chapter 2, I discussed how informal workers' organisations enhance capabilities of informal workers through the provision of resources and promotion of conversion factors. Informal workers' organisations provide a range of services such as literacy programmes, education for children, vocational training, health awareness, legal awareness, insurance etc for workers.

Moreover, Hill points out that simply by bringing together informal workers in one place organisations significantly enhances workers' capabilities.[15] Based on her study of SEWA members, Hill shows that there is a marked change in the demeanour of informal workers once they join the trade union; the once timid, insecure, vulnerable workers are transformed into assertive, confident and empowered individuals after they join the union.[16] The union inculcated a sense of identity, recognition, respect and public status amongst its members.[17]

Hill notes that SEWA's organisation of informal women workers generates mutual recognition and respect that produces individual self-confidence, self-respect and self-esteem amongst self-employed informal women workers in India.[18] She further observes: '[b]y formally coming together and establishing their own institutions, workers recognise themselves both as individuals and as part of a larger community of workers who have a legitimate claim to public resources.'[19]

---

13   Interview conducted on 22 June 2011 at the ILO Office (India Habitat Centre) in New Delhi, India.
14   Kompier was referring to the numerical and wage-based definition of worker, which excludes a section of workers from being recognised under Indian labour laws. I have discussed this issue in ch 2.
15   See Hill (n 7) 97–100.
16   ibid 97–100, 104–12.
17   ibid 101–102, 109–12.
18   ibid 116.
19   ibid 119.

Organisations thus have intrinsic value in informal workers' lives[20] in the sense that 'structures of living together' such as a trade union determines its members' capabilities by contributing towards their personal development (or influencing personal conversion factors).[21] Accordingly, positive influence on personal conversion factors of women members of the union (discussed above as delineated by Hill) would not have been possible if those individuals were not part of the collective.[22] Although the analytical focus of the capability approach is individual, Amartya Sen notes that collective capabilities and collective action can be conceptualised within the capability approach.[23]

Solava S Ibrahim argues that in developing countries development of capabilities is a communal process rather than an individual one.[24] His argument is based on his study of poor communities in Egypt. He found that poor communities organised self-help groups[25] and that these initiatives not only promoted economic opportunities, but also facilitated grassroots political participation, developed social capital and enhanced bargaining power of the poor.[26] The promotion of capabilities in these economic, social and political fronts would not have been possible except for communal (self-help group) action.[27]

Thus, collective action is significant in promoting intrinsic freedom of individual informal workers, especially in a developing country context. In its promotional capacity of intrinsic freedom, collective action contributes to individual capabilities (as distinct from collective capabilities), thereby enabling individual informal workers to perform as effective agents. However, collective organisation of informal workers also contributes to the promotion of collective capabilities as discussed below.

20 Peter Evans, 'Collective capabilities, culture, and Amartya Sen's *Development as Freedom*' (2002) 37(2) *Studies in Comparative International Development* 54 at 56; Martha C Nussbaum, *Women and Human Development: the Capabilities Approach* (Cambridge: Cambridge University Press, 2000) 79; Frances Stewart, 'Groups and capabilities' (2005) 6(2) *Journal of Human Development* 185 at 185, 187–88.

21 Severine Deneulin, *The Capability Approach and the Praxis of Development* (New York: Palgrave Macmillan, 2006) 60, 67–68, 72–76, 86; Jérôme Ballet, Jean-Luc Dubois and François-Régis Mahieu, 'Responsibility for each other's freedom: agency as the source of collective capability' (2007) 8(2) *Journal of Human Development* 185 at 188, 196–99.

22 Deneulin (n 21) 63–65; Evans (n 20) 56–59.

23 Amartya Sen, 'Response to commentaries' (2002) 37(2) *Studies in Comparative International Development* 78 at 85; Amartya Sen, 'The place of capability in a theory of justice' in Harry Brighouse, Ingrid Robeyns (eds), *Measuring Justice: Primary Goods and Capabilities* (Cambridge: Cambridge University Press, 2010) 239 at 249–50.

24 See Solava S Ibrahim, 'From individual to collective capabilities: the capability approach as a conceptual framework for self-help' (2006) 7(3) *Journal of Human Development* 397 at 398, 402–404, 407–408, 411; Evans (n 20) 56.

25 Ibrahim (n 24) 398–99, 405–406, 411–13.

26 ibid 398–99, 411–13.

27 ibid 407–408, 411.

7.2.2 Negotiating with government

Unorganised waste pickers in Kolkata are at a disadvantage in communicating their interests to the government. In view of the significant impact waste pickers have on the waste management system of Kolkata (discussed in Chapter 6), integration of waste pickers into the municipal waste management system of the city could be beneficial for both the municipality and the waste pickers. However, such a proposal was never discussed with government officials. On being asked whether the Kolkata Municipal Corporation could employ waste pickers in its solid waste management system, the incumbent Minister-in-Charge of Labour of the Government of West Bengal reflected:

> Municipalities [around the state] are already overburdened because of over-staffing. Therefore, it will be difficult for the municipalities to bring in new waste pickers in their regular roles.

Echoing the Labour Minister's observation, Debabrata Mazumdar, the Mayor-in-Council for Solid Waste Management of the Kolkata Municipal Corporation, pointed out that they have adequate staff for solid waste management.[28] Majumdar noted:

> While segregating solid waste, waste pickers litter on city roads and *vats* [garbage dumping places].[29] They pollute the city. Only a small portion of waste picker collected waste goes for recycling – the rest of the waste is dumped in Dhapa [landfill site]. It is difficult to employ waste pickers as part of the regular workforce of the Municipality. Their [waste pickers] attitude is not conducive for a disciplined regular labour force. Moreover, since educated workforce is available even for waste-collection jobs, it is difficult to integrate uneducated waste pickers with the municipal solid waste management system. Even though the Municipality cannot integrate waste pickers in its waste management system, we definitely encourage NGOs to work with waste pickers. However, there may be ways in which the Municipality can help waste pickers. But to do that, we need to know what their problems are. Because these people [waste pickers] do not have a representative organisation, there is a communication gap between authorities and them [waste pickers]. If waste pickers can organise themselves into a union it becomes much easier for us [the Municipality] to communicate with them.

The Mayor-in-Council attributed the lack of communication and effective dialogue between waste pickers and the government to the absence of a representative organisation of waste pickers.

---

28 Interview conducted on 4 July 2011 at the Mayor-in-Council's office at the Kolkata Municipal Corporation Building in Kolkata, India.

29 Amongst the 141 wards of the Kolkata Municipal Corporation, municipal staff segregate solid waste in only seven wards. See ch 6 for a detailed discussion.

Kompier also pointed out the need for a representative organisation of informal workers in order to negotiate and bargain with the government. He noted that workers can make use of the ILO complaint procedure to improve their conditions. If a registered trade union files a *comment* (ie a complaint) to the ILO, mentioning that, in spite of ratifying an ILO convention, the government is violating the convention's provisions, the ILO can take the issue up with the respective government. He mentioned a recent ILO initiative with the Government of India:

> For instance . . . we have been able to do something on manual scavenging. India has ratified Convention 111 on discrimination in occupation and employment, which is one of these eight fundamental conventions; there are two on discrimination. The unions were filing complaints to our supervisory body, which is the Committee of Experts. This is an independent body; they meet every year in December for almost a month to look into the application[s] [ie complaints] against a ratified convention by a country.

Upon receipt of a complaint (comment) from different unions that, since the work of manual scavenging is based on caste, it is in violation of Convention 111, the ILO Committee of Experts brought it to the notice of the Government of India. The ILO has then taken up a US$100,000 project with manual scavengers in India.[30]

Kompier was of the view that this mechanism could be utilised even by waste pickers in India.[31] When asked whether waste pickers could initiate a complaint (comment) to the ILO Committee of Experts if they are not part of a trade union, Kompier reflected: 'the complaint procedure can only work if you are registered as a trade union; [otherwise] we [the ILO] would be very embarrassed'.[32] Noting that the ILO cannot help waste pickers' cause in the absence of their representative union, Kompier advised that the waste pickers in Kolkata should try to form a trade union. I will describe their unionisation initiative in section 7.3 of the chapter.

In Chapter 2, I discussed how informal workers' organisations constantly negotiate and bargain with the government at different levels (central, provincial and local) in order to ensure concrete social and economic support for informal workers. Organisations such as the Kagad Kach Patra Kashtakari Panchayat (KKPKP) and Chintan have bargained with local governments to secure recognition and integration of waste pickers into the formal municipal waste management system. Hill, too, notes the centrality of bargaining with the government: 'SEWA interventions for work-life reform rely on public action and support from the state, its institutions and officials to make productive resources accessible to

---

30 Interview conducted on 22 June 2011 at the ILO Office (India Habitat Centre) in New Delhi, India.
31 ibid.
32 ibid.

informal workers.'[33] However, bargaining with the government is not limited only to workers' socio-economic needs; organisations such as SEWA lobby with the government in order to amend and enact laws for informal workers.[34]

In her study on Indian informal workers' organisations, Agarwala documents the nature of negotiations and bargaining between informal workers' organisations and the government.[35] Agarwala points out that informal workers' unions must negotiate with government: 'unlike the formal sector unions, informal workers' unions make their demands directly to the state, because their employers are not constant and are often unknown'.[36] She further observes that: 'the tone of the new movement is non-violent, framed as a bargain between the citizen and the state'.[37] Agarwala shows that in some Indian states such as Tamil Nadu, West Bengal and Maharashtra, certain categories of informal workers (construction workers and *bidi* workers) have been able to secure legal rights to economic benefits by continuously negotiating with the government.[38]

Although certain categories of informal workers have been able to negotiate with the government in availing themselves of some economic benefits, the majority of informal workers in India remain excluded from legislative and executive assistance.[39] However, informal workers' organisations are increasingly generating socio-economic benefits for a large number of workers who remain excluded from government welfare programmes. In Chapter 2, I discussed how informal workers' organisations provide socio-economic resources to their members and beneficiaries. In what follows, I briefly describe why socio-economic resources are not available to waste pickers in Kolkata and how waste pickers' organisations can become important in realising socio-economic benefits for them.

7.2.3 Providing social and economic benefits

In Chapter 6, I discussed the different legally mandated beneficial schemes available to certain categories of informal workers in the state of West Bengal. Waste pickers are excluded from government beneficial measures designed for informal workers. When asked why waste pickers are excluded from the purview of the legally mandated SASPFUW provident fund scheme (see Chapter 6 for a discussion of the scheme), Sarkari Munsi,[40] a government official at the Labour Department of the Government of West Bengal, replied:

---

33 See Hill (n 7) 136.
34 See ch 4; Hill (n 7) 137–39, 142–45.
35 Hill (n 7) 61–63, 66–69.
36 Rina Agarwala, 'From Work to Welfare: Informal Workers' Organizations and the State in India' (unpublished PhD Thesis, Princeton University, 2006) 32.
37 ibid 70.
38 ibid 80–81, 89–90, 107–108, 114–16, 141–43.
39 See generally NCEUS, 'Conditions of work' (n 12).
40 This is a pseudonym that I use upon a request from my research participant.

We cannot include anyone [everyone] within the purview of the Scheme by ourselves. If there are some such workers and if they have a union they can apply to the government for the inclusion of their name in the Schedule of the law. If there are only fifty or hundred people waste picking it is not possible to include them under a different professional category. If a union is able to organise about thousand or so waste pickers, they can apply to be included within the SASPFUW Scheme.[41]

Although an unofficial account estimates the number of waste pickers in and around Kolkata to be about 20,000,[42] waste pickers are not visible for policy-making purposes.[43] The government official also seems to be taking the position that if only some insignificant minorities of people are engaged in an economic activity that cannot qualify to be work (at least for the purpose of social protection). However, more importantly, for the purpose of the present discussion, the official makes it amply clear that, in the absence of a union, waste pickers would not be brought within the purview of the social protection legislation of the state.

This official's views were corroborated by Purnendu Bose, the Minister-in-Charge of Labour, a revolutionary Marxist (Maoist/Naxal) turned proponent of neo-liberalism. Although he was sympathetic to these workers' cause,[44] he noted that it is better if a request for inclusion in the SASPFUW scheme comes from a union of waste pickers. However, he did not insist that waste pickers could only be included within the scheme if a union applies on their behalf, stating that, if a report documenting waste pickers' situation in Kolkata was submitted to him, he would consider including waste pickers within the purview of the law.[45] Delineating the newly formed government's informal worker policy,[46] the minister noted:

we already have laws and schemes for informal workers.[47] There is no use of having more legislation for them. What is required is appropriate imple-mentation of existing legislation. The days are over when the governments used

41 Interview conducted on 9 June 2011 at the State Secretariat Building in Kolkata, India.
42 See Martin Medina, 'Waste picker cooperatives in developing countries' El Colegio de la Frontera Norte, Mexico 1 at 12, available at http://wiego.org/sites/wiego.org/files/publications/files/Medina-wastepickers.pdf (last visited 23 May 2012); 'Trash talk: gaining value from waste, as it relates to the global poor', 2012 Yunus Challenge Waste: Put it to use, available at http://web.mit.edu/idi/yunus_2012/Yunus_2012.pdf (last visited 23 May 2012).
43 Such ignorance might also be a carefully crafted strategy on the government's part. If the government claims ignorance about the existence of waste pickers, they can easily excuse themselves from dealing with issues involving waste pickers.
44 Interview conducted on 29 June 2011 at the Writers' Building in Kolkata, India.
45 What the minister implied by this statement is that I submit a report documenting living standard and working conditions of waste pickers in Kolkata to him. He would consider including waste pickers within the legislative scheme if he is satisfied with my report.
46 The new coalition Government of West Bengal was formed in May 2011. See ch 6 for detailed discussion on the socio-political situation in West Bengal.
47 Such as the West Bengal Unorganised Sector Workers' Welfare Act 2007; West Bengal Beedi Workers' Welfare Scheme (WBBWWS); the Building and Other Construction Workers'

to protect workers. This is an era of *hire and fire*; there is no employment guarantee. Concepts such as minimum wages should be obliterated in the open market system; it should be the market that will decide wages of informal workers. [Our] government cannot protect workers. It is an open market – workers have to compete in that market. Our government proposes to create an *employment bank*; an employment bank will be a repository of informal workers. Whenever employers need they can draw from this pool of informal workers [to be enlisted in the employment bank]. We plan to provide on-hand training such as knitting, ironing of clothes etc. to informal workers. [emphasis mine]

Although the present government has not discontinued any of the existing welfare schemes for informal workers, the Labour Minister made it clear that the government does not envisage developing new frameworks to promote informal workers' interests.

State support for informal workers is meagre considering the multiple capability deficiencies suffered by such workers (discussed in Chapter 2 and Chapter 6). Moreover, state support is limited to only certain categories of informal workers such as construction workers, *bidi* workers, head-load workers etc. Under such circumstances, informal workers' organisations provide economic benefits and social services to their members and beneficiaries.

In Chapter 2, I discussed the range of social and economic services and assistance provided to informal workers by their organisations. SEWA, for example, arranges for banking services, housing services, health care services, child care services, insurance schemes and legal assistance for its members; KKPKP provides its members with group insurance, credit facilities and vocational training; Chintan has arranged for door-to-door waste collection by its beneficiaries. The ILO has documented a comprehensive list of services and benefits offered by informal workers' organisations to their members and beneficiaries.[48]

Thus, collective organisation is also of instrumental value (apart from intrinsic value) in the sense that collective action helps in attaining social, economic and political conditions necessary for the development of capabilities of all workers.[49] If waste pickers did not undertake collective action through organisations such as the SEWA, the KKPKP or the Chintan, they would not have been able to secure municipal contracts, beneficial statutes, banking services, insurance, credit facilities etc – all of which contributes to the enhancement of capabilities of these informal workers' collectives (or aggregate[50] of all informal workers).[51]

(Regulation of Employment and Conditions of Service) Act 1996, the Rashtriya Swastha Bima Yojana (RSBY). See ch 6 for a discussion of the different schemes available to informal workers.

48 See Piush Antony, *Towards Empowerment: Experiences of Organizing Women Workers* (New Delhi: ILO, 2001); Pong-Sul Ahned, *Organizing for Decent Work in the Informal Economy: Strategies, Methods and Practices* (New Delhi: Sub-regional Office for South Asia, ILO, 2007).

49 See Amartya Sen, *Development as Freedom* (New York: Alfred A. Knopf, 1999) 116; Evans (n 20) 57; Stewart (n 20) 185, 188, 190.

50 Even though it might appear self-evident, a brief note is in order here: legal fiction envisages an organisation (union or cooperative) as a separate legal entity apart from its members. However,

Their collective action is instrumental in furtherance of their collective capabilities.[52] Evans notes that organised collectives such as unions are central for *less privileged* groups in order to promote their capabilities.[53]

Frances Stewart shows how collective action has *intrinsic* and *instrumental* significance for impoverished groups and promotes their capabilities around the world.[54] Sen himself notes that collective capabilities emanating from collective action is capable of addressing larger public policy issues.[55]

Thus, informal workers' organisations play a developmental role in the lives of their members and beneficiaries. By providing for resources and social conditions of capability enhancement, informal workers' organisations promote workers' development in terms of freedom. These organisations provide for the necessary conditions for capability development of informal workers. As discussed in Chapter 2, informal workers' organisations promote constitutional labour rights for informal workers in India.

However, waste pickers in West Bengal remain excluded from any capability-development initiative. My interviews in West Bengal indicated that one of the prominent reasons for the exclusion of waste pickers from the purview of government welfare schemes is the absence of organisation amongst waste pickers. The incumbent minister and other government officials emphasised the importance of unionisation in order to access government welfare schemes. During the course of my fieldwork in Kolkata, waste pickers of the city organised themselves into a trade union.

While it is too early to analyse the significance of the unionisation initiative, some early indications point at the advantages of the unionisation. In the next section of the chapter, I discuss how within a very short span of time the waste pickers' union in Kolkata has been able to draw attention from various quarters, which is useful in promoting visibility of the waste pickers and drawing attention to their predicament.

7.3 Waste pickers organise in Kolkata

While I was conducting my fieldwork in Kolkata, during the course of an informal meeting between the organisers of the Calcutta Samaritans (the NGO), a few waste pickers, some city intellectuals and activists, the idea of organising waste pickers

in the discussion of collective capabilities one needs to be careful that enhancement of collective capability of a group actually means that capabilities of all the group members are enhanced, rather than the group as an abstract entity.

51   Ibrahim (n 24) 398, 402–404, 407–408, 411.

52   F Comim, F Carey, 'Social capital and the capability approach: are Putnam and Sen incompatible bedfellows?' (Paper delivered at the EAEPE Conference 'Comparing economic institutions', Siena, November 2001, as cited in Ibrahim (n 24) 403; Evans (n 20) 56.

53   See Evans (n 20) 56; Aili Mari Tripp, 'Creating collective capabilities: women, agency and the politics of representation' (2010) 19(1) *Columbia Journal of Gender and Law* 219; Ibrahim (n 24) 405.

54   Stewart (n 20) 189, 195–99.

55   Sen, 'Response' (n 23) 85.

into a trade union was discussed.[56] The Calcutta Samaritans have been involved with issues related to waste pickers and other homeless populations in Kolkata since 1971, and Pratim Roba, a Calcutta Samaritans organiser, enthusiastically supported the idea of unionisation.[57] The Calcutta Samaritans campaigned for the inclusion of the homeless population in Kolkata under the below the poverty line (BPL) scheme in order to enable homeless people to seek government assistance.[58] In 2009, they prepared a report on the socio-economic situation of waste pickers in Kolkata.[59] Recently, the Calcutta Samaritans conducted a survey on homeless people in Kolkata with assistance from the Government of West Bengal.[60]

Armed with the idea of forming a trade union, the Calcutta Samaritans' organisers reached out to waste pickers in different locations of the city. The organisers received a positive response from the waste pickers in the city and they proposed that a meeting of waste pickers be convened with a view to initiating the formation of a trade union and delineating a road map for the union activities.

Reshmi Ganguly, another organiser with the Calcutta Samaritans, planned the meeting with financial assistance from Action Aid.[61] We (Calcutta Samaritans' organisers, city intellectuals and I) approached the Legal Aid Society of the West Bengal National University of Juridical Sciences (WB NUJS),[62] Kolkata, India, to provide us with a venue for the meeting of waste pickers. The then Vice-Chancellor and Registrar of the law university enthusiastically agreed to allow us the use of the university auditorium free of cost for the meeting.

The Calcutta Samaritans' organisers went to the different localities in order to brief waste pickers about the advantages of unionisation and the tentative agendas for a waste pickers' union in Kolkata. After this phase of reaching out to waste pickers, the Calcutta Samaritans' organisers sensed immense enthusiasm amongst waste pickers to form a trade union of their own. The organisers estimated about 600 waste pickers' presence for the proposed meeting.[63]

---

56 Meeting on 12 June 2011 at the Calcutta Samaritans Office at Ripon Street in Kolkata, India.
57 Interview conducted on 30 June 2011 at the Calcutta Samaritans Office at Ripon Street in Kolkata, India.
58 In this respect several NGOs in Kolkata have moved the High Court of Calcutta in a public interest litigation in order to enlist homeless population in the BPL list. *Griha Adhikar Mancha and Others* v *Union of India and Others* Writ Petition Number 19802 (W) of 2008 (on file with author).
59 Supriya Routh and others, *Situational Analysis of Ragpickers in Kolkata* (Kolkata: Calcutta Samaritans, 2009).
60 Sharmistha Banerjee and others, *A Report on Rapid Assessment Survey of Homeless Population within Kolkata Municipal Corporation Area* (Kolkata: Calcutta Samaritans, undated).
61 'Action Aid is an anti-poverty agency, working in India since 1972 with the poor people to end poverty and injustice together.' See 'who we are', available at http://www.actionaid.org/india/who-we-are (last visited 23 May 2012). As I mention in ch 6, I was directly involved with the organisation initiative of waste pickers in Kolkata. During the unionisation initiative I actively worked with the Calcutta Samaritans, the West Bengal National University of Juridical Sciences and waste pickers.
62 The West Bengal National University of Juridical Sciences (WB NUJS) is a premier law university of India, located in the city of Kolkata.
63 Meeting of Calcutta Samaritans' organisers at the Calcutta Samaritans Office on 4 July 2011 at Ripon Street, Kolkata, India.

On 6 July 2011 about 500 waste pickers assembled at the WBNUJS auditorium for their meeting in furtherance of formation of a trade union. Many of the women waste pickers came with their children because they did not want to miss the occasion but at the same time they had no one at home to take care of their children. During the meeting, waste pickers were asked to identify their problems. Waste pickers identified the factors inhibiting their capability enhancement during the meeting, many of which were similar to those I discovered in my interviews with waste pickers (discussed in Chapter 6). Once this exercise was completed, the idea of formation of a trade union was advanced.

Once the idea of membership of the trade union and of the executive committee (office bearers) was discussed, all the waste pickers present at the meeting became members of the union by paying a membership fee of Rs 1 for a year. The women waste pickers were enthusiastic and eager to represent their locality in the executive committee of the union. The union members elected 20 executive committee members, with Kalu Das, a waste picker himself, elected its general secretary.[64] On the same day the executive committee held its first meeting and decided a name for the union: Barjya Punarbyawaharikaran Shilpa Shramik Sangathan (BPSSS), which was translated into English as Association of Workers engaged in Waste Recycling Industry (AWWRI). Kalu Das enthusiastically pointed out that the union must have a symbol like other political parties.[65] In their second meeting, the executive committee of BPSSS decided on their symbol.[66]

Having already discussed the problems faced by waste pickers in the general members meeting, it was incumbent on the executive committee of the union to frame such problems in terms of a more focused agenda, which the union could pursue. Based on the discussion with the members the BPSSS identified five primary action plans: first, to provide their members with safety gear such as Wellington boots, gloves and aprons; secondly, to lobby with the Government of West Bengal in order to bring waste pickers within the purview of the existing legislative protection for informal workers (discussed in the previous chapter); thirdly, to lobby with the Kolkata Municipal Corporation so that waste pickers could be integrated with the municipal solid waste management system; fourthly, to prepare a comment on their deprivations to be submitted to the ILO; and, finally, to generate a fund in order to institute a group health insurance scheme for waste pickers.

64 After I returned from my fieldwork in India, I was informed that the executive committee had to meet to reduce the strength of the committee to nine members, on the basis of their possession of an official identity document. This was necessitated when the union members applied for the registration of their trade union. The executive committee was informed by the Department of Labour that, for the registration of the union, all executive committee members have to submit identity proof and residential certificate. Accordingly, executive committee members who did not possess a valid identification document or residential certificate had to be removed from the committee.

65 Meeting of the executive committee of BPSSS on 6 July 2011 at the West Bengal National University of Juridical Sciences, Kolkata, India.

66 Meeting of the executive committee of BPSSS on 12 July 2011 at the Calcutta Samaritans, Kolkata, India.

During the first executive committee meeting, the WB NUJS Legal Aid Society expressed interest in providing legal and other assistance to BPSSS.[67] The WB NUJS Legal Aid Society has adopted BPSSS as one of their projects, thereby enabling students of the law university to work in furtherance of promoting BPSSS's interests.[68] Students engaged with the Legal Aid Society have undertaken to educate waste pickers' children.[69]

Students have also undertaken a membership drive on behalf of the union through awareness campaigns amongst waste pickers in Kolkata.[70] The Legal Aid Society is also providing legal assistance to individual members of the union if they are arrested or harassed by law enforcement officials.[71] Recently, the WB NUJS Legal Aid Society devoted an Open House Discussion session to discussing their role in promoting BPSSS initiatives.[72] The Legal Aid Society prepared a petition to be filed with the Ministry of Urban Affairs, Government of India, National Human Rights Commission and the Supreme Court of India, advocating the right to work and livelihood for homeless waste pickers in Kolkata.[73]

What is evident from the above description is that the waste pickers who were living at the margins of society have become significantly more visible with their unionisation initiative. Within days of formation of the union, the Legal Aid Society began collaborating with waste pickers on different issues. Within months of the formation of the union, the Legal Aid Society brought the waste pickers to the notice of academics and policy-makers through a national conference. What is much more significant is that unionisation works as an instrument of social dialogue. However, as important as unions may be for the promotion of informal workers' visibility and social dialogue, the fact is that only a small section of informal workers are organised in membership-based unions and non-membership organisations. Accordingly, the policy challenge for these unorganised informal workers is to make themselves more visible and engage in social dialogue in furtherance of their capability enhancement.

In the next section, I propose a way through which informal workers could be made participants in the social dialogue process in furtherance of enhancing their capabilities, which is based on the specific case of informal waste pickers in Kolkata.

---

67 Meeting of the executive committee of BPSSS on 6 July 2011 at the West Bengal National University of Juridical Sciences, Kolkata, India.

68 Legal Aid Society: Brief report of activities undertaken over the period from July 2011 to January 2012; also email conversation with Prof Anirban Chakraborty, Assistant Professor and Faculty Advisor of the Legal Aid Society, the West Bengal National University of Juridical Sciences, Kolkata, India on 8 February 2012.

69 Email conversation with Prof Anirban Chakraborty (n 68) on 5 February 2012.

70 ibid.

71 ibid.

72 'Open house discussion on deemed homeless', AWWRI Project of NUJS Legal Aid Society & Centre for Human Rights, National Conference on place of deemed homeless in good governance and Inclusive growth in India (27–29 January 2012) WB NUJS Campus (on file with author).

73 Email conversation (5 February 2012) (n 69).

7.4 Role of integrated institutions in the social dialogue process

In Chapter 5, I proposed a capability-based approach for developing labour law for informal economic activities. I developed the proposed approach in three stages. First, I advocated that the normative goal of labour law for informal workers must be enhancement and equality of capability. Secondly, invoking Anderson's insights, I proposed that labour law must be based on the concept of democratic equality in the cooperative production process. Thirdly, based on Drèze and Sen, I argued that labour law for informal economic activities should be operationalised through social dialogue amongst integrated institutions in a democratic society, which integrates informal workers into the dialogue process.

In the absence of an organisation of informal workers, integrated institutions can become immensely important in promoting social dialogue involving informal workers. In this section of the chapter, by using the example of waste pickers in Kolkata, I propose how integrated institutions can promote social dialogue for waste pickers in the absence of a waste pickers' organisation.

In Chapter 6, I delineated factors (resources) identified by waste pickers as necessary for the development of their capabilities. As I argued in Chapter 5, if development of capability is to be the normative goal of labour law, then one of the prerequisites for developing a labour law framework for informal economic activities would be the ascertainment of factors necessary for capability enhancement. Since the capability approach is a choice-based conceptualisation of development, it is the perspective of the specific group of informal workers that is relevant in determining necessary valuable capabilities. Once capabilities valuable for specific categories of informal workers are identified, the next task is the identification of resources and socio-economic-political-cultural factors that are necessary for enhancing identified capabilities. Accordingly, a labour law approach for specific informal economic activities would involve identification of valuable capabilities and determination of necessary factors responsible for promoting such capabilities.

While participation of the specific category of informal workers is a *sine qua non* in identifying valuable capabilities, their participation is not a sufficient condition in determining necessary factors to promote capabilities. This insufficiency is the result of the possibility that informal workers might suffer from adaptive preferences (discussed in Chapter 3) arising from their deprivation of basic capabilities such as health, nutrition and education. As a result of their marginalisation and adaptive preferences, it might be difficult for them to identify factors necessary for their capability enhancement (I discuss more on adaptive preference in section 7.5 of this chapter). Accordingly, capability-enhancing factors need to be determined through the involvement of a wider range of stakeholders. Therefore, at a preliminary level, the challenge is to devise a mechanism through which capabilities and necessary factors could be decided upon for a labour law for specific categories of informal workers. I address this challenge in the context of waste pickers in Kolkata.

In order to meet this two-pronged challenge, an institutional platform for the promotion of social dialogue (amongst stakeholders) has to be devised. Such an institutional platform has to ensure the participation of informal workers as its principal objective. If informal workers are organised, it becomes much easier to ensure their representative participation in such a platform for social dialogue. In the context of waste pickers in Kolkata, the waste pickers' union BPSSS can be one such representative organisation. However, it must be remembered that the BPSSS is a very new initiative (and to date has only a small membership base); to all intents and purposes waste pickers in Kolkata were unorganised until recently. This lack of organisation characterises not only waste pickers in Kolkata, but a significant majority of informal workers in India.[74]

Reflecting on the problem of the lack of organisation of informal workers in India, Kompier noted: 'There is a kind of catch-22 situation'.[75] He reflected that to receive some benefits, such as the advantage of the ILO complaint mechanism, informal workers (or for that matter, formal workers) must be part of a trade union. However, to register as a trade union informal workers have to be employed by an employer.[76] Trade union registrars in different jurisdictions refuse to register informal workers' trade unions because informal workers are mostly self-employed and, accordingly, there are no employers to bargain with. Although registration of informal workers' trade unions such as SEWA has shown the futility of this approach (as noted earlier in Chapter 2), Kompier observed that many trade union registrars in the country refuse to register trade unions of informal workers because these workers are not employed. He further noted:

> Amongst the big trade unions in India it is only the HMS [Hind Mazdoor Sabha] and BMS [Bharatiya Mazdoor Sangh] who are trying to organise informal home-based workers. Formal sector unions are reluctant to venture into organising informal workers. . . . With informal workers social dialogue can happen through any group: self-help group, cooperative, etc.[77]

---

74   Lack of organisation is one of the central features of informal workers in India. Therefore, unsurprisingly, informal workers are termed as unorganised workers in policy parlance and government documents in India.

75   Interview conducted on 22 June 2011 at the ILO Office (India Habitat Centre) in New Delhi, India.

76   Trade Unions Act 1926. The Act defines a 'trade union' as 'any combination, whether temporary or permanent, formed primarily for the purpose of regulating the relations between workmen and employers or between workmen and workmen, or between employers and employers, or for imposing restrictive conditions on the conduct of any trade or business . . .' (s 2(h)). The Act defines 'trade dispute' as 'any dispute between employers and workmen or between workmen and workmen, or between employers and employers which is connected with the employment or non-employment, or the terms of employment or the conditions of labour, of any person, and "workmen" means all persons employed in trade or industry whether or not in the employment of the employer with whom the trade dispute arises' (s 2(g)).

77   Interview conducted on 22 June 2011 at the ILO Office (India Habitat Centre) in New Delhi, India.

Thus, Kompier advised that if trade union registrars are unwilling to register trade unions of informal workers under the Trade Unions Act 1926, informal workers should try to organise as self-help groups or cooperatives in order to promote their involvement in the social dialogue process.

Kompier's reflection on the big trade unions' lack of involvement in organising informal workers was confirmed by leaders of two of the biggest trade unions in India. Mrinal Das, a secretary of the Centre of Indian Trade Unions (CITU) for 20 years, observed that, although the CITU has affiliated unions in the informal sector such as brick-kilns, auto-rickshaw workers, *bidi* workers, construction workers and street vendors, it has been unable to reach out to the majority of workers employed in informal activities.[78] Das frankly admitted that CITU's orientation still lies in the employment relationship-based concept of workers.

Accordingly, self-employed own-account informal workers mostly remain outside the union's radar. When asked whether CITU organises informal domestic workers or waste pickers in Kolkata or West Bengal, Das replied in the negative. Similarly, Pradip Bhattacharya of the Indian National Trade Union Congress (INTUC) pointed out that INTUC organises agricultural workers, construction workers, *bidi* workers, street vendors etc.[79] However, like the CITU, the INTUC has also not been able to organise either domestic workers or waste pickers.

Organisation or unionism is one of the prerequisites for workers' democratic participation in the policy-making process. However, if organising initiatives amongst workers is absent or inadequate, there may be other ways in which workers could be integrated into a democratic dialogue process. In the context of informal workers, one of the ways of integrating workers into a dialogue process other than through union organising could be through the multiple institutions of a democratic society with which informal workers regularly interact. In the following section with a few examples in the context of waste pickers in Kolkata, India, I discuss how multiple institutions can integrate waste pickers into the social dialogue process.

7.5 In what ways can integrated institutions facilitate integration of waste pickers into the social dialogue process?

Under circumstances where informal workers are not represented by unions or other kinds of organisations, their integration into the process of social dialogue is challenging. In this scenario, integrated institutions of a democratic society might be able to provide a mechanism through which unorganised informal workers could be integrated into the social dialogue process. Using the example of waste pickers

78 Interview with Mrinal Das, Centre of Indian Trade Unions (CITU) on 1 June 2011 at the CITU Office, Kolkata, India.
79 Interview with Pradip Bhattacharya, Indian National Trade Union Congress (INTUC) on 2 June 2011 at the INTUC Office, Kolkata, India.

in Kolkata, I indicate how integrated institutions could bring informal workers within the fold of the social dialogue process.

In the context of my fieldwork in Kolkata, I argue that integrated institutions such as police, NGOs, elected representatives, universities and media might be able to integrate waste pickers into an effective social dialogue process. One of the institutions that waste pickers regularly interact with is the institution of law enforcement officials. Waste pickers in Kolkata have a love–hate relationship with the police. While most waste pickers complain about the police, many waste pickers point out the cordial and helpful role that police officers play in their work-lives.[80]

In the preceding chapter I described how police play a helpful and cooperative role in the lives of waste pickers in Kolkata. Although the police are aware that waste pickers' squatter settlements are illegal encroachments on public space, some of the police officers adopt a tolerant approach towards waste pickers' slums and their work. There have been instances when, prior to conducting a raid or eviction drive, police personnel warned waste pickers to vacate their slums and return only after things have quietened down.[81] Showing a remarkable understanding of the law enforcement officials' limitations, waste pickers reflected that they understand that the police have to do their job (ie evicting them from their slums) when ordered from above.[82] However, as waste pickers point out, in spite of such limitations, many police personnel cooperate with them in allowing them to collect waste and live in their slums without interference.

However, as waste pickers also point out, helpful and cooperative police personnel are a minority. The police are generally perceived as a threat to their work-lives by the waste pickers.[83] Some police regularly arrest waste pickers on allegations of theft and other petty offences.[84] Others regularly extract bribes from waste pickers and keep them under continuous observation.[85] Police are aware that on account of ignorance, illiteracy and lack of education, waste pickers are vulnerable and, therefore, cannot complain against police atrocities. They are also aware that, in order to have access to waste-collection sites, waste pickers need to negotiate with police on a regular basis. Thus, the police are not only aware of the *modus operandi* of waste picking and waste-recycling activities, they also regularly interact with waste pickers. Accordingly, the police might be one of the institutions amongst many that could be involved in a social dialogue process in the absence of representative organisations of waste pickers.[86]

---

80 See discussion in ch 6.
81 Interview conducted on 20 April 2011 in the Tollygunj-Golfgreen area, Kolkata, India.
82 ibid.
83 Interview conducted on 20 April 2011 in the Tala Park area, Kolkata, India; interview conducted on 20 April 2011 in the Aajkaal area, Kolkata, India.
84 Interviews conducted on 20 April 2011 in the Tala Park area; 9 May 2011, 10 May 2011, 11 May 2011 in the Rajabazar area; 19 April 2011 in the Golfgreen area; 5 June 2011 in the BNR area in Kolkata, India.
85 ibid. This is a general perception about law enforcement officials shared by waste pickers across different locations in Kolkata.
86 However there is a possibility that police personnel might not be empathetic (or at least, sympathetic) to the issues involving waste pickers, because, if they are sympathetic to the waste

NGOs can be important institutions in promoting integration of informal workers in the social dialogue process. Registered under the Societies Registration Act 1860,[87] the Calcutta Samaritans undertake crisis counselling, rehabilitation of drug addicts, aftercare for children and adult drug addicts, harm minimisation of drug addicts, treatment of sexually transmitted diseases, AIDS awareness and prevention, campaign and advocacy for marginalised population, vocational training and workplace care and counselling programmes.[88]

The Calcutta Samaritans organise medical camps for waste pickers; the NGO helps waste pickers' children get into schools, and campaigns and lobbies against eviction of waste pickers from their shelters.[89] Moreover, they are involved in day-to-day interaction with waste pickers at several levels. Since they are involved with multi-dimensional issues of waste pickers, the Calcutta Samaritans are in a very good position to analyse the work-life conditions of waste pickers in Kolkata. Accordingly, the Calcutta Samaritans would not only be important to integrate waste pickers in the social dialogue process, they can also provide important reflections on the required factors necessary for the enhancement of capabilities of waste pickers in Kolkata.

Locally elected representatives could be another institution which is important in integrating informal workers in the social dialogue process. Waste pickers have to interact with locally elected representatives on a regular basis. However, one must be mindful that these interactions are not always positive or for the benefit of waste pickers. Sometimes the waste pickers have to negotiate their very existence with these locally elected representatives. Waste pickers have to seek permission from local representatives to live in a squatter settlement or collect waste. I discuss some of the indications in this respect in the concluding chapter.

In Aajkaal and Kestopur Khal, waste pickers seemed to be scared of locally elected representatives. In the Aajkaal area the local representative has tried to evict waste pickers from their shanties, whereas in the Kestopur Khal area waste pickers were instructed not to talk to strangers without the local representative's permission. However, as I discussed in the previous chapter, one of the waste pickers, Jehadi Bewa, notes that the former local representative used to help waste pickers secure ration cards. Ration cards have a twofold purpose: first, they act as identification for waste pickers; and, secondly, they entitle waste pickers to state-subsidised rations. Thus, elected representatives deeply interact with waste pickers. Some of them also appear to be sympathetic to the informal workers' cause. Accordingly, in the absence of waste pickers' organisations, locally elected representatives can promote the integration of waste pickers into the social dialogue process.

---

pickers' cause, they cannot extract bribes from waste pickers. The police might not want to risk the loss of some additional income.

87 See the Calcutta Samaritans, available at http://thecalcuttasamaritans.org/contact.htm (last visited 21 February 2012).

88 Projects of Calcutta Samaritans, available at http://thecalcuttasamaritans.org/project.htm (last visited 21 February 2012).

89 Interview with Reshmi Ganguly on 9 June 2011 at the Calcutta Samaritans Office at Ripon Street in Kolkata, India.

A final institution that I will discuss here is a university. A premier law university, the WB NUJS has undertaken a pioneering initiative in promoting waste pickers' interests in Kolkata. The WB NUJS has been working with waste pickers in Kolkata since 2009. The Legal Aid Society and students of the Legal Clinic of the university have undertaken a study on situational analysis of waste pickers in Kolkata with assistance from the Calcutta Samaritans.[90]

More recently, the Legal Aid Society is working closely with BPSSS, the newly formed trade union of waste pickers in Kolkata as I discussed earlier in this chapter. In addition to initiatives discussed earlier, the Legal Aid Society is also devising ways to secure identity cards for BPSSS members[91] and enabling waste pickers to claim social protection from the state.[92] Such an intricate relationship between the Legal Aid Society of the WB NUJS and the waste pickers in Kolkata suggests that in absence of an organisation of waste pickers the university could be an institution that is also capable of integrating waste pickers into the social dialogue process.

In this context the role of media also needs to be appreciated. For about a decade the media have been reporting on different aspects of waste pickers' lives and livelihood in Kolkata. Such media reports have drawn attention towards the lives of waste pickers;[93] discussed proposals of door-to-door waste-collection by waste pickers;[94] reported on rehabilitation plans for waste pickers;[95] discussed municipal plans to undertake awareness for and organise waste pickers;[96] and reported on private and government initiatives undertaken by some states in order better to understand waste pickers and their work-lives.[97] Therefore, quite naturally, the media can be one of the institutions that are capable of integrating waste pickers into the social dialogue process.

---

90 I was a participant in the Legal Aid Society, and Legal Clinic initiative of the WB NUJS on waste pickers in Kolkata in 2009.

91 Email conversation (n 69).

92 ibid.

93 See Prasanta Paul, 'Pujas bring bonanza for Bengal ragpickers'; A Dalit-Bahujan, 'Media, Dr Babasaheb Ambedkar and his people' (undated) available at http://www.ambedkar.org/News/Pujasbring.htm (last visited 22 February 2012).

94 See 'Ragpickers: NGOs to help collect household plastic waste' *The Hindu Business Line* (1 May 2004) available at http://www.thehindubusinessline.in/2004/05/01/stories/2004050101 611900.htm (last visited 22 February 2012).

95 See Ajanta Chakraborty, 'Rehab plan for city's ragpicker community' *The Times of India* (13 August 2010) available at http://articles.timesofindia.indiatimes.com/2010-08-13/kolkata/28304234_1_ rag-pickers-solid-waste-urban-development (last visited 22 February 2012).

96 See 'Ragpickers to help recycle waste' *The Times of India* (11 May 2002), available at http://articles.timesofindia.indiatimes.com/2002-05-11/kolkata/27142733_1_solid-waste-ragpickers-recyclable-material (last visited 22 February 2012).

97 'Study to determine the role of rag pickers: outsourcing and innovation mantra for solid waste management in urban centres' *The Telegraph* (29 December 2010), available at http://www.telegraphindia.com/1101229/jsp/bihar/story_13362268.jsp (last visited 22 February 2012); Antara Bose, 'Rag-pickers take to reading, saving: interactive session motivates underprivileged children to join schools' *The Telegraph* (22 August 2009), available at http://www.telegraph india.com/1090822/jsp/jharkhand/story_11394087.jsp (last visited 22 February 2012).

The above discussion shows that waste pickers closely interact with multiple institutions at several levels. The nature of interaction differs depending on the orientation and capacity of an institution. For example, while the police are non-committal to the issues involving waste pickers, the Calcutta Samaritans have been constructively working with waste pickers for quite some time. The purpose of this discussion is to drive home the point that even if waste pickers are not organised[98] there are avenues through which they can become visible if the state wants to take note of them. This finding about waste pickers might be generalisable for all informal workers. Multiple institutions such as NGOs, police and the media interact with informal workers at different levels on a day-to-day basis. These multiple institutions are immensely important in furtherance of the promotion of informal workers' capabilities.

The involvement of integrated institutions in the social dialogue process is not only important when informal workers are unorganised. The role of such institutions is significant also when informal workers have their own organisation. Integrated institutions are a safeguard against adaptive preference,[99] which might be inherent in the choices made and valuable capabilities identified, by informal workers. Adaptive preference is a subjective state of mind that determines preference commensurate to one's actual surrounding circumstances.[100]

Preferences are conditioned by circumstances. Informal workers live under conditions of insecurity, uncertainty, exploitation and marginalisation and are outside the scope of public policy. Accordingly, their preferences are adapted to their precarious situation. They might consider themselves undeserving of even an insignificant act of charity. Because of their adaptive preference informal workers might lack 'the courage to demand any radical change' in their work-lives.[101] While working alongside informal workers during the social dialogue process integrated institutions can help remove this lack of courage to demand radical changes from the minds of informal workers.

The multiple institutions envisaged above as social partners do not share similar socio-economic-political circumstances and marginalisation that are faced by informal workers. These institutions are free from the influence of adaptive preference, which might shape informal workers' behaviour. Therefore, while the interface between informal workers and integrated institutions could help chart a comprehensive framework for the benefit of informal workers engaged in a specific informal activity, both informal workers and integrated institutions would bring different perspectives into dialogue. Since integrated institutions are, to a large extent, free from the subjective considerations characterising informal workers, they are capable of offering reasonably objective but empathetic insights into the law-making process for specific informal workers. Accordingly, integrated

---

98 One has to remember that waste pickers in Kolkata have begun to organise only in 2011.
99 Sen, *Development* (n 49) 62–63.
100 Benedetta Giovanola, 'Personhood and human richness: good and well-being in the capability approach and beyond' (2005) 63(2) *Review of Social Economy* 249 at 250.
101 ibid 254.

institutions could also be important in helping to identify factors that are important for the facilitation of capabilities of informal workers.

As I have noted above, in order to ensure social, economic, political and cultural factors necessary for the enhancement of valuable capabilities identified by informal workers, such informal workers should be heard through the social dialogue process. However, while informal workers might be able to identify valuable capabilities important to them, they might not be able to identify the factors necessary for the promotion of such capabilities. Accordingly, multiple institutions should be involved in the social dialogue process to help identify factors necessary for the enhancement of capabilities. The integration of informal workers and multiple institutions into a process of social dialogue is necessary. If informal workers are organised as a trade union or a cooperative (which are also integrated institutions), their integration into the social dialogue process in a representative capacity is, at least in a formal sense, possible. But, in reality, informal workers in India are mostly unorganised. Therefore, it would be difficult to integrate informal workers into the social dialogue process through their representative organisations.

In such a scenario, other integrated (multiple) institutions can ensure informal workers' participation in the social dialogue process. Such participation can be conceptualised at two levels: as institutions involved in the social dialogue process in a representative capacity, or as institutions assisting informal workers to participate in the social dialogue process. While participation of integrated institutions is essential they still may not optimise the identification of valuable capabilities of informal workers. It would be a far better approach to enable informal workers to speak for themselves. If informal workers are allowed to speak for themselves their emergent points of views could be sharpened and sophisticated with the participation of integrated institutions through the social dialogue process.

Thus, in the context of the specific example of waste pickers in Kolkata, integrated institutions such as the police, NGOs (including the Calcutta Samaritans), locally elected officials, the university (WB NUJS) and the media need to be involved in the social dialogue process with waste pickers and the government. The hope is that such a social dialogue process will be capable of identifying valuable capabilities for waste pickers. Once the range of valuable capabilities is identified, integrated institutions (including the government) along with waste pickers should be able to identify factors that are necessary for the promotion of informal workers' capabilities.

Drèze and Sen's institutionally integrated approach[102] envisages that institutions (such as NGOs and the media) have to be assessed collectively in an integrated manner[103] on the basis of their collective capacity to promote individual capabilities.[104] Noting that mere existence of institutions is not enough for the enhancement of capabilities, Sen calls for the examination of institutions based on

---

102   See Jean Drèze, Amartya Sen, *India Development and Participation* (New Delhi: Oxford University Press, 2002) 20.
103   Sen, *Development* (n 49) 142.
104   Amartya Sen, *The Idea of Justice* (Cambridge, MA: Harvard University Press, 2009) 75–86.

their contribution to capability development.[105] Sen advocates for actual participation of people in the social dialogue process.[106] According to Sen, it is through the involvement of people in the social dialogue process that valuable capabilities and functionings should be identified for a particular society.[107]

Accordingly, it is the responsibility of the participants in the social dialogue process to institutionalise factors necessary for the enhancement of capabilities. Sen is not in favour of trusting government to institutionalise factors necessary for the enhancement of capabilities as a benevolent provider.[108] He calls upon integrated institutions to mediate government action.[109] In the context of formulation of labour law for waste pickers integrated institutions are expected to do just that – mediate government and legislative action. In order to formulate labour law for waste pickers integrated institutions of NGOs, the police, elected officials, the university and the media[110] are to engage in a democratic deliberation process to assist the government and the legislature to institutionalise factors promoting capabilities of waste pickers.

Thus, one of the prerequisites of labour law for informal workers is an institutional mechanism ensuring social dialogue involving integrated institutions. From a substantive point of view labour law for informal workers needs to institutionalise factors that promote capabilities of such informal workers. One additional element that needs to characterise such labour law for informal economic activities is democratic equality amongst participants in a cooperative production system.[111] I want to conclude this chapter by looking into a concrete implication of the idea of democratic equality in the context of waste pickers in Kolkata. Before venturing into that discussion, the following is a brief explanation of the diagram in which I chart my proposed labour law framework.

The diagram explains the labour law framework that I propose in the context of informal waste pickers in the Indian context. Waste pickers, who could either belong to organisations in the form of trade unions, cooperative societies or charitable trusts, or who could be unorganised (ie who do not belong to an organisation) are charted at the bottom of the diagram. According to the framework I propose, a social dialogue process integrating waste pickers should be the precursor of labour law for waste pickers.

The large oval-shaped circle represents the social dialogue process. Integration of waste pickers into the dialogue process, as the figure indicates, could be done

105 ibid 81–83.
106 Sen, *Development* (n 49) 156–59; Sen, *Idea of Justice* (n 104) 91, 324–27, 392.
107 See Sen, *Development* (n 49) 31–32, 36–40, 51–53, 123, 147–48, 152–55; Sen, *Idea of Justice* (n 104) 91, 324–27, 392; Amartya Sen, 'Human rights and capabilities' (2005) 6(2) *Journal of Human Development* 151 at 158–63; Shelley Marshall (undated) 'Main findings concerning the role of labour law in promoting decent work' in *Promoting Decent Work: the Role of Labour Law* (on file with author).
108 Drèze and Sen, *India Development* (n 102) 45.
109 ibid.
110 Etc, because depending on specific circumstances opposition political parties, and other groups can be part of integrated institutions.
111 Elizabeth Anderson, 'What is the point of equality?' (1999) 109(2) *Ethics* 287 at 317–18.

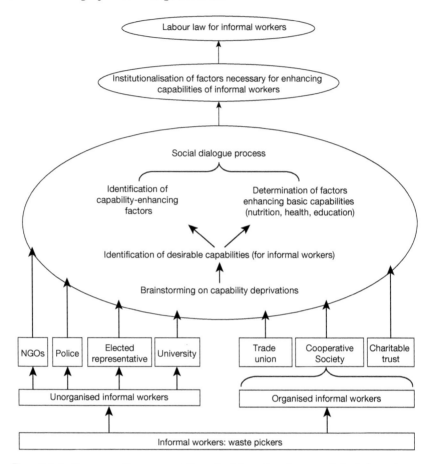

Figure 7.1 A diagrammatic representation of a labour law framework for informal waste
pickers

through the representative institutions (such as trade unions, cooperative societies
or charitable trusts), or through other integrated institutions (such as NGOs, police,
elected representatives, universities). The diagram indicates that during the social
dialogue process waste pickers need to interact with several institutions of the
democratic society that interface with their work and their lives.

The diagram illustrates how the social dialogue process needs to discuss means
of capability-enhancement for waste pickers in three stages: first, by recognising
capability deprivations of waste pickers; secondly, by identifying desirable capabilities for waste pickers; and, thirdly, by determining factors necessary for the
enhancement of desirable capabilities. Once the social dialogue process has
determined the factors necessary for the capability development of waste pickers,
such factors need to be institutionalised through legislative guarantee. These legislative guarantees would constitute labour law for waste pickers in the context of
my study.

7.6 The idea of democratic equality in the concrete context of labour law for informal workers

According to Elizabeth Anderson, democratic equality envisages the creation of equal opportunity for participants in a cooperative production system (discussed in Chapter 5).[112] Such equality is based on principles of recognition and respect.[113] All participants in a cooperative production system ought to have an obligation to recognise and respect other participants.[114] The purpose of democratic equality is to remove the social basis of inequality so that participants in a cooperative production system can have effective voice in self-determination.[115]

Accordingly, institutional arrangements need to remove socially created relations of oppression, violence, marginalisation, domination, exploitation and cultural imperialism.[116] In the context of my study, it is important to remove relations of oppression, violence, marginalisation, domination, exploitation and cultural imperialism in order to enhance capabilities of informal workers.

Therefore, the challenge is to conceptualise a concrete framework that ensures democratic equality while enhancing and equalising capabilities of informal workers. By looking at an Indian example I offer one concrete framework through which the concept of democratic equality could be assimilated into labour law for informal economic activities.

In the Indian state of Kerala a law was passed that required fish traders and fish exporters to pay welfare benefit to workers in the fishing industry.[117] Although fish workers do not have an employment relationship with fish traders and fish exporters, they sell their collect to such traders and exporters. In the absence of a direct employment relationship between fish workers and fish traders (or fish exporters), the law asserted that entities benefiting from fish workers (ie fish traders and fish exporters) should contribute towards fish workers' welfare.[118] However, when the fish traders and fish exporters challenged the legislation, the Supreme Court held that the law envisaging such a contributory scheme is unconstitutional:[119]

[t]he State cannot in an Act under Entry 23 of List III, place the burden of an impost by way of contribution for giving effect to the Act and the scheme made thereunder for the social security and social welfare for a section of society upon a person who is not a member of such section of society nor an employer of a person who is a member of such section of society. The burden of the impost may be placed only when there exists the relationship of

---

112 ibid 288–89.
113 ibid 313, 315.
114 ibid 315, 319.
115 ibid 288–89, 291, 313.
116 ibid 308–309, 313, 315.
117 Kerala Fishermen's Welfare Fund Act 1985, available at http://wiego.org/sites/wiego.org/files/resources/files/fw_kerala_1985.pdf (last visited 24 February 2012).
118 ibid.
119 *Koluthara Exports Ltd* v *State of Kerala* (2002) MANU 0070 (SC) para 25.

employer and employee between the contributor and the beneficiary of the provisions of the Act and the scheme made thereunder.[120] . . . In the instant case, the only nexus between the categories or persons covered by the sweep . . . of the Act . . . is that the former [fish-exporters] are the purchasers and the latter [fish-workers] are the catchers and sellers of fish.[121]

Thus, the Supreme Court held that collectors (ie catchers of fish) and purchasers (ie fish exporters) are not in an employment relationship; and since they are not in an employment relationship, purchasers cannot be compelled to contribute towards the welfare of collectors. The Supreme Court found itself unable to move beyond the employer–employee relationship in establishing a mutual obligation amongst participants in a cooperative production system. What this case shows is that the court did not have the theoretical tools necessary to justify a contributory scheme arranged amongst participants in a cooperative production system.

However, it could be argued that by mandating an obligation on fish traders and fish exporters for the welfare of workers in the fishing industry (fishermen), the state of Kerala envisaged a mechanism that recognised that a production system (ie fisheries industry) necessarily involves the cooperation of a diverse range of participants, even if there is no employer–employee nexus between them.[122] These participants share an obligation of recognition and respect towards their co-participants.[123] From this point of view, all participants share a responsibility to remove socially created relations of oppression, violence, marginalisation, domination, exploitation and cultural imperialism vitiating other participants in the production system.[124] This is precisely what Anderson's *democratic equality* seeks to achieve.

Unfortunately, however, the court failed to perceive such equality amongst participants in the fishing industry. Interestingly, in order to overcome the court judgment, the state of Kerala enacted the Kerala Fishermen's and Allied Workers' Welfare Cess Act 2007.[125] The 2007 Act provides:

> . . . for the levy and collection of cess [ie tax] on the sale proceeds of fish, fish products allied objects and equipments within the State with a view to augmenting the resources of the Kerala Fishermen's Welfare Fund constituted under section 3 of the Kerala Fishermen's Welfare Fund Act, 1985 (30 of 1985).[126]

---

120 ibid para 20.
121 ibid para 24.
122 It might be useful to note here that the state of Kerala is one of the states in India which has a tradition of organised left movement. A Left Front led by the Communist Party of India (Marxist) governs the state in regular intervals (every five years the government in Kerala changes).
123 Anderson (n 111) 313, 315.
124 ibid 308–309, 313, 315.
125 See Kerala Fishermen's and Allied Workers' Welfare Cess Act 2007, available at http://wiego. org/sites/wiego.org/files/resources/files/fw_keralafishermen_2007.pdf (last visited 24 February 2012).
126 See 'Object' of the Kerala Fishermen's and Allied Workers' Welfare Cess Act 2007 (n 125).

Taking account of the court judgment, the 2007 Act imposes tax on 'sale proceeds' on fish products, rather than mandating welfare contributions by fish traders and fish exporters, as was envisaged in the 1985 Act. This initiative of the Kerala legislature shows that, although the legislature had to accept the judicial reasoning on the non-imposition of financial obligation in the absence of an employment relationship, the legislature was unwilling to let fish traders and fish exporters evade their responsibility of contributing towards the welfare of fishermen.

Kerala's mandatory contribution by fish traders and fish exporters for the welfare of fishermen could serve as an example of how the theoretical idea of democratic equality amongst participants in a cooperative production system could work in practice. In the *Koluthara Exports Ltd v State of Kerala* case,[127] if the Supreme Court had analysed mandatory contributions through the theoretical framework of democratic equality, it would have been possible for the court to justify such contribution even in the absence of an employment relationship between workers and traders.

Taking its cue from the Kerala law contributory scheme, which has been held unconstitutional by the Supreme Court, the WIEGO Law Pilot Project proposes that participants in the waste-recycling industry (a cooperative production system) such as municipalities, itinerant waste traders, the (formal) recycling industry etc need to 'contribute towards a fund that will provide welfare benefits' for waste pickers.[128] The WIEGO report further notes: '[t]he idea that such forest workers, fish workers and waste collectors are "workers" outside of an employment relationship, but nevertheless capable of raising a claim upon the industry is crucial'.[129] The idea of democratic equality provides for a theoretical basis where workers outside an employment relationship can raise a claim upon the industry (production system).

7.7 Conclusion

By considering the concrete example of informal waste pickers in Kolkata, in this chapter I have offered a mechanism through which a labour law framework for such waste pickers could be devised. My proposal is designed to improve the conditions of informal workers in India on the basis of their work. In my proposal, labour law moves beyond the narrow employer–employee notion and takes work as its point of reference, as I discussed earlier.

In my proposed scheme, waste pickers attain central significance in the formulation of a statutory framework for themselves. Such a scheme allows informal workers (waste pickers) to decide what they want to do or want to be and,

---

127 (2002) MANU 0070 (SC).
128 Kamala Sankaran, 'Informal economy, own-account workers and the law: an overview', WIEGO Law Pilot Project on the Informal Economy, at para 6.7, available at http://wiego.org/sites/wiego.org/files/resources/files/iei_background_paper_oaw_and_law.pdf (last visited 24 February 2012).
129 ibid para 6.8.

accordingly, to identify factors that would be necessary for the attainment of such doing or being. Once those factors are identified, labour law needs to institutionalise them. Informal waste pickers are to be integrated into the law-making process through a social dialogue mechanism. I envisage such a social dialogue process in an expansive manner so that any number of integrated institutions in a democratic society can engage in the social dialogue.

I contemplate two situations for the participation of waste pickers in the social dialogue process: first, when they are organised; and, secondly, when they are unorganised. When waste pickers are organised, their organisation can represent their perspectives in the social dialogue process. But, when waste pickers are unorganised, I propose integrated institutions play an additional role in integrating waste pickers in the social dialogue process.

Under both of these scenarios, the participation of integrated institutions is essential. Integrated institutions are not only important to help to identify capability-enhancing factors for the waste pickers (or any other group of specific informal workers), but their participation in the social dialogue process is important in order to ward off any adaptive preferences held by waste pickers. Finally, drawing upon a concrete example in the Indian state of Kerala, I indicate a taxation mechanism capable of striking democratic equality between informal waste pickers and formal recycling industry. In the following concluding chapter, instead of offering any new insights, I summarise the different chapters of my study and identify future areas of research.

Conclusion

The purpose of this book is to ascertain whether a legislative framework is capable of improving the work-life experiences of informal workers. Since informal economic activities are heterogeneous in nature and unique to particular regions and places, a legislative framework that might work for one particular category of informal workers might not be effective for other categories of informal workers. Accordingly, I select one specific informal economic activity as my frame of reference. In this study, I analyse the specific informal economic activity of waste picking in order to see whether a definite idea of labour law could be invoked for the purpose of improving the conditions of waste pickers in India.

I undertake the case study of waste picking in Kolkata for the purpose of understanding the work-lives of waste pickers and the *modus operandi* of the activity of waste picking. Waste pickers are self-employed informal workers who collect recyclable solid waste, segregate such waste and sell it to the intermediary (or middle-person). Intermediaries supply the recyclable waste to the recycling factories. Even though waste pickers mostly sell their collect to one or two definite intermediaries, an employment relationship does not exist between waste pickers and intermediaries or between an intermediary and a recycling factory. The different entities in the recycling production process – waste pickers, intermediaries and recycling factory – are related as sellers and buyers.

The recycling production process is a continuum constitutive of the informal economic activities of waste-collection, waste-segregation and supply, and the (mostly) formal economic activity of factory-based production of recycled goods. Being engaged in the informal part of the production process, waste pickers in Kolkata are excluded from the purview of labour rights guaranteed under the numerous labour laws in India; they are also excluded from the scope of social security protections available to certain categories of informal workers in West Bengal. As a result of such exclusion, waste pickers in Kolkata live vulnerable, marginalised and invisible lives outside the domain of public policy.

Through the case study of the informal economic activity of waste picking I unearth the capability deprivations of waste pickers in Kolkata in their work-lives. However, understanding the capability deprivations of waste pickers is not the only objective of the case study. A much more important aim of the case study is the ascertainment of valuable capabilities from the perspective of the waste pickers.

The waste pickers in Kolkata identified some of the desirable capabilities for them: the capability to be able to work and recognition as workers; access to work-sites; being in possession of an identification document proving citizenship of the country; shelter or housing; protection against forced eviction from their shelters; physical and mental security at worksites; access to a regular channel of paid labour (or selling of their collect); appropriate payment for their work; provision for economic (and other) assistance during emergencies; and provision for health. Whilst all of these capabilities are considered valuable by waste pickers, they need not necessarily become part of a labour law dispensation; capabilities that are valuable primarily for waste pickers' *work* should become part of a labour law framework.

While a labour rights-based framework might be able to address some of these concerns raised by waste pickers in Kolkata, some of the other concerns, such as access to worksites, access to identification documentation (in the sense I discussed in Chapter 6) do not traditionally fall within the domain of labour rights.

The capability approach, on the other hand, is more sensitive to intergroup (and interpersonal) variations, and accounts for the unique characteristics and requirements of each specific group of people. The capability approach envisages an analytical framework in which the objective of public policy is to ensure appropriate social, economic, political, environmental and physical conditions in which desirable capabilities of an individual or a specific group of people could be promoted. Accordingly, the theoretical underpinning of the capability approach provides an appropriate analytical basis for the purpose of accounting for the typical necessities (ie desirable capabilities) of informal waste pickers.

The traditional idea of labour law is not well equipped to address problems involving the informal economic activity of waste picking at two levels. First, since the traditional idea of labour law is based on the juridical concept of employment relationship, it excludes waste pickers who are not in an employment relationship from its purview. Secondly, as I indicate, being based on the idea of definite labour rights that are (theoretically) available to all categories of workers irrespective of the nature and *modus operandi* of their work, it fails to account for the typical characteristics of waste picking and waste pickers.

Accordingly, based on an emerging idea of labour law, in my study I offer a way to conceptualise a labour law framework which can address the challenges posed by the informal economic activity of waste picking. Waste pickers are self-employed workers without an employer or any definite workplace and, accordingly, an employment relationship or a workplace is absent in their working lives. Although waste pickers are not, a significant number of informal workers are waged workers. Even when informal workers are waged workers, it is difficult to determine an employer for such workers, because an employment relationship is hidden or disguised for many informal workers.

Additionally, many informal workers work for more than one entity, which may or may not be an employer. Thus, the domain of informal economic activities poses a conceptual challenge to the traditional scope of labour law. The phenomenon of informal economic activities is conceptually problematic because it is incapable of being framed in terms of an existing theoretical framework of labour law. It characterises a messy situation wherein it is difficult for the traditional labour law framework to address the typical problems posed by informal economic activities and the activity of waste picking in particular. The absence of law and policy resulting from this conceptual difficulty adversely affects the work-lives of informal workers in general and waste pickers in particular.

The logic behind the traditional normative goal of labour law is that if labour law can strike a better balance of power between employer and employees they can bargain between themselves in order to determine the nature and extent of benefits that each party would enjoy. In the absence of an employment relationship the normative goal of balance of bargaining power cannot function. Accordingly, a proposal for a labour law for the advancement of informal waste pickers needs to look for other normative goals that are independent of an employment relationship.

Under such circumstances, human development of waste pickers emerges as an attractive contender as a normative goal of labour law. Labour law for waste pickers should aim to promote human development of waste pickers, regardless of whether or not an employment relationship exists. I invoke Amartya Sen's capability approach, a flexible and non-deterministic human development approach, as a normative goal of labour law for informal waste pickers.

According to Sen, public policy needs to promote individual capabilities. Based on Sen's insight I propose that labour law for waste pickers needs to institutionalise factors that are capable of promoting desired capabilities of waste pickers. Since the capability approach is a choice-based development theory, it is necessary to integrate waste pickers themselves in the process of institutionalisation of factors that can promote their capabilities. Integration of waste pickers in the legislative institutionalisation process could be ensured through the ILO-promoted strategy of social dialogue. Dialogue is also central in the capability approach. Sen envisages a participatory democratic dialogue process for the determination of desired capabilities for particular societies.

According to this approach, the law-making process needs to be attentive to the voices of different stakeholders directly or indirectly engaged in or related to the informal economic activity of waste picking. However, institutionalisation of the social dialogue principle must be carefully devised in order to make such institutionalisation effective. An effective social dialogue mechanism might be devised only when such mechanism is alert to the subtleties involving the specific activity of waste picking and the waste pickers involved in the process. Since the legislative policy I propose seeks to institutionalise factors that can promote capabilities as desired by waste pickers themselves, the proposed legislative policy for waste pickers needs to be shaped to a great extent by the waste pickers themselves.

Since informal workers are heterogeneous, I have grouped together one specific category of workers – waste pickers in Kolkata, and I offer a proposal through which waste pickers could be integrated into the social dialogue process that shapes the legal regime promoting waste pickers' interests. In addition to waste pickers, I propose that integrated institutions of the democratic society, such as law enforcement officials, NGOs, trade unions (if existent), elected representatives, the media, political parties, universities and research institutions etc need to be integrated into the social dialogue process.

The Kerala fishermen's dispute I discussed in the Chapter 7 proves the significance of integrated institutions in promoting capabilities of informal workers. In that particular dispute the social basis of capability enhancement (ie traders' contributions towards workers' welfare) emerged out of the conflict between the fish traders, the government and the judiciary. While it might be expected that a government committed to the cause of the downtrodden and marginalised people will facilitate their interests, government benevolence might not always stand the test of time. Accordingly, membership-based organisations of informal workers should become participants in the process of determining the social basis of capability development. The challenge is to institute a social dialogue framework which is respectful of informal workers and a range of other institutions. Informal workers are not mere passive victims of fate.

As my case study shows, given an opportunity waste pickers (one of the most marginalised of all informal workers) can become active agents of change. Their awareness, articulation, negotiation and bargaining skills could be substantially improved by instituting a social basis for capability enhancement, such as trade unions.

Indications of newly attained functionings were visible after the waste pickers in Kolkata organised themselves into a trade union. In the second executive committee meeting of the BPSSS, Najma Biwi, a waste picker and an executive committee member, described an incident of a recent eviction attempt by local hooligans in the Gariahat area of Kolkata.[1] She described how five or six local strongmen, who were working at the behest of a local real estate promoter, came to her neighbourhood and threatened the residents with eviction from their slum. She recounted how she gathered a number of slum dwellers in order to encounter the thugs, informing them that the residents were part of a trade union, and if they were forcibly evicted they would take the matter to the police, the court and 'lawyers from the university' would put the thugs behind bars. Not accustomed to such a collective backlash, the thugs retreated from the neighbourhood.

This incident shows that waste pickers, living at the margins of society, are capable of being assertive and fighting their own cause by employing a range of negotiation tools. These tools – the threat of police, court and lawyers from the university – emanates from their participation in the trade union BPSSS. This vignette illustrates that the informal workers need appropriate institutions and frameworks that create conditions in which they can effectively exercise their agency. Moreover, as Elizabeth Hill shows, agency itself is also the creation of these institutions and frameworks.[2]

---

1   Meeting of the executive committee of BPSSS on 12 July 2011 at the Calcutta Samaritans, Kolkata, India.
2   Elizabeth Hill, *Worker Identity, Agency and Economic Development: Women's Empowerment in the Indian Informal Economy* (New York: Routledge, 2010) 97–100, 104–12, 116, 131–32.

Although legal institutions and legislative safeguards cannot be a panacea for all injustices suffered by informal workers, they are still important and they must involve informal workers through a process of democratic deliberation during the legislative institutionalisation of capability-enhancing factors. Changes in governance attitude and democratic culture are preconditions for the law-making process. For this reason, the proposal I offer cannot work in a vacuum. It requires a receptive and open democratic culture that believes in democratic equality in the production process.

I use the capabilities approach to explore a framework for labour law for one category of informal workers. Other researchers need to engage with other groups of informal workers in different socio-economic-political settings in order to ascertain how labour law could be adapted to address their specific needs. A social justice-based conceptualisation of labour law inspired by the capability approach might provide an overarching labour law framework for informal employment. However, it is undisputed that labour law cannot satisfactorily function within its traditional scope of an employment relationship if it is to enhance the capabilities of informal workers and provide them with decent work and dignified lives.

While the specific model needed for different groups of informal workers in India (and elsewhere) is an open question, it is clear that a legislative framework developed with the participation of informal workers would not only further the Indian constitutional guarantee of equality, but that it would also significantly contribute to promote a dignified life for informal workers, which the Constitution of India promises to its people.

Bibliography

Monographs

Agarwala, Rina, *From Work to Welfare: Informal Workers' Organizations and the State in India* (unpublished PhD Thesis, Faculty of Princeton University, 2006).

Ahn, Pong-Sul (ed), *Organizing for Decent Work in the Informal Economy: Strategies, Methods and Practices* (New Delhi: ILO, 2007).

Alexander, John, *Capabilities and Social Justice: the Political Philosophy of Amartya Sen and Martha Nussbaum* (Farnham & Burlington: Ashgate, 2008).

Alkire, Sabina, *Valuing Freedoms: Sen's CA and Poverty Reduction* (New York: Oxford, 2002).

Anker, Richard, *Gender and Jobs: Sex segregation of occupations in the world* (Geneva: ILO, 1998).

Antony, Piush, *Towards Empowerment: Experiences of Organizing Women Workers* (New Delhi: ILO, 2001).

Aristotle, *Nicomachean Ethics, Book I*, 2nd edn, translated by Terence Irwin (Indianapolis/Cambridge: Hackett Publishing, 1999).

Austin, Granville, *The Indian Constitution: Cornerstone of a Nation* (Bombay: Oxford University Press, 1976).

Bacchetta, Marc, Ekkehard Ernst and Juana P. Bustamante, *Globalization and Informal Jobs in Developing Countries* (Geneva: WTO & ILO, 2009).

Barnard, Catherine, Simon Deakin and Gillian Morris (eds), *The Future of Labour Law: Liber Amicorum Sir Bob Hepple QC* (Portland, Oregon: Hart Publishing, 2004).

Beaud, Michel, *A History of Capitalism 1500–2000* (New York: Monthly Review Press, 2001).

Beneria, Lourdes, *Changing Employment Patterns and the Informalization of Jobs: General Trends and Gender Dimensions* (Geneva: ILO, 2001).

Bhat, Ela R., *We Are Poor But So Many: the Story of Self-Employed Women in India* (New York: Oxford University Press, 2006).

Boeri, Tito and others, *The Role of Unions in the Twenty-First Century: a Report for the Fondazione Rodolfo Debenedetti* (New York: Oxford University Press, 2001).

Breman, Jan, *Footloose Labour: Working in India's Informal Economy* (Cambridge: Cambridge University Press, 1996).

Breman, Jan, *The Making and Unmaking of an Industrial Working Class: Sliding Down the Labour Hierarchy in Ahmedabad, India* (New Delhi: Oxford University Press, 2004).

Chatterjee, Partha, *The Present History of West Bengal: Essays in Political Criticism* (Delhi: Oxford University Press, 1997).

Chen, Martha Alter, Renana Jhabvala and Frances Lund, *Supporting Workers in the Informal Economy*, Working Paper on the Informal Economy, Employment Sector 2002/2 (Geneva: International Labour Office, 2002).

Chikarmane, Poornima, Lakshmi Narayan, *Rising from the Waste: Organising Wastepickers in India, Thailand and the Philippines* (Bangkok: Committee for Asian Women, 2009).

Conaghan, Joanne, Richard Michael Fischl and Karl Klaree (eds), *Labour Law in an Era of Globalization: Transformative Practices and Possibilities* (Oxford & New York: Oxford University Press, 2002).

Creswell, John W, *Research Design: Qualitative, Quantitative, and Mixed Methods Approaches* (London: Sage, 2009).

David, Natacha, *Worlds Apart: Women and the Global Economy* (Geneva: ICFTU, 1996).

Davis, Paul, Mark Freedland, *Kahn-Freund's Labour and the Law* (3rd edn London: Stevens & Sons, 1983).

Davies, Paul, Mark Freedland, *Labour Law: Text and Materials* (London: Weidenfeld and Nicolson, 1984).

De Soto, Hernando, *The Other Path: the Invisible Revolution in the Third World* (New York: Harper & Row, 1989).

Deakin, Simon, Gillian S. Morris, *Labour Law* (4th edn Portland: Hart Publishing, 2005).

Deakin, Simon, Frank Wilkinson, *The Law of the Labour Market: Industrialization, Employment, and Legal Evolution* (Oxford: Oxford University Press, 2005).

Deneulin, Severine, *The Capability Approach and the Praxis of Development* (New York: Palgrave Macmillan, 2006).

Denscombe, Martyn, *The Good Research Guide for small-scale social research projects* (Berkshire: Open University Press, McGraw-Hill, 2007).

DeWalt, Kathleen M., Billie R. DeWalt, *Participant Observation: A Guide for Fieldworkers* (Walnut Creek: Altamira, 2002).

Drèze, Jean, Amartya Sen, *India Development and Participation* (New Delhi: Oxford University Press, 2002).

Freeman, Richard B., James L. Medoff, *What Do Unions Do?* (New York: Basic Books, 1984).

Fudge, Judy, Eric Tucker and Leah Vosko, *The Legal Concepts of Employment: Marginalizing Workers* (Ottawa, Ontario: Law Commission of Canada, 2002).

Gajendragadkar, P. B., *The Constitution of India: Its Philosophy and Basic Postulates*, Gandhi Memorial Lectures, University College, Nairobi, First Series (Nairobi: Oxford University Press, 1969).

Gibson-Graham, J.K., *The End of Capitalism (as we knew it): a Feminist Critique of Political Economy* (Oxford: Blackwell, 1996).

Gibson-Graham, J.K., *Postcapitalist Politics* (Minneapolis & London: University of Minnesota Press, 2006).

Gill, Kaveri, *Of Poverty and Plastic: Scavenging and Scrap Trading Entrepreneurs in India's Urban Informal Economy* (New Delhi: Oxford University Press, 2010).

Gothoskar, Sujata, *New Initiatives in Organizing Strategy in the Informal Economy: a Case Study of Domestic Workers Organizing in India* (Bangkok: Committee for Asian Women, 2005).

Hammersley, Martyn, *The Dilemma of Qualitative Method: Herbert Blumer and the Chicago Tradition* (London and New York: Routledge, 1989).

Harding, Philip, Richard Jenkins, *The Myth of the Hidden Economy: Towards a New Understanding of Informal Economic Activity* (Philadelphia: Open University Press, 1989).

Hepple, Bob, *Labour Law, Inequality and Global Trade*, Sinzheimer Lecture 2002 (Amsterdam: Hugo Sinzheimer Instituut, 2002).

Hepple, Bob, *Labour Laws and Global Trade* (Oxford and Portland: Hart, 2005).

Héthy, L., *Hungary: Social Dialogue Within and Outside of the Framework of Tripartism*, InFocus Programme on Strengthening Social Dialogue, WP. 4 (Geneva: ILO, 2000).

Hill, Elizabeth, *Worker Identity, Agency and Economic Development: Women's Empowerment in the Indian Informal Economy* (New York: Routledge, 2010).

Hughes, Steve, Nigel Haworth, *The International Labour Organisation (ILO)* (New York: Routledge, 2011).

Hussmanns, Ralf, *Statistical Definition of Informal Employment: Guidelines Endorsed by the Seventeenth International Conference of Labour Statisticians (2003)* (Geneva: ILO, 2004).

Hussmanns, Ralf, *Measuring the Informal Economy: From Employment in the Informal Sector to Informal Employment*, Working Paper No 53, Policy Integration Department, Bureau of Statistics (Geneva: ILO, 2004).

ICFTU, *Building Workers' Human Rights into the Global Trading System* (Geneva: ICFTU, 1999).

ILO, *Freedom of Association and Collective Bargaining* (Geneva: ILO, 1994).

ILO, *Conclusions Concerning Tripartite Consultation at the National Level on Economic and Social Policy* (Geneva: ILO, 1996).

ILO, *Women and Men in the Informal Economy: a Statistical Picture* (Geneva: ILO, 2002).

Jose, A. V., *The ILO Declaration on Fundamental Principles and Rights at Work: Role of Social Partners in South Asia* (Geneva: ILO, IILS, 2002).

Kahn-Freund, Otto, *Labour and the Law* (1st edn London: Stevens & Sons, 1972).

Kahn-Freund, Otto, *Labour and the Law* (2ndedn London: Stevens & Sons, 1977).

Kahn-Freund, Otto, *Labour and the Law* (3rd edn London: Stevens & Sons, 1983).

Kemp, Tom, *Industrialization in the non-Western World* (New York: Longman, 1983).

Kemp, Tom, *Historical Patterns of Industrialization* (London & New York: Longman, 1993).

Kohli, Atul, *The State and Poverty in India: the Politics of Reform* (Cambridge: Cambridge University Press, 1987).

Kohli, Atul, *Democracy and Discontent: India's Growing Crisis of Governability* (Cambridge: Cambridge University Press, 1990).

Kohli, Atul, *Democracy and Development in India* (New Delhi: Oxford University Press, 2009).

Lapierre, Dominique, *The City of Joy* (New York: Warner Books, 1986).

Luebbert, Gregory M., *Liberalism, Fascism, or Social Democracy* (New York: Oxford University Press, 1991).

Marjit, Sugata, Saibal Kar, *The Outsiders: Economic Reforms and Informal Labour in a Developing Economy* (New Delhi: Oxford University Press, 2011).

Marx, Karl, *Capital Vol. III: the Process of Capitalist Production as a Whole*, available at http://www.marxists.org/archive/marx/works/1894-c3/ch20.htm (last visited 13 August 2010).

Mason, Jennifer, *Qualitative Researching* (London: Sage, 2002).

Maul, Daniel, *Human Rights, Development and Decolonization: the International Labour Organization, 1940–70* (Basingstoke: Palgrave Macmillan & Geneva: ILO, 2012).

Moorhouse, Geoffrey, *Calcutta: the City Revealed* (New York: Penguin Books, 1984).

Morse, David A., *The Origin and Evolution of the ILO and Its Role in the World Community* (New York: Cornell University, 1969).

Namboodiripad, E. M. S., *The Republican Constitution in the Struggle for Socialism*, R.R. Kale Memorial Lecture 1968 Gokhale Institute of Politics and Economics, Poona (Bombay: Asia Publishing House, 1968).

Nozick, Robert, *Anarchy, State, and Utopia* (New York: Basic Books, 1974).

Nussbaum, Martha C., *Women and Human Development: the Capabilities Approach* (Cambridge: Cambridge University Press, 2000).

Payne, A., *The Global Politics of Unequal Development* (New York: Palgrave Macmillan, 2005).

Perry, Guillermo E. and others, (eds), *Informality: Exit and Exclusion* (Washington DC: The World Bank, 2007).

Pogge, Thomas, *John Rawls* (New York: Oxford University Press, 2007).

Polanyi, Karl, *The Great Transformation* (Boston: Beacon Press, 1957).

Rawls, John, *A Theory of Justice* (Cambridge: Harvard University Press, 1971).

Reddy, O. Chinnappa, *The Court and the Constitution of India: Summits and Shallows* (New Delhi: Oxford University Press, 2010).

Rodgers, Gerry and others, *The International Labour Organization and the Quest for Social Justice, 1919–2009* (Geneva: ILO, 2009).

Roy, Ananya, *City Requiem, Calcutta: Gender and the Politics of Poverty* (Minneapolis & London: University of Minnesota Press, 2003).

Samaddar, Ranabir, *The Marginal Nation: Transborder Migration from Bangladesh to West Bengal* (New Delhi: Sage, 1999).

Sankaran, Kamala, *Labour Laws in South Asia: the need for an inclusive approach* (Geneva: International Institute for Labour Studies, 2007).

Sarkar, Ashis, *Urban System, Urban Growth and Urbanisation in 20th Century West Bengal* (Delhi: New Academic Publishers, 1998).

Schwartz, Howard, Jerry Jacobs, *Qualitative Sociology: a Method to the Madness* (New York: Free Press, 1979).

Sen, Amartya, *Resources, Values and Development* (Cambridge: Harvard University Press, 1984).

Sen, Amartya, *Commodities and Capabilities* (Amsterdam & New York: North Holland, 1985).

Sen, Amartya, *Hunger and Entitlements* (Helsinki: World Institute for Development Economics Research, 1987).

Sen, Amartya, *Inequality Reexamined* (New York: Russell Sage Foundation/Cambridge: Harvard University Press, 1992).

Sen, Amartya, *Development as Freedom* (New York: Alfred A. Knopf, 1999).

Sen, Amartya, *The Idea of Justice* (Cambridge: Harvard University Press, 2009).

Sen, Anupam, *The State, Industrialization and Class Formations in India: a neo-Marxist Perspective on Colonialism, Underdevelopment and Development* (London: Routledge & Kegan Paul, 1982).

Shankar, Shylashri, *Scaling Justice: India's Supreme Court, Anti-terror Laws, and Social Rights* (New Delhi: Oxford University Press, 2009).

Silverman, David, Amir Marvasti, *Doing Qualitative Research: a Comprehensive Guide* (Thousand Oaks: Sage, 2008).

Singh, M P, *V.N. Shukla Constitution of India* (10th edn Lucknow: Eastern Book Company, 2001).

Singleton, Royce A., Jr., Bruce C. Straits, *Approaches to Social Research* (New York: Oxford University Press, 2005).

Society for Participatory Research in Asia, *People's Autonomy in Government Schemes* (Kolkata: PRIA, 2008).

Standing, Guy, *Beyond the New Paternalism: Basic Security as Equality* (London & New York: Verso, 2002).

Stone, Katherine V. W., *From Widgets to Digits: Employment Regulation for the Changing Workplace* (New York: Cambridge University Press, 2004).

Supiot, Alain and others, *Beyond Employment Changes in Work and the Future of Labour Law in Europe* (Oxford & New York: Oxford University Press, 2001).

Szentes, Tamás, *The Transformation of the World Economy: New Directions and New Interests* (London & New Jersey: Zed Books, 1988).

Unni, Jeemol, Uma Rani, *Insecurities of Informal Workers in Gujarat, India* (Geneva: ILO, 2002).

Wallerstein, Immanuel, *The Modern World-System Capitalist Agriculture and the Origins of the European World-Economy in the Sixteenth Century* (New York and London: Academic Press, 1974).

Yin, R. K., *Case Study Research: Design and Methods* (2nd edn Thousand Oaks: Sage Publications, 1994).

Articles

Agarwala, Ramgopal, Nagesh Kumar and Michelle Riboud, 'Reforms, labour markets, and social security policy in India: an introduction' in Ramgopal Agarwala, Nagesh Kumar and Michelle Riboud (eds), *Reforms, Labour Markets, and Social Security in India* (New Delhi: Oxford University Press, 2004) 1.

Ahluwalia, Montek Singh, 'Economic reforms in India since 1991: has gradualism worked?' (2002) 16(3) *Journal of Economic Perspectives* 67.

Ahmed, Iftikhar, 'Decent work and human development' (2003) 142(2) *International Labour Review* 263.

Alexander, John M., 'Capabilities, human rights and moral pluralism' (2004) 8(4) *International Journal of Human Rights* 451.

Alkire, Sabina, 'Dimensions of human development' (2002) 30(2) *World Development* 181.

Alkire, Sabina, 'Why the capability approach?' (2005) 6(1) *Journal of Human Development* 115.

Alston, Philip, '"Core labour standards" and the transformation of the international labour rights regime' (2004) 15(3) *European Journal of International Law* 457.

Anderson, Elizabeth S., 'What is the point of equality?' (1999) 109(2) *Ethics* 287.

Anderson, Elizabeth, 'Justifying the capabilities approach to justice' in Harry Brighouse and Ingrid Robeyns (eds), *Measuring Justice Primary Goods and Capabilities* (Cambridge: Cambridge University Press, 2010) 81.

Anderson, Michael, 'India 1858–1930: the illusion of free labour' in Douglas Hay and Paul Craven (eds), *Masters, Servants, and Magistrates in Britain and the Empire, 1562–1955* (Chapel Hill & London: The University of North Carolina Press, 2004) 422.

Anderson, David M., 'Kenya, 1895–1939: registration and rough justice' in Douglas Hay and Paul Craven (eds), *Masters, Servants, and Magistrates in Britain and the Empire, 1562–1955* (Chapel Hill & London: The University of North Carolina Press, 2004) 498.

Anker, Richard, and others, 'Measuring decent work with statistical indicators' (2003) 142(2) *International Labour Review* 147.

Arthurs, Harry, 'Labour law after labour' in Guy Davidov and Brian Langille (eds), *The Idea of Labour Law* (New York: Oxford University Press, 2011) 13.

Austin, Granville, 'The expected and the unintended in working a democratic constitution' in Zoya Hasan, E. Sridharan and R. Sudarshan (eds), *India's Living Constitution: Ideas, Practices, Controversies* (London: Anthem Press, 2005) 319.

Bag, Kheya, 'Red Bengal's rise and fall' (2011) 70 *New Left Review* 69.

Bagchi, Amiya Kumar, 'Studies on the economy of West Bengal since Independence' (1998) 33(47/48) *Economic and Political Weekly* 2973.

Ballet, Jerome, Jean-Luc Dubois and Francois-Regis Mahieu, 'Responsibility for each other's freedom: agency as the source of collective capability' (2007) 8(2) *Journal of Human Development* 185.

Banakar, Reza, Max Travers, 'Introduction' in Reza Banakar and Max Travers (eds), *An Introduction to Law and Social Theory* (Oxford & Portland, Oregon: Hart, 2002) 1.

Banakar, Reza, Max Travers, 'Introduction' in Reza Banakar and Max Travers (eds), *Theory and Method in Socio-Legal Research* (Oxford & Portland, Oregon: Hart, 2005) ix.

Banakar, Reza, Max Travers, 'Law, sociology and method' in Reza Banakar and Max Travers (eds), *Theory and Method in Socio-Legal Research* (Oxford & Portland, Oregon: Hart, 2005) 1.

Bardhan, Pranab, 'Poverty and employment characteristics of urban households in West Bengal' (1987) 22(35) *Economic and Political Weekly* 1496.

Baxi, Upendra, '"The little done, the vast undone" – some reflections on reading Glanville Austin's *The Indian Constitution*' (1967) 9 *Journal of the Indian Law Institute* 323.

Baxi, Upendra, 'The (Im)possibility of constitutional justice: seismmographic notes on Indian constitutionalism' in Zoya Hasan, E. Sridharan, and R. Sudarshan (eds), *India's Living Constitution: Ideas, Practices, Controversies* (London: Anthem Press, 2005) 31.

Beneria, Lourdes, 'Subcontracting and employment dynamics in Mexico City' in Alejandro Portes, Manuel Castells and Lauren A. Benton (eds), *The Informal Economy: Studies in Advanced and Less developed Countries* (Baltimore & London: The Johns Hopkins University Press, 1989) 173.

Beneria, Lourdes, Maria Floro, 'Distribution, gender, and labor market informalization: a conceptual framework with a focus on homeworkers' in Neema Kudva and Lourdes Baneria (eds), *Rethinking Informalization: Poverty, Precarious Jobs and Social Protection* (Cornell University Open Access Repository, 2005) 9.

Bensusan, Graciela, 'Labour law in Latin America: the gap between norms and reality' in Tzehainesh Tekle (ed), *Labour Law and Worker Protection in Developing Countries* (Oxford and Portland, Oregon: Hart; Geneva: ILO, 2010) 135.

Benton, Lauren A., 'Industrial subcontracting and the informal sector: the politics of restructuring in the Madrid electronics industry' in Alejandro Portes, Manuel Castells and Lauren A. Benton (eds), *The Informal Economy: Studies in Advanced and Less developed Countries* (Baltimore & London: The Johns Hopkins University Press, 1989) 228.

Bescond, David, Anne Chataignier and Farhad Mehran, 'Seven indicators to measure decent work: an international comparison' (2003) 142(2) *International Labour Review* 179.

Bhattacharya, Nikhilesh, Manabendu Chattopadhyay and Ashok Rudra, 'Changes in level of living in rural West Bengal: perceptions of the people' (1987) 22(48) *Economic and Political Weekly* 2071.

Blackett, Adelle, 'Situated reflections on international labour law, capabilities, and decent work: the case of centre *Maraîcher* Eugène Guinois' (2007) *Revue québécoise de droit international (Hors-série)* 223.

Blackett, Adelle, 'Emancipation in the idea of labour law' in Guy Davidov and Brian Langille (eds), *The Idea of Labour Law* (New York: Oxford University Press, 2011) 420.

Bonnet, Florence, Jose B. Figueiredo and Guy Standing, 'A family of decent work indexes' (2003) 142(2) *International Labour Review* 213.

Bronstein, Arturo, 'Labour law and the informal sector' *Workshop on Regulatory Frameworks and their Economic and Social Impact* (unpublished paper) Geneva (4–5 February 1999).

Browne, Jude, Simon Deakin and Frank Wilkinson, 'Capabilities, social rights and European market integration' in Robert Salais and Robert Villeneuve (eds), *Europe and the Politics of Capabilities* (New York: Cambridge University Press, 2004) 205.

Castells, Manuel, Alejandro Portes, 'World underneath: the origins, dynamics, and effects of the informal economy' in Alejandro Portes, Manuel Castells and Lauren A. Benton (eds), *The Informal Economy: Studies in Advanced and Less Developed Countries* (Baltimore & London: The Johns Hopkins University Press, 1989) 11.

Chakrabarty, Bidyut, 'The Left Front's 2009 Lok Sabha Poll debacle in West Bengal, India' (2011) 51(2) *Asian Survey* 290.

Chanock, Martin, 'South Africa, 1841–1924: race, contract, and coercion' in Douglas Hay and Paul Craven (eds), *Masters, Servants, and Magistrates in Britain and the Empire, 1562–1955* (Chapel Hill & London: The University of North Carolina Press, 2004) 338.

Chatterjee, Mirai, Jayshree Vyas, 'Organising insurance for women workers' in Renana Jhabvala and R. K. A. Subrahmanya (eds), *The Unorganised Sector: Work Security and Social Protection* (New Delhi: Sage Publications, 2001) 74.

Chaturvedi, Bharati, 'Santraj Maurya and Lipi in India: tales of two waste pickers in Delhi, India' in Melanie Samson (ed), *Refusing to be Cast Aside: Waste Pickers Organising Around the World* (Cambridge, MA: WEIGO, 2009) 8.

Chen, Martha, Jennefer Sebstad and Lesley O'Connell, 'Counting the invisible workforce: the case of homebased workers' (1999) 27(3) *World Development* 603.

Chen, Martha Alter, 'Rethinking the informal economy: linkages with the formal economy and the formal regulatory environment' in Basudeb Guha-Khasnobis, Ravi Kanbur and Elinor Ostrom (eds), *Linking the Formal and Informal Economy Concepts and Policies* (New York: Oxford University Press, 2006) 75.

Chen, Marty, 'Rethinking the informal economy: from enterprise characteristics to employment relations' in Neema Kudva and Lourdes Baneria (eds), *Rethinking Informalization: Poverty, Precarious Jobs and Social Protection* (Cornell University Open Access Repository, 2005) 28.

Chikarmane, Poornima, Lakshmi Narayanan, 'Transform or perish: changing conceptions of work in recycling' in Judy Fudge, Shae McCrystal and Kamala Sankaran (eds), *Challenging the Legal Boundaries of Work Regulation* (Oxford & Portland, Oregon: Hart Publishing, 2012) 49.

Christensen, Robert K., 'The global path: soft law and non-sovereigns formalizing the potency of the informal sector' in Basudeb Guha-Khasnobis, Ravi Kanbur and Elinor Ostrom (eds), *Linking the Formal and Informal Economy Concepts and Policies* (New York: Oxford University Press, 2006) 36.

Cohen, G.A., 'Equality of what? On welfare, goods and capabilities' in Martha C. Nussbaum and Amartya Sen (eds), *The Quality of Life* (Oxford: Clarendon, 1993) 9.

Collins, Hugh, 'Justifications and techniques of legal regulation of the employment relation' in Hugh Collins, M. Davies and Roger Rideout (eds), *Legal Regulation of the Employment Relation* (London: Kluwer Law International, 2003) 3.

Cox, Robert W., 'The idea of international labour regulation' (1953) 67 *International Labour Review* 191.

Cox, Robert W., 'Labor and hegemony' (1977) 31(3) *International Organization* 385.

Daele, Jasmien Van, 'The International Labour Organization (ILO) in past and present research' (2008) 53 *International Review of Social History* 485.

Das, Keshab, 'Income and employment in informal manufacturing: a case study' in Renana Jhabvala, Ratna M. Sudarshan and Jeemol Unni eds, *Informal Economy Centrestage: New Structures of Employment* (New Delhi: Sage Publications, 2003) 62.

Dasgupta, Biplab, 'The 1972 election in West Bengal' (1972) 7(16) *Economic and Political Weekly* 804.

Dash, S, 'Human capital as a basis of comparative advantage equations in services outsourcing: a cross country comparative study' (2006) *International Conference on Information and Communication Technologies and Development* 165.

Datta, Pranati, 'Push-Pull factors of Undocumented migration from Bangladesh to West Bengal: a perception study' (2004) 9(2) *The Qualitative Report* 335.

Dave, Janhavi, Manali Shah and Yamini Parikh, 'The Self Employed Women's Association (SEWA) organising through union and co-operative in India' in Melanie Samson (ed),

Refusing to be Cast Aside: Waste Pickers Organising Around the World (Cambridge, MA: WEIGO, 2009) 27.

Davidov, Guy, 'The (changing?) idea of labour law' (2007) 146(3–4) *International Labour Review* 311.

De Haan, Arjan, 'Calcutta's labour migrants: encounters with modernity' (2003) 37 *Contributions to Indian Sociology* 189.

Deakin, Simon, Jude Browne, 'Social rights and market order: adapting the CA' in Tamara K Hervey and Jeff Kenner (eds), *Economic and Social Rights under the EU Charter of Fundamental Rights: a Legal Perspective* (Oxford and Portland, Oregon: Hart, 2003) 27.

Deakin, Simon, 'The contribution of labour law to economic and human development' in Guy Davidov and Brian Langille (eds), *The Idea of Labour Law* (New York: Oxford University Press, 2011) 156.

Deolalikar, Anil B., 'Human development in India: past trends and future challenges' in Raghbendra Jha (ed), *The Indian Economy Sixty Years After Independence* (London: Palgrave Macmillan, 2008) 155.

Dev, S. Mahendra, 'Social security in the unorganized sector in India' in Ramgopal Agarwala, Nagesh Kumar and Michelle Riboud (eds), *Reforms, Labour Markets, and Social Security in India* (New Delhi: Oxford University Press, 2004) 198.

Dukes, Ruth, 'Constitutionalizing employment relations: Sinzheimer, Kahn-Freund, and the role of labour law' (2008) 35 *Journal of Law and Society* 341.

Dukes, Ruth, 'Hugo Sinzheimer and the constitutional function of labour law' in Guy Davidov and Brian Langille (eds), *The Idea of Labour Law* (New York: Oxford University Press, 2011) 57.

Dworkin, Ronald, 'What is equality? Part 2: Equality of resources' (1981) 10(4) *Philosophy and Public Affairs* 283.

Evans, Peter, 'Collective capabilities, culture, and Amartya Sen's development as freedom' (2002) 37(2) *Studies in Comparative International Development* 54.

Fashoyin, Tayo, 'Tripartite cooperation, social dialogue and national development' (2004) 143(4) *International Labour Review* 341.

Fenwick, Colin, Evance Kalula and Ingrid Landau, 'Labour law: a southern African perspective' in Tzehainesh Tekle (ed), *Labour Law and Worker Protection in Developing Countries* (Oxford and Portland, Oregon: Hart; Geneva: ILO, 2010) 175.

Fields, Gary S., 'Decent work and development policies' (2003) 142(2) *International Labour Review* 239.

Foster, Andrew D., Mark R. Rosenzweig, 'Comparative advantage, information and the allocation of workers to tasks: evidence from an agricultural labour market' (1996) 63(3) *Review of Economic Studies* 347.

Fudge, Judy, 'The new discourse of labor rights' (2007) 29 *Comparative Labor Law and Policy Journal* 29.

Fudge, Judy, 'Labour as a "Fictive commodity": radically reconceptualizing labour law' in Guy Davidov and Brian Langille (eds), *The Idea of Labour Law* (New York: Oxford University Press, 2011) 120.

Fudge, Judy, 'Blurring legal boundaries' in Judy Fudge, Shae McCrystal and Kamala Sankaran (eds), *Challenging the Legal Boundaries of Work Regulation* (Oxford & Portland, Oregon: Hart Publishing, 2012) 1.

Gangoli, Geetanjali, 'Sex work, poverty and migration in Eastern India' in Sadhna Arya and Anupama Roy (eds), *Poverty, Gender and Migration* (New Delhi, Thousand Oaks & London: Sage Publications, 2006) 214.

Gerxhani, Klarita, 'The informal sector in developed and less developed countries: a literature survey' (2004) 120(3/4) *Public Choice* 267.

Ghai, Dharam, 'Decent work: universality and diversity' in Dharam Ghai (ed), *Decent Work: Objectives and Strategies* (Geneva: IILS, ILO, 2006) 1.

Ghosh, Madhusudan, 'Agricultural development, agrarian structure and rural poverty in West Bengal' (1998) 33(47/48) *Economic and Political Weekly* 2987.

Ginnekenn, Wouter van, 'Social protection for the informal sector in India' in Ramgopal Agarwala, Nagesh Kumar and Michelle Riboud (eds), *Reforms, Labour Markets, and Social Security in India* (New Delhi: Oxford University Press, 2004) 186.

Giovanola, Benedetta, 'Personhood and human richness: good and well-being in the capability approach and beyond' (2005) 63(2) *Review of Social Economy* 249.

Goldin, Adrian, 'Global conceptualizations and local constructions of the idea of labour law' in Guy Davidov and Brian Langille (eds), *The Idea of Labour Law* (New York: Oxford University Press, 2011) 69.

Grindle, Merilee S., 'Agrarian class structures and state policies: past, present and future' (1993) 28(1) *Latin American Research Review* 174.

Guha-Khasnobis, Basudeb, Ravi Kanbur and Elinor Ostrom, 'Beyond formality and informality' in Basudeb Guha-Khasnobis, Ravi Kanbur and Elinor Ostrom (eds), *Linking the Formal and Informal Economy Concepts and Policies* (New York: Oxford University Press, 2006) 1.

Gumbrell-McCormick, Rebecca, 'European trade unions and "atypical" workers' (2011) 42(3) *Industrial Relations Journal* 293.

Guruswamy, Mohan, Kamal Sharma and Jeevan Prakash Mohanty, 'Economic growth and development in West Bengal: reality versus perception' (2005) 40(21) *Economic and Political Weekly* 2151.

Halliday, Fred, 'The pertinence of imperialism' in Mark Rupert and Hazel Smith (eds), *Historical Materialism and Globalization* (London: Routledge, 2002) 75.

Harris, John R, Michael P Todaro, 'Migration, unemployment and development: a two-Sector analysis' (1970) 60(1) *The American Economic Review* 126.

Harriss-White, Barbara, 'Globalization, the financial crisis and petty production in India's socially regulated informal economy' (2010) 1(1) *Global Labour Journal* 152.

Harriss-White, Barbara, 'Globalization, the financial crisis and petty commodity production in India's socially regulated informal economy' in Paul Bowles and John Harriss (eds), *Globalization and Labour in China and India: Impacts and Responses* (New York: Palgrave Macmillan, 2010) 131.

Harriss-White, Barbara, Anushree Sinha, 'Introduction' in Barbara Harriss-White and Anushree Sinha (eds), *Trade Liberalization and India's Informal Economy* (New Delhi: Oxford University Press, 2007) 1.

Harriss-White, Barbara, 'Work and wellbeing in informal economies: the regulative roles of institutions of identity and the state' (2010) 38(2) *World Development* 170.

Hart, Keith, 'Informal income opportunities and urban employment in Ghana' (1973) 11(1) *Journal of Modern African Studies* 61.

Hart, Keith, 'Bureaucratic form and the informal economy' in Basudeb Guha-Khasnobis, Ravi Kanbur and Elinor Ostrom (eds), *Linking the Formal and Informal Economy Concepts and Policies* (New York: Oxford University Press, 2006) 23.

Harvey, David, 'From globalization to the new imperialism' in R. Appelbaum and W. I. Robinson (eds), *Critical Globalization Studies* (New York: Routledge, 2005) 91.

Harvey, David, 'Neo-liberalism and the restoration of class power' in David Harvey, *Spaces of Global Capitalism: towards a Theory of Uneven Geographical Development* (London: Verso, 2006) 9.

Haworth, Nigel, Stephen Hughes, 'Trade and international labour standards: issues and debates over a social clause' (1997) 39(2) *Journal of Industrial Relations* 179.

Heintz, James, Robert Pollin, 'Informalization, economic growth, and the challenge of creating viable labor standards in developing countries' in Neema Kudva and Lourdes Baneria (eds), *Rethinking Informalization: Poverty, Precarious Jobs and Social Protection* (Cornell University Open Access Repository, 2005) 44.

Helfer, Laurence R., 'Understanding change in international organizations: globalization and innovation in the ILO' (2006) 59 *Vanderbilt Law Review* 649.

Hepple, Bob, 'Introduction' in Bob Hepple (ed), *The Making of Labour Law in Europe: a Comparative Study of Nine Countries up to 1945* (London: Mansell, 1986) 1.

Hepple, Bob, 'The future of labour law' (1995) 24(4) *Industrial Law Journal* 303.

Hepple, Bob, 'Rights at work' in Dharam Ghai (ed), *Decent Work: Objectives and Strategies* (Geneva: IILS, ILO, 2006) 33.

Hensman, Rohini, 'Labour and globalization: union responses in India' in Paul Bowles and John Harriss (eds), *Globalization and Labour in China and India: Impacts and Responses* (New York: Palgrave Macmillan, 2010) 189.

Hill, Elizabeth, 'Women in the Indian informal economy: collective strategies for work life improvement and development' (2001) 15(3) *Work, Employment & Society* 443.

Huysman, Marijk, 'Waste picking as a survival strategy for women in Indian cities' (1994) 6(2) *Environment and Urbanization* 155.

Hyde, Alan, 'What is labour law?' in Guy Davidov and Brian Langille (eds), *Boundaries and Frontiers of Labour Law* (Portland: Hart Publishing, 2006) 37.

Hyde, Alan, 'The idea of the idea of labour law: a parable' in Guy Davidov and Brian Langille (eds), *The Idea of Labour Law* (Oxford & New York: Oxford University Press, 2011) 88.

Ibrahim, Solava S., 'From individual to collective capabilities: the capability approach as a conceptual framework for self-help' (2006) 7(3) *Journal of Human Development* 397.

Jha, Raghbendra, 'The Indian economy: current performance and short-Term prospects' in Raghbendra Jha (ed), *The Indian Economy Sixty Years After Independence* (London: Palgrave Macmillan, 2008) 20.

Jhabvala, Renana, 'Participatory approaches: emerging trends in social security' in Renana Jhabvala and R. K. A. Subrahmanya (eds), *The Unorganised Sector: Work Security and Social Protection* (New Delhi: Sage Publications, 2001) 30.

KKPKP Central Secretariat, 'The SWACHH National Alliance of Waste Pickers, India' in Melanie Samson (ed), *Refusing to be Cast Aside: Waste Pickers Organising Around the World* (Cambridge, MA: WEIGO, 2009) 37.

Kannan, K.P., T.S. Papola, 'Workers in the informal sector: initiatives by India's National Commission for Enterprises in the unorganized sector (NCEUS)' (2007) 146(3–4) *International Labour Review* 321.

Kanwar, J. S., S. M. Virmani and S. K. Das, 'Farming systems research in India: a historical Perspective' (1992) 28(1) *Experimental Agriculture* 1.

Kapoor, Aditi, 'The SEWA way: shaping another future for informal labour' (2007) 39 *Futures* 554.

Karat, Prakash, 'On democratic centralism' (2010) 26(1) *The Marxist* 3.

Khan, Mohd. Afaq, 'India's comparative advantage in business process outsourcing' (2004) 1(2) *Aim Explore* 33.

Khosla, Madhav, 'Making social rights conditional: lessons from India' (2010) 8(4) *I.CON* 739.

Kolben, Kevin, 'A development approach to trade and labor regimes' (2010) 45(2) *Wake Forest Law Review* 355.

Kucera, David and Leanne Roncolato, 'Informal employment: two contested policy issues' (2008) 147(4) *International Labour Review* 321.

Kudva, Neema, Lourdes Baneria, 'Introduction' in Neema Kudva and Lourdes Baneria (eds), *Rethinking Informalization: Poverty, Precarious Jobs and Social Protection* (Cornell University Open Access Repository, 2005) 6.

Kuruvilla, Sarosh, 'Social dialogue for decent work' in Dharam Ghai (ed), *Decent Work: Objectives and Strategies* (Geneva: IILS, ILO, 2006) 175.

Lalitha, N., 'Unorganised manufacturing and the gross domestic product' in Renana Jhabvala, Ratna M. Sudarshan and Jeemol Unni (eds), *Informal Economy Centrestage: New Structures of Employment* (New Delhi: Sage Publications, 2003) 157.

Langille, Brian A, 'Core labour rights: the true story (Reply to Alston)' (2005) 16(3) *European Journal of International Law* 409.

Langille, Brian, 'Labour law's back pages' in Guy Davidov and Brian Langille (eds), *Boundaries and Frontiers of Labour Law* (Portland: Hart Publishing, 2006) 13.

Langille, Brian, 'Labour law's theory of justice' in Guy Davidov and Brian Langille (eds), *The Idea of Labour Law* (Oxford & New York: Oxford University Press, 2011) 101.

Lewis, W.A., 'Economic development with unlimited supplies of labour' (1954) 22(2) *The Manchester School* 139.

Low, Linda, T C Aw 'The human development index revisited' (1997) *Singapore Management Review* 1.

Ludden, David, 'The formation of modern agrarian economies in South India' in Binay Bhushan Chaudhuri (ed), *Economic History of India from Eighteenth to Twentieth Century* (New Delhi: Centre for Studies in Civilizations, 2005) 1.

Marshall, Shelley (undated) 'Main findings concerning the role of labour law in promoting decent work' in *Promoting Decent Work: the Role of Labour Law* (on file with author).

Maupain, Francis, 'New foundation or new façade? The ILO and the 2008 Declaration on Social Justice for a Fair Globalization' (2009) 20(3) *EJIL* 823.

McGillivray, Mark, Howard White, 'Measuring development? The UNDP's human development index' (1993) 5(2) *Journal of International Development* 183.

McNally, David, 'The colour of money: race, gender, and the many oppressions of global capital' in David McNally (ed), *Another World is Possible: Globalization and Anti-Capitalism*, revised edition (Winnipeg: Arbeiter Ring Publishing, 2006) 137.

Meknassi, Rachid Filali, 'The effectiveness of labour law and decent work aspirations in the developing countries: a framework for analysis' in Tzehainesh Tekle (ed), *Labour Law and Worker Protection in Developing Countries* (Oxford and Portland, Oregon: Hart; Geneva: ILO, 2010) 51.

Mitchell, Richard, 'Introduction: a new scope and a new task for labour law?' in Richard Mitchell (ed), *Redefining Labour Law: New Perspectives on the Future of Teaching and Research* (Melbourne: Centre for Employment and Labour Relations Law, Occasional Monograph Series No 3, 1995) vii.

Mitchell, Richard, Christopher Arup, 'Labour law and labour market regulation' in Christopher Arup and others (eds), *Labour Law and Labour Market Regulation: Essays on the Construction, Constitution and Regulation of Labour Markets and Work Relationships* (Sydney: Federation Press, 2006) 3.

Mohapatra, Prabhu P., 'Assam and the West Indies, 1860–1920: immobilizing plantation labour' in Douglas Hay and Paul Craven (eds), *Masters, Servants, and Magistrates in Britain and the Empire, 1562–1955* (Chapel Hill & London: The University of North Carolina Press, 2004) 455.

Mukherji, Saugata, 'Evolution of the non-Agrarian formal sector of the Indian economy through the nineteenth and twentieth century' in Binay Bhushan Chaudhuri (ed), *Economic History of India from Eighteenth to Twentieth Century* (New Delhi: Centre for Studies in Civilizations, 2005) 356.

Mukhopadhyay, Ishita, 'Calcutta's informal sector: Changing pattern of labour use' (1998) 33(47/48) *Economic and Political Weekly* 3075.

Narayana, M. R., 'Formal and informal enterprises: concept, definition, and measurement issues in India' in Basudeb Guha-Khasnobis, Ravi Kanbur and Elinor Ostrom (eds), *Linking the Formal and Informal Economy Concepts and Policies* (New York: Oxford University Press, 2006) 93.

Noorbakhsh, Farhad, 'The human development index: some technical issues and alternative indices' (1998) 10 *Journal of International Development* 589.

Nussbaum, Martha, 'Nature, function and capability: Aristotle on political distribution' (1987) WIDER Working Papers, WP 31 (December 1987) World Institute for Development Economics Research of the United Nations University.

Nussbaum, Martha C., 'Capabilities as fundamental entitlements: Sen and social justice' (2003) 9(2/3) *Feminist Economics* 33.

Nussbaum, Martha, 'Violence on the left: Nandigram and the communists of West Bengal' (2008) *Dissent* 27.

Paul, Shutapa, 'East Bengal in West Bengal', *India Today* (24 January 2011).

Perelman, Michael, 'The history of capitalism' in Alfredo Saad-Filho (eds), *Anti-Capitalism* (London: Pluto Press, 2003) 119.

'Perspectives: towards a policy framework for decent work' (2002) 141(1–2) *International Labour Review* 161.

Petit, Philip, 'Freedom in the spirit of Sen' in Christopher W Morris (ed), *Amartya Sen* (New York: Cambridge University Press, 2010) 91.

Portes, Alejandro, Lauren Benton, 'Industrial development and labor absorption: a reinterpretation' (1984) 10(4) *Population and Development Review* 589.

Radovanovic, Bojana, 'Human development index as a measure of human development' (2011) *FilozofijaiDrustvo* 193.

Ramm, Thilo, 'Epilogue: the new ordering of labour law 1918–45' in Bob Hepple (ed), *The Making of Labour Law in Europe: a Comparative Study of Nine Countries up to 1945* (London: Mansell, 1986) 277.

Rani, Uma, Jeemol Unni, 'Do economic reforms influence home-based work? Evidence from India' (2009) 15(3) *Feminist Economics* 191.

Ranis, Gustav, Frances Stewart and Emma Samman, 'Human development: beyond the human development index' (2006) 7(3) *Journal of Human Development* 323.

Rathbone, Richard, 'West Africa, 1874–1948: employment legislation in a nonsettler peasant economy' in Douglas Hay and Paul Craven (eds), *Masters, Servants, and Magistrates in Britain and the Empire, 1562–1955* (Chapel Hill & London: The University of North Carolina Press, 2004) 481.

Rawal, Vikas, Madhura Swaminathan, 'Changing trajectories: agricultural growth in West Bengal, 1950 to 1996' (1998) 33(40) *Economic and Political Weekly* 2595.

Robeyns, Ingrid, 'Sen's capability approach and gender inequality: selecting relevant capabilities' (2003) 9(2–3) *Feminist Economics* 61.

Robeyns, Ingrid, 'The capability approach: a theoretical survey' (2005) 6(1) *Journal of Human Development* 93.

Rodgers, Gerry, 'The goal of decent work' (2008) 39(2) *IDS Bulletin* 63.

Routh, Supriya, 'Globalizing labor standards: the developed-developing divide' (2010) 2(1) *Jindal Global Law Review* 153.

Sachs, Ignacy, 'Inclusive development and decent work for all' (2004) 143(1–2) *International Labour Review* 161.

Salais, Robert, Robert Villeneuve, 'Introduction: Europe and the politics of capabilities' in Robert Salais and Robert Villeneuve (eds), *Europe and the Politics of Capabilities* (New York: Cambridge University Press, 2004) 1.

Salais, Robert, 'Incorporating the CA into social and employment policies' in Robert Salais and Robert Villeneuve (eds), *Europe and the Politics of Capabilities* (New York: Cambridge University Press, 2004) 287.

Samson, Melanie, 'Formal integration into municipal waste management systems' in Melanie Samson (ed), *Refusing to be Cast Aside: Waste Pickers Organising Around the World* (Cambridge, MA: WEIGO, 2009) 50.

Samson, Melanie, 'Using the law" in Melanie Samson (ed), *Refusing to be Cast Aside: Waste Pickers Organising Around the World* (Cambridge, MA: WEIGO, 2009) 60.

Sankaran, Kamala, 'Protecting the worker in the informal economy: the role of labour law' in Guy Davidov and Brian Langille (eds), *Boundaries and Frontiers of Labour Law* (Portland: Hart Publishing, 2006) 205.

Sankaran, Kamala, 'Labour laws in South Asia: the need for an inclusive approach' in Tzehainesh Tekle (ed), *Labour Law and Worker Protection in Developing Countries* (Oxford and Portland, Oregon: Hart; Geneva: ILO, 2010) 225.

Sankaran, Kamala, 'Informal employment and the challenges for labour law' in Guy Davidov and Brian Langille (eds), *The Idea of Labour Law* (Oxford & New York: Oxford University Press, 2011) 223.

Sanyal, Kalyan, Rajesh Bhattacharya, 'Beyond the factory: globalization, informalization of production and the changing locations of labour' in Paul Bowles and John Harriss (eds), *Globalization and Labour in China and India: Impacts and Responses* (New York: Palgrave Macmillan, 2010) 151.

Sassen-Koob, Saskia, 'New York City's informal economy' in Alejandro Portes, Manuel Castells and Lauren A. Benton (eds), *The Informal Economy: Studies in Advanced and Less Developed Countries* (Baltimore & London: The Johns Hopkins University Press, 1989) 60.

Sen, Amartya, 'Equality of what?' The Tanner Lecture on Human Values, delivered at Stanford University (22 May 1979) in *The Tanner Lectures on Human Values, Vol. I* (Salt Lake City: University of Utah Press/Cambridge, London, Melbourne and Sydney: Cambridge University Press, 1980).

Sen, Amartya, 'Well-being, agency and freedom: the Dewey Lectures 1984' (1985) 82(4) *Journal of Philosophy* 169.

Sen, Amartya, 'Freedom of choice: concepts and content' (1988) 32 *European Economic Review* 269.

Sen, Amartya, 'Capability and well-being' in Martha Nussbaum and Amartya Sen, (eds), *The Quality of Life* (Oxford: Oxford University Press, 1993) 30.

Sen, Amartya, 'Work and rights' (2000) 139(2) *International Labour Review* 119.

Sen, Amartya, 'Response to commentaries' (2002) 37(2) *Studies in Comparative International Development* 78.

Sen, Amartya, 'Human rights and capabilities' (2005) 6(2) *Journal of Human Development* 151.

Sen, Amartya, 'Human rights and the limits of law' (2006) 27 *Cardozo Law Rev* 2913.

Sen, Amartya, 'The place of capability in a theory of justice' in Harry Brighouse and Ingrid Robeyns (eds), *Measuring Justice Primary Goods and Capabilities* (Cambridge: Cambridge University Press, 2010) 239.

Sen Gupta, Prasanta, 'Politics in West Bengal: the Left Front versus the Congress (I)' (1989) 29(9) *Asian Survey* 883.

Servais, Jean-Michel, 'Globalization and decent work policy: reflections upon a new legal approach' (2004) 143(1–2) *International Labour Review* 185.

Sharma, Alakh N., 'Employment generation policy and social safety nets in India' in Ramgopal Agarwala, Nagesh Kumar and Michelle Riboud (eds), *Reforms, Labour Markets, and Social Security in India* (New Delhi: Oxford University Press, 2004) 236.

Shekar, Nalini, 'Suman More: KKPKP, Pune, India' in Melanie Samson (ed), *Refusing to be Cast Aside: Waste Pickers Organising Around the World* (Cambridge, MA: WEIGO, 2009) 11.

Sicular, Daniel T., 'Pockets of peasants in Indonesian cities: the case of scavengers' (1991) 19(2/3) *World Development* 137.

Siggel, Eckhard, 'The Indian informal sector: the impact of globalization and reform' (2010) 149(1) *International Labour Review* 93.

Sindzingre, Alice, 'The relevance of the concepts of formality and informality: a theoretical appraisal' in Basudeb Guha-Khasnobis, Ravi Kanbur and Elinor Ostrom (eds), *Linking the Formal and Informal Economy Concepts and Policies* (New York: Oxford University Press, 2006) 59.

Singh, Arbind, Rakesh Saran, 'NIDAN Swachdhara Private Ltd: forming a company with waste pickers in India' in Melanie Samson (ed), *Refusing to be Cast Aside: Waste Pickers Organising Around the World* (Cambridge, MA: WEIGO, 2009) 17.

Singh, M. P., 'The statics and the dynamics of the fundamental rights and the directive principles: a human rights perspective' (2003) 5 *Supreme Court Cases Journal* 1.

Smit, Nicola, Elmarie Fourie, 'Extending protection to atypical workers, including workers in the informal economy, in developing countries' (2010) 26(1) *International Journal of Comparative Labor Law & Industrial Relations* 43.

Somavia, Juan, 'Promoting the MDGs: the role of employment and decent work' (2007) 4 *UN Chronicle* 28.

Spector, Horacio, 'Philosophical foundations of labor law' (2006) 33 *Florida State University Law Review* 1119.

Srivastava, S. C., 'Development and disparity: agriculture in North East India' (1998) 79(313) *Indian Journal of Economics* 195.

Standing, Guy, 'From people's security surveys to a decent work index' (2002) 141(4) *International Labour Review* 441.

Standing, Guy, 'The ILO: an agency for globalization?' (2008) 39(3) *Development and Change* 355.

Stepick, Alex, 'Miami's two informal sectors' in Alejandro Portes, Manuel Castells and Lauren A. Benton (eds), *The Informal Economy: Studies in Advanced and Less Developed Countries* (Baltimore & London: The Johns Hopkins University Press, 1989) 111.

Stewart, Frances, 'Groups and capabilities' (2005) 6(2) *Journal of Human Development* 185.

Subrahmanya, R. K. A., Renana Jhabvala, 'Meeting basic needs: the unorganised sector and social security' in Renana Jhabvala and R. K. A. Subrahmanya (eds), *The Unorganised Sector: Work Security and Social Protection* (New Delhi: Sage Publications, 2001) 17.

Subrahmanya, R. K. A., 'Strategies for protective social security' in Renana Jhabvala and R. K. A. Subrahmanya (eds), *The Unorganised Sector: Work Security and Social Protection* (New Delhi: Sage Publications, 2001) 38.

Subrahmanya, R. K. A., 'Support for the unorganised sector: existing social security measures' in Renana Jhabvala and R. K. A. Subrahmanya (eds), *The Unorganised Sector: Work Security and Social Protection* (New Delhi: Sage Publications, 2001) 45.

Subrahmanya, R. K. A., 'Welfare funds: an Indian model for workers in the unorganised sector' in Renana Jhabvala and R. K. A. Subrahmanya (eds), *The Unorganised Sector: Work Security and Social Protection* (New Delhi: Sage Publications, 2001) 65.

Sudarshan, Ratna M., Jeemol Unni, 'Measuring the informal economy' in Renana Jhabvala, Ratna M. Sudarshan and Jeemol Unni (eds), *Informal Economy Centrestage: New Structures of Employment* (New Delhi: Sage Publications, 2003) 19.

Supiot, Alain, 'Perspectives on work: introduction' (1996) 135(6) *International Labour Review* 603.

Swaminathan, Mina, 'Worker, mother or both: maternity and child care services for women in the unorganised sector' in Renana Jhabvala and R. K. A. Subrahmanya (eds), *The Unorganised Sector: Work Security and Social Protection* (New Delhi: Sage Publications, 2001) 122.

Tekle, Tzehainesh, 'Labour law and worker protection in the South: an evolving tension between models and reality' in Tzehainesh Tekle (ed), *Labour Law and Worker Protection in Developing Countries* (Oxford and Portland, Oregon: Hart; Geneva: ILO, 2010) 3.

Trebilcock, Anne, 'Using development approaches to address the challenge of the informal economy for labour law' in Guy Davidov and Brian Langille (eds), *Boundaries and Frontiers of Labour Law* (Oxford: Hart Publishing, 2006) 63.

Tripp, Aili Mari, 'Creating collective capabilities: women, agency and the politics of representation' (2010) 19(1) *Columbia Journal of Gender and Law* 219.

Unni, Jeemol, 'Gender and informality in labour market in South Asia' (2001) 36(26) *Economic and Political Weekly* 2360.

Unni, Jeemol, Namrata Bali, 'Subcontracted women workers in the garment industry in India' in R Balakrishnan (ed), *The Hidden Assembly Line: Gender Dynamics of subcontracted Work in a Global Economy* (Bloomfield, Connecticut: Kumarian Press, 2002) 115.

Unni, Jeemol, Uma Rani, 'Employment and income in the informal economy: a micro-perspective' in Renana Jhabvala, Ratna M. Sudarshan and Jeemol Unni (eds), *Informal Economy Centrestage: New Structures of Employment* (New Delhi: Sage Publications, 2003) 39.

Vaidyanathan, A., 'The pursuit of social justice' in Zoya Hasan, E. Sridharan, and R. Sudarshan (eds), *India's Living Constitution: Ideas, Practices, Controversies* (London: Anthem Press, 2005) 284.

Valticos, Nicolas, 'Fifty years of standard-setting activities by the International Labour organisation' (1996) 135(3–4) *International Labour Review* 393.

Vosko, Leah, '"Decent work": the shifting role of the ILO and the struggle for global social justice' (2002) 19(2) *Global Social Policy* 19.

Wallerstein, Immanuel, 'The rise and future demise of the world capitalist system: concepts for comparative analysis' (1974) 16(4) *Comparative Studies in Society and History* 387.

Weiss, Manfred, 'Re-Inventing labour law?' in Guy Davidov and Brian Langille (eds), *The Idea of Labour Law* (New York: Oxford University Press, 2011) 43.

Wilson, David C., Costas Velis and Chris Cheeseman, 'Role of informal sector recycling in waste management in developing countries' (2006) 30 *Habitat International* 797.

Wisskirchen, Alfred, 'The standard-setting and monitoring activity of the ILO: legal questions and practical experience' (2005) 144(3) *International Labour Review* 253.

Yhdego, Michael, 'Scavenging solid wastes in Dar es Salaam, Tanzania' (1991) 9 *Waste Management and Research* 259.

Reports and electronic resources

'About the informal economy: definitions and theories', Women in Informal Employment: Globalizing and Organizing, available at http://www.wiego.org/about_ie/definitions AndTheories.php (last visited 22 June 2010).

Banerjee, Sharmistha and others, *A Report on Rapid Assessment Survey of Homeless Population within Kolkata Municipal Corporation Area* (Kolkata: Calcutta Samaritans, Undated).

Becker, Kristina Flodman, 'The informal economy', Sida Fact Finding Study, March 2004 at 21, available at http://rru.worldbank.org/Documents/PapersLinks/Sida.pdf (last visited 20 July 2010).

Bhalla, Sheila, *Definitional and Statistical Issues Relating to Workers in Informal Employment*, Working Paper No 3, National Commission for Enterprises in the Unorganised Sector (New Delhi: NCEUS, 2008).

Blaxall, John, 'India's Self Employed Women's Association (SEWA): empowerment through mobilization of poor women on a large scale', available at http://info.worldbank.org/etools/docs/reducingpoverty/case/79/fullcase/India%20SEWA%20Full%20Case.pdf (last visited 6 June 2012).

Bose, Antara, 'Rag-pickers take to reading, saving: interactive session motivates under-privileged children to join schools' *The Telegraph* (22 August 2009).

Bureau of International Labor Affairs, United States Department of Labor, 'ILO standards', available at http://www.dol.gov/ilab/programs/oir/PC-ILO-page2.htm (30 March 2012).

'Cabinet okays fund for unorganized sector' *The Times of India* (29 July 2011).

Chakraborty, Ajanta, 'Rehab plan for city's ragpicker community' *The Times of India* (13 August 2010).

Chapter 8, para 8.1, The Ministry of Labour Annual Report 2008–2009 (Chapter 8: Unorganised Labour), available at http://labour.nic.in/annrep/annrep0809/Chapter-8.pdf (last visited 17 December 2009).

Chen, Martha Alter, 'The informal economy: definitions, theories and policies' (2012) WIEGO Working Paper No 1, available at http://wiego.org/sites/wiego.org/files/publications/files/Chen_WIEGO_WP1.pdf (last visited 2 November 2012).

Chikarmane, Poornima, Laxmi Narayan, 'Organising the unorganised: a case study of the Kagad Kach Patra Kashtakari Panchayat' (Trade Union of Waste Pickers), available at http://www.wiego.org/program_areas/org_rep/case-kkpkp.pdf (last visited 23 April 2010).

Chikarmane, Poornima, Medha Deshpande and Lakshmi Narayan, 'Untitled' at 13, 17, 27, available at http://ilo-mirror.library.cornell.edu/public/english/region/asro/newdelhi/download/puneabst.pdf (last visited 20 May 2012).

Chikarmane, Poornima, 'Policy outline', *Workshop to Discuss Policy on Community-based and Decentralised Integrated Sustainable Solid Waste Management in the Country* (22–23 July 2008), available at http://wiego.org/sites/wiego.org/files/resources/files/wp_consultation_report.pdf (last visited 16 June 2012).

Clark, David A., 'The capability approach: its development, critiques and recent advances', GPRG-WPS-032, Global Poverty Research Group, available at http://www.gprg.org/pubs/workingpapers/pdfs/gprg-wps-032.pdf (last visited 26 December 2010).

Constituent Assembly of India Debates (Proceedings), Vol II, No 3 (22 January 1947).

Contribution of the Unorganised Sector to GDP Report of the Sub Committee of a NCEUS Task Force, Working Paper No 2 (June 2008) National Commission for Enterprises in the Unorganised Sector (New Delhi: NCEUS, 2008), available at http://nceus.gov.in/ Final_Booklet_Working_Paper_2.pdf (last visited 22 June 2010).

'Decent work agenda', available at http://www.ilo.org/global/about-the-ilo/decent-work-agenda/lang--en/index.htm (last visited 26 May 2012).

Fifteenth International Conference of Labour Statisticians, Geneva (19–28 January 1993) ICLS/15/D.6(Rev.1, Resolution II: Resolution concerning statistics of employment in the informal sector (Geneva: ILO, 1993).

Government of India, 'India and the ILO', available at http://labour.nic.in/ilas/indiaandilo.htm (last visited 30 March 2012).

Government of India, *Resolution No 5(2)/2004-ICC* of 20 September 2004.

Government of India, 'Area, population, decennial growth rate and density for 2001 and 2011 at a glance for West Bengal and the districts, provisional population totals for West Bengal' *Census of India 2011*, Ministry of Home Affairs, Government of India, available at http://www.censusindia.gov.in/2011-prov-results/prov_data_products_wb.html (last visited 3 February 2012).

Government of India, 'Statement 1, ranking of districts by population size in 2001 and 2011, provisional population totals for West Bengal' *Census of India 2011*, Ministry of Home Affairs, Government of India, available at http://www.censusindia.gov.in/2011-prov-results/prov_data_products_wb.html (last visited 3 February 2012).

Government of West Bengal, *Labour Department Resolution Nos 180-IR dated 24/01/2001 and 305-IR* of 19/02/2001.

Government of West Bengal, 'Annexure-A', Vide clause I of the *State Assisted Scheme of Provident Fund for Unorganised Workers in West Bengal* (SASPFUW) under *Labour Department Resolution No 180-IR* of 24/01/2001.

Government of West Bengal, Labour Department, *Resolution No 658-LW/2B-02/07* of 23/08/2007.

Government of West Bengal, Labour Department, *Notification No 1025-IR* of 06/11/2009.

Government of West Bengal, Labour Department, *Resolution No 907-IR/EIL/1-A-4/10* of 13/08/2010.

Government of West Bengal, *Labour in West Bengal 2010: Annual Report* (Kolkata: Government of WB, undated).

Government of West Bengal, *Social Security for the Working Class and Left-Front Government* (*Shramik-shrenir Samajik Suraksha O Bam-Front Sarkar*) (Kolkata: Government of WB, 2010) [English title provided by author].

Government of West Bengal, *The West Bengal Unorganised Sector Workers Health Security Scheme* (WBUSWHS), Labour Department, *Government of West Bengal Resolution No 34-IR, IR/MISC-06/10* of 05/01/2011.

Himanshu, 'Poverty's definitional woes', *Livemint.com* and *The Wall Street Journal* (27 May 2010).

Human Development Report 2009, 'India: the human development index: going beyond income', available at http://hdrstats.undp.org/en/countries/country_fact_sheets/cty_fs_IND.html (last visited 21 June 2010).

Human Development Report 2009, 'Overcoming barriers: human mobility and development' (UNDP, New York, 2009), available at http://hdr.undp.org/en/media/HDR_2009_EN_Complete.pdf (last visited 21 June 2010).

Human Development Report 2005, 'International cooperation at a crossroads: aid, trade and security in an unequal world', available at http://hdr.undp.org/en/media/HDR05_complete.pdf (last visited 21 June 2010).

ILO, *Decent work agenda: Promoting decent work for all*, available at http://www.ilo.org/global/about-the-ilo/decent-work-agenda/lang--en/index.htm (last visited 1 December 2010).

ILO, *Declaration concerning the aims and purposes of the International Labour Organisation*, available at http://www.ilo.org/ilolex/english/constq.htm (last visited 22 April 2012).

ILO, *Mission and objectives*, available at http://www.ilo.org/global/about-the-ilo/mission-and-objectives/lang--en/index.htm (last visited 4 August 2012).

ILO, *Programmes and projects*, available at http://www.ilo.org/global/programmes-and-projects/lang--en/index.htm (last visited 22 April 2012).

ILO, *Social Dialogue*, available at http://www.ilo.org/global/about-the-ilo/decent-work-agenda/social-dialogue/lang--en/index.htm (last visited 20 May 2012).

ILO, *Social Dialogue Sector*, available at http://www.ilo.org/public/english/dialogue/ (last visited 4 August 2012).

ILO, *InFocus Programme on Strengthening Social Dialogue*, Social Dialogue Sector (Geneva: ILO, undated).

ILO, *ILO History*, available at http://www.ilo.org/public/english/about/history.htm (last visited 14 September 2011).

ILO, Report VII, *Consideration of a possible Declaration of principles of the International Labour Organization concerning fundamental rights and its appropriate follow-up mechanism*, 86th Session, Geneva (June 1998), available at http://www.ilo.org/public/english/standards/relm/ilc/ilc86/rep-vii.htm (last visited 20 September 2011).

ILO, *Declaration on Fundamental Principles and Rights at Work and its Follow-up*, available at http://www.ilo.org/declaration/thedeclaration/textdeclaration/lang--en/index.htm (last visited 20 May 2012).

ILO, *Ratifications of the Fundamental human rights Conventions by country*, ILOLEX, available at http://www.ilo.org/ilolex/english/docs/declworld.htm (last visited 30 March 2012).

ILO, *The US: a Leading Role in the ILO*, available at http://www.ilo.org/washington/ilo-and-the-united-states/the-usa-leading-role-in-the-ilo/lang--en/index.htm (last visited 30 March 2012).

ILO, *United States, List of Ratifications of International Labour Conventions, International Labour Standards*, available at http://webfusion.ilo.org/public/applis/appl-byCtry.cfm?lang=EN&CTYCHOICE=0610 (last visited 30 March 2012).

ILO, *Employment, Incomes and Equality: a strategy for increasing productive employment in Kenya*, Report of an Inter-Agency Team Financed by the United Nations Development Programme and Organised by the International Labour Office (Geneva: ILO, 1972).

ILO, *The dilemma of the informal sector*, Report of the Director-General, International Labour Conference, 78th Session (Geneva: ILO, 1991).

ILO, *Resolution concerning the International Classification of Status in Employment (ICSE), adopted by the Fifteenth International Conference of Labour Statisticians*, the Fifteenth International Conference of Labour Statisticians (January 1993), available at http://www.ilo.org/wcmsp5/groups/public/---dgreports/---stat/documents/normativeinstrument/wcms_087562.pdf (last visited 5 June 2012).

ILO, *Decent Work*, Report of the Director-General, International Labour Conference (June 1999) 87th Session (Geneva: ILO, 1999).

ILO, *Reducing the Decent Work Deficit: a Global Challenge*, Report of the Director-General, International Labour Conference, 89th Session (Geneva: ILO, 2001).

ILO, *Decent work and the informal economy*, International Labour Conference, 90th Session, 2002 (Geneva: International Labour Office, 2002).

ILO, 'Measurement of decent work', Discussion paper for the Tripartite Meeting of Experts on the Measurement of Decent Work (8–10 September 2008) TMEMDW/2008 (Geneva: ILO, 2008).

ILO, *Tripartite Meeting of Experts on the Measurement of Decent Work* (8–10 September 2008) (Geneva: ILO).

'India pilot project: Law and informality', Women in Informal Employment: Globalizing and Organizing, available at http://wiego.org/informal_economy_law/india-pilot-project (last visited 16 June 2012).

Jha, Praveen, 'Globalization and labour in India: the emerging challenges', available at http://www.nottingham.ac.uk/shared/shared_scpolitics/documents/gwcprojectPapers/India.pdf (last visited 16 June 2012).

Kagad Kach Patra Kashtakari Panchayat (KKPKP), available at http://www.wastepickers collective.org/ (last visited 7 June 2012).

Kolkata Municipal Corporation (KMC), *Basic Statistics of Kolkata*, available at https://www.kmcgov.in/KMCPortal/jsp/KolkataStatistics.jsp (last visited 10 December 2011).

Kundu, Nitai, 'The case of Kolkata, India', available at http://www.ucl.ac.uk/dpu-projects/Global_Report/pdfs/Kolkata.pdf (last visited 11 June 2012).

'Legal empowerment and the informal economy: SEWA experience', paper presented at the Regional Dialogue on Legal Empowerment for the Poor, Bangkok (Thailand, 3–5 March 2009), available at http://www.snap-undp.org/lepknowledgebank/Public%20Document%20Library/SEWA%20-%20Legal%20Empowerment%20and%20the%20informal%20economy.pdf (last visited 18 December 2009).

Medina, Martin, 'Waste picker cooperatives in developing countries', El Colegio de la FronteraNorte, Mexico, available at http://wiego.org/sites/wiego.org/files/publications/files/Medina-wastepickers.pdf (last visited 23 May 2012).

NCEUS, *Report on Conditions of Work and Promotion of Livelihoods in the Unorganised Sector*, National Commission for Enterprises in the Unorganised Sector's (NCEUS) (New Delhi: NCEUS, 2007).

NCEUS, *Report on Definitional and Statistical Issues Relating to Informal Economy*, National Commission for Enterprises in the Unorganised Sector (New Delhi: NCEUS, 2008).

NCEUS, *The Challenge of Employment in India: an Informal Economy Perspective*, Volume 1 Main Report (New Delhi: NCEUS, 2009).

Nidan, 'Activities, empowering the informal workers and children', available at http://www.nidan.in/otherpage.php?page_code_no=3 (last visited 16 January 2012).

Ofreneo, Rene, *Informal Sector: Labour Laws and Industrial Relations, Interdepartmental Project on the Urban Informal Sector: Philippines*, Assessment Report Series No 6 (Manila: ILO, 1994).

OneWorld South Asia, available at http://southasia.oneworld.net/todaysheadlines/planning-commission-accepts-37-pc-live-below-poverty-line (last visited 21 June 2010).

Open House Discussion on Deemed Homeless, AWWRI Project of NUJS Legal Aid Society & Center for Human Rights, National Conference on Place of Deemed Homeless in Good Governance and Inclusive Growth in India (27–29 January 2012) WB NUJS Campus (on file with author).

Party Constitution of the Communist Party of India (Marxist), available at http://www.cpim.org/content/party-constitution#Principles%20of%20Democratic%20Centralism (last visited 12 June 2012).

Paul, Prasanta, 'Pujas bring bonanza for Bengal ragpickers', A Dalit-Bahujan 'Media, Dr BabasahebAmbedkar and his people' (undated) available at http://www.ambedkar.org/News/Pujasbring.htm (last visited 22 February 2012)

'Ragpickers to help recycle waste' *The Times of India* (11 May 2002).

'Ragpickers, NGOs to help collect household plastic waste' *The Hindu Business Line* (1 May 2004).

Rashtriya Swastha Bima Yojana website at http://www.rsby.gov.in/index.aspx (last visited 12 June 2012).

'Reich urges adherence to "core" labor standards (reconciliation of trade, labor rules needed', available at http://www.usembassy-israel.org.il/publish/press/labor/archive/june/dl1_6-12.htm (last visited 30 March 2012).

Report of the Expert Group to Review the methodology for Estimation of Poverty, Government of India, Planning Commission, 2009, available at http://www.planningcommission.nic.in/reports/genrep/rep_pov.pdf (last visited 21 June 2010).

Reserve Bank of India, *Internal Working Group to Review the Recommendations of the NCEUS Report on Conditions of Work and Promotion of Livelihoods in the Unorganised Sector* (Mumbai: Reserve Bank of India, 2008).

'Revised office proposal for the measurement of decent work based on guidance received at the TME on the measurement of decent work' (to be read in conjunction with the Discussion Paper and the detailed comments made by experts as reflected in the Chairperson's report), available at http://www.ilo.org/wcmsp5/groups/public/---dgreports/---integration/documents/meetingdocument/wcms_115402.pdf (last visited 19 November 2011).

Routh, Supriya and others, 'Situational analysis of ragpickers in Kolkata' (Kolkata: Calcutta Samaritans, 2009).

Saith, Ruhi, 'Capabilities: the concept and its operationalization' (2001) Working Paper Number 66, QEH Working Paper Series: QEHWPS66, University of Oxford, available at http://www3.qeh.ox.ac.uk/pdf/qehwp/qehwps66.pdf (last visited 11 June 2012).

Sankaran, Kamala, Shalini Sinha and Roopa Madhav, 'Domestic workers: background document', WIEGO Law Pilot Project on the Informal Economy, available at http://wiego.org/sites/wiego.org/files/resources/files/dw_background_note.pdf (last visited 16 June 2012).

Sankaran, Kamala, Shalini Sinha and Roopa Madhav, 'Waste pickers background note', *WIEGO Law Pilot Project on the Informal Economy*, available at http://wiego.org/sites/wiego.org/files/resources/files/wp_background_note.pdf (last visited 16 June 2012).

Sankaran, Kamala, Shalini Sinha and Roopa Madhav, 'Concept note: national consultation of waste pickers' (22–23 July 2008) KKPKP and WIEGO Pilot Project, available at http://wiego.org/sites/wiego.org/files/resources/files/wp_consultation_concept_note.pdf (last visited 16 June 2012).

Sankaran, Kamala, 'Informal economy, own-account workers and the law: an overview', WIEGO Law Pilot Project on the Informal Economy, available at http://wiego.org/sites/wiego.org/files/resources/files/iei_background_paper_oaw_and_law.pdf (last visited 24 February 2012).

'Scavengers to managers', available at http://www.chintan-india.org/initiatives_scavengers_to_managers.htm (last visited 16 January 2012).

Self Employed Women's Association (SEWA), at http://www.sewa.org/ (last visited 5 January 2012).

Somavia, Juan, 'Decent work in the global economy' *Vigyan Bhawan* New Delhi (18 February 2000), available at http://www.ilo.org/public/english/bureau/dgo/speeches/somavia/2000/delhi.htm (last visited 25 March 2012).

'State Assisted Scheme of Provident Fund for Unorganised Workers in West Bengal' (SASPFUW), Labour Department, *Resolution Nos 180-IR* of 24/01/2001 and *305-IR* of 19/02/2001 of the Government of West Bengal.

'Study to determine the role of rag pickers: outsourcing and innovation mantra for solid waste management in urban centres' *The Telegraph* (29 December 2010).

The Calcutta Samaritans, available at http://thecalcuttasamaritans.org/contact.htm (last visited 21 February 2012).

The Chintan Environmental Research and Action Group, at http://www.chintan-india.org/ (last visited 20 May 2012).

'The terms of reference', Chapter-I, *Report of the National Commission on Labour* (New Delhi: Government of India, 2002), available at http://labour.nic.in/lcomm2/2nlc-pdfs/Chap1-2.pdf (last visited 28 May 2012).

'Trash talk: gaining value from waste, as it relates to the global poor', the 2012 Yunus Challenge Waste: Put it to use, available at http://web.mit.edu/idi/yunus_2012/Yunus_2012.pdf (last visited 23 May 2012).

Trebilcock, Anne, 'Decent work and the informal economy', Discussion Paper No 2005/04 (January 2005), available at http://62.237.131.23/publications/dps/dps2005/dp2005%2004%20Trebilcock.pdf (last visited 20 July 2010).

United Nations Development Programme (UNDP), available at http://www.undp.org/content/undp/en/home.html (last visited 24 September 2010).

UNDP, 'Human development index', available at http://hdr.undp.org/en/statistics/hdi/ (last visited 11 August 2012).

UNDP, 'International human development indicators', available at http://hdrstats.undp.org/en/indicators/default.html (last visited 11 August).

United Nations, 'Structure and organization', available at http://www.un.org/en/aboutun/structure/index.shtml (last visited 22 April 2012).

United Nations, *Report of the World Summit for Social Development*, World Summit for Social Development, Copenhagen, Denmark (6–12 March 1995), available at http://daccess-dds-ny.un.org/doc/UNDOC/GEN/N95/116/51/PDF/N9511651.pdf?OpenElement (last visited 30 March 2012).

United States Council for International Business, 'Issue analysis: US ratification of ILO core labor standards' (April 2007), available at http://www.uscib.org/docs/US_Ratification_of_ILO_Core_Conventions.pdf (last visited 30 March 2012).

WB NUJS, Legal Aid Society: *Brief Report of Activities Undertaken over the Period from July 2011 to January 2012.*

'Who we are', ActionAid, available at http://www.actionaid.org/india/who-we-are (last visited 23 May 2012).

Women in Informal Employment: Globalizing and Organizing (WIEGO), available at http://wiego.org (last visited 20 October 2010).

WIEGO, *Workshop to Discuss Policy on Community-based and Decentralised Integrated Sustainable Solid Waste Management in the Country* (22–23 July 2008), available at http://wiego.org/sites/wiego.org/files/resources/files/wp_consultation_report.pdf (last visited 16 June 2012).

Working out of Poverty: Report of the Director General, International Labour Conference, 91st Session (Geneva: ILO, 2003), available at http://www.ilo.org/wcmsp5/groups/public/---dgreports/---dcomm/documents/publication/kd00116.pdf (last visited 20 July 2010).

Index

For Product Safety Concerns and Information please contact our EU
representative GPSR@taylorandfrancis.com
Taylor & Francis Verlag GmbH, Kaufingerstraße 24, 80331 München, Germany